NILS

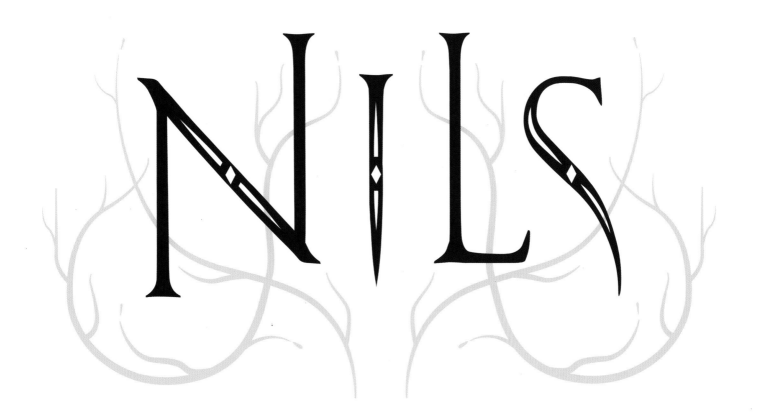

MAGNETIC™

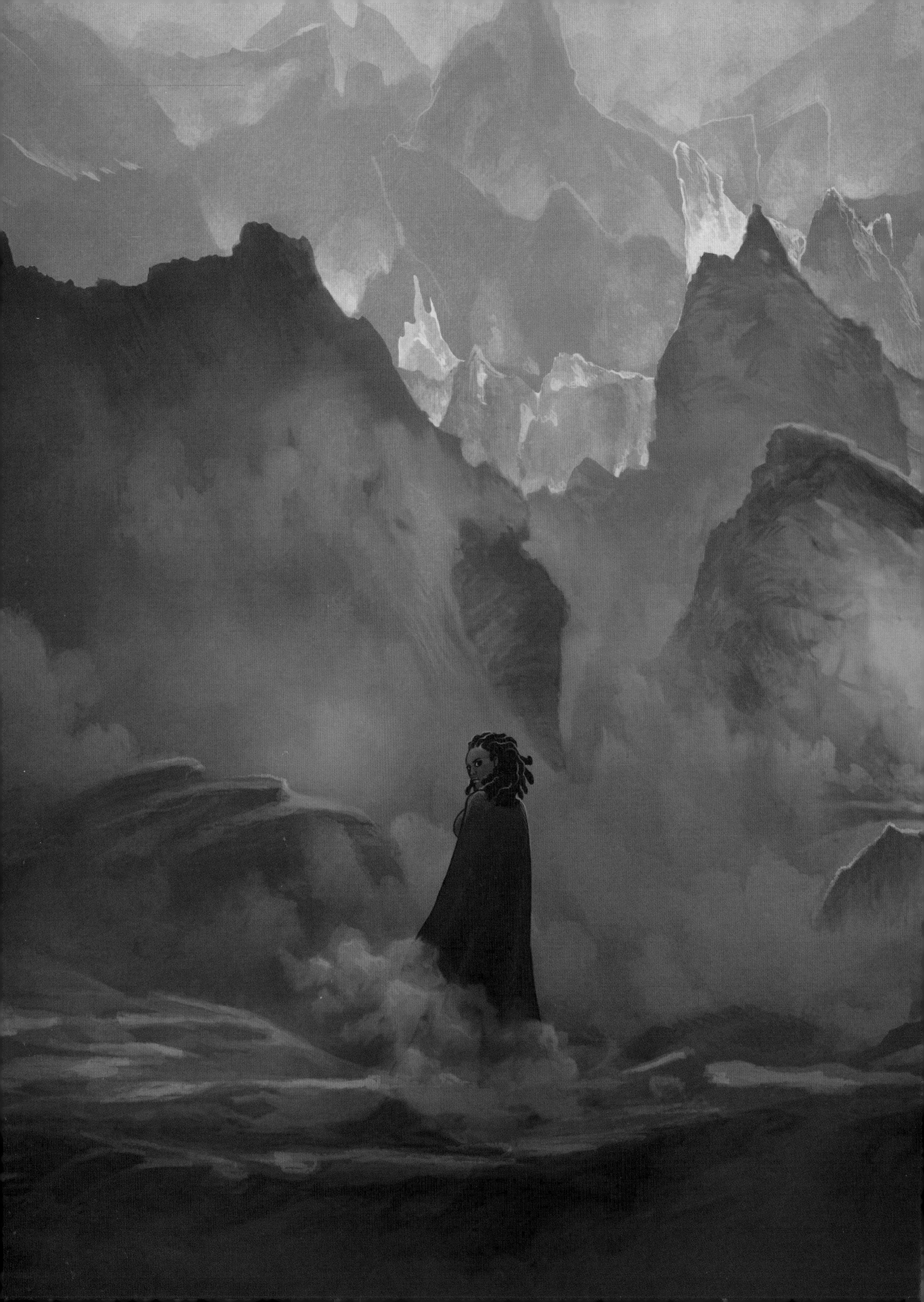

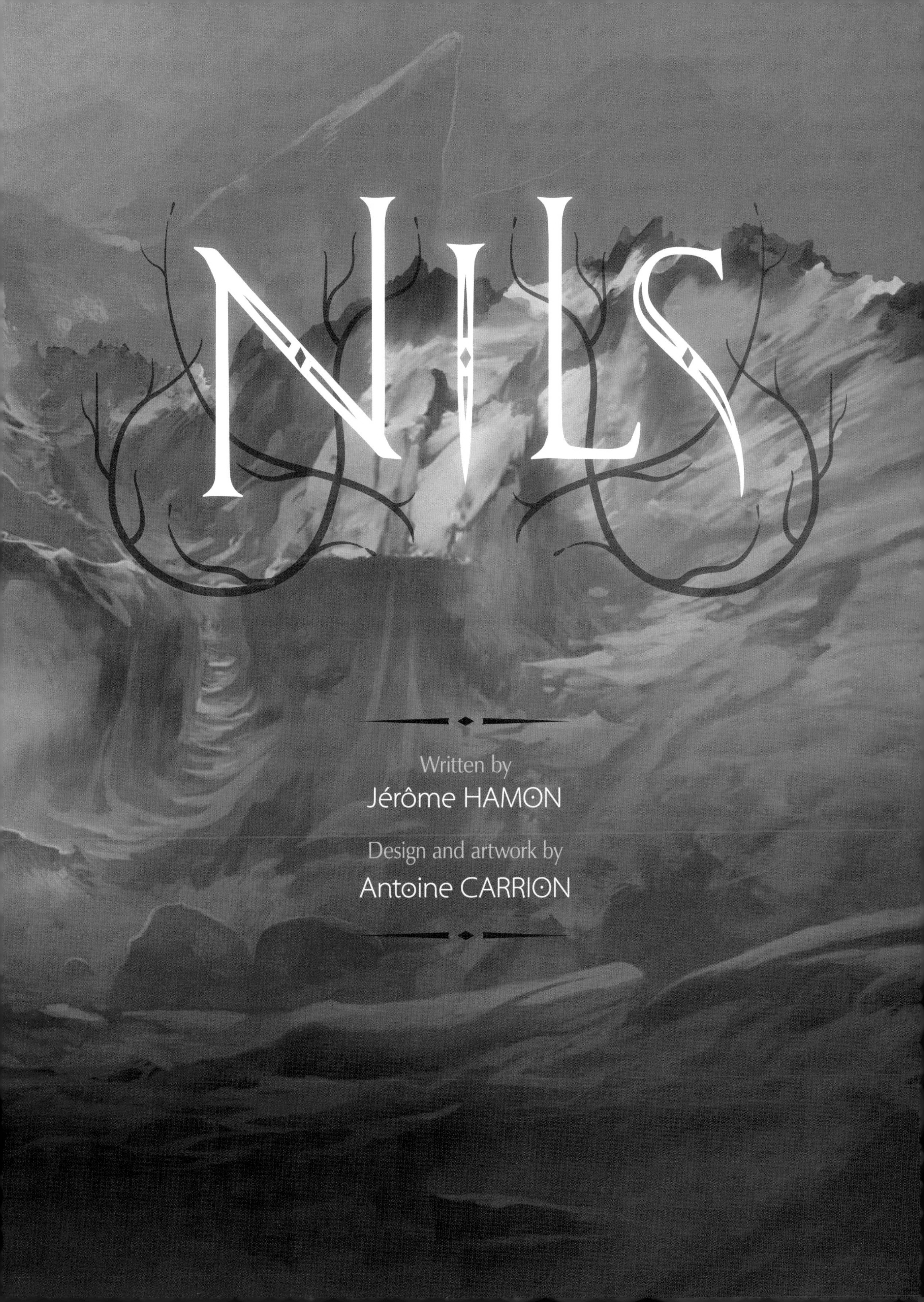

NILS

Written by
Jérôme HAMON

Design and artwork by
Antoine CARRION

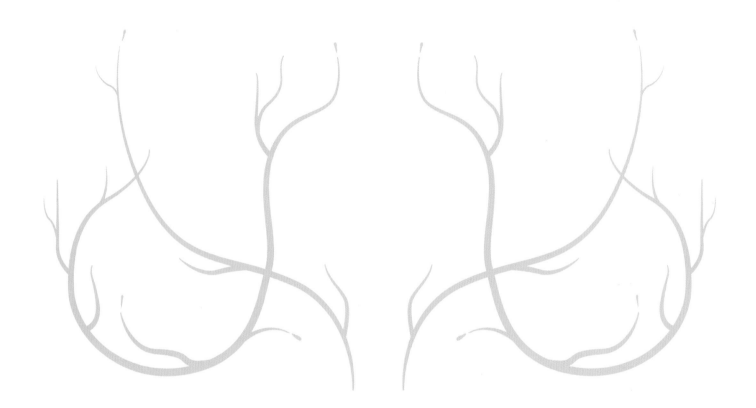

Chapter One
THE ELEMENTALS

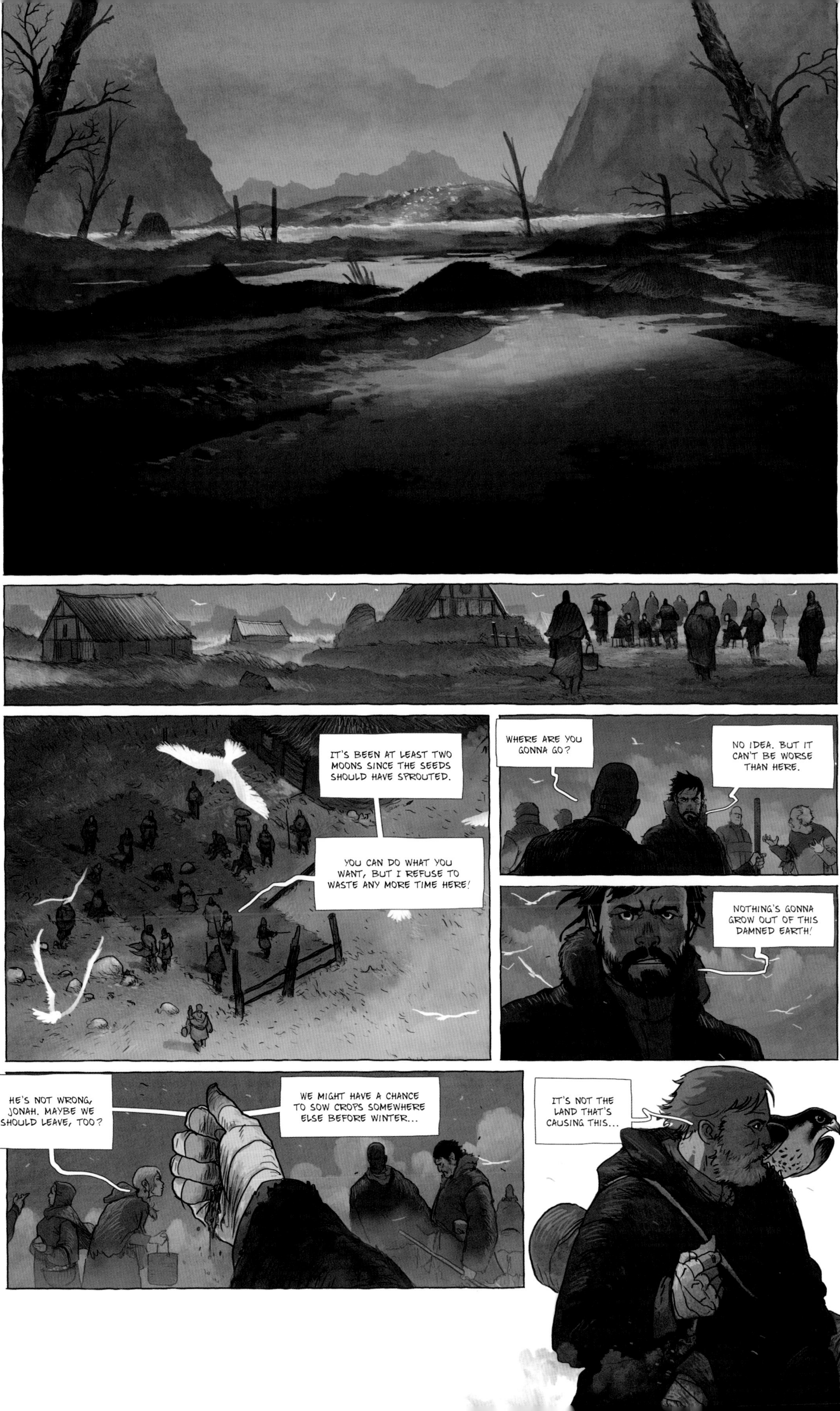
IT'S BEEN AT LEAST TWO MOONS SINCE THE SEEDS SHOULD HAVE SPROUTED.
YOU CAN DO WHAT YOU WANT, BUT I REFUSE TO WASTE ANY MORE TIME HERE!
WHERE ARE YOU GONNA GO?
NO IDEA. BUT IT CAN'T BE WORSE THAN HERE.
NOTHING'S GONNA GROW OUT OF THIS DAMNED EARTH!
HE'S NOT WRONG, JONAH. MAYBE WE SHOULD LEAVE, TOO?
WE MIGHT HAVE A CHANCE TO SOW CROPS SOMEWHERE ELSE BEFORE WINTER...
IT'S NOT THE LAND THAT'S CAUSING THIS...

LOOK -- IT'S FULL OF ORGANIC MATTER!

WE SHOULD EASILY HARVEST THREE OR FOUR CROPS IN A ROW.

EASY TO SAY, FOR THE GUY WHO BROUGHT US HERE!

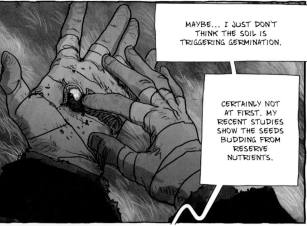

MAYBE... I JUST DON'T THINK THE SOIL IS TRIGGERING GERMINATION.

CERTAINLY NOT AT FIRST. MY RECENT STUDIES SHOW THE SEEDS BUDDING FROM RESERVE NUTRIENTS.

SO THEN WHY ISN'T ANYTHING GROWING?

I HAVE NO IDEA. IT'S BEEN SEVERAL WEEKS SINCE I'VE BEEN ABLE TO SPROUT ANY SEEDS. TO BE HONEST, IT'S BEEN A LONG TIME SINCE I'VE SEEN ANYTHING SPROUT ANYWHERE...

IT'S AS IF NATURE IS BROKEN.

AND I'M AFRAID NOT ONLY NATURE WILL BE AFFECTED...

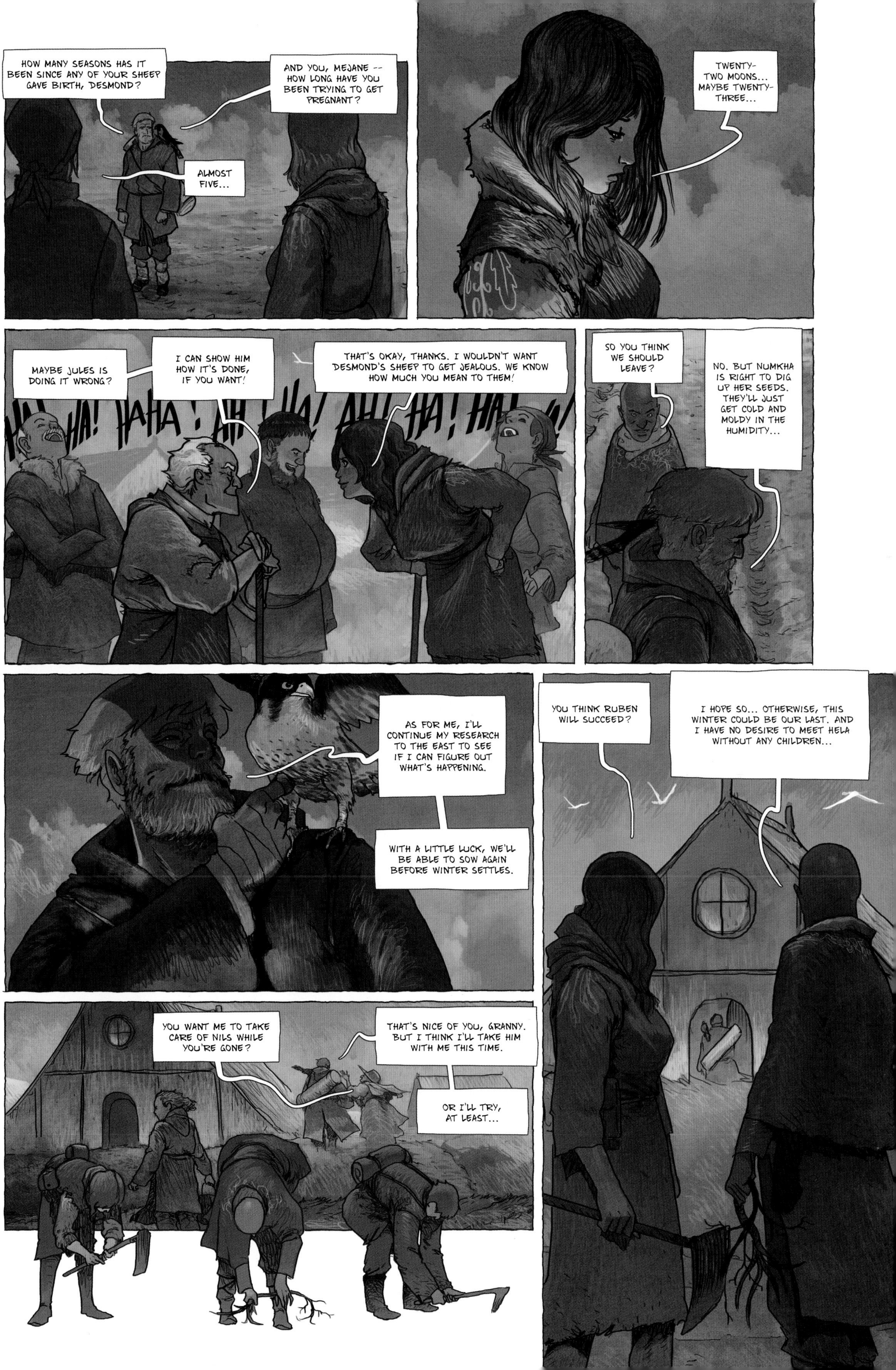
HOW MANY SEASONS HAS IT BEEN SINCE ANY OF YOUR SHEEP GAVE BIRTH, DESMOND?
AND YOU, MEJANE -- HOW LONG HAVE YOU BEEN TRYING TO GET PREGNANT?
ALMOST FIVE...
TWENTY-TWO MOONS... MAYBE TWENTY-THREE...
MAYBE JULES IS DOING IT WRONG?
I CAN SHOW HIM HOW IT'S DONE, IF YOU WANT!
THAT'S OKAY, THANKS. I WOULDN'T WANT DESMOND'S SHEEP TO GET JEALOUS. WE KNOW HOW MUCH YOU MEAN TO THEM!
HA! HA! HAHA! AH! HA! AH! HA! HA!
SO YOU THINK WE SHOULD LEAVE?
NO. BUT NUMKHA IS RIGHT TO DIG UP HER SEEDS. THEY'LL JUST GET COLD AND MOLDY IN THE HUMIDITY...
AS FOR ME, I'LL CONTINUE MY RESEARCH TO THE EAST TO SEE IF I CAN FIGURE OUT WHAT'S HAPPENING.
WITH A LITTLE LUCK, WE'LL BE ABLE TO SOW AGAIN BEFORE WINTER SETTLES.
YOU WANT ME TO TAKE CARE OF NILS WHILE YOU'RE GONE?
THAT'S NICE OF YOU, GRANNY. BUT I THINK I'LL TAKE HIM WITH ME THIS TIME.
OR I'LL TRY, AT LEAST...
YOU THINK RUBEN WILL SUCCEED?
I HOPE SO... OTHERWISE, THIS WINTER COULD BE OUR LAST. AND I HAVE NO DESIRE TO MEET HELA WITHOUT ANY CHILDREN...

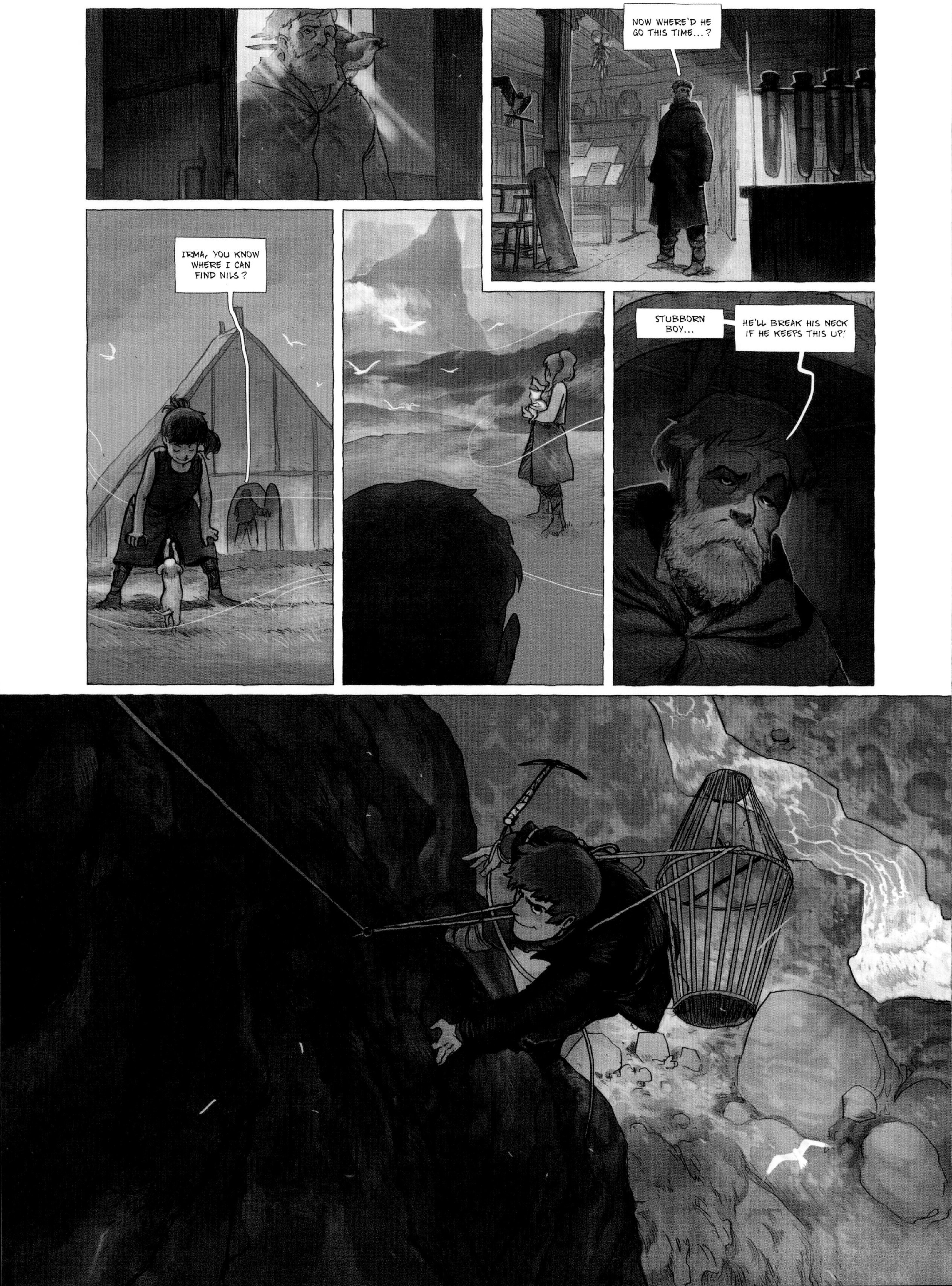
NOW WHERE'D HE GO THIS TIME...?
IRMA, YOU KNOW WHERE I CAN FIND NILS?
STUBBORN BOY...
HE'LL BREAK HIS NECK IF HE KEEPS THIS UP!

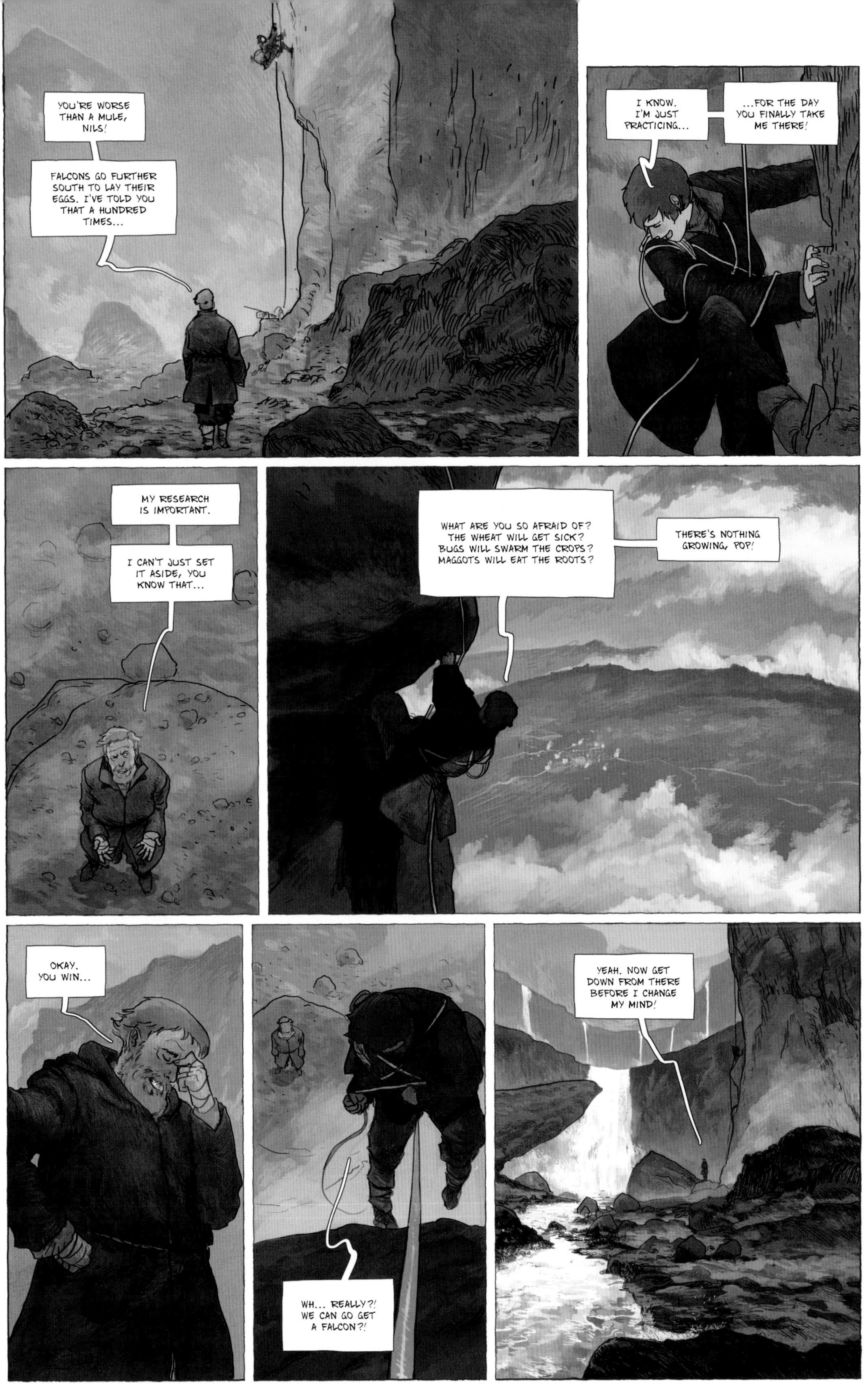
YOU'RE WORSE THAN A MULE, NILS!
FALCONS GO FURTHER SOUTH TO LAY THEIR EGGS. I'VE TOLD YOU THAT A HUNDRED TIMES...
I KNOW. I'M JUST PRACTICING...
...FOR THE DAY YOU FINALLY TAKE ME THERE!
MY RESEARCH IS IMPORTANT.
I CAN'T JUST SET IT ASIDE, YOU KNOW THAT...
WHAT ARE YOU SO AFRAID OF? THE WHEAT WILL GET SICK? BUGS WILL SWARM THE CROPS? MAGGOTS WILL EAT THE ROOTS?
THERE'S NOTHING GROWING, POP!
OKAY. YOU WIN...
WH... REALLY?! WE CAN GO GET A FALCON?!
YEAH. NOW GET DOWN FROM THERE BEFORE I CHANGE MY MIND!

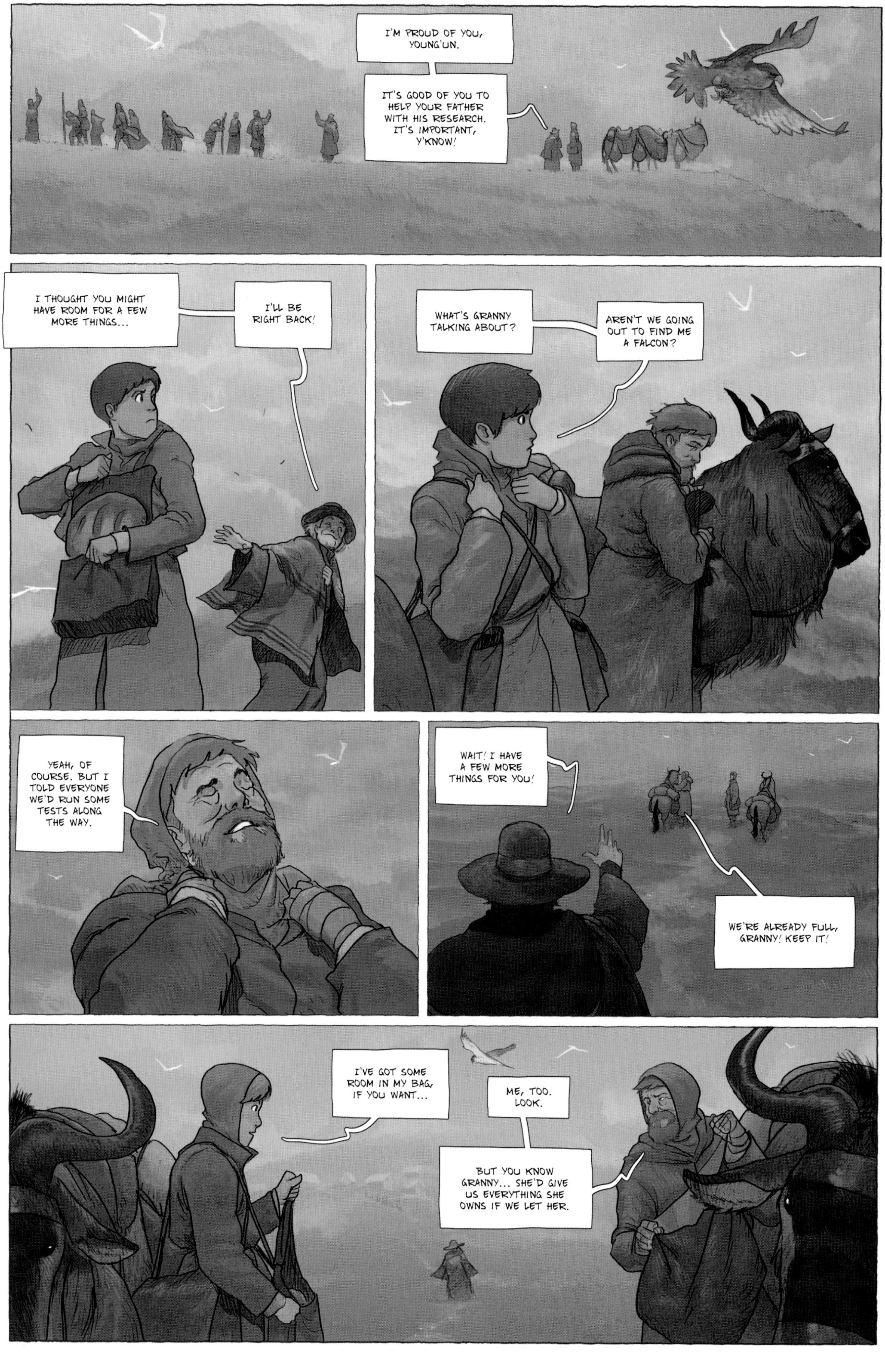
I'M PROUD OF YOU, YOUNG'UN.
IT'S GOOD OF YOU TO HELP YOUR FATHER WITH HIS RESEARCH. IT'S IMPORTANT, Y'KNOW!
I THOUGHT YOU MIGHT HAVE ROOM FOR A FEW MORE THINGS...
I'LL BE RIGHT BACK!
WHAT'S GRANNY TALKING ABOUT?
AREN'T WE GOING OUT TO FIND ME A FALCON?
YEAH, OF COURSE. BUT I TOLD EVERYONE WE'D RUN SOME TESTS ALONG THE WAY.
WAIT! I HAVE A FEW MORE THINGS FOR YOU!
WE'RE ALREADY FULL, GRANNY! KEEP IT!
I'VE GOT SOME ROOM IN MY BAG, IF YOU WANT...
ME, TOO. LOOK.
BUT YOU KNOW GRANNY... SHE'D GIVE US EVERYTHING SHE OWNS IF WE LET HER.

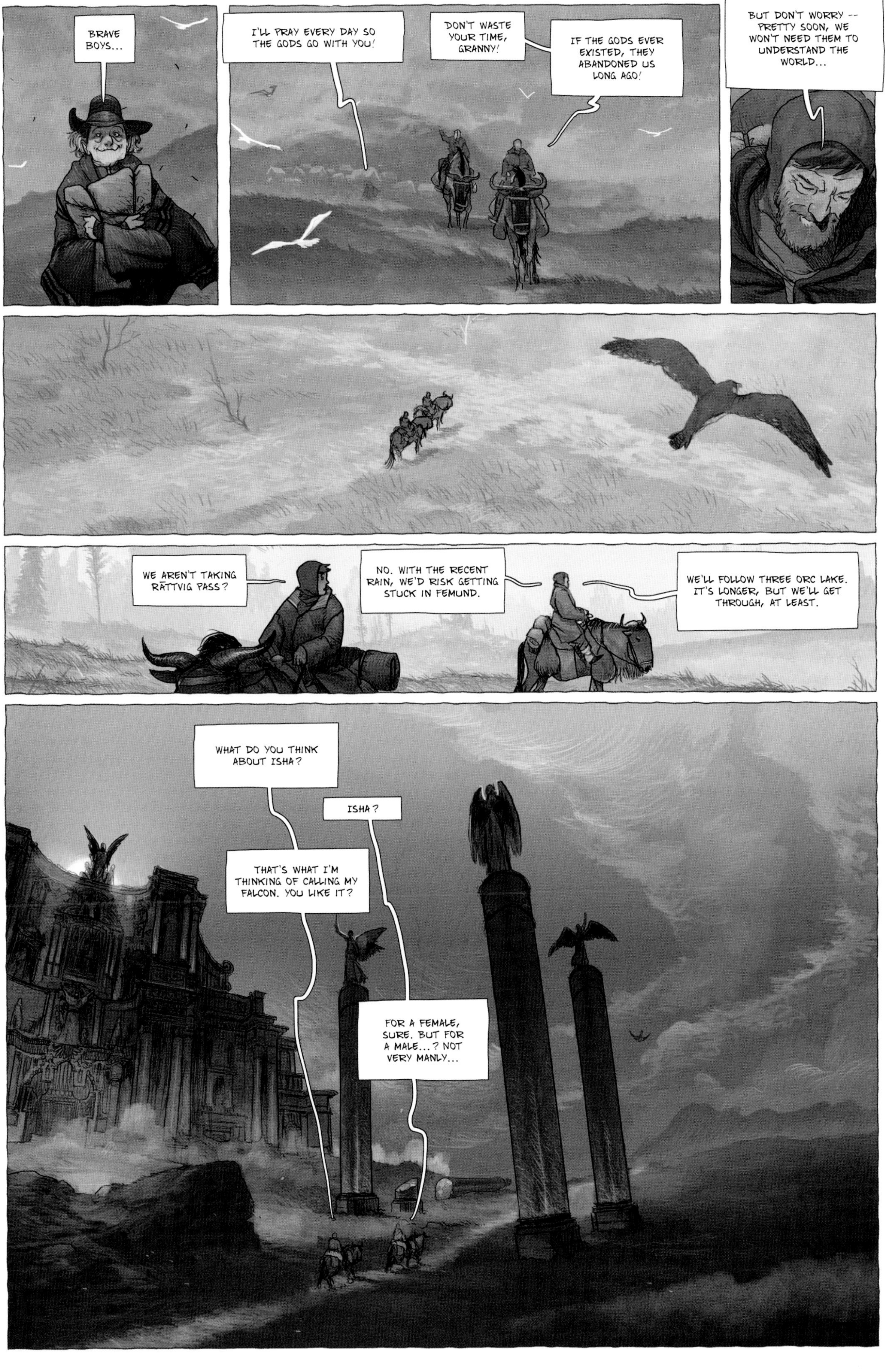
BRAVE BOYS...
I'LL PRAY EVERY DAY SO THE GODS GO WITH YOU!
DON'T WASTE YOUR TIME, GRANNY!
IF THE GODS EVER EXISTED, THEY ABANDONED US LONG AGO!
BUT DON'T WORRY -- PRETTY SOON, WE WON'T NEED THEM TO UNDERSTAND THE WORLD...
WE AREN'T TAKING RÄTTVIG PASS?
NO. WITH THE RECENT RAIN, WE'D RISK GETTING STUCK IN FEMUND.
WE'LL FOLLOW THREE ORC LAKE. IT'S LONGER, BUT WE'LL GET THROUGH, AT LEAST.
WHAT DO YOU THINK ABOUT ISHA?
ISHA?
THAT'S WHAT I'M THINKING OF CALLING MY FALCON. YOU LIKE IT?
FOR A FEMALE, SURE. BUT FOR A MALE...? NOT VERY MANLY...

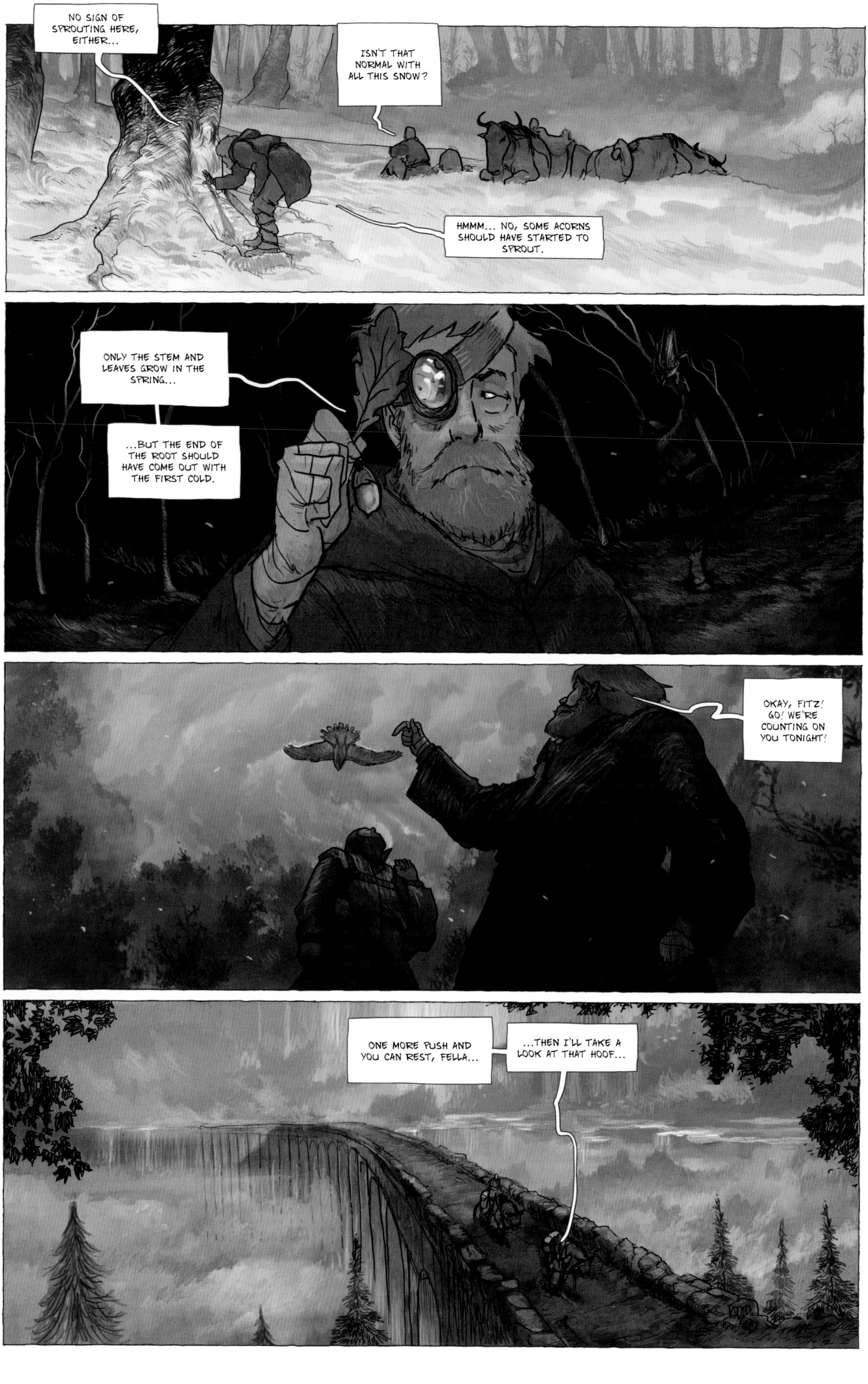
NO SIGN OF SPROUTING HERE, EITHER...
ISN'T THAT NORMAL WITH ALL THIS SNOW?
HMMM... NO, SOME ACORNS SHOULD HAVE STARTED TO SPROUT.
ONLY THE STEM AND LEAVES GROW IN THE SPRING...
...BUT THE END OF THE ROOT SHOULD HAVE COME OUT WITH THE FIRST COLD.
OKAY, FITZ! GO! WE'RE COUNTING ON YOU TONIGHT!
ONE MORE PUSH AND YOU CAN REST, FELLA...
...THEN I'LL TAKE A LOOK AT THAT HOOF...

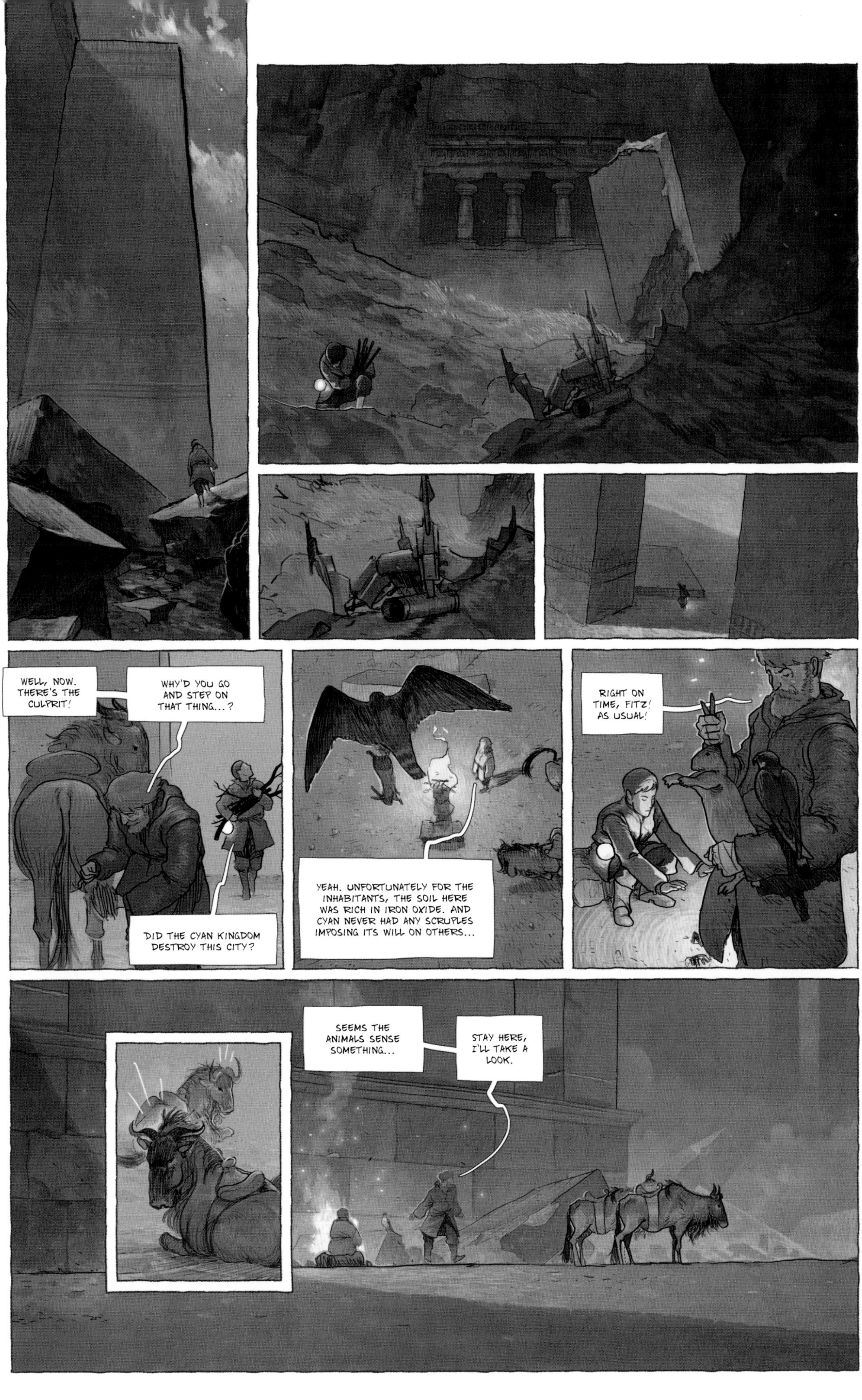
WELL, NOW. THERE'S THE CULPRIT!
WHY'D YOU GO AND STEP ON THAT THING...?
DID THE CYAN KINGDOM DESTROY THIS CITY?
YEAH. UNFORTUNATELY FOR THE INHABITANTS, THE SOIL HERE WAS RICH IN IRON OXIDE. AND CYAN NEVER HAD ANY SCRUPLES IMPOSING ITS WILL ON OTHERS...
RIGHT ON TIME, FITZ! AS USUAL!
SEEMS THE ANIMALS SENSE SOMETHING...
STAY HERE, I'LL TAKE A LOOK.

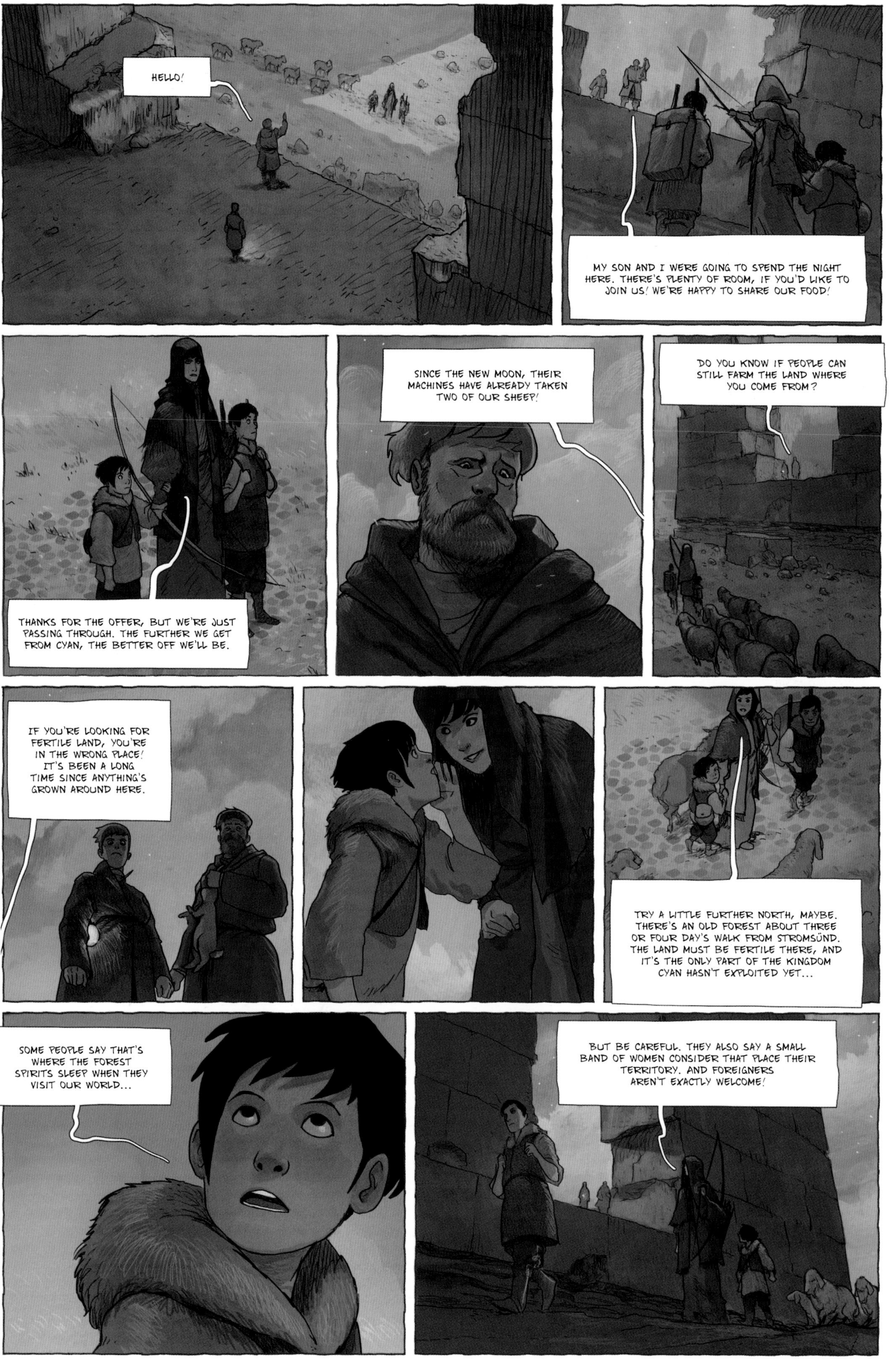
HELLO!
MY SON AND I WERE GOING TO SPEND THE NIGHT HERE. THERE'S PLENTY OF ROOM, IF YOU'D LIKE TO JOIN US! WE'RE HAPPY TO SHARE OUR FOOD!
THANKS FOR THE OFFER, BUT WE'RE JUST PASSING THROUGH. THE FURTHER WE GET FROM CYAN, THE BETTER OFF WE'LL BE.
SINCE THE NEW MOON, THEIR MACHINES HAVE ALREADY TAKEN TWO OF OUR SHEEP!
DO YOU KNOW IF PEOPLE CAN STILL FARM THE LAND WHERE YOU COME FROM?
IF YOU'RE LOOKING FOR FERTILE LAND, YOU'RE IN THE WRONG PLACE! IT'S BEEN A LONG TIME SINCE ANYTHING'S GROWN AROUND HERE.
TRY A LITTLE FURTHER NORTH, MAYBE. THERE'S AN OLD FOREST ABOUT THREE OR FOUR DAY'S WALK FROM STROMSÜND. THE LAND MUST BE FERTILE THERE, AND IT'S THE ONLY PART OF THE KINGDOM CYAN HASN'T EXPLOITED YET...
SOME PEOPLE SAY THAT'S WHERE THE FOREST SPIRITS SLEEP WHEN THEY VISIT OUR WORLD...
BUT BE CAREFUL. THEY ALSO SAY A SMALL BAND OF WOMEN CONSIDER THAT PLACE THEIR TERRITORY. AND FOREIGNERS AREN'T EXACTLY WELCOME!

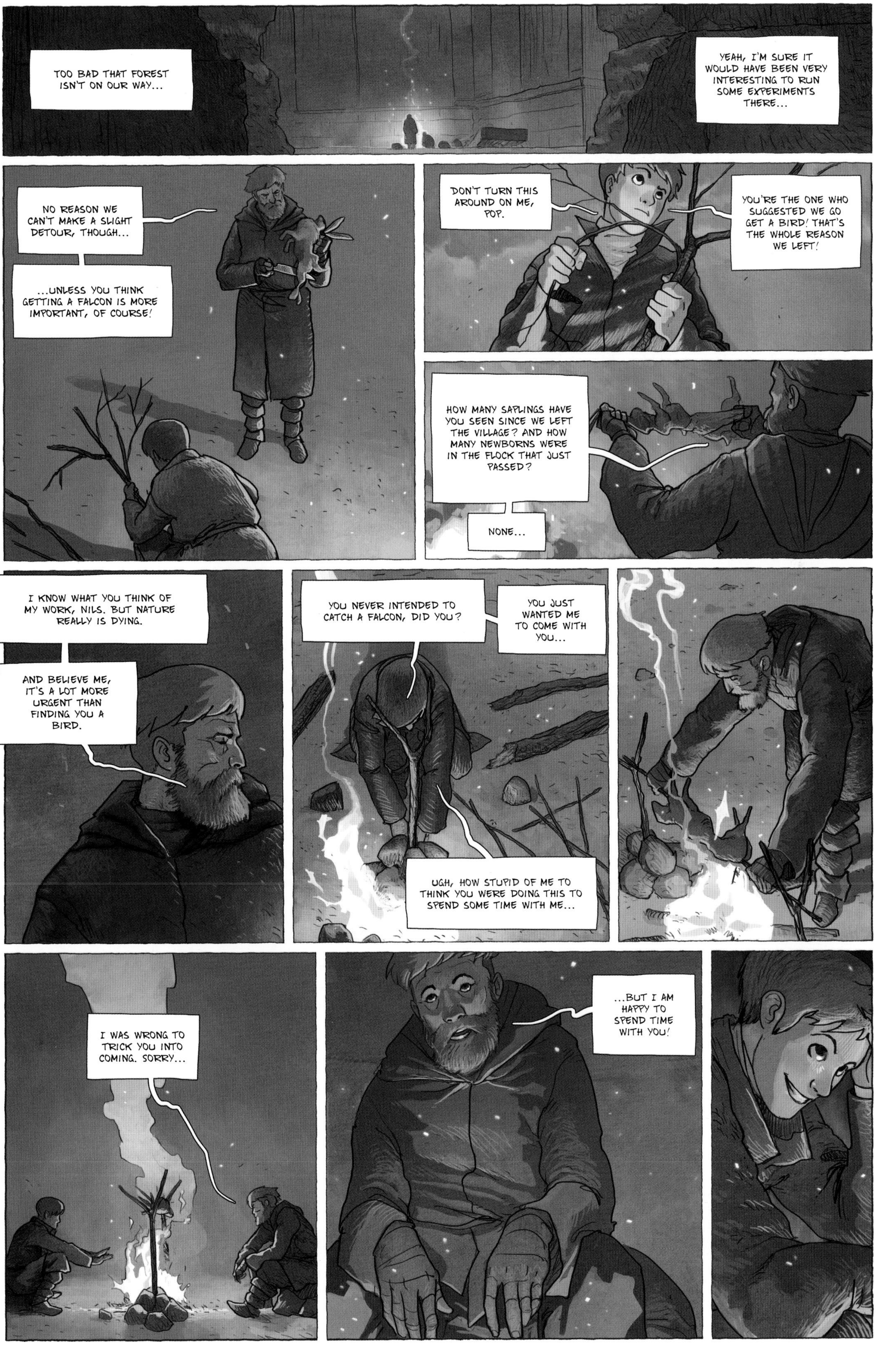

TOO BAD THAT FOREST ISN'T ON OUR WAY...
YEAH, I'M SURE IT WOULD HAVE BEEN VERY INTERESTING TO RUN SOME EXPERIMENTS THERE...
NO REASON WE CAN'T MAKE A SLIGHT DETOUR, THOUGH...
...UNLESS YOU THINK GETTING A FALCON IS MORE IMPORTANT, OF COURSE!
DON'T TURN THIS AROUND ON ME, POP.
YOU'RE THE ONE WHO SUGGESTED WE GO GET A BIRD! THAT'S THE WHOLE REASON WE LEFT!
HOW MANY SAPLINGS HAVE YOU SEEN SINCE WE LEFT THE VILLAGE? AND HOW MANY NEWBORNS WERE IN THE FLOCK THAT JUST PASSED?
NONE...
I KNOW WHAT YOU THINK OF MY WORK, NILS. BUT NATURE REALLY IS DYING.
AND BELIEVE ME, IT'S A LOT MORE URGENT THAN FINDING YOU A BIRD.
YOU NEVER INTENDED TO CATCH A FALCON, DID YOU?
YOU JUST WANTED ME TO COME WITH YOU...
UGH, HOW STUPID OF ME TO THINK YOU WERE DOING THIS TO SPEND SOME TIME WITH ME...
I WAS WRONG TO TRICK YOU INTO COMING. SORRY...
...BUT I AM HAPPY TO SPEND TIME WITH YOU!

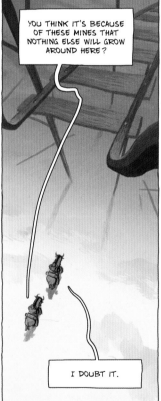

YOU THINK IT'S BECAUSE OF THESE MINES THAT NOTHING ELSE WILL GROW AROUND HERE?

I DOUBT IT.

MEN ARE RECKLESS ENOUGH TO CAUSE THIS KIND OF DISASTER, BUT I TRUST THEY KNOW ENOUGH NOT TO PUT ALL LIFE IN DANGER.

AT LEAST, I HOPE SO.

WHAT ARE WE DOING, THEN?

ARE WE GONNA LOOK FOR A FALCON OR CHASE SOME ANSWERS IN THAT FOREST?

IF NATURE REALLY HAS GONE OUT OF ORDER, WHAT CAN WE EVEN DO ABOUT IT?

I DON'T HAVE THE FAINTEST IDEA. BUT WE CAN START BY FINDING OUT WHAT'S WRONG...

SOUNDS LIKE QUITE A PLAN...

I'M BEGINNING TO UNDERSTAND WHY NO ONE EVER HELPS YOU WITH YOUR RESEARCH.

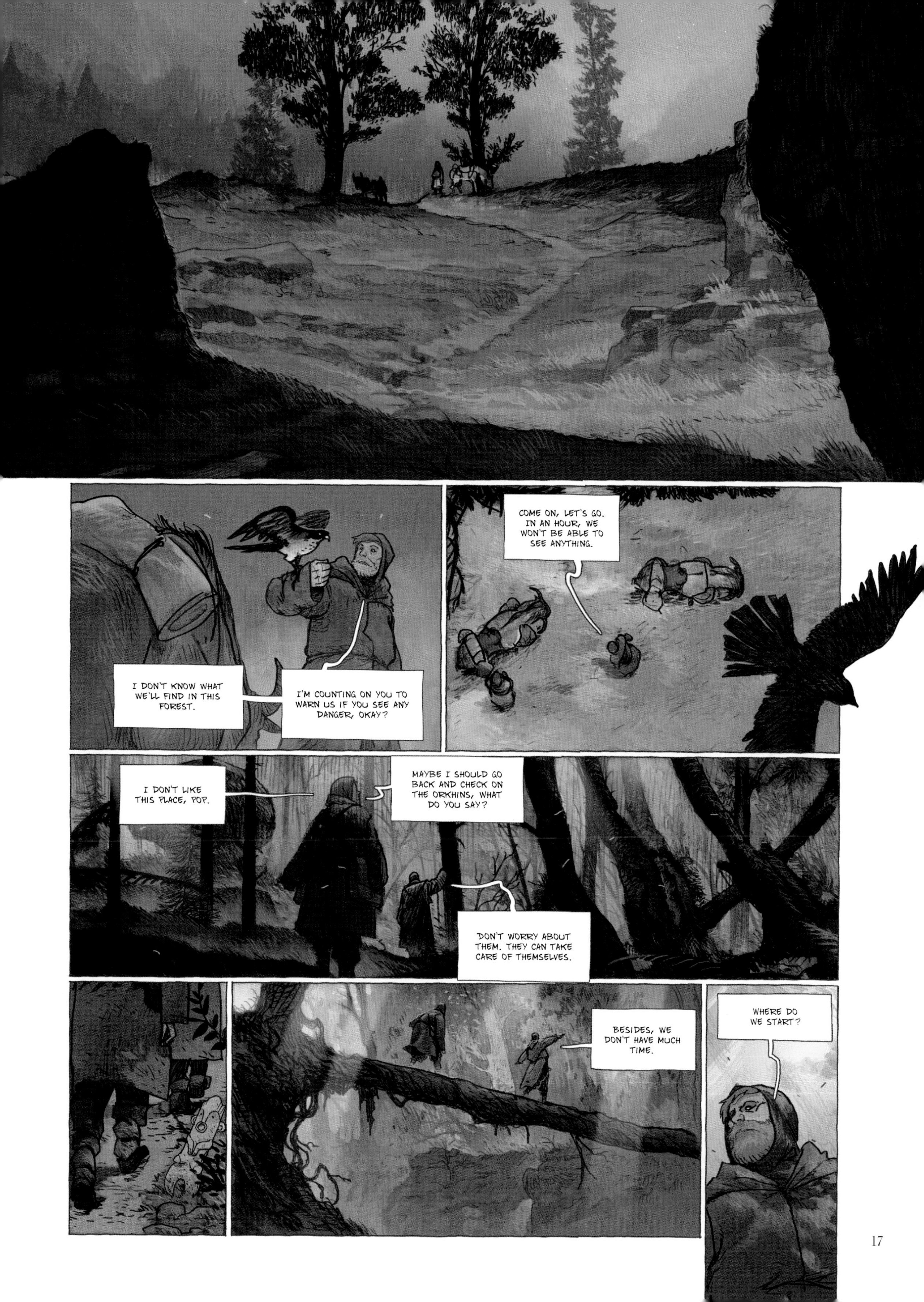
I DON'T KNOW WHAT WE'LL FIND IN THIS FOREST.
I'M COUNTING ON YOU TO WARN US IF YOU SEE ANY DANGER, OKAY?
COME ON, LET'S GO. IN AN HOUR, WE WON'T BE ABLE TO SEE ANYTHING.
I DON'T LIKE THIS PLACE, POP.
MAYBE I SHOULD GO BACK AND CHECK ON THE ORKHINS, WHAT DO YOU SAY?
DON'T WORRY ABOUT THEM. THEY CAN TAKE CARE OF THEMSELVES.
BESIDES, WE DON'T HAVE MUCH TIME.
WHERE DO WE START?

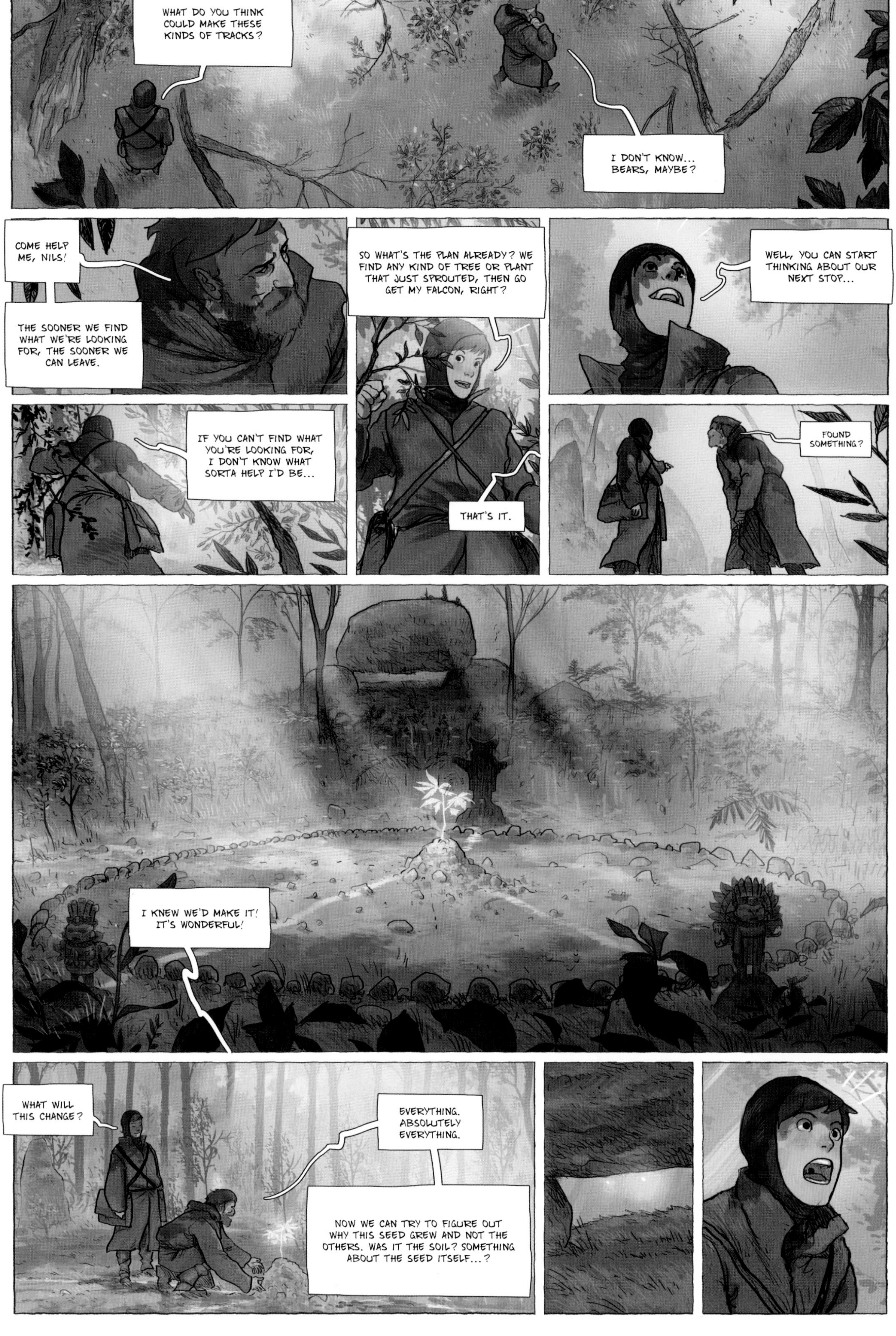
WHAT DO YOU THINK COULD MAKE THESE KINDS OF TRACKS?
I DON'T KNOW... BEARS, MAYBE?
COME HELP ME, NILS!
THE SOONER WE FIND WHAT WE'RE LOOKING FOR, THE SOONER WE CAN LEAVE.
SO WHAT'S THE PLAN ALREADY? WE FIND ANY KIND OF TREE OR PLANT THAT JUST SPROUTED, THEN GO GET MY FALCON, RIGHT?
WELL, YOU CAN START THINKING ABOUT OUR NEXT STOP...
IF YOU CAN'T FIND WHAT YOU'RE LOOKING FOR, I DON'T KNOW WHAT SORTA HELP I'D BE...
THAT'S IT.
FOUND SOMETHING?
I KNEW WE'D MAKE IT! IT'S WONDERFUL!
WHAT WILL THIS CHANGE?
EVERYTHING. ABSOLUTELY EVERYTHING.
NOW WE CAN TRY TO FIGURE OUT WHY THIS SEED GREW AND NOT THE OTHERS. WAS IT THE SOIL? SOMETHING ABOUT THE SEED ITSELF...?

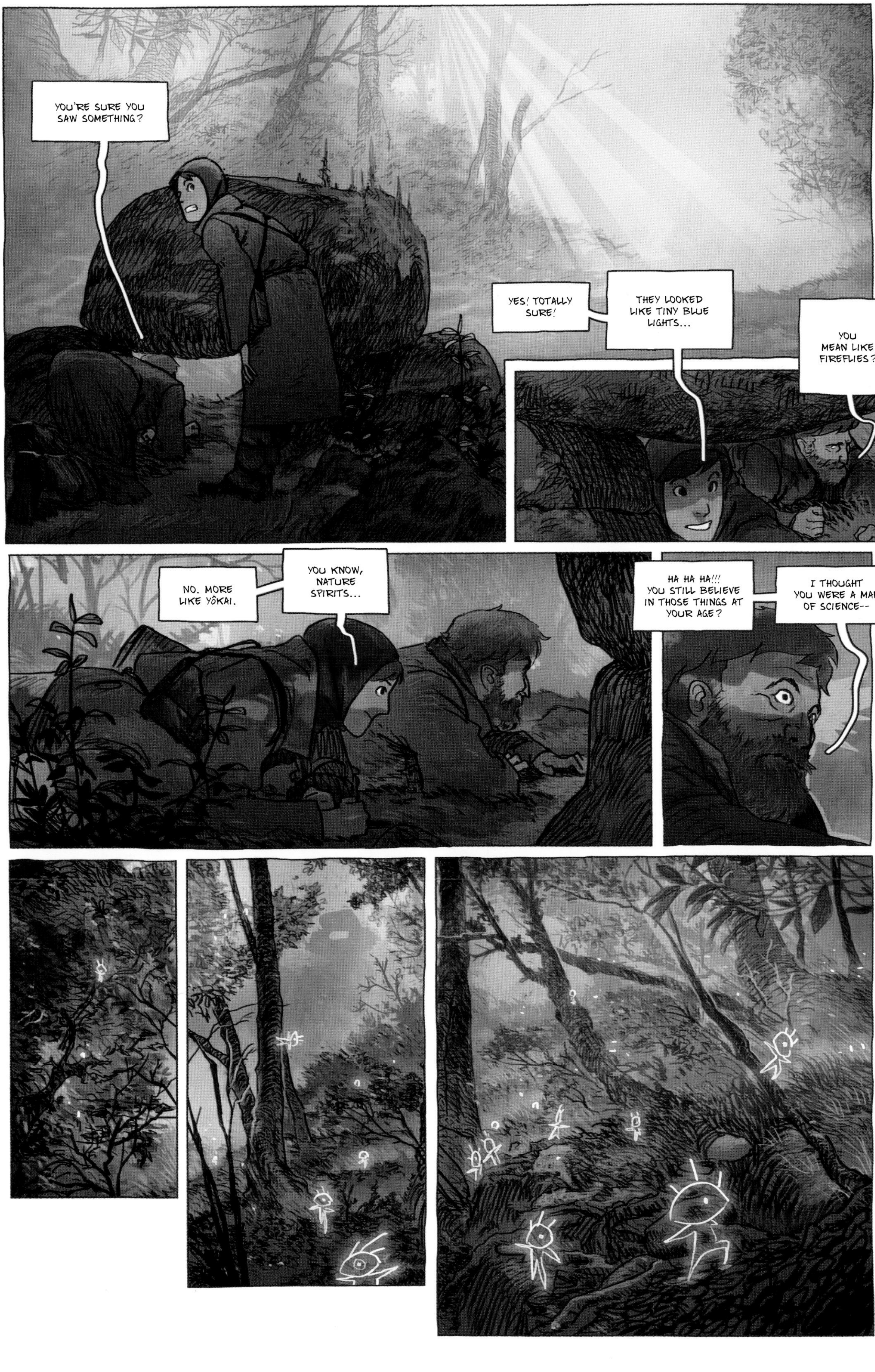
YOU'RE SURE YOU SAW SOMETHING?
YES! TOTALLY SURE!
THEY LOOKED LIKE TINY BLUE LIGHTS...
YOU MEAN LIKE FIREFLIES?
NO. MORE LIKE YÔKAI.
YOU KNOW, NATURE SPIRITS...
HA HA HA!!! YOU STILL BELIEVE IN THOSE THINGS AT YOUR AGE?
I THOUGHT YOU WERE A MAN OF SCIENCE--

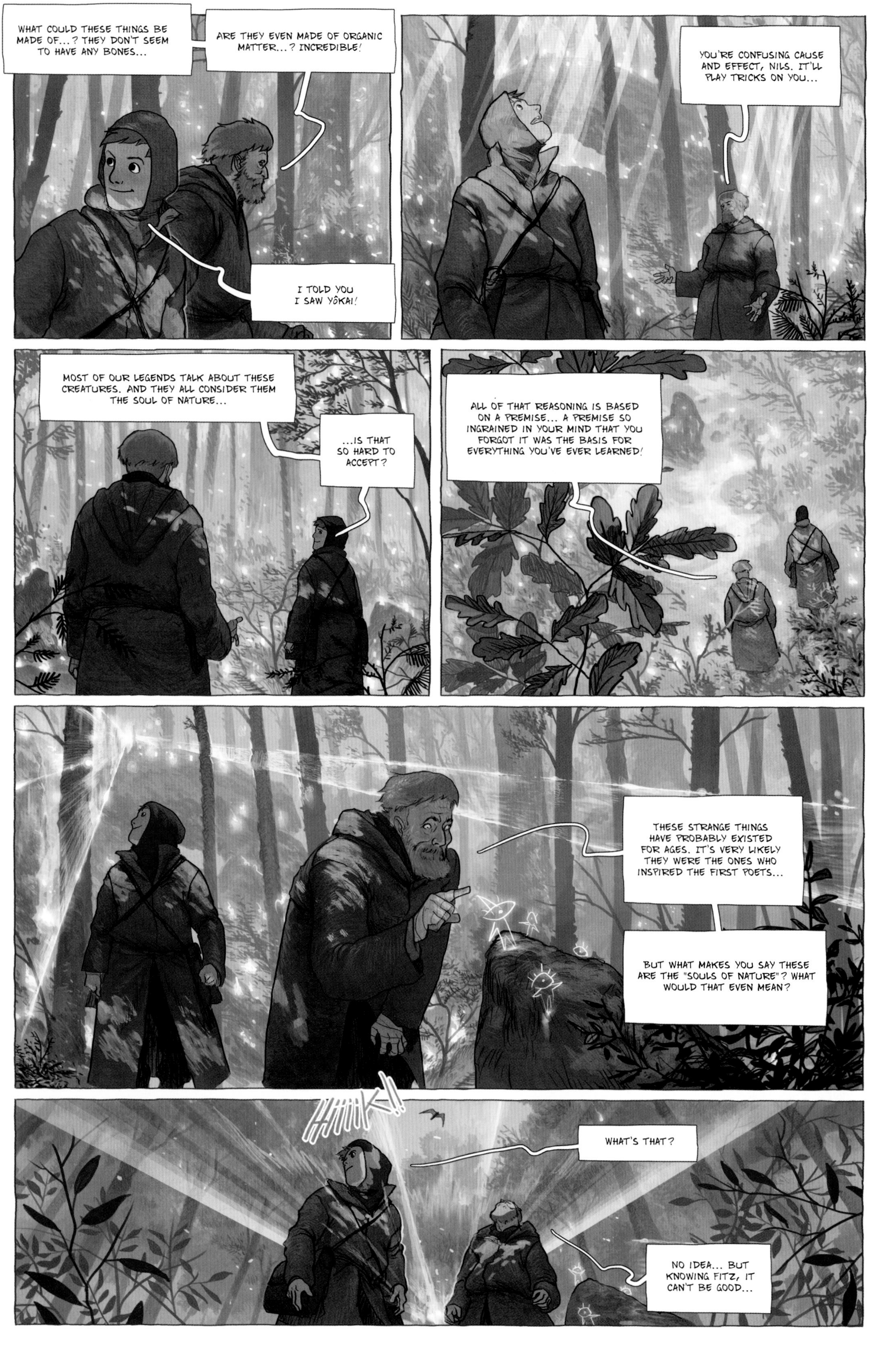
WHAT COULD THESE THINGS BE MADE OF...? THEY DON'T SEEM TO HAVE ANY BONES...
ARE THEY EVEN MADE OF ORGANIC MATTER...? INCREDIBLE!
I TOLD YOU I SAW YŌKAI!
YOU'RE CONFUSING CAUSE AND EFFECT, NILS. IT'LL PLAY TRICKS ON YOU...
MOST OF OUR LEGENDS TALK ABOUT THESE CREATURES. AND THEY ALL CONSIDER THEM THE SOUL OF NATURE...
...IS THAT SO HARD TO ACCEPT?
ALL OF THAT REASONING IS BASED ON A PREMISE... A PREMISE SO INGRAINED IN YOUR MIND THAT YOU FORGOT IT WAS THE BASIS FOR EVERYTHING YOU'VE EVER LEARNED!
THESE STRANGE THINGS HAVE PROBABLY EXISTED FOR AGES. IT'S VERY LIKELY THEY WERE THE ONES WHO INSPIRED THE FIRST POETS...
BUT WHAT MAKES YOU SAY THESE ARE THE "SOULS OF NATURE"? WHAT WOULD THAT EVEN MEAN?
HIIIIK!!
WHAT'S THAT?
NO IDEA... BUT KNOWING FITZ, IT CAN'T BE GOOD...

NILS, COME ON. I ONLY KNOW ONE KINGDOM WITH TECHNOLOGY LIKE THAT... AND BELIEVE ME, IT'S BETTER NOT TO STICK AROUND!

THE CYAN KINGDOM?

YEAH, I'M AFRAID SO...

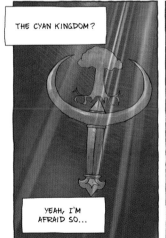

#@%!

WHAT COULD THEY POSSIBLY WANT WITH THE YŌKAI?

YOUR GUESS IS AS GOOD AS MINE... BUT I DON'T CARE TO HANG AROUND TO FIND OUT!

A FEW MORE SECONDS, SASCHA! I'M ALMOST THERE...

GO WARN THE OTHERS!

Roc!

I'M AFRAID WE CAN'T DO IT ALONE THIS TIME...

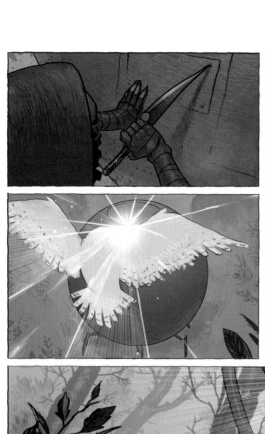

NILS... WHAT ARE YOU DOING, DAMMIT?

SHE WON'T MAKE IT WITHOUT OUR HELP, POP! WE GOTTA DO SOMETHING!

I'VE SEEN MACHINES LESS SOPHISTICATED THAN THAT CRUSH A DOZEN MEN! WITH OR WITHOUT US, THAT WOMAN DOESN'T STAND A CHANCE!

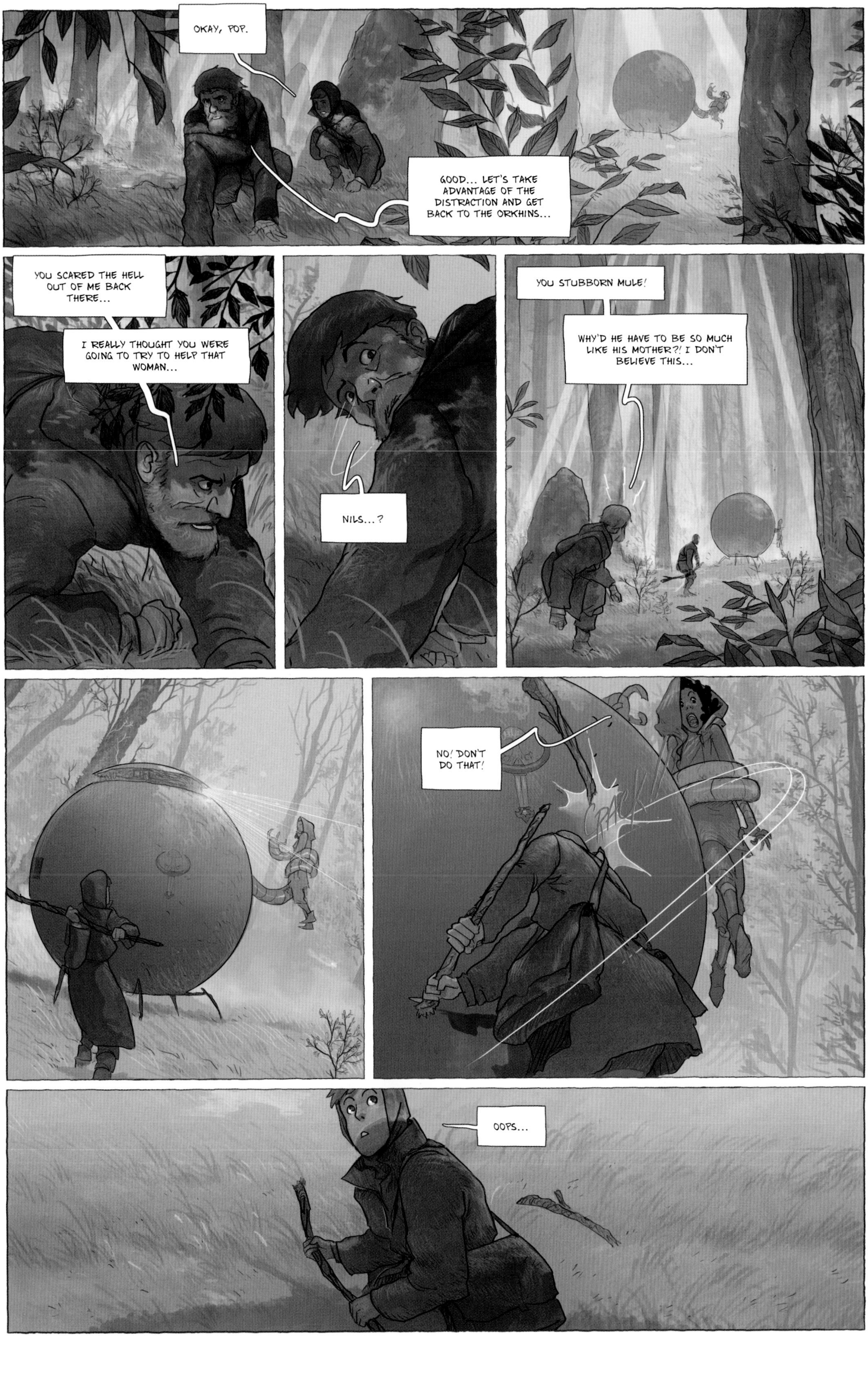
OKAY, POP.
GOOD... LET'S TAKE ADVANTAGE OF THE DISTRACTION AND GET BACK TO THE ORKHINS...
YOU SCARED THE HELL OUT OF ME BACK THERE...
I REALLY THOUGHT YOU WERE GOING TO TRY TO HELP THAT WOMAN...
NILS...?
YOU STUBBORN MULE!
WHY'D HE HAVE TO BE SO MUCH LIKE HIS MOTHER?! I DON'T BELIEVE THIS...
NO! DON'T DO THAT!
CRACK
OOPS...

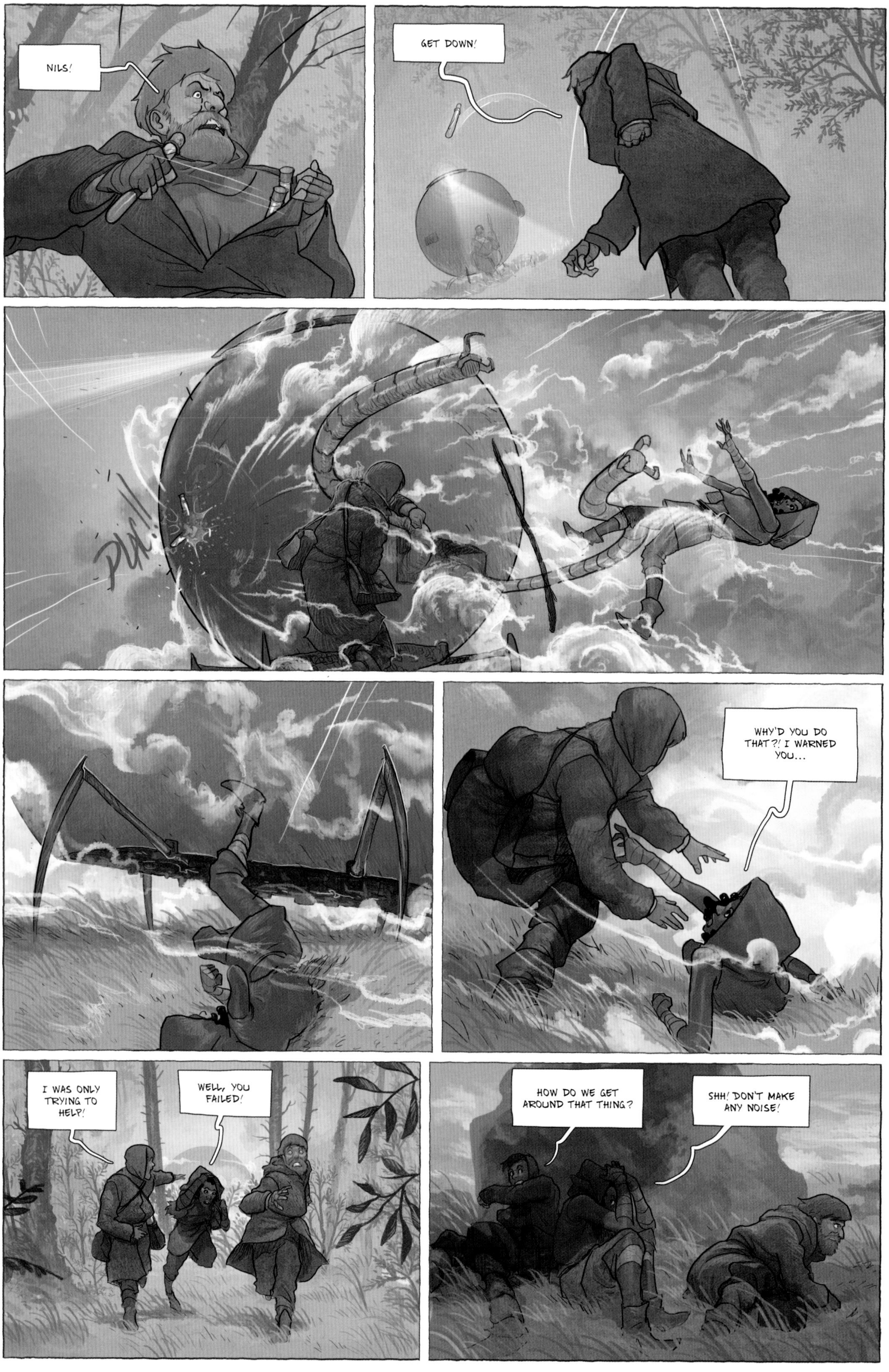
NILS!
GET DOWN!
PLIC!!
WHY'D YOU DO THAT?! I WARNED YOU...
I WAS ONLY TRYING TO HELP!
WELL, YOU FAILED!
HOW DO WE GET AROUND THAT THING?
SHH! DON'T MAKE ANY NOISE!

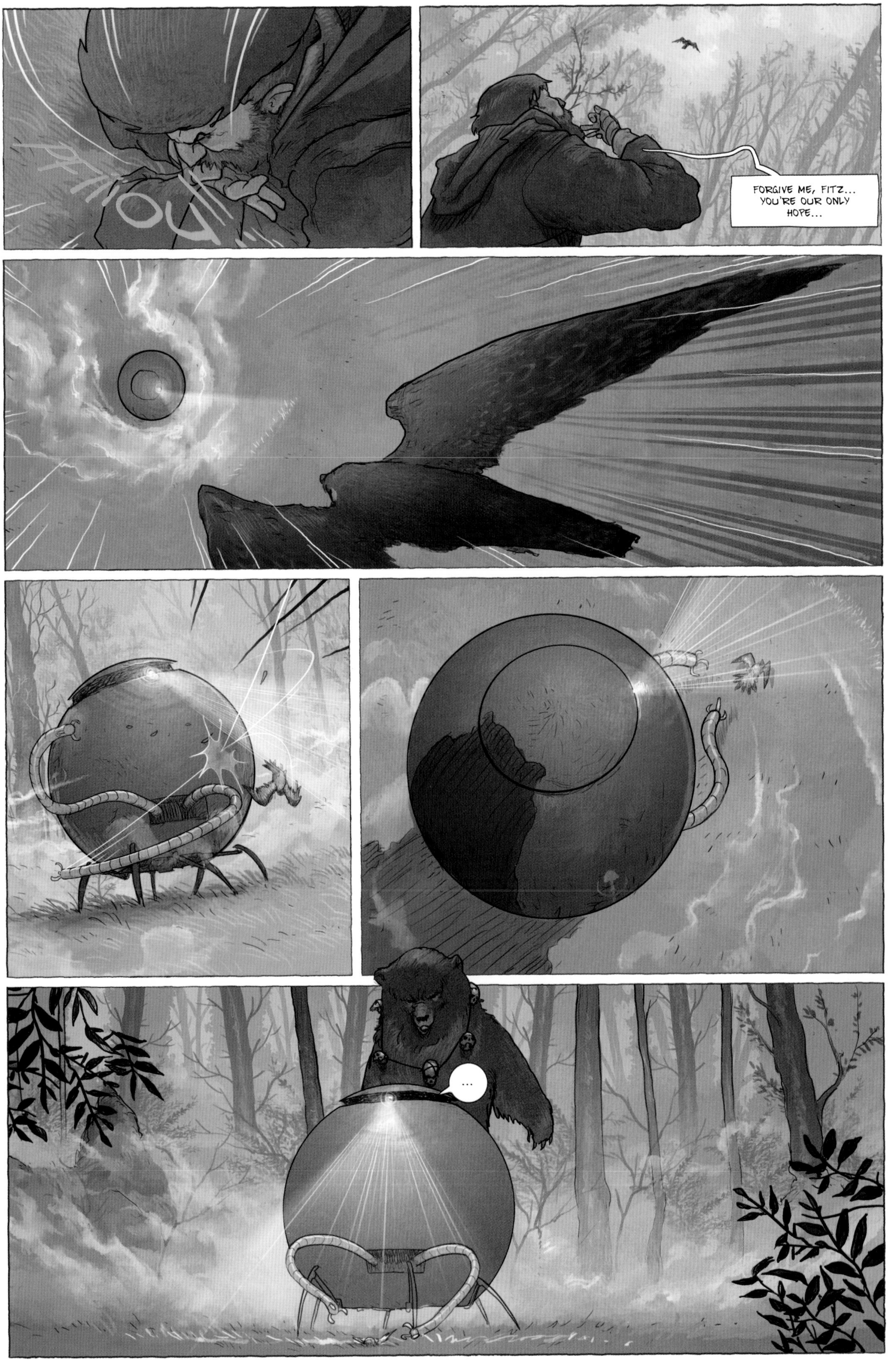
FORGIVE ME, FITZ... YOU'RE OUR ONLY HOPE...
...

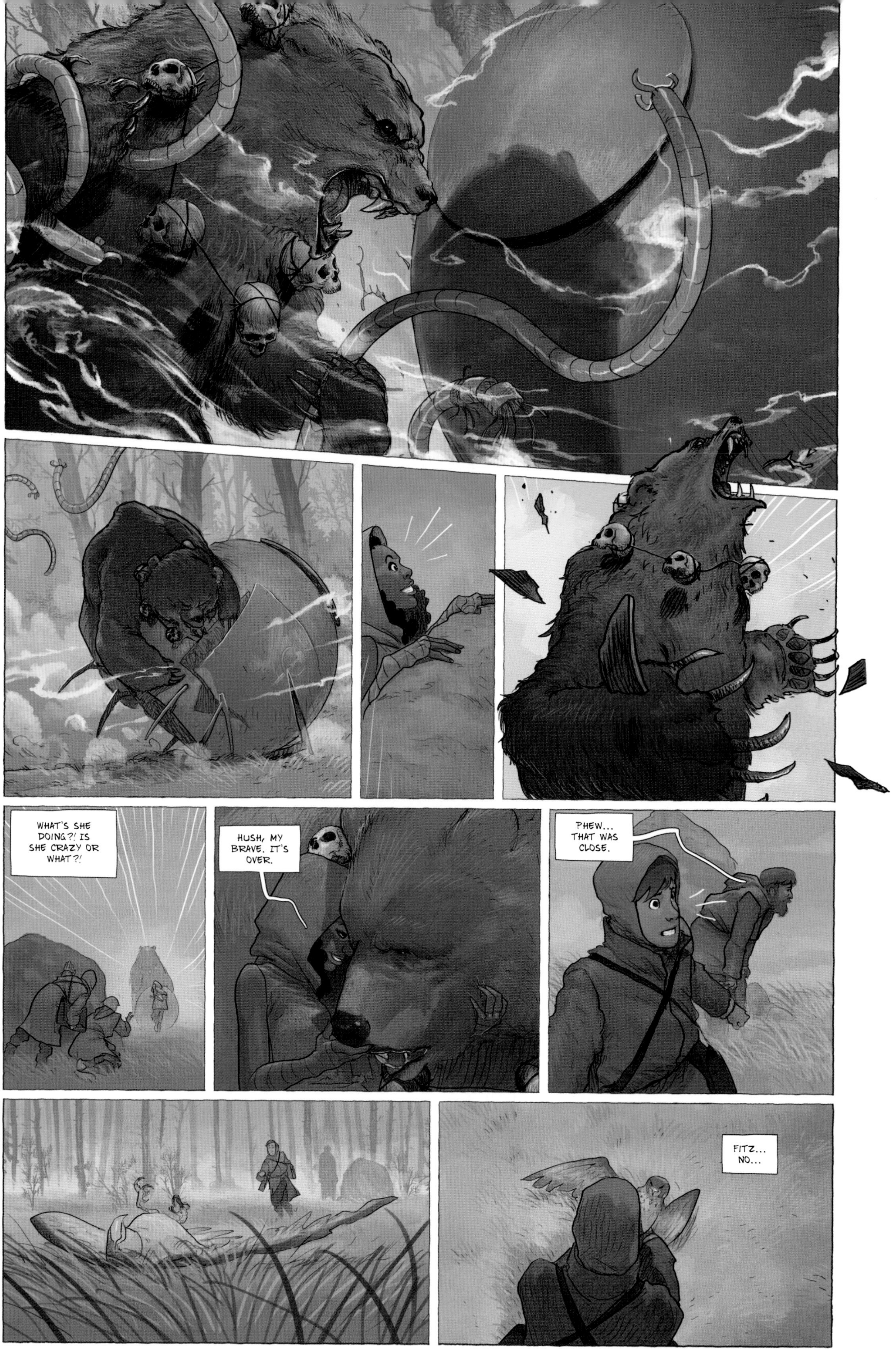
WHAT'S SHE DOING?! IS SHE CRAZY OR WHAT?!
HUSH, MY BRAVE. IT'S OVER.
PHEW... THAT WAS CLOSE.
FITZ... NO...

I'M SORRY, IT'S ALL MY FAULT.

YOU DID NOTHING, NILS. I'M THE ONE THAT ASKED FITZ TO HELP US.

IF THAT MACHINE WAS YOUR SIZE, IT WOULDN'T HAVE STOOD A CHANCE...

YOU FOUGHT WELL. THANK YOU!

THAT WAS STUPID!

TRUE, IT WAS A HUGE MISTAKE TO HELP YOU!

YEAH, BUT IT WAS EVEN MORE STUPID TO SEND THIS CREATURE TO CERTAIN DEATH...

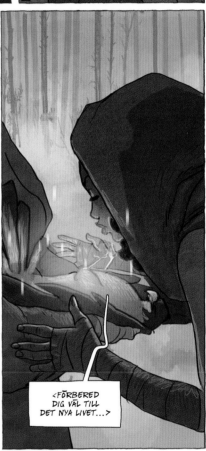

<FÖRBERED DIG VÄL TILL DET NYA LIVET...>

<...SOM SNART KOMMER ATT BLI DIN.>

WHAT'S HAPPENING...?

WHAT WAS THAT LIGHT THAT JUST DISAPPEARED?

NOW YOU CAN HONOR YOUR FRIEND'S OLD BODY.

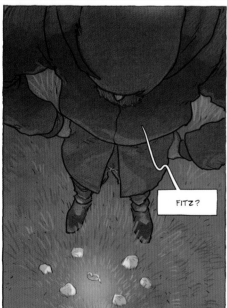

FITZ?

THAT'S IMPOSSIBLE! HOW CAN FITZ'S SPIRIT END UP IN THAT PLANT?

WHO MENTIONED SPIRITS?

I DON'T UNDERSTAND... WHAT WAS THAT LUMINOUS THING?

JUST AS I THOUGHT... THEY ADDED A CAMERA AND SOME EXTRA ARMORED PLATING.

?!

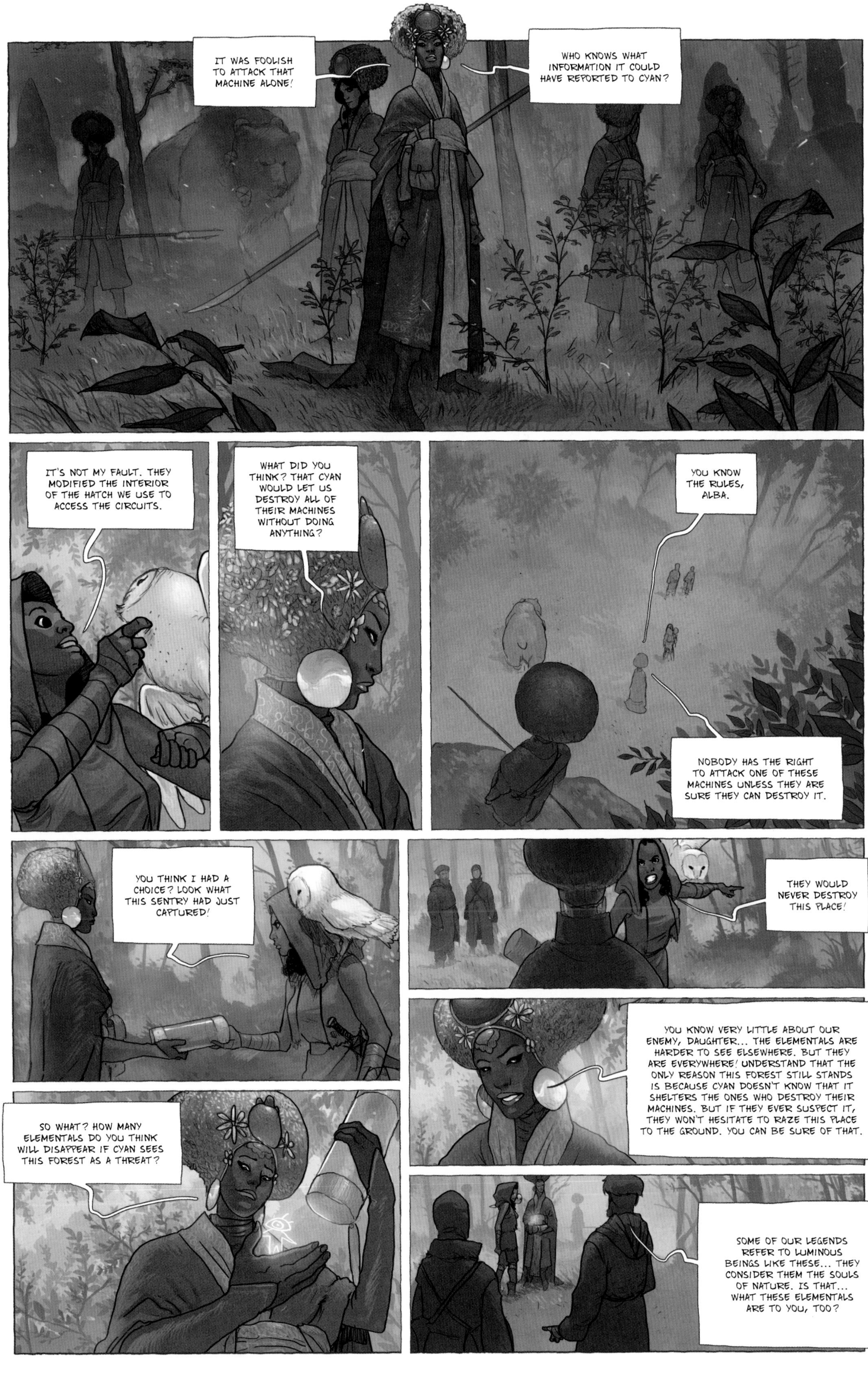
IT WAS FOOLISH TO ATTACK THAT MACHINE ALONE!
WHO KNOWS WHAT INFORMATION IT COULD HAVE REPORTED TO CYAN?
IT'S NOT MY FAULT. THEY MODIFIED THE INTERIOR OF THE HATCH WE USE TO ACCESS THE CIRCUITS.
WHAT DID YOU THINK? THAT CYAN WOULD LET US DESTROY ALL OF THEIR MACHINES WITHOUT DOING ANYTHING?
YOU KNOW THE RULES, ALBA.
NOBODY HAS THE RIGHT TO ATTACK ONE OF THESE MACHINES UNLESS THEY ARE SURE THEY CAN DESTROY IT.
YOU THINK I HAD A CHOICE? LOOK WHAT THIS SENTRY HAD JUST CAPTURED!
THEY WOULD NEVER DESTROY THIS PLACE!
YOU KNOW VERY LITTLE ABOUT OUR ENEMY, DAUGHTER... THE ELEMENTALS ARE HARDER TO SEE ELSEWHERE. BUT THEY ARE EVERYWHERE! UNDERSTAND THAT THE ONLY REASON THIS FOREST STILL STANDS IS BECAUSE CYAN DOESN'T KNOW THAT IT SHELTERS THE ONES WHO DESTROY THEIR MACHINES. BUT IF THEY EVER SUSPECT IT, THEY WON'T HESITATE TO RAZE THIS PLACE TO THE GROUND. YOU CAN BE SURE OF THAT.
SO WHAT? HOW MANY ELEMENTALS DO YOU THINK WILL DISAPPEAR IF CYAN SEES THIS FOREST AS A THREAT?
SOME OF OUR LEGENDS REFER TO LUMINOUS BEINGS LIKE THESE... THEY CONSIDER THEM THE SOULS OF NATURE. IS THAT... WHAT THESE ELEMENTALS ARE TO YOU, TOO?

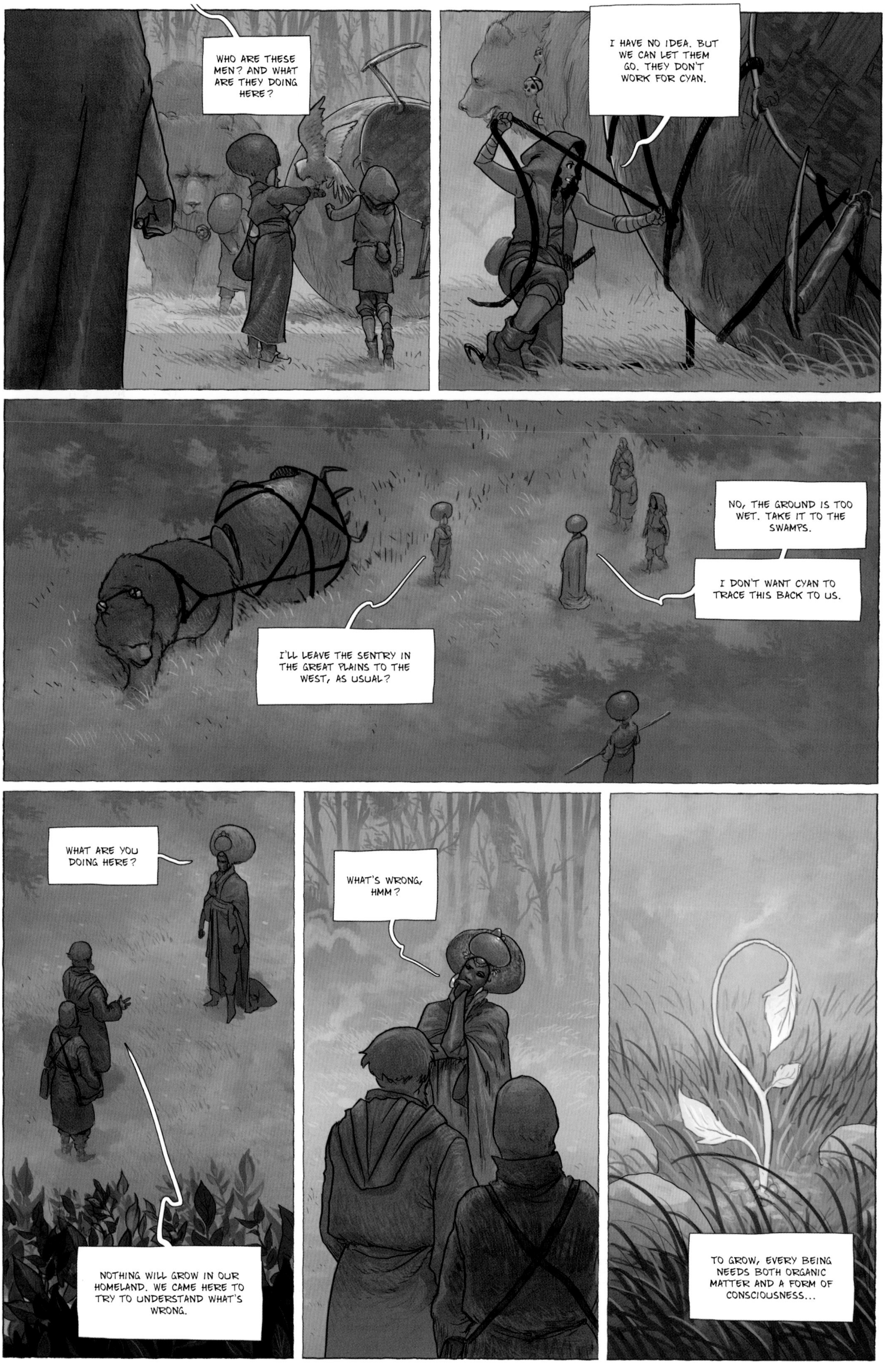
WHO ARE THESE MEN? AND WHAT ARE THEY DOING HERE?
I HAVE NO IDEA. BUT WE CAN LET THEM GO. THEY DON'T WORK FOR CYAN.
I'LL LEAVE THE SENTRY IN THE GREAT PLAINS TO THE WEST, AS USUAL?
NO, THE GROUND IS TOO WET. TAKE IT TO THE SWAMPS.
I DON'T WANT CYAN TO TRACE THIS BACK TO US.
WHAT ARE YOU DOING HERE?
NOTHING WILL GROW IN OUR HOMELAND. WE CAME HERE TO TRY TO UNDERSTAND WHAT'S WRONG.
WHAT'S WRONG, HMM?
TO GROW, EVERY BEING NEEDS BOTH ORGANIC MATTER AND A FORM OF CONSCIOUSNESS...

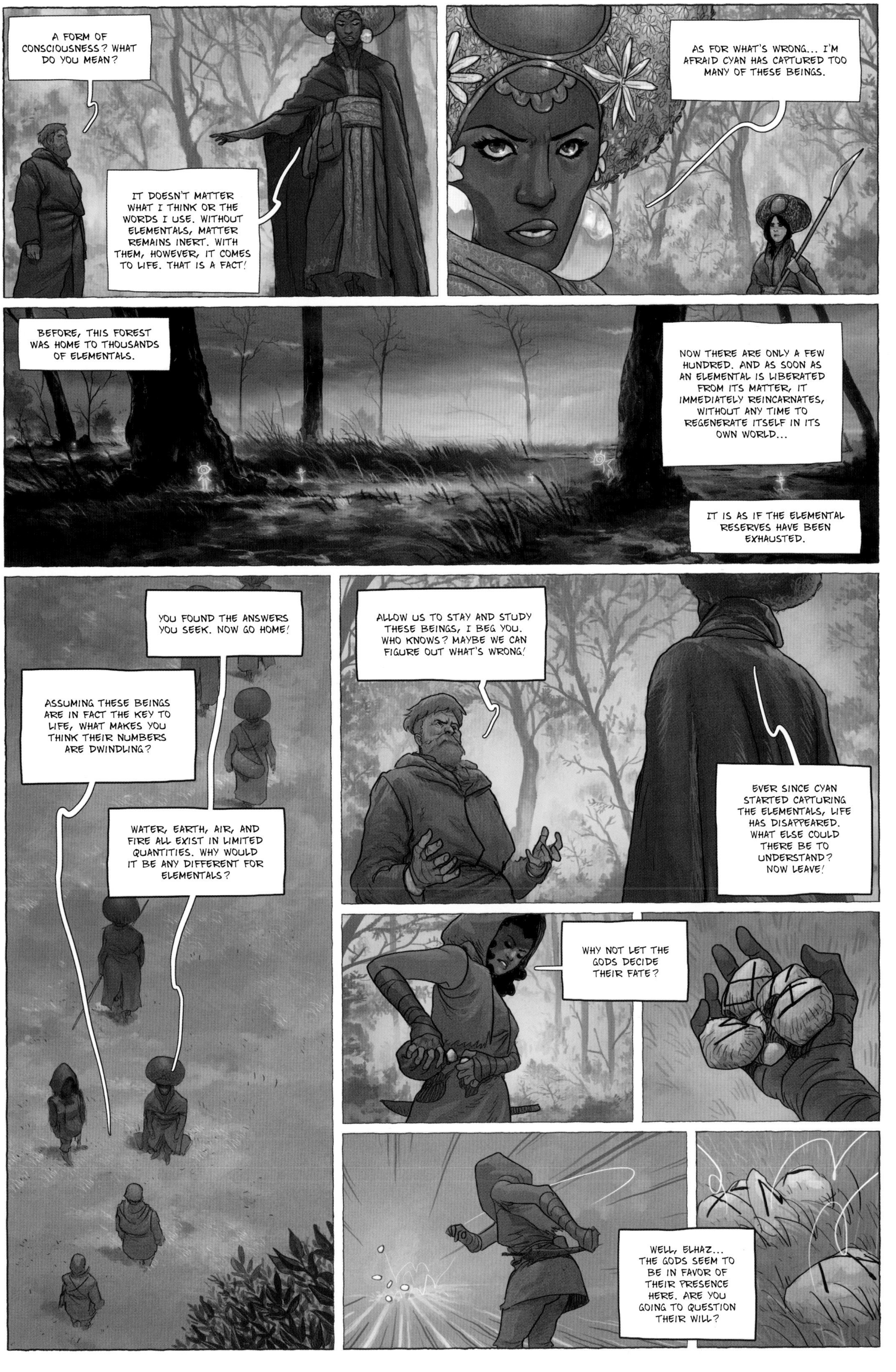
A FORM OF CONSCIOUSNESS? WHAT DO YOU MEAN?
IT DOESN'T MATTER WHAT I THINK OR THE WORDS I USE. WITHOUT ELEMENTALS, MATTER REMAINS INERT. WITH THEM, HOWEVER, IT COMES TO LIFE. THAT IS A FACT!
AS FOR WHAT'S WRONG... I'M AFRAID CYAN HAS CAPTURED TOO MANY OF THESE BEINGS.
BEFORE, THIS FOREST WAS HOME TO THOUSANDS OF ELEMENTALS.
NOW THERE ARE ONLY A FEW HUNDRED. AND AS SOON AS AN ELEMENTAL IS LIBERATED FROM ITS MATTER, IT IMMEDIATELY REINCARNATES, WITHOUT ANY TIME TO REGENERATE ITSELF IN ITS OWN WORLD...
IT IS AS IF THE ELEMENTAL RESERVES HAVE BEEN EXHAUSTED.
YOU FOUND THE ANSWERS YOU SEEK. NOW GO HOME!
ASSUMING THESE BEINGS ARE IN FACT THE KEY TO LIFE, WHAT MAKES YOU THINK THEIR NUMBERS ARE DWINDLING?
WATER, EARTH, AIR, AND FIRE ALL EXIST IN LIMITED QUANTITIES. WHY WOULD IT BE ANY DIFFERENT FOR ELEMENTALS?
ALLOW US TO STAY AND STUDY THESE BEINGS, I BEG YOU. WHO KNOWS? MAYBE WE CAN FIGURE OUT WHAT'S WRONG!
EVER SINCE CYAN STARTED CAPTURING THE ELEMENTALS, LIFE HAS DISAPPEARED. WHAT ELSE COULD THERE BE TO UNDERSTAND? NOW LEAVE!
WHY NOT LET THE GODS DECIDE THEIR FATE?
WELL, ELHAZ... THE GODS SEEM TO BE IN FAVOR OF THEIR PRESENCE HERE. ARE YOU GOING TO QUESTION THEIR WILL?

SINCE IT IS THE WILL OF THE GODS, YOU CAN STAY IN THIS FOREST UNTIL DAWN!

BUT IF YOU WANT TO STUDY THE ELEMENTALS, I SUGGEST YOU GO FURTHER NORTH, TOWARD THE BIG LAKES. WITH ALL OF THE RUCKUS HERE, I DOUBT THEY WILL REAPPEAR IN THIS PART OF THE FOREST FOR SEVERAL DAYS.

THE GODS TELL US WHAT WE NEED TO HEAR IN ORDER TO ACHIEVE THEIR WILL, ALBA.

BUT I WARN YOU, THAT IS SOMETIMES VERY DIFFERENT FROM WHAT YOU THINK IT IS.

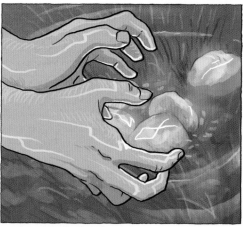

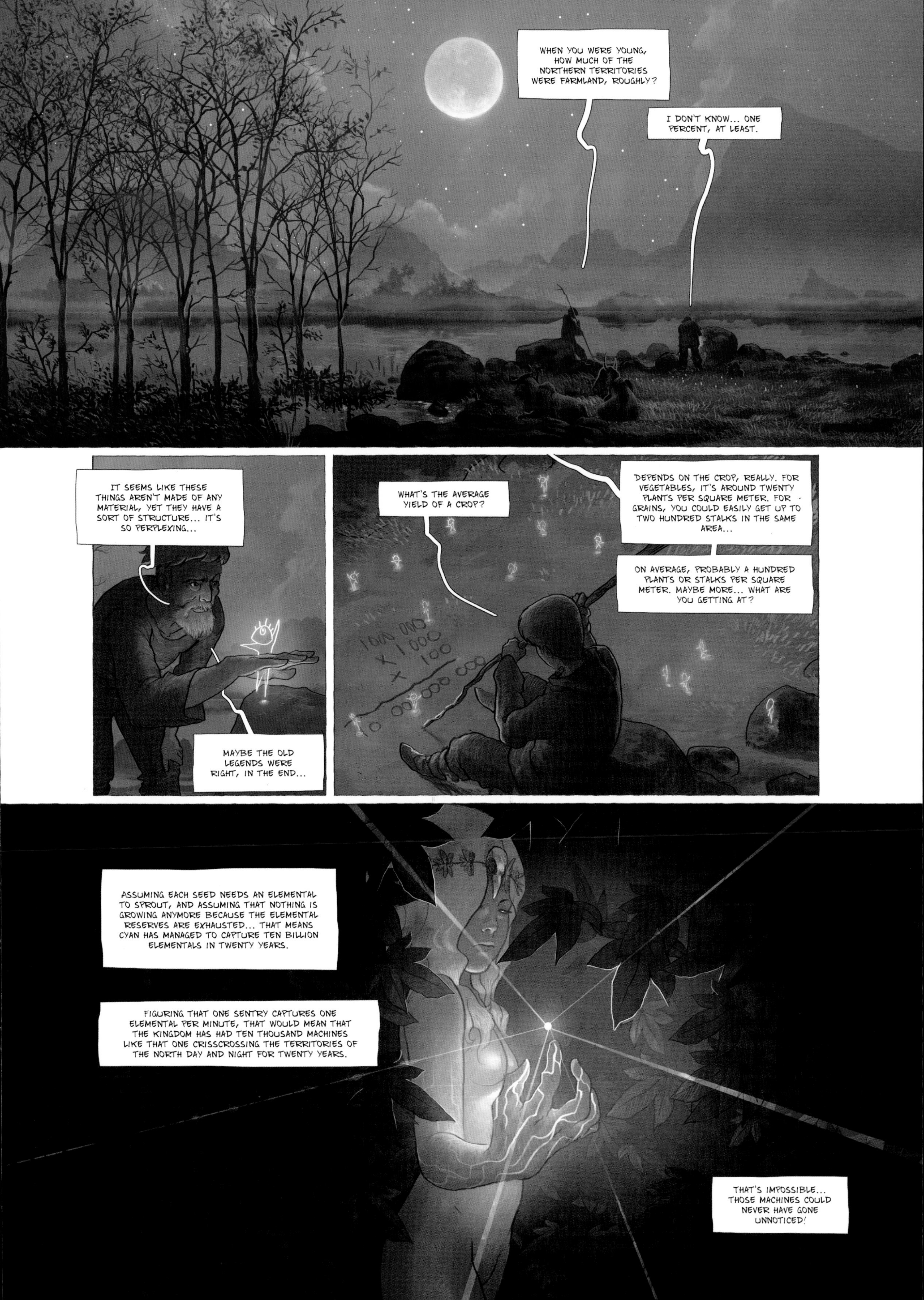

WHEN YOU WERE YOUNG, HOW MUCH OF THE NORTHERN TERRITORIES WERE FARMLAND, ROUGHLY?
I DON'T KNOW... ONE PERCENT, AT LEAST.
IT SEEMS LIKE THESE THINGS AREN'T MADE OF ANY MATERIAL, YET THEY HAVE A SORT OF STRUCTURE... IT'S SO PERPLEXING...
MAYBE THE OLD LEGENDS WERE RIGHT, IN THE END...
WHAT'S THE AVERAGE YIELD OF A CROP?
DEPENDS ON THE CROP, REALLY. FOR VEGETABLES, IT'S AROUND TWENTY PLANTS PER SQUARE METER. FOR GRAINS, YOU COULD EASILY GET UP TO TWO HUNDRED STALKS IN THE SAME AREA...
ON AVERAGE, PROBABLY A HUNDRED PLANTS OR STALKS PER SQUARE METER. MAYBE MORE... WHAT ARE YOU GETTING AT?
ASSUMING EACH SEED NEEDS AN ELEMENTAL TO SPROUT, AND ASSUMING THAT NOTHING IS GROWING ANYMORE BECAUSE THE ELEMENTAL RESERVES ARE EXHAUSTED... THAT MEANS CYAN HAS MANAGED TO CAPTURE TEN BILLION ELEMENTALS IN TWENTY YEARS.
FIGURING THAT ONE SENTRY CAPTURES ONE ELEMENTAL PER MINUTE, THAT WOULD MEAN THAT THE KINGDOM HAS HAD TEN THOUSAND MACHINES LIKE THAT ONE CRISSCROSSING THE TERRITORIES OF THE NORTH DAY AND NIGHT FOR TWENTY YEARS.
THAT'S IMPOSSIBLE... THOSE MACHINES COULD NEVER HAVE GONE UNNOTICED!

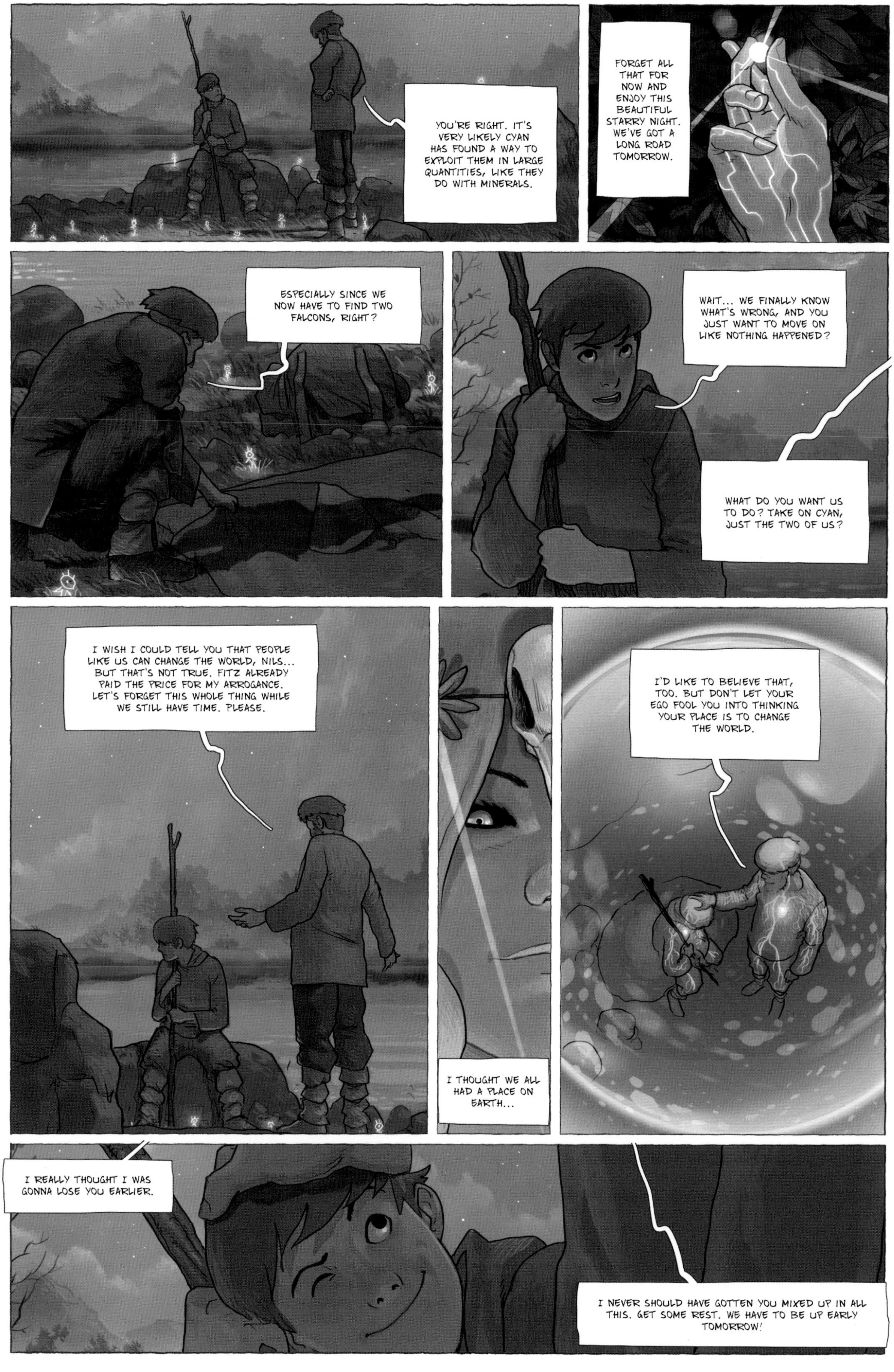
YOU'RE RIGHT. IT'S VERY LIKELY CYAN HAS FOUND A WAY TO EXPLOIT THEM IN LARGE QUANTITIES, LIKE THEY DO WITH MINERALS.
FORGET ALL THAT FOR NOW AND ENJOY THIS BEAUTIFUL STARRY NIGHT. WE'VE GOT A LONG ROAD TOMORROW.
ESPECIALLY SINCE WE NOW HAVE TO FIND TWO FALCONS, RIGHT?
WAIT... WE FINALLY KNOW WHAT'S WRONG, AND YOU JUST WANT TO MOVE ON LIKE NOTHING HAPPENED?
WHAT DO YOU WANT US TO DO? TAKE ON CYAN, JUST THE TWO OF US?
I WISH I COULD TELL YOU THAT PEOPLE LIKE US CAN CHANGE THE WORLD, NILS... BUT THAT'S NOT TRUE. FITZ ALREADY PAID THE PRICE FOR MY ARROGANCE. LET'S FORGET THIS WHOLE THING WHILE WE STILL HAVE TIME. PLEASE.
I THOUGHT WE ALL HAD A PLACE ON EARTH...
I'D LIKE TO BELIEVE THAT, TOO. BUT DON'T LET YOUR EGO FOOL YOU INTO THINKING YOUR PLACE IS TO CHANGE THE WORLD.
I REALLY THOUGHT I WAS GONNA LOSE YOU EARLIER.
I NEVER SHOULD HAVE GOTTEN YOU MIXED UP IN ALL THIS. GET SOME REST. WE HAVE TO BE UP EARLY TOMORROW!

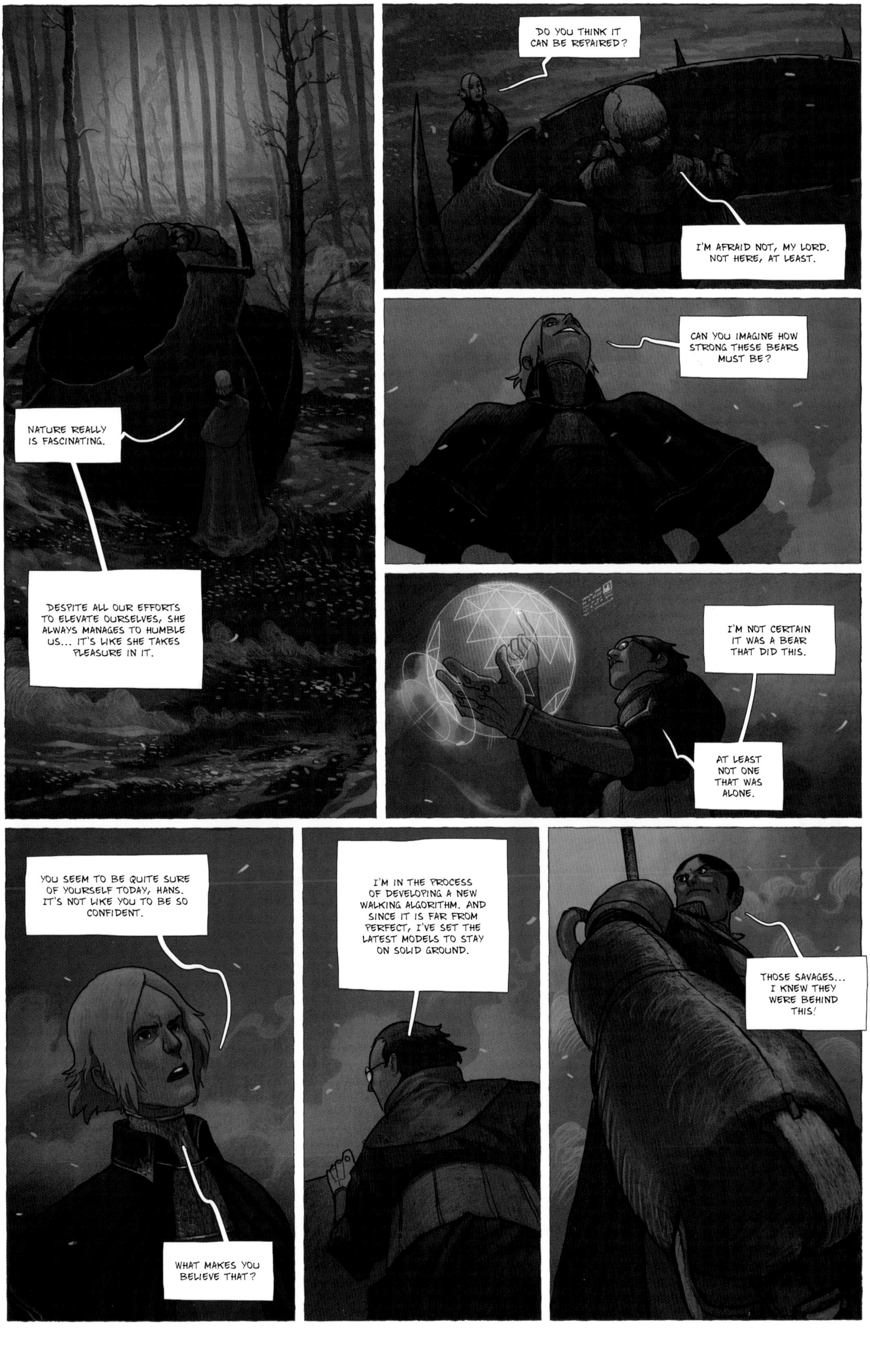
NATURE REALLY IS FASCINATING.
DESPITE ALL OUR EFFORTS TO ELEVATE OURSELVES, SHE ALWAYS MANAGES TO HUMBLE US... IT'S LIKE SHE TAKES PLEASURE IN IT.
DO YOU THINK IT CAN BE REPAIRED?
I'M AFRAID NOT, MY LORD. NOT HERE, AT LEAST.
CAN YOU IMAGINE HOW STRONG THESE BEARS MUST BE?
I'M NOT CERTAIN IT WAS A BEAR THAT DID THIS.
AT LEAST NOT ONE THAT WAS ALONE.
YOU SEEM TO BE QUITE SURE OF YOURSELF TODAY, HANS. IT'S NOT LIKE YOU TO BE SO CONFIDENT.
WHAT MAKES YOU BELIEVE THAT?
I'M IN THE PROCESS OF DEVELOPING A NEW WALKING ALGORITHM. AND SINCE IT IS FAR FROM PERFECT, I'VE SET THE LATEST MODELS TO STAY ON SOLID GROUND.
THOSE SAVAGES... I KNEW THEY WERE BEHIND THIS!

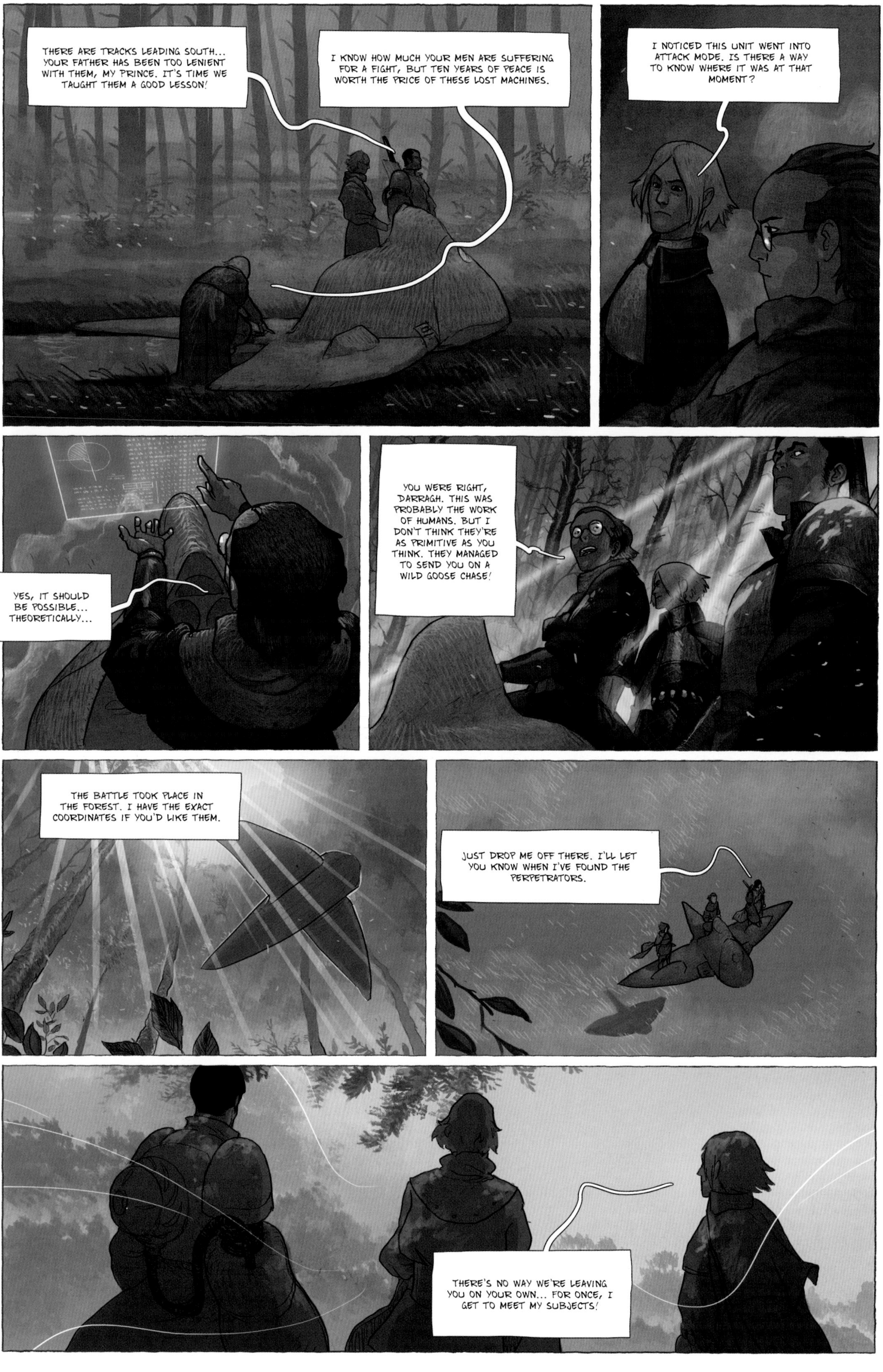
THERE ARE TRACKS LEADING SOUTH... YOUR FATHER HAS BEEN TOO LENIENT WITH THEM, MY PRINCE. IT'S TIME WE TAUGHT THEM A GOOD LESSON!
I KNOW HOW MUCH YOUR MEN ARE SUFFERING FOR A FIGHT, BUT TEN YEARS OF PEACE IS WORTH THE PRICE OF THESE LOST MACHINES.
I NOTICED THIS UNIT WENT INTO ATTACK MODE. IS THERE A WAY TO KNOW WHERE IT WAS AT THAT MOMENT?
YES, IT SHOULD BE POSSIBLE... THEORETICALLY...
YOU WERE RIGHT, DARRAGH. THIS WAS PROBABLY THE WORK OF HUMANS. BUT I DON'T THINK THEY'RE AS PRIMITIVE AS YOU THINK. THEY MANAGED TO SEND YOU ON A WILD GOOSE CHASE!
THE BATTLE TOOK PLACE IN THE FOREST. I HAVE THE EXACT COORDINATES IF YOU'D LIKE THEM.
JUST DROP ME OFF THERE. I'LL LET YOU KNOW WHEN I'VE FOUND THE PERPETRATORS.
THERE'S NO WAY WE'RE LEAVING YOU ON YOUR OWN... FOR ONCE, I GET TO MEET MY SUBJECTS!

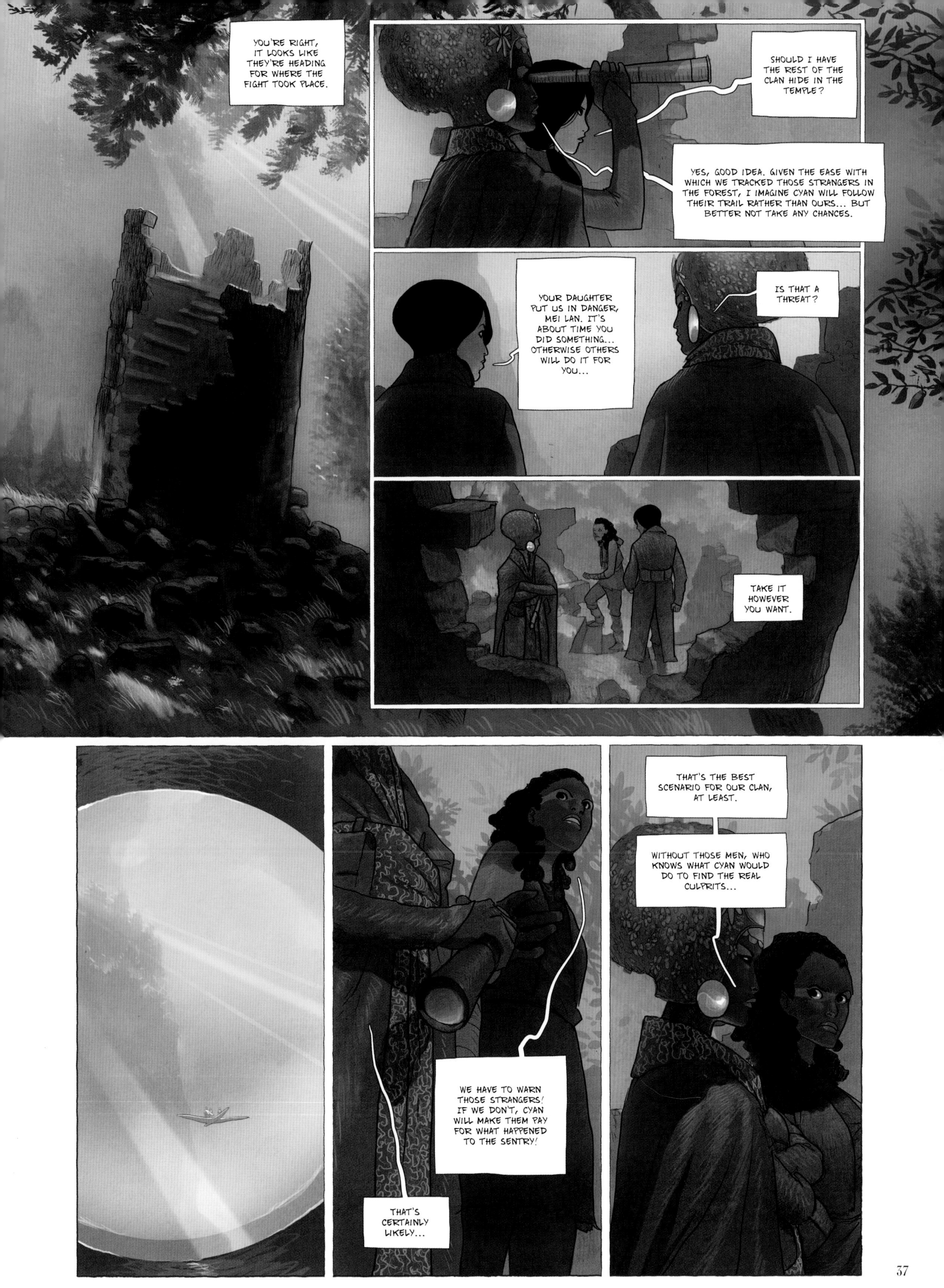
YOU'RE RIGHT, IT LOOKS LIKE THEY'RE HEADING FOR WHERE THE FIGHT TOOK PLACE.
SHOULD I HAVE THE REST OF THE CLAN HIDE IN THE TEMPLE?
YES, GOOD IDEA. GIVEN THE EASE WITH WHICH WE TRACKED THOSE STRANGERS IN THE FOREST, I IMAGINE CYAN WILL FOLLOW THEIR TRAIL RATHER THAN OURS... BUT BETTER NOT TAKE ANY CHANCES.
YOUR DAUGHTER PUT US IN DANGER, MEI LAN. IT'S ABOUT TIME YOU DID SOMETHING... OTHERWISE OTHERS WILL DO IT FOR YOU...
IS THAT A THREAT?
TAKE IT HOWEVER YOU WANT.
WE HAVE TO WARN THOSE STRANGERS! IF WE DON'T, CYAN WILL MAKE THEM PAY FOR WHAT HAPPENED TO THE SENTRY!
THAT'S CERTAINLY LIKELY...
THAT'S THE BEST SCENARIO FOR OUR CLAN, AT LEAST.
WITHOUT THOSE MEN, WHO KNOWS WHAT CYAN WOULD DO TO FIND THE REAL CULPRITS...

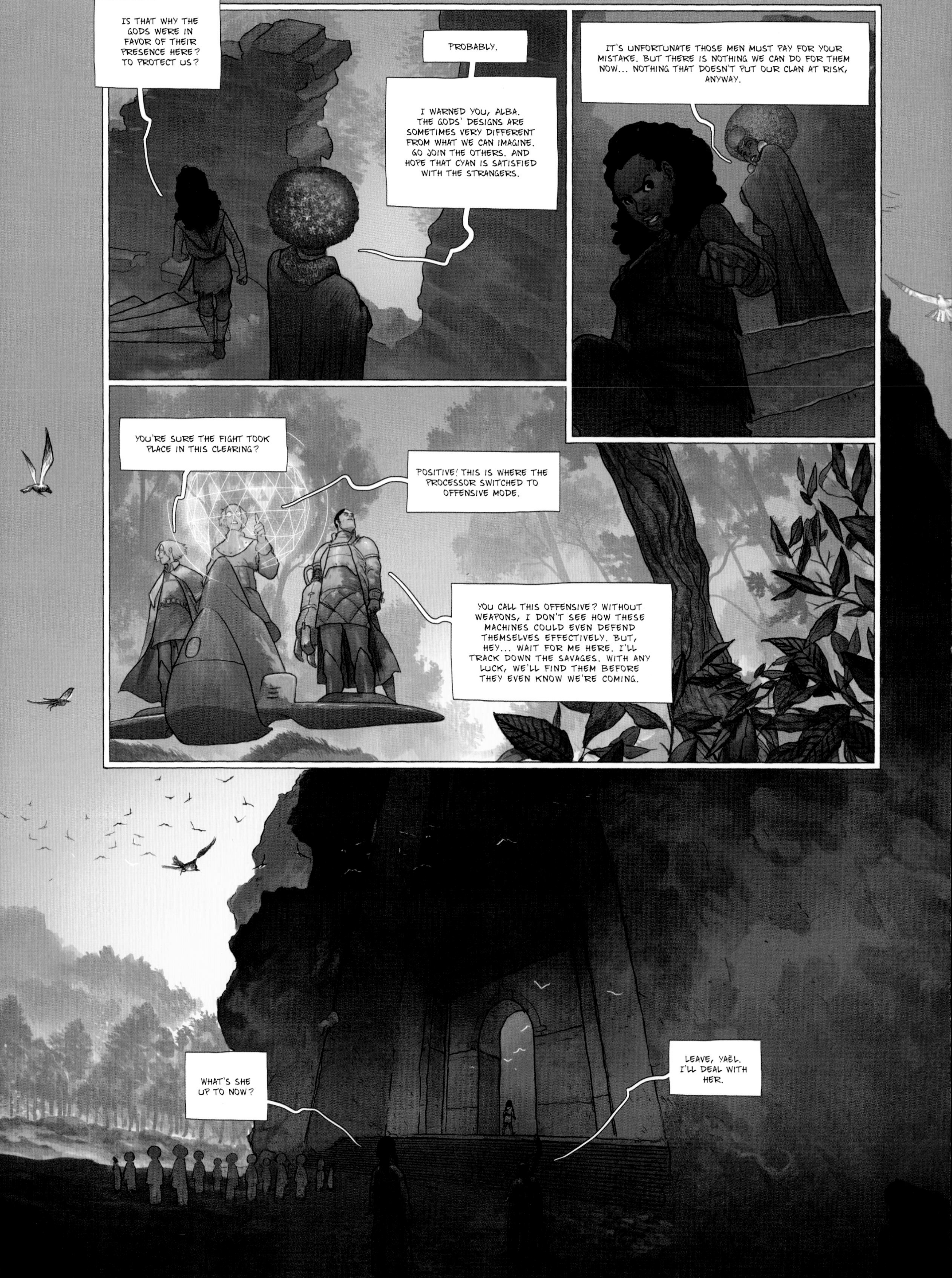
IS THAT WHY THE GODS WERE IN FAVOR OF THEIR PRESENCE HERE? TO PROTECT US?
PROBABLY.
I WARNED YOU, ALBA. THE GODS' DESIGNS ARE SOMETIMES VERY DIFFERENT FROM WHAT WE CAN IMAGINE. GO JOIN THE OTHERS. AND HOPE THAT CYAN IS SATISFIED WITH THE STRANGERS.
IT'S UNFORTUNATE THOSE MEN MUST PAY FOR YOUR MISTAKE. BUT THERE IS NOTHING WE CAN DO FOR THEM NOW... NOTHING THAT DOESN'T PUT OUR CLAN AT RISK, ANYWAY.
YOU'RE SURE THE FIGHT TOOK PLACE IN THIS CLEARING?
POSITIVE! THIS IS WHERE THE PROCESSOR SWITCHED TO OFFENSIVE MODE.
YOU CALL THIS OFFENSIVE? WITHOUT WEAPONS, I DON'T SEE HOW THESE MACHINES COULD EVEN DEFEND THEMSELVES EFFECTIVELY. BUT, HEY... WAIT FOR ME HERE. I'LL TRACK DOWN THE SAVAGES. WITH ANY LUCK, WE'LL FIND THEM BEFORE THEY EVEN KNOW WE'RE COMING.
WHAT'S SHE UP TO NOW?
LEAVE, YAËL. I'LL DEAL WITH HER.

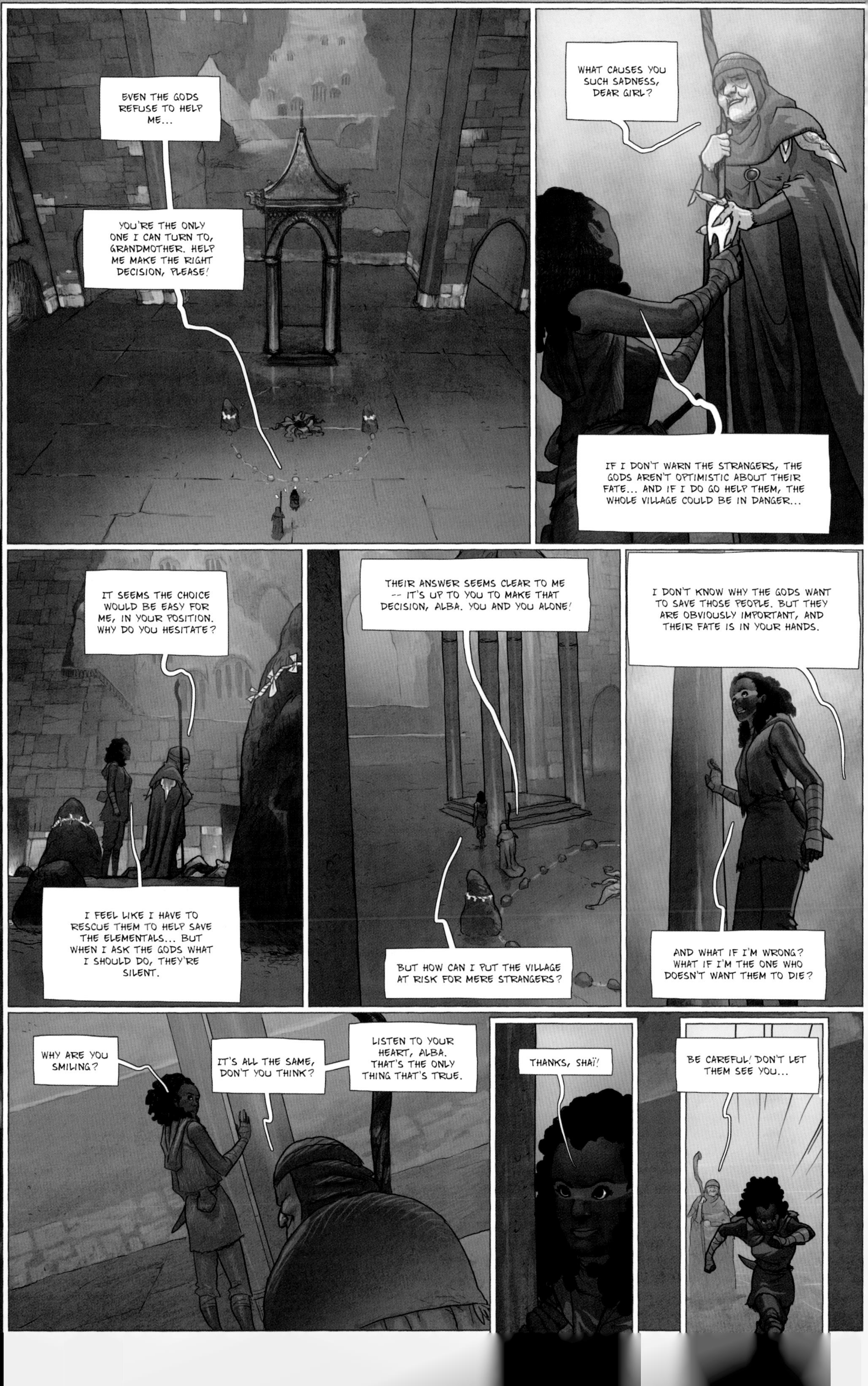
EVEN THE GODS REFUSE TO HELP ME...
YOU'RE THE ONLY ONE I CAN TURN TO, GRANDMOTHER. HELP ME MAKE THE RIGHT DECISION, PLEASE!
WHAT CAUSES YOU SUCH SADNESS, DEAR GIRL?
IF I DON'T WARN THE STRANGERS, THE GODS AREN'T OPTIMISTIC ABOUT THEIR FATE... AND IF I DO GO HELP THEM, THE WHOLE VILLAGE COULD BE IN DANGER...
IT SEEMS THE CHOICE WOULD BE EASY FOR ME, IN YOUR POSITION. WHY DO YOU HESITATE?
I FEEL LIKE I HAVE TO RESCUE THEM TO HELP SAVE THE ELEMENTALS... BUT WHEN I ASK THE GODS WHAT I SHOULD DO, THEY'RE SILENT.
THEIR ANSWER SEEMS CLEAR TO ME -- IT'S UP TO YOU TO MAKE THAT DECISION, ALBA. YOU AND YOU ALONE!
BUT HOW CAN I PUT THE VILLAGE AT RISK FOR MERE STRANGERS?
I DON'T KNOW WHY THE GODS WANT TO SAVE THOSE PEOPLE. BUT THEY ARE OBVIOUSLY IMPORTANT, AND THEIR FATE IS IN YOUR HANDS.
AND WHAT IF I'M WRONG? WHAT IF I'M THE ONE WHO DOESN'T WANT THEM TO DIE?
WHY ARE YOU SMILING?
IT'S ALL THE SAME, DON'T YOU THINK?
LISTEN TO YOUR HEART, ALBA. THAT'S THE ONLY THING THAT'S TRUE.
THANKS, SHAÏ!
BE CAREFUL! DON'T LET THEM SEE YOU...

DID YOU DO THAT?

WHAT'S THE MATTER?

SKULD IS STARTING A NEW WAR BETWEEN MEN.

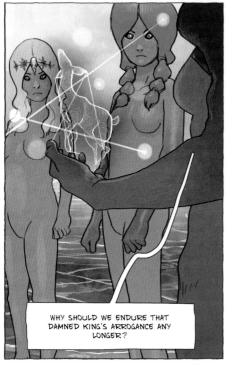

WHY SHOULD WE ENDURE THAT DAMNED KING'S ARROGANCE ANY LONGER?

BESIDES, WHAT ELSE COULD WE HAVE DONE? DO YOU SERIOUSLY BELIEVE YOUR YOUNG PROTÉGÉ HAS ANY CHANCE OF SAVING THE WORLD?

BEFORE YOU INTERVENED, YES, NOTHING HAD BEEN DETERMINED. FAR FROM IT... BUT AT LEAST HE HAD A CHANCE! BUT NOW... NOW, EVERYTHING MUST BE REDONE. AND FOR WHAT? SIMPLE REVENGE?

YOU'VE BEEN SPENDING TOO MUCH TIME WITH THE HUMANS, SKULD. I'M AFRAID THEY'VE RUBBED OFF ON YOU.

DON'T BE MISTAKEN, THIS HAS NOTHING TO DO WITH REVENGE.

THE GODS SHOULD HAVE PUNISHED THE KING OF CYAN A LONG TIME AGO!

WE'VE BECOME WEAK, VERDANDI... FAR TOO WEAK. THAT'S WHY THE HUMANS HAVE TURNED AWAY FROM US. AND I DON'T BLAME THEM! FAR FROM IT... WHY SHOULD THEY CONTINUE TO BELIEVE IN US WHEN SUCH CRIMES GO UNPUNISHED?

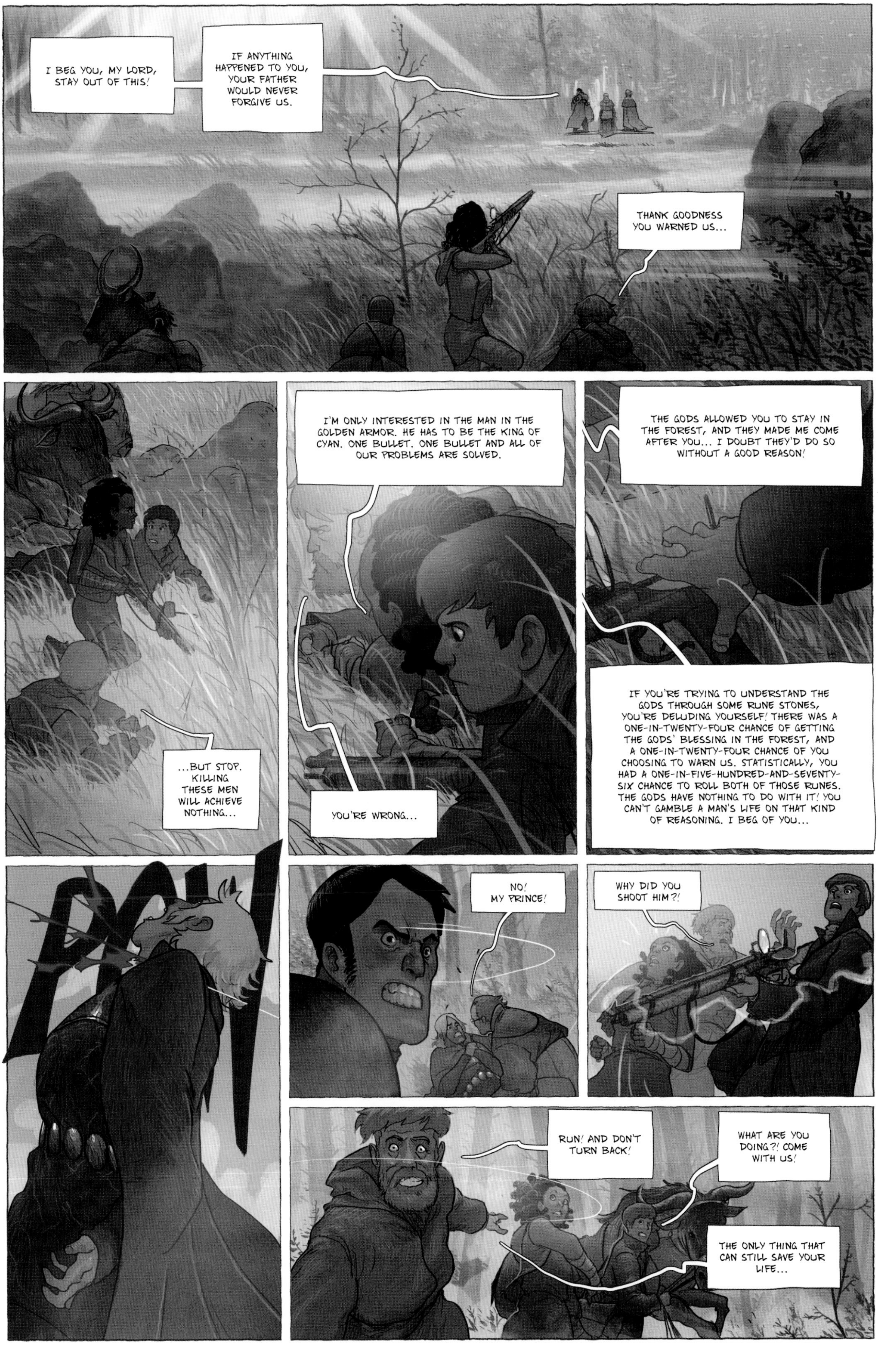
I BEG YOU, MY LORD, STAY OUT OF THIS!
IF ANYTHING HAPPENED TO YOU, YOUR FATHER WOULD NEVER FORGIVE US.
THANK GOODNESS YOU WARNED US...
...BUT STOP. KILLING THESE MEN WILL ACHIEVE NOTHING...
I'M ONLY INTERESTED IN THE MAN IN THE GOLDEN ARMOR. HE HAS TO BE THE KING OF CYAN. ONE BULLET. ONE BULLET AND ALL OF OUR PROBLEMS ARE SOLVED.
YOU'RE WRONG...
THE GODS ALLOWED YOU TO STAY IN THE FOREST, AND THEY MADE ME COME AFTER YOU... I DOUBT THEY'D DO SO WITHOUT A GOOD REASON!
IF YOU'RE TRYING TO UNDERSTAND THE GODS THROUGH SOME RUNE STONES, YOU'RE DELUDING YOURSELF! THERE WAS A ONE-IN-TWENTY-FOUR CHANCE OF GETTING THE GODS' BLESSING IN THE FOREST, AND A ONE-IN-TWENTY-FOUR CHANCE OF YOU CHOOSING TO WARN US. STATISTICALLY, YOU HAD A ONE-IN-FIVE-HUNDRED-AND-SEVENTY-SIX CHANCE TO ROLL BOTH OF THOSE RUNES. THE GODS HAVE NOTHING TO DO WITH IT! YOU CAN'T GAMBLE A MAN'S LIFE ON THAT KIND OF REASONING. I BEG OF YOU...
NO! MY PRINCE!
WHY DID YOU SHOOT HIM?!
RUN! AND DON'T TURN BACK!
WHAT ARE YOU DOING?! COME WITH US!
THE ONLY THING THAT CAN STILL SAVE YOUR LIFE...

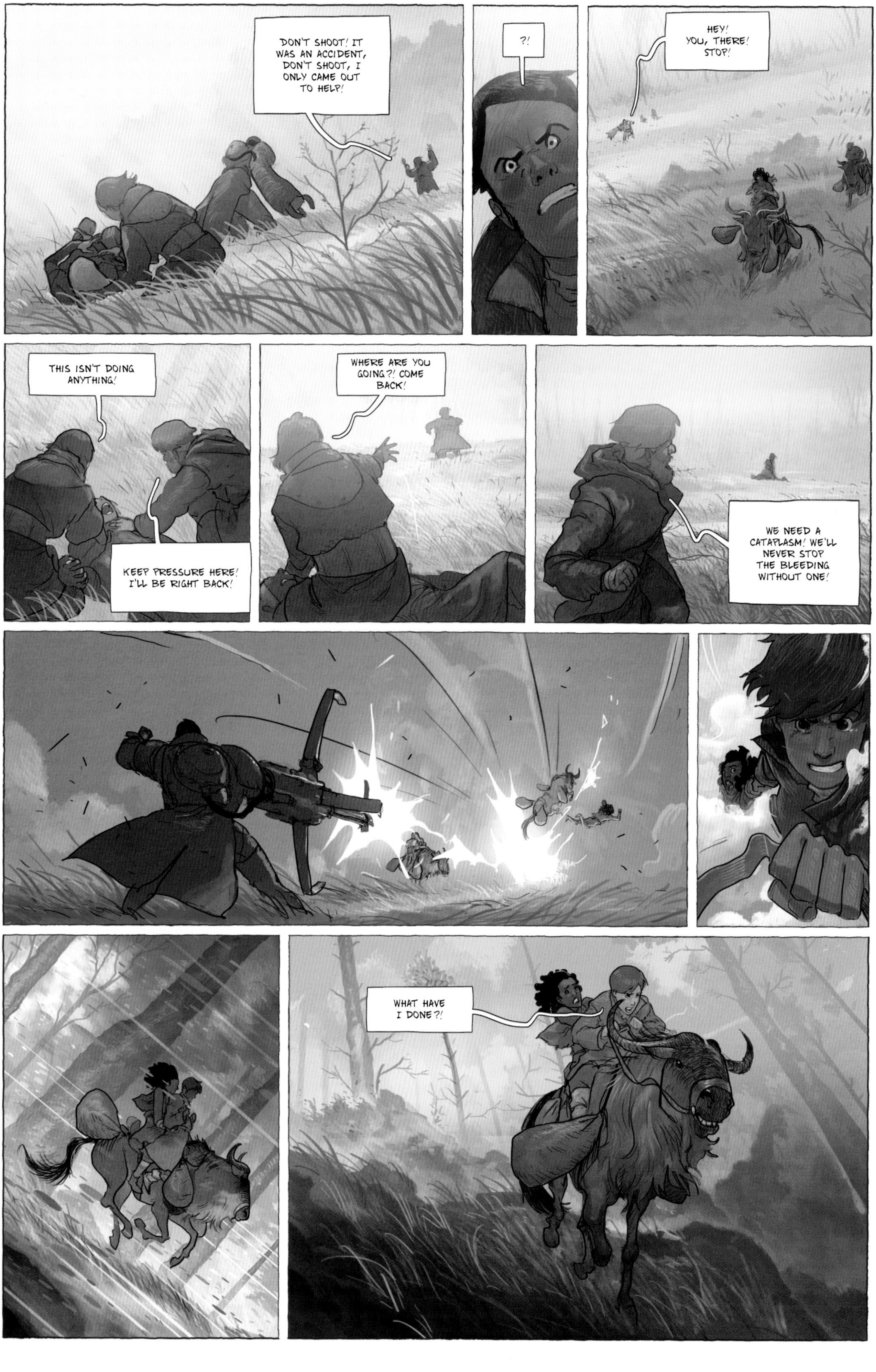
DON'T SHOOT! IT WAS AN ACCIDENT, DON'T SHOOT, I ONLY CAME OUT TO HELP!
?!
HEY! YOU, THERE! STOP!
THIS ISN'T DOING ANYTHING!
KEEP PRESSURE HERE! I'LL BE RIGHT BACK!
WHERE ARE YOU GOING?! COME BACK!
WE NEED A CATAPLASM! WE'LL NEVER STOP THE BLEEDING WITHOUT ONE!
WHAT HAVE I DONE?!

HOLD ON, MY PRINCE. WE'LL TAKE YOU HOME.

I FOUND WHAT WE NEED. THESE PLANTS WILL HELP THE BLOOD CLOT!

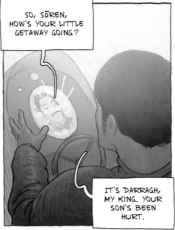

SO, SÖREN, HOW'S YOUR LITTLE GETAWAY GOING?

IT'S DARRAGH, MY KING. YOUR SON'S BEEN HURT.

WHAT HAPPENED?!

IT'S ALL MY FAULT, FATHER. WE WERE AMBUSHED. YOU WERE RIGHT, IT'S THE MEN WHO ATTACKED THE PATROLS IN SECTOR FORTY TWO. I SHOULD HAVE LISTENED TO YOU AND STAYED IN CYAN. SORRY.

AS SOON AS THEIR CARRIER LEAVES SECTOR FORTY-TWO, I WANT IT WIPED OFF THE MAP!

THE WHOLE SECTOR?

YES! UNLESS YOU KNOW WHERE THE ANIMALS WHO DID THIS TO MY SON ARE HIDING?

WHY'D YOU DO THAT BACK THERE?

I DON'T KNOW. I BELIEVED YOU. I THOUGHT THAT REALLY WAS THE KING OF CYAN. AND FOR THE FIRST TIME IN MY LIFE, I WANTED TO CHANGE THINGS. SO STUPID...

WHAT'S THAT?

CYAN'S ANSWER, I GUESS...

STUPID!

HOW COULD I BELIEVE I COULD SAVE THE ELEMENTALS ON MY OWN?!

43

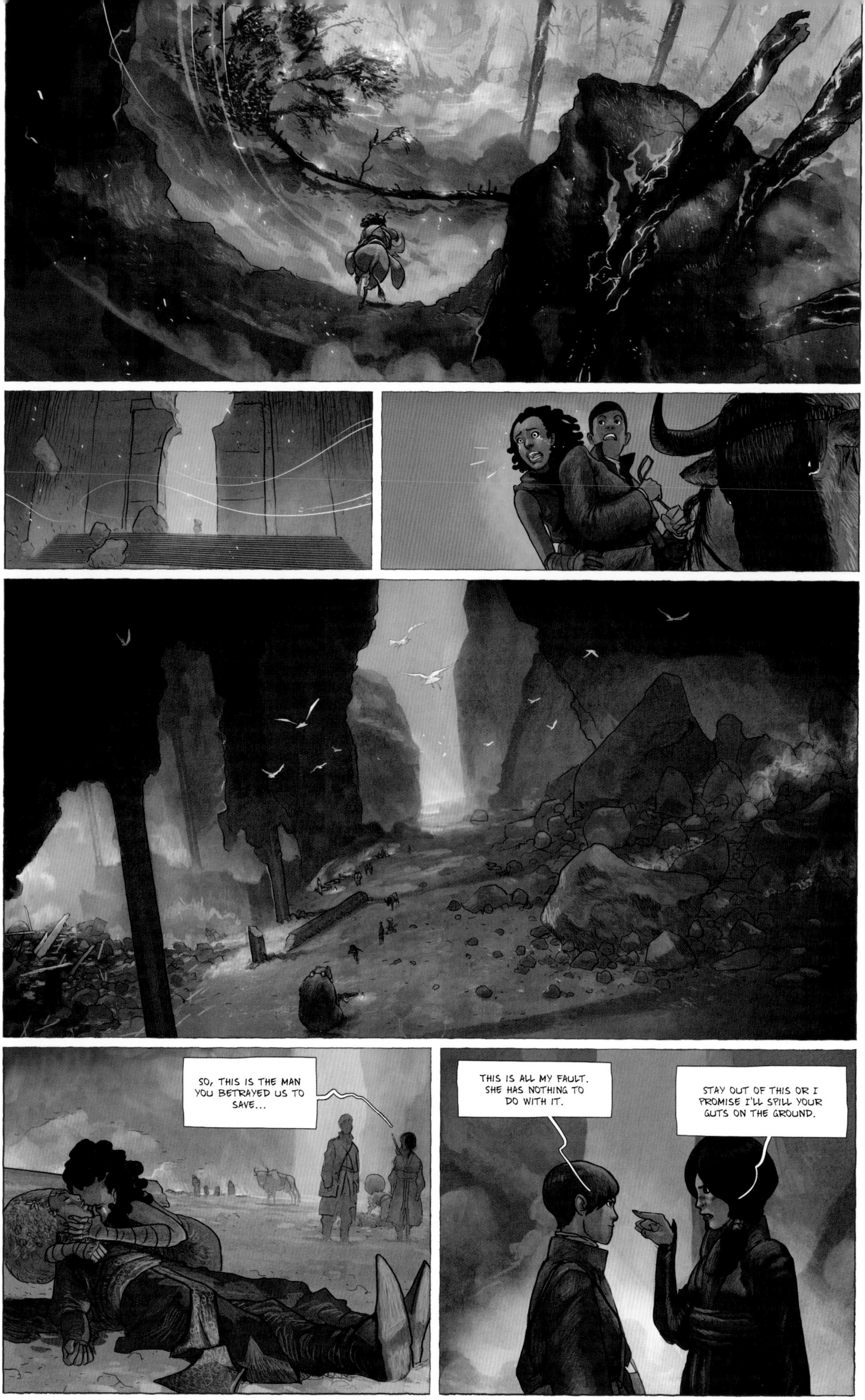

SO, THIS IS THE MAN YOU BETRAYED US TO SAVE...
THIS IS ALL MY FAULT. SHE HAS NOTHING TO DO WITH IT.
STAY OUT OF THIS OR I PROMISE I'LL SPILL YOUR GUTS ON THE GROUND.

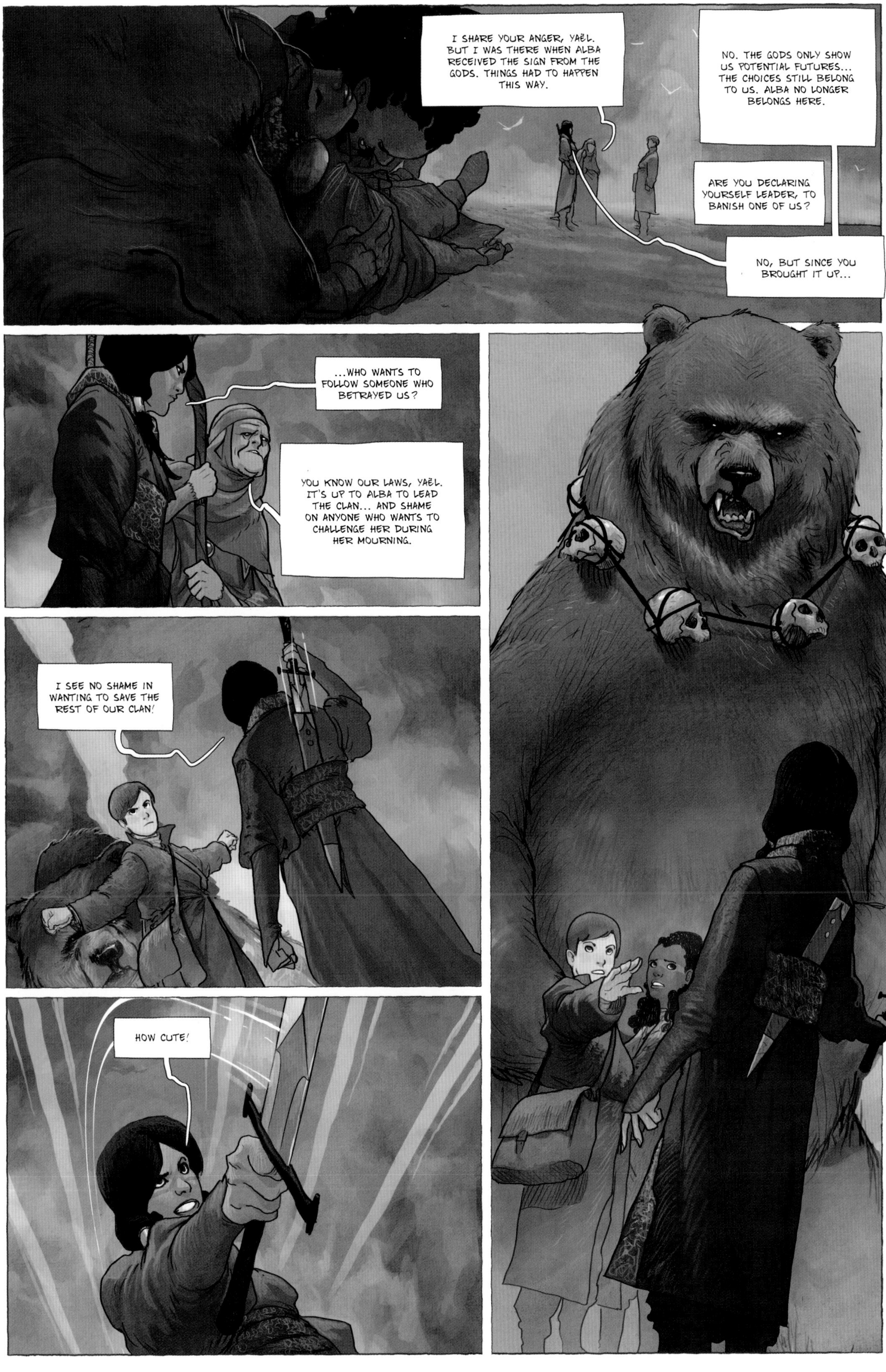
I SHARE YOUR ANGER, YAËL. BUT I WAS THERE WHEN ALBA RECEIVED THE SIGN FROM THE GODS. THINGS HAD TO HAPPEN THIS WAY.
NO. THE GODS ONLY SHOW US POTENTIAL FUTURES... THE CHOICES STILL BELONG TO US. ALBA NO LONGER BELONGS HERE.
ARE YOU DECLARING YOURSELF LEADER, TO BANISH ONE OF US?
NO, BUT SINCE YOU BROUGHT IT UP...
...WHO WANTS TO FOLLOW SOMEONE WHO BETRAYED US?
YOU KNOW OUR LAWS, YAËL. IT'S UP TO ALBA TO LEAD THE CLAN... AND SHAME ON ANYONE WHO WANTS TO CHALLENGE HER DURING HER MOURNING.
I SEE NO SHAME IN WANTING TO SAVE THE REST OF OUR CLAN!
HOW CUTE!

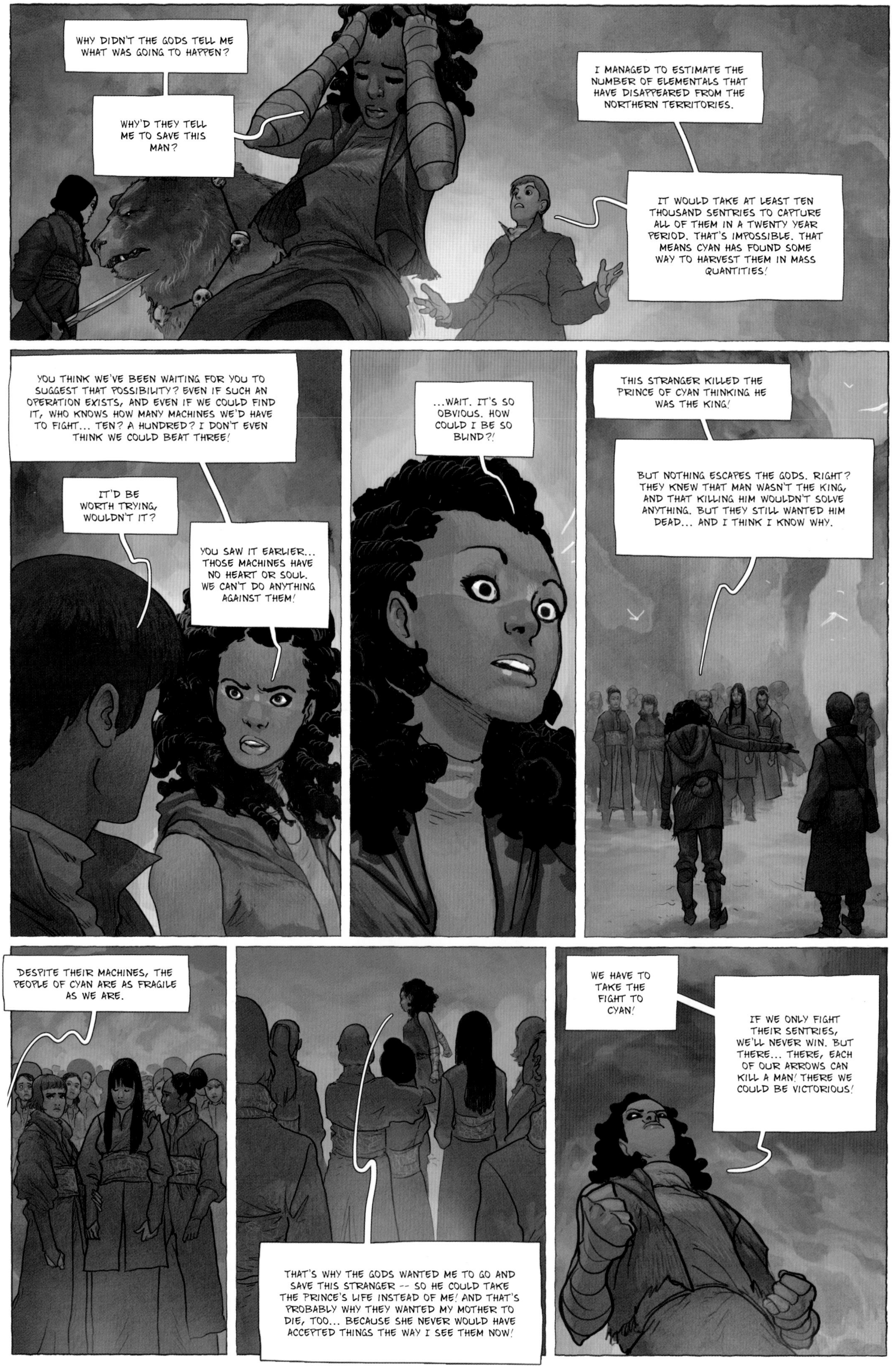
WHY DIDN'T THE GODS TELL ME WHAT WAS GOING TO HAPPEN?
WHY'D THEY TELL ME TO SAVE THIS MAN?
I MANAGED TO ESTIMATE THE NUMBER OF ELEMENTALS THAT HAVE DISAPPEARED FROM THE NORTHERN TERRITORIES.
IT WOULD TAKE AT LEAST TEN THOUSAND SENTRIES TO CAPTURE ALL OF THEM IN A TWENTY YEAR PERIOD. THAT'S IMPOSSIBLE. THAT MEANS CYAN HAS FOUND SOME WAY TO HARVEST THEM IN MASS QUANTITIES!
YOU THINK WE'VE BEEN WAITING FOR YOU TO SUGGEST THAT POSSIBILITY? EVEN IF SUCH AN OPERATION EXISTS, AND EVEN IF WE COULD FIND IT, WHO KNOWS HOW MANY MACHINES WE'D HAVE TO FIGHT... TEN? A HUNDRED? I DON'T EVEN THINK WE COULD BEAT THREE!
IT'D BE WORTH TRYING, WOULDN'T IT?
YOU SAW IT EARLIER... THOSE MACHINES HAVE NO HEART OR SOUL. WE CAN'T DO ANYTHING AGAINST THEM!
...WAIT. IT'S SO OBVIOUS. HOW COULD I BE SO BLIND?!
THIS STRANGER KILLED THE PRINCE OF CYAN THINKING HE WAS THE KING!
BUT NOTHING ESCAPES THE GODS, RIGHT? THEY KNEW THAT MAN WASN'T THE KING, AND THAT KILLING HIM WOULDN'T SOLVE ANYTHING. BUT THEY STILL WANTED HIM DEAD... AND I THINK I KNOW WHY.
DESPITE THEIR MACHINES, THE PEOPLE OF CYAN ARE AS FRAGILE AS WE ARE.
THAT'S WHY THE GODS WANTED ME TO GO AND SAVE THIS STRANGER -- SO HE COULD TAKE THE PRINCE'S LIFE INSTEAD OF ME! AND THAT'S PROBABLY WHY THEY WANTED MY MOTHER TO DIE, TOO... BECAUSE SHE NEVER WOULD HAVE ACCEPTED THINGS THE WAY I SEE THEM NOW!
WE HAVE TO TAKE THE FIGHT TO CYAN!
IF WE ONLY FIGHT THEIR SENTRIES, WE'LL NEVER WIN. BUT THERE... THERE, EACH OF OUR ARROWS CAN KILL A MAN! THERE WE COULD BE VICTORIOUS!

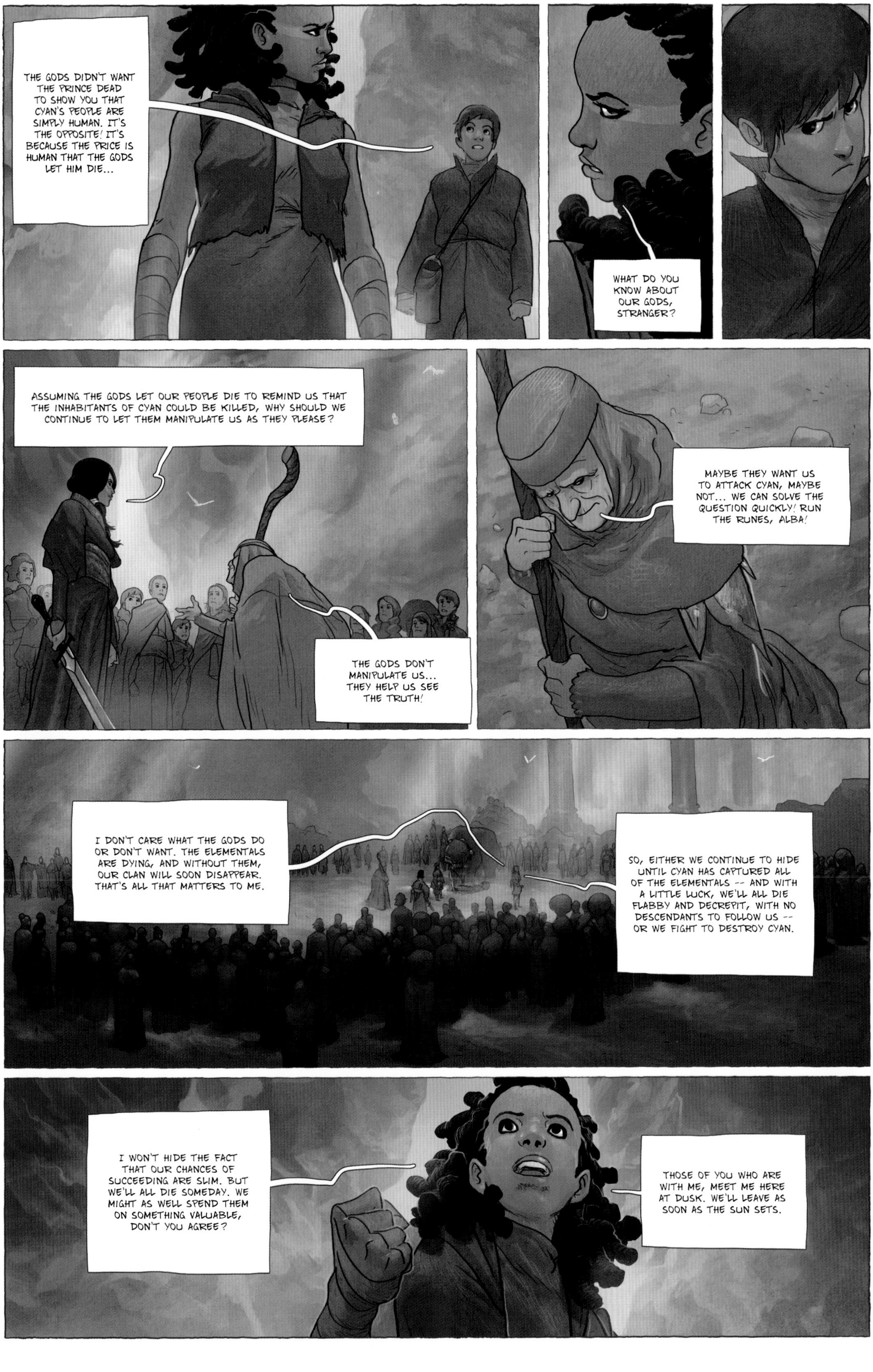
THE GODS DIDN'T WANT THE PRINCE DEAD TO SHOW YOU THAT CYAN'S PEOPLE ARE SIMPLY HUMAN. IT'S THE OPPOSITE! IT'S BECAUSE THE PRICE IS HUMAN THAT THE GODS LET HIM DIE...
WHAT DO YOU KNOW ABOUT OUR GODS, STRANGER?
ASSUMING THE GODS LET OUR PEOPLE DIE TO REMIND US THAT THE INHABITANTS OF CYAN COULD BE KILLED, WHY SHOULD WE CONTINUE TO LET THEM MANIPULATE US AS THEY PLEASE?
THE GODS DON'T MANIPULATE US... THEY HELP US SEE THE TRUTH!
MAYBE THEY WANT US TO ATTACK CYAN, MAYBE NOT... WE CAN SOLVE THE QUESTION QUICKLY! RUN THE RUNES, ALBA!
I DON'T CARE WHAT THE GODS DO OR DON'T WANT. THE ELEMENTALS ARE DYING, AND WITHOUT THEM, OUR CLAN WILL SOON DISAPPEAR. THAT'S ALL THAT MATTERS TO ME.
SO, EITHER WE CONTINUE TO HIDE UNTIL CYAN HAS CAPTURED ALL OF THE ELEMENTALS -- AND WITH A LITTLE LUCK, WE'LL ALL DIE FLABBY AND DECREPIT, WITH NO DESCENDANTS TO FOLLOW US -- OR WE FIGHT TO DESTROY CYAN.
I WON'T HIDE THE FACT THAT OUR CHANCES OF SUCCEEDING ARE SLIM. BUT WE'LL ALL DIE SOMEDAY. WE MIGHT AS WELL SPEND THEM ON SOMETHING VALUABLE, DON'T YOU AGREE?
THOSE OF YOU WHO ARE WITH ME, MEET ME HERE AT DUSK. WE'LL LEAVE AS SOON AS THE SUN SETS.

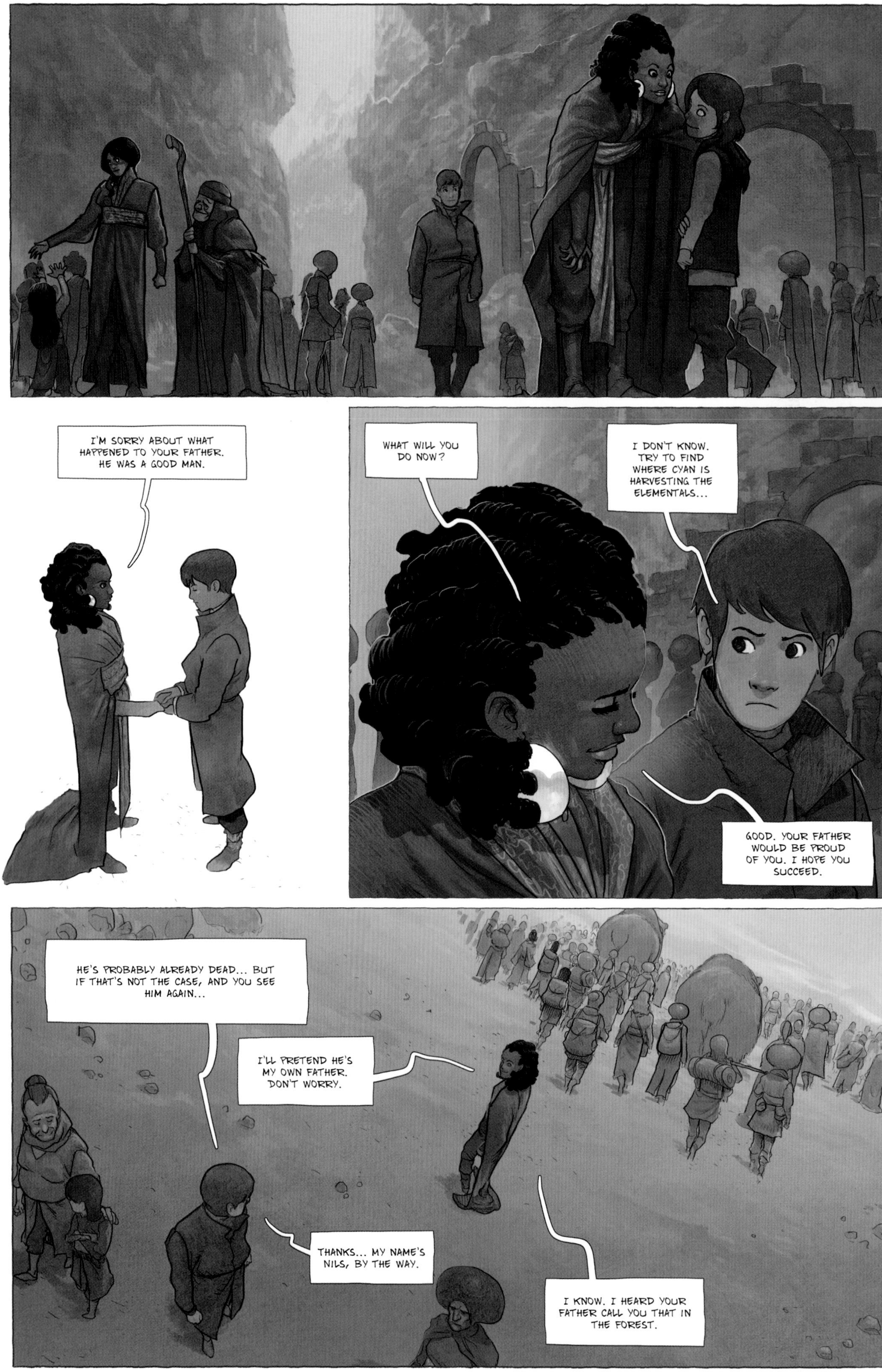

I'M SORRY ABOUT WHAT HAPPENED TO YOUR FATHER. HE WAS A GOOD MAN.
WHAT WILL YOU DO NOW?
I DON'T KNOW. TRY TO FIND WHERE CYAN IS HARVESTING THE ELEMENTALS...
GOOD. YOUR FATHER WOULD BE PROUD OF YOU. I HOPE YOU SUCCEED.
HE'S PROBABLY ALREADY DEAD... BUT IF THAT'S NOT THE CASE, AND YOU SEE HIM AGAIN...
I'LL PRETEND HE'S MY OWN FATHER. DON'T WORRY.
THANKS... MY NAME'S NILS, BY THE WAY.
I KNOW. I HEARD YOUR FATHER CALL YOU THAT IN THE FOREST.

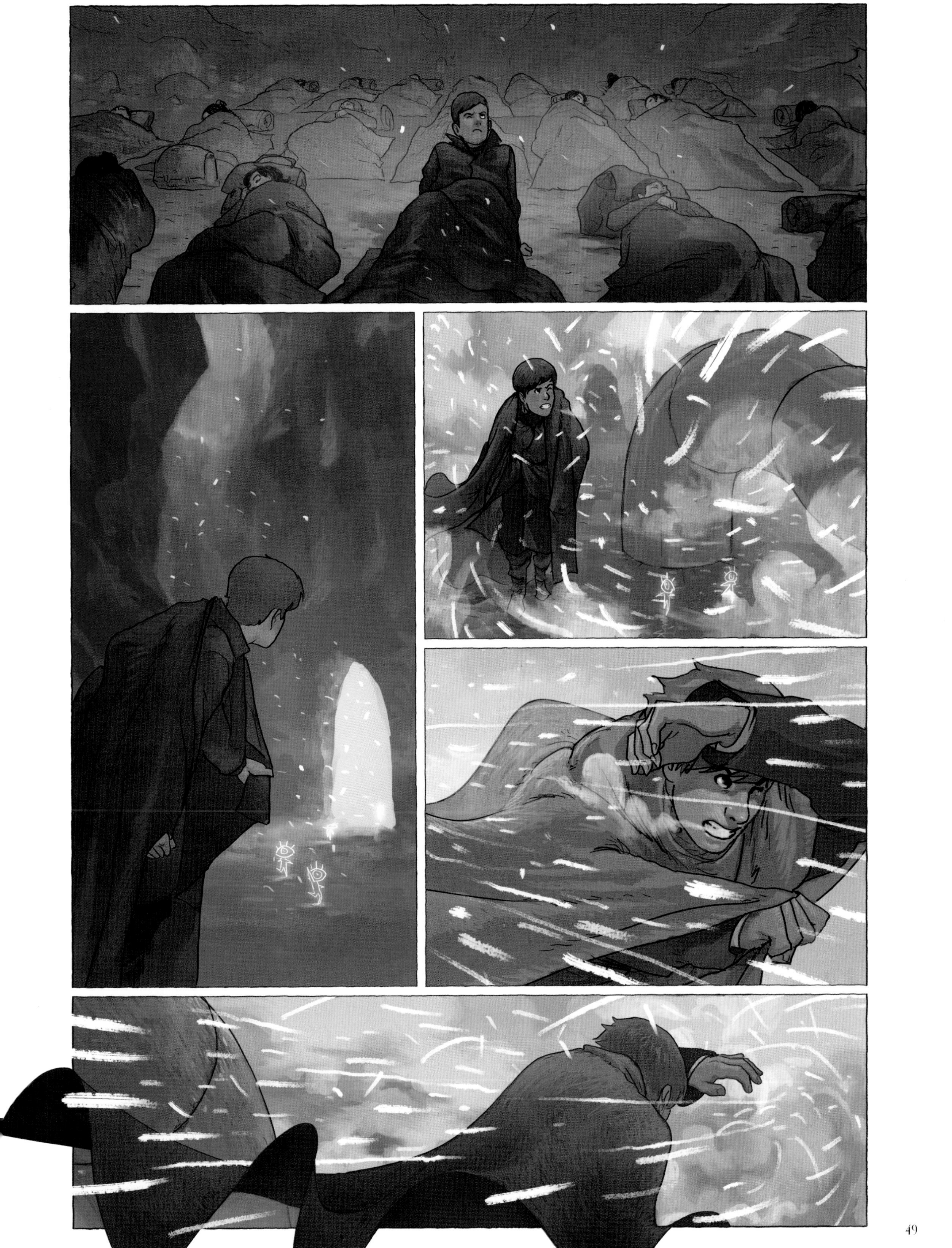

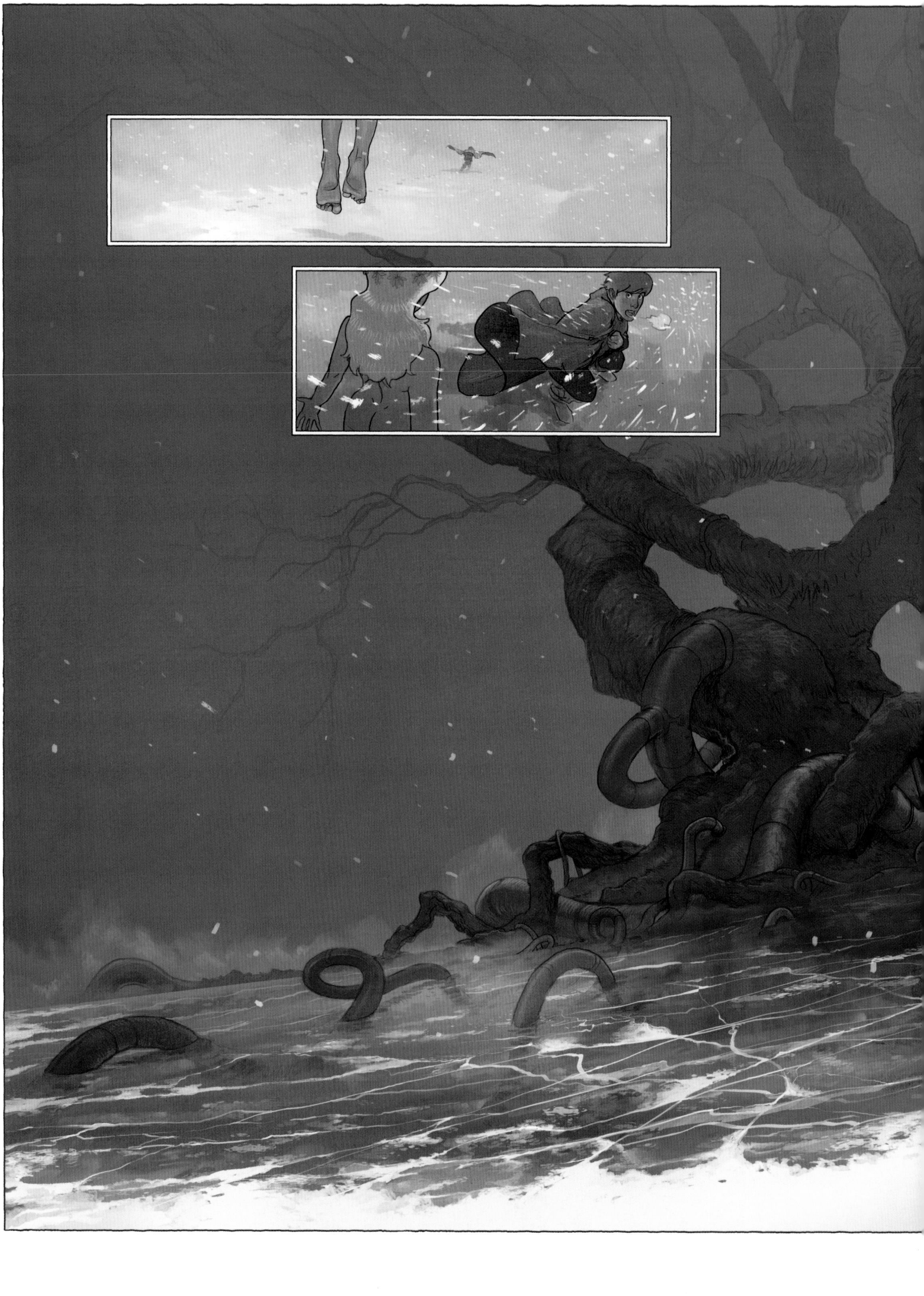

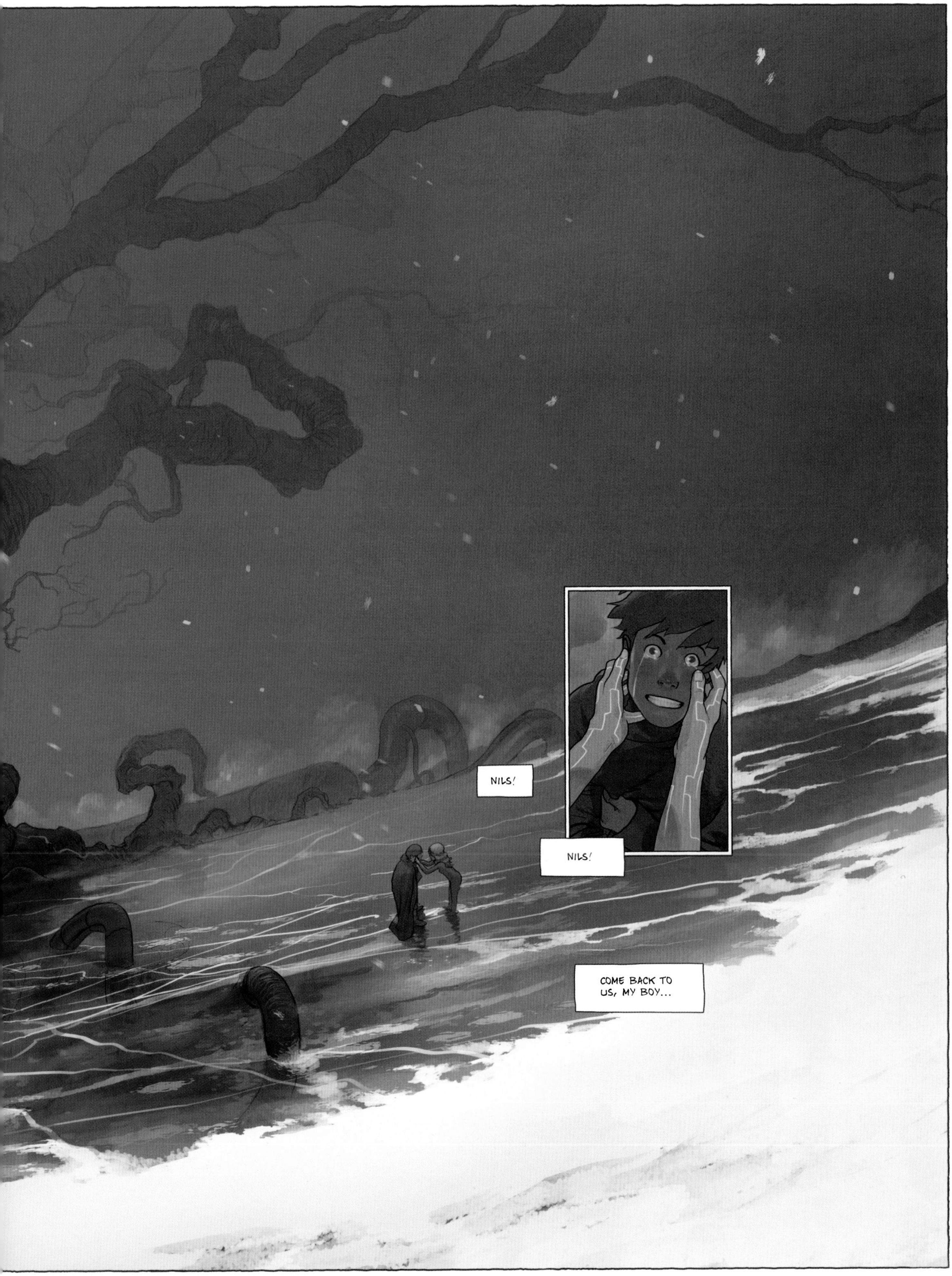
NILS!
NILS!
COME BACK TO US, MY BOY...

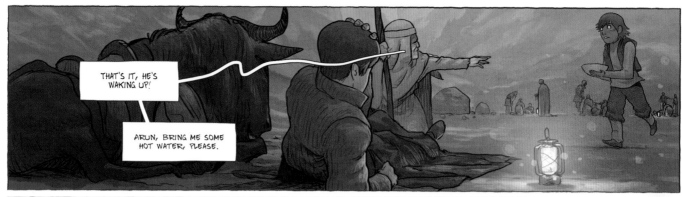

THAT'S IT, HE'S WAKING UP!

ARUN, BRING ME SOME HOT WATER, PLEASE.

HERE, MY BOY. THIS WILL WARM YOU UP.

THE ELEMENTALS... I SAW THEM IN MY DREAM. IT WAS LIKE THEY WANTED TO SHOW ME SOMETHING. BUT... IT WAS FAR, FAR AWAY. AND SO COLD... I COULDN'T FOLLOW THEM ALL THE WAY. I STOPPED ON A BIG, FROZEN LAKE...

...THAT'S WHERE I MET HER. SHE WAS BEAUTIFUL, LIKE A GODDESS...

A GODDESS... THAT MUST SOUND RIDICULOUS.

WHAT MAKES YOU SAY THAT?

NOT AT ALL. YOU MET A GODDESS.

YOUR EYES... THEY'RE LIKE ARUN'S.

SHE ONCE HAD A DREAM SIMILAR TO YOURS. SHE FOLLOWED THE ELEMENTALS TO A FROZEN LAKE WHERE SHE SAW THREE GODDESSES... WHEN SHE WOKE UP, HER EYES WERE AS WHITE AS SNOW.

SOME THINK IT'S THE PRICE SHE PAID FOR DARING TO LOOK UPON THE FACES OF THE GODS. OTHERS SEE IT AS A FORM OF BLESSING: THE INEVITABLE FINGERPRINT SUCH PURE BEINGS LEAVE ON LESSER BEINGS SUCH AS US.

ALBA'S GRANDMOTHER WAS CONVINCED THAT THE GODS WANTED TO SHOW US SOMETHING THROUGH HER VISION. SHE AND A SMALL GROUP TRAVELED THE ICE PACKS FOR MANY MOONS... BUT ONLY ONE WOMAN CAME BACK TO THE VILLAGE: MEÏ LAN, HER DAUGHTER. THEY FOUND NO TRACE OF THE PLACE ARUN HAD SEEN, SO THEY CONCLUDED THAT IT DIDN'T EXIST. AND SHE REMAINED CONVINCED THAT THE GODS HAD GIVEN THIS GIRL A VISION IN ORDER TO GET RID OF HER MOTHER AND PUT HER AT THE HEAD OF THE CLAN.

DID YOU NOTICE ANYTHING SPECIAL ABOUT THE PLACE THAT COULD HELP US FIND IT?

I... I DON'T RECALL MUCH... APART FROM A TREE LOST IN THE MIDDLE OF NOWHERE...

YOU SAW THE TREE?

YEAH, WHY? WHAT'S SO IMPORTANT ABOUT A TREE?

THAT'S YGGDRASIL... THE TREE OF LIFE THAT CONNECTS THE NINE WORLDS...

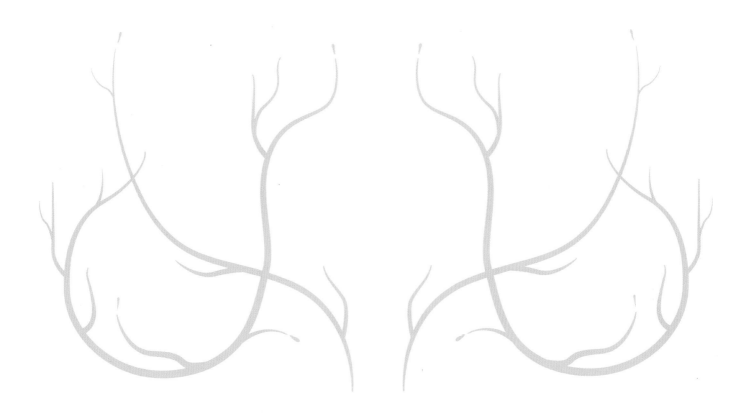

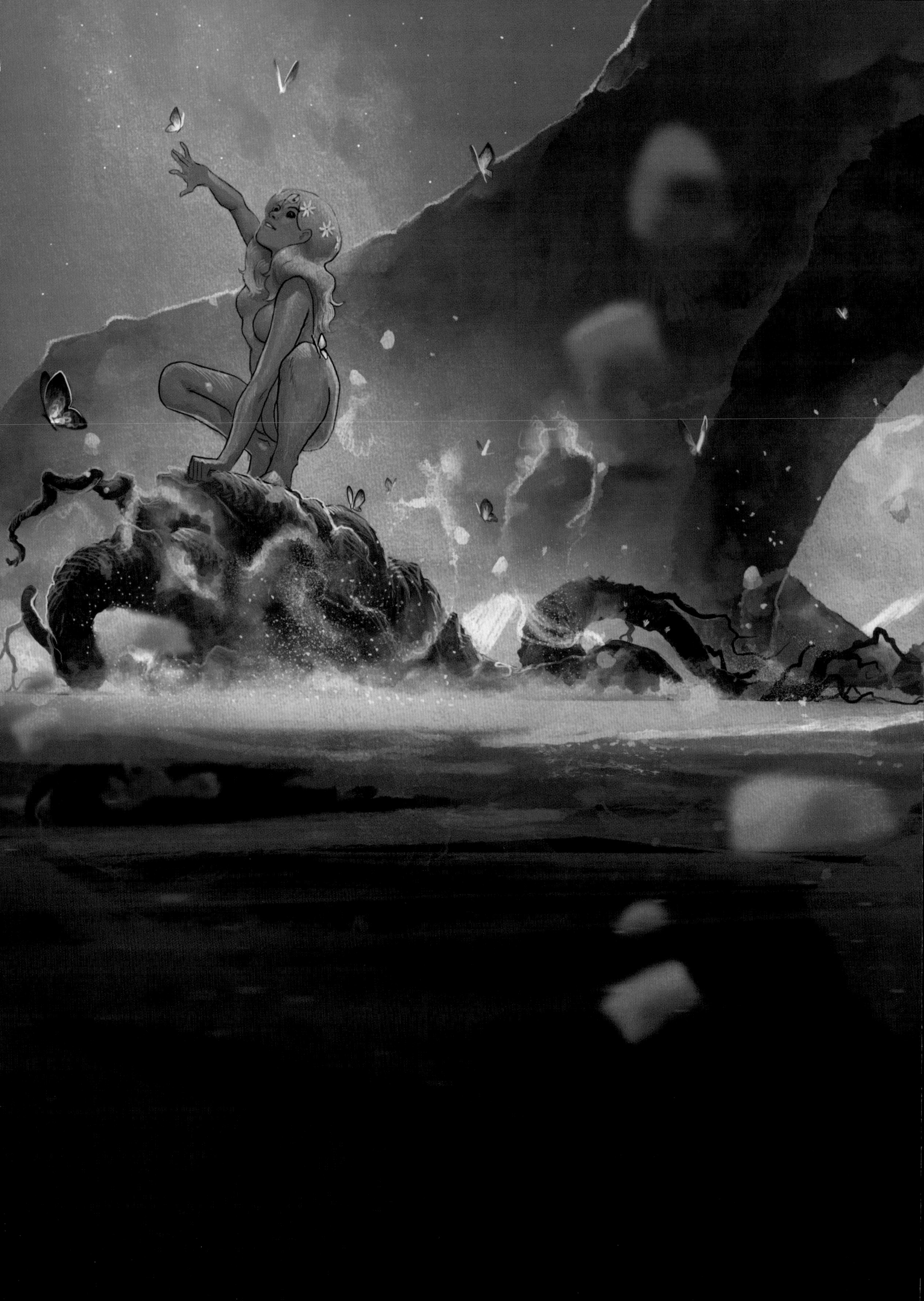

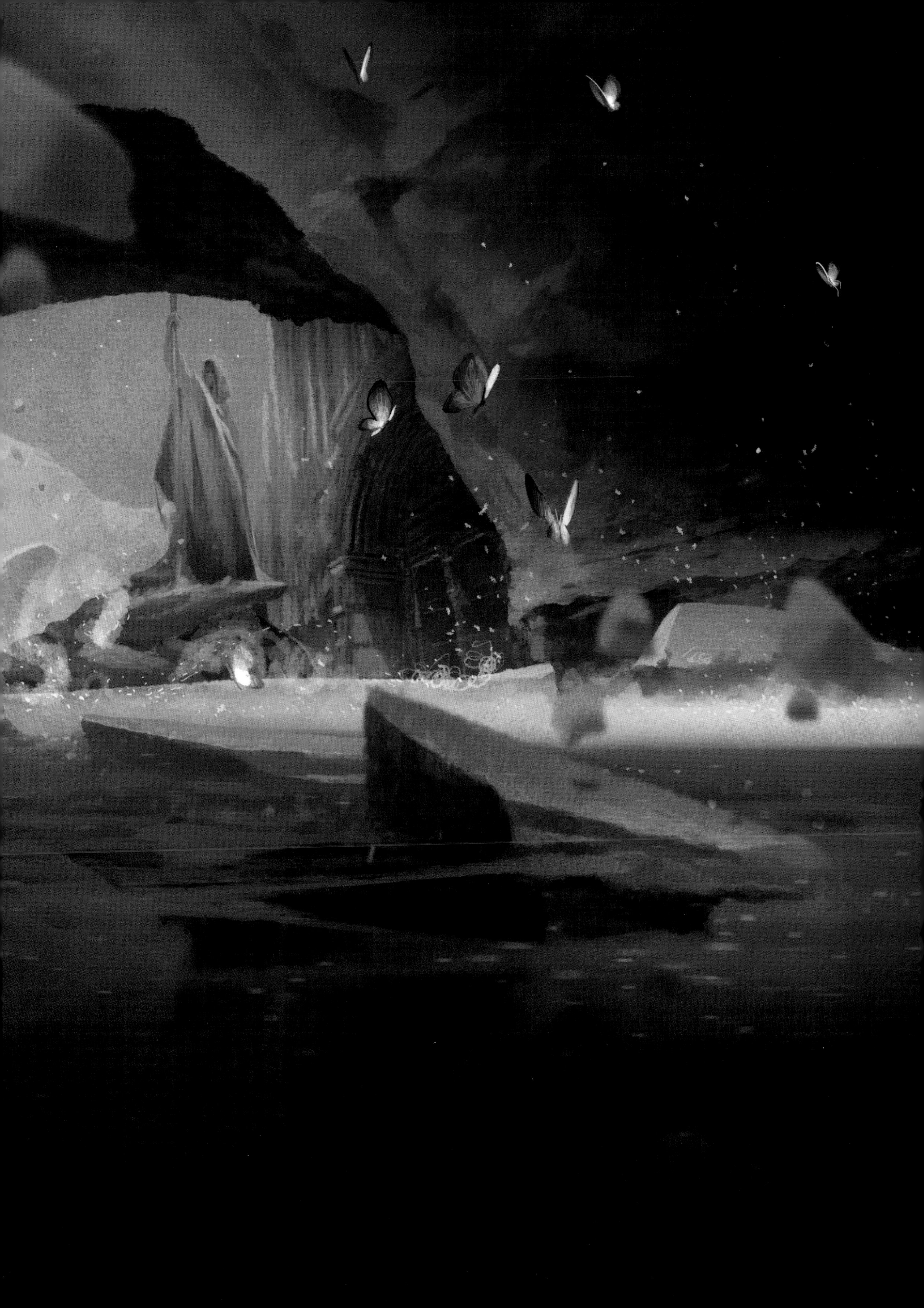

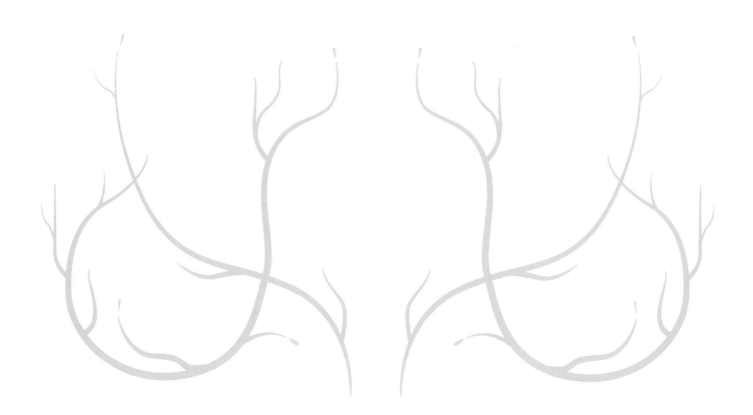

Chapter Two
CYAN

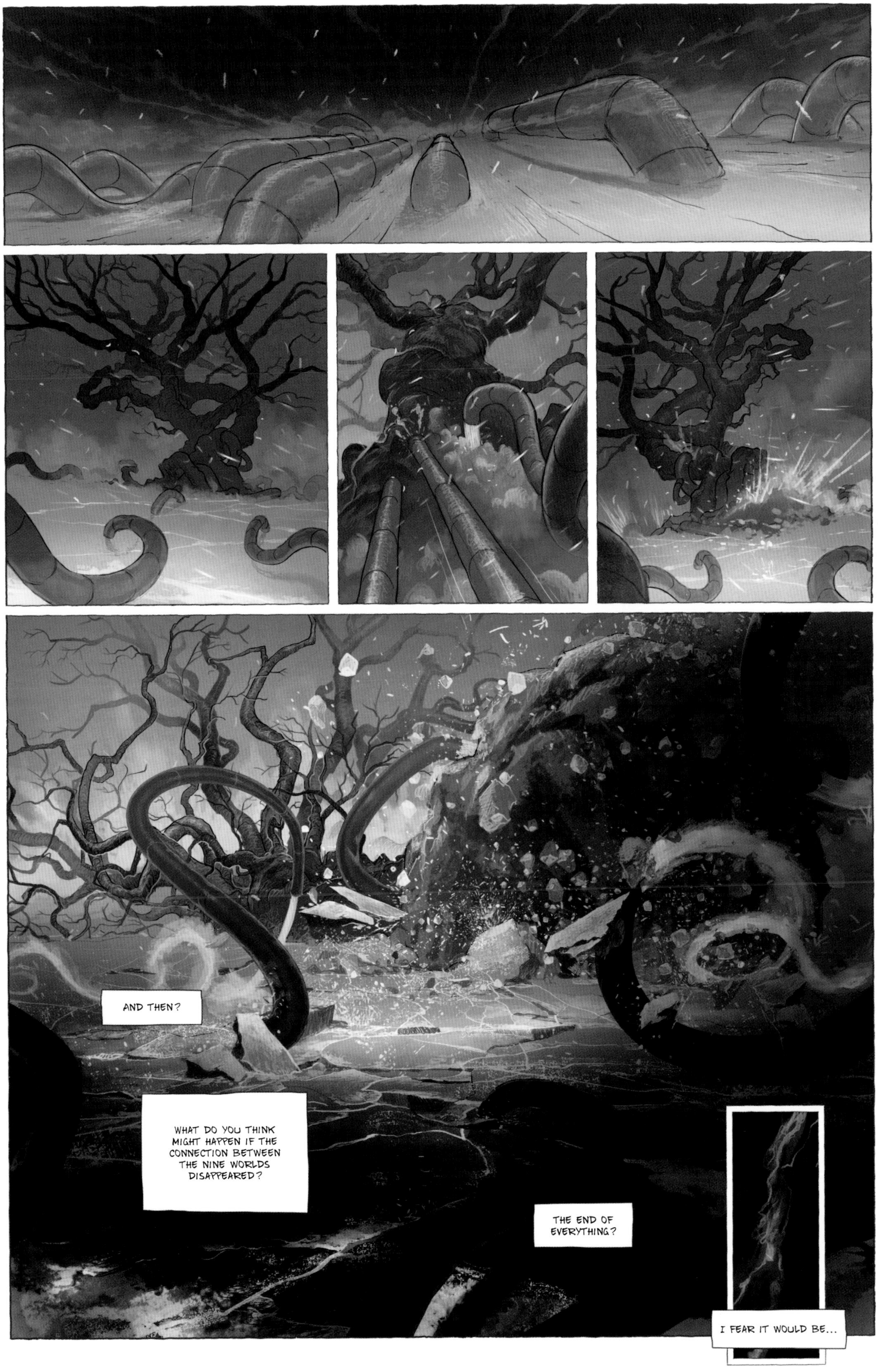
AND THEN?
WHAT DO YOU THINK MIGHT HAPPEN IF THE CONNECTION BETWEEN THE NINE WORLDS DISAPPEARED?
THE END OF EVERYTHING?
I FEAR IT WOULD BE...

YOU MUST REALLY LOVE THESE HUMANS TO PROTECT THEM LIKE THAT...

WHY DIDN'T YOU TELL US ABOUT THESE VISIONS EARLIER?

WHAT DIFFERENCE WOULD IT HAVE MADE?

YOU KNOW AS WELL AS I DO... THE CLOSER WE GET TO AN EVENT, THE MORE LIKELY IT IS TO COME TRUE.

WE MUST DESTROY CYAN AS SOON AS POSSIBLE!

YOU THINK I HAVEN'T CONSIDERED THAT?

WHAT IF IN TRYING TO AVOID IT WE END UP CAUSING IT?

INTERESTING QUESTION...

SO WHAT SHOULD WE DO?

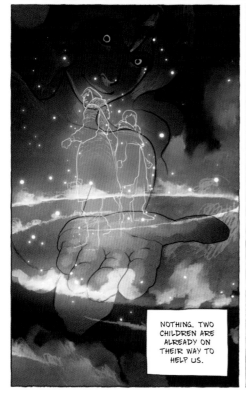

NOTHING. TWO CHILDREN ARE ALREADY ON THEIR WAY TO HELP US.

WORLDS ARE ABOUT TO DISAPPEAR, AND YOU'RE COUNTING ON TWO CHILDREN?

YES.

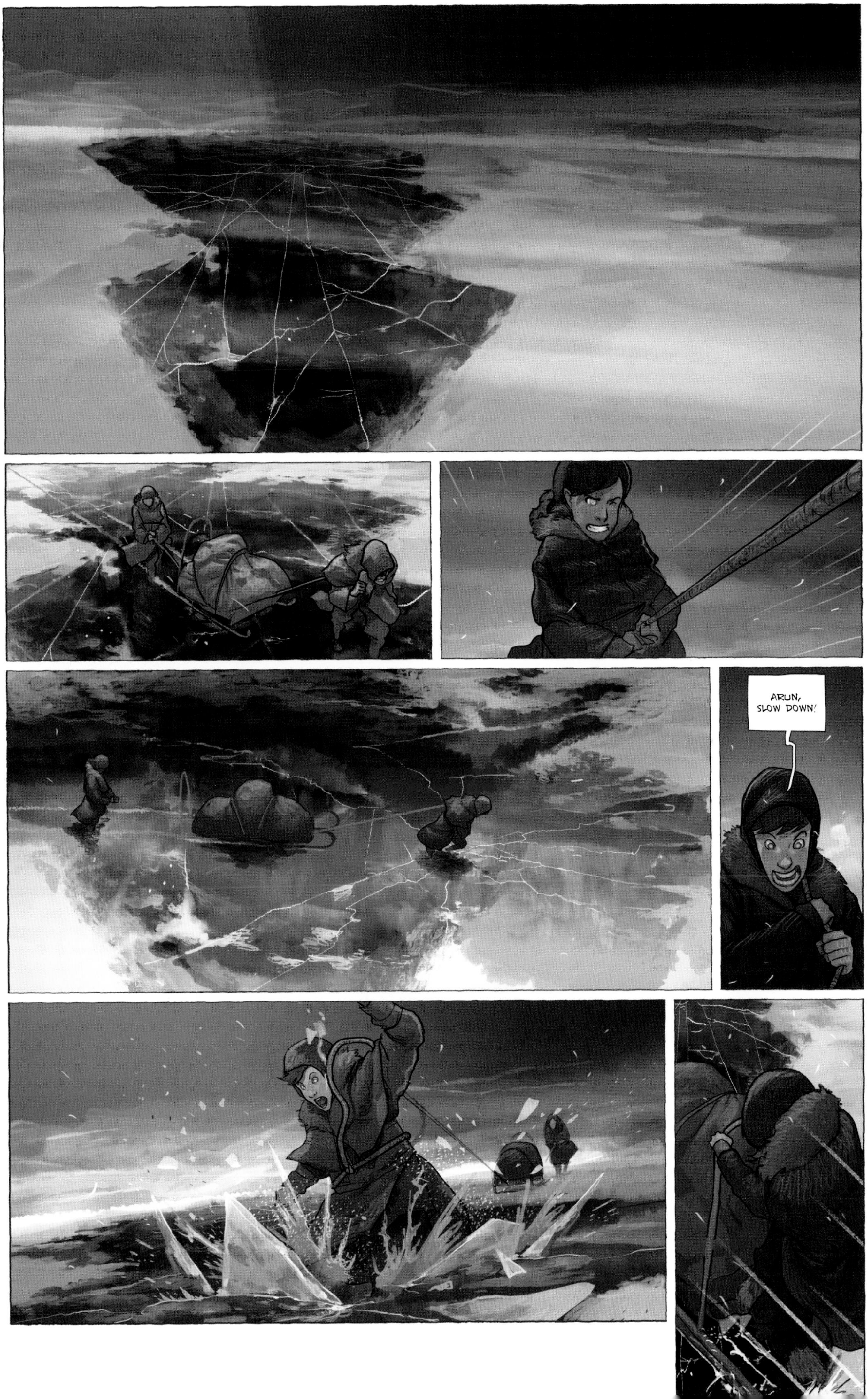
ARUN, SLOW DOWN!

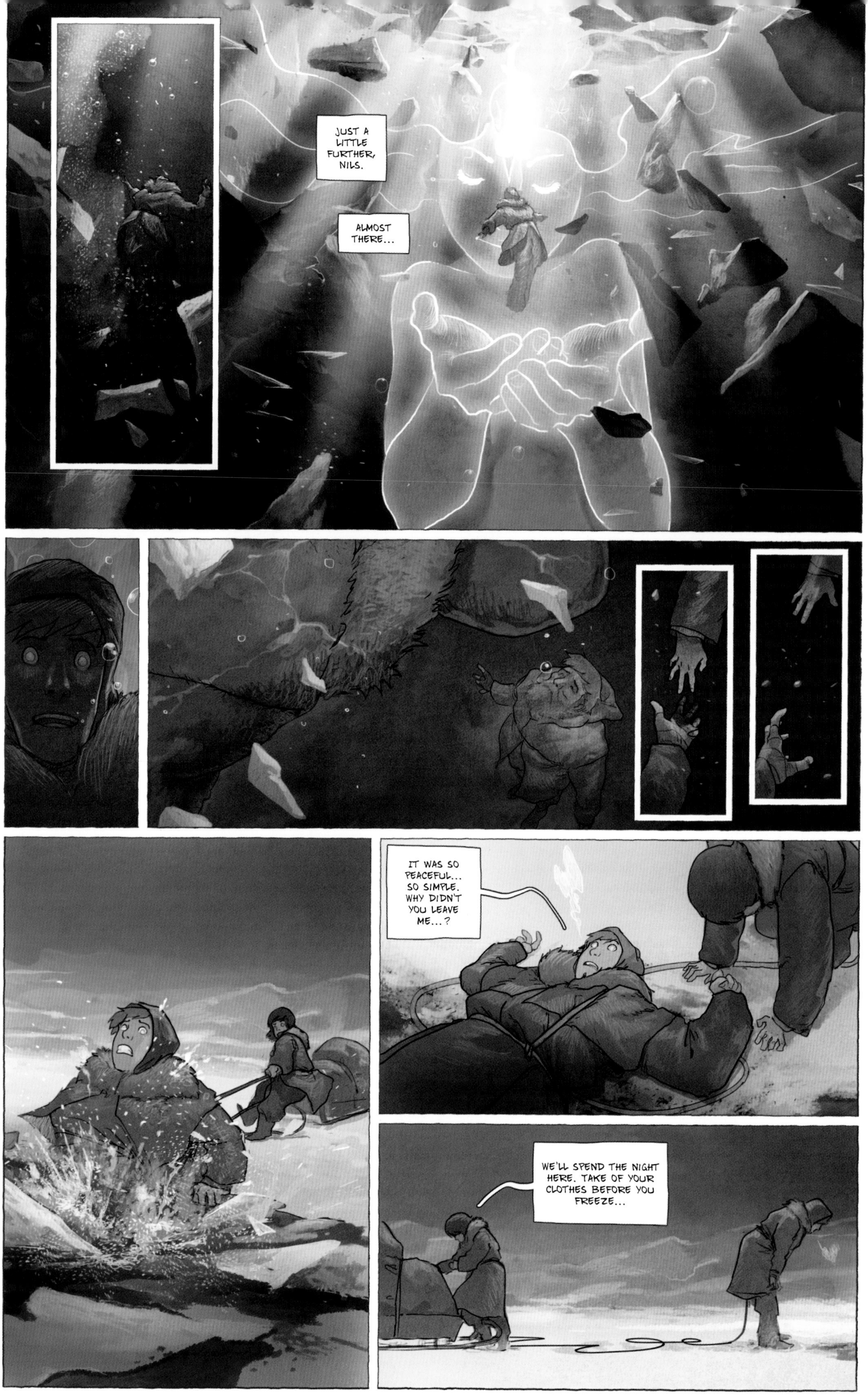
JUST A LITTLE FURTHER, NILS.
ALMOST THERE...
IT WAS SO PEACEFUL... SO SIMPLE. WHY DIDN'T YOU LEAVE ME...?
WE'LL SPEND THE NIGHT HERE. TAKE OF YOUR CLOTHES BEFORE YOU FREEZE...

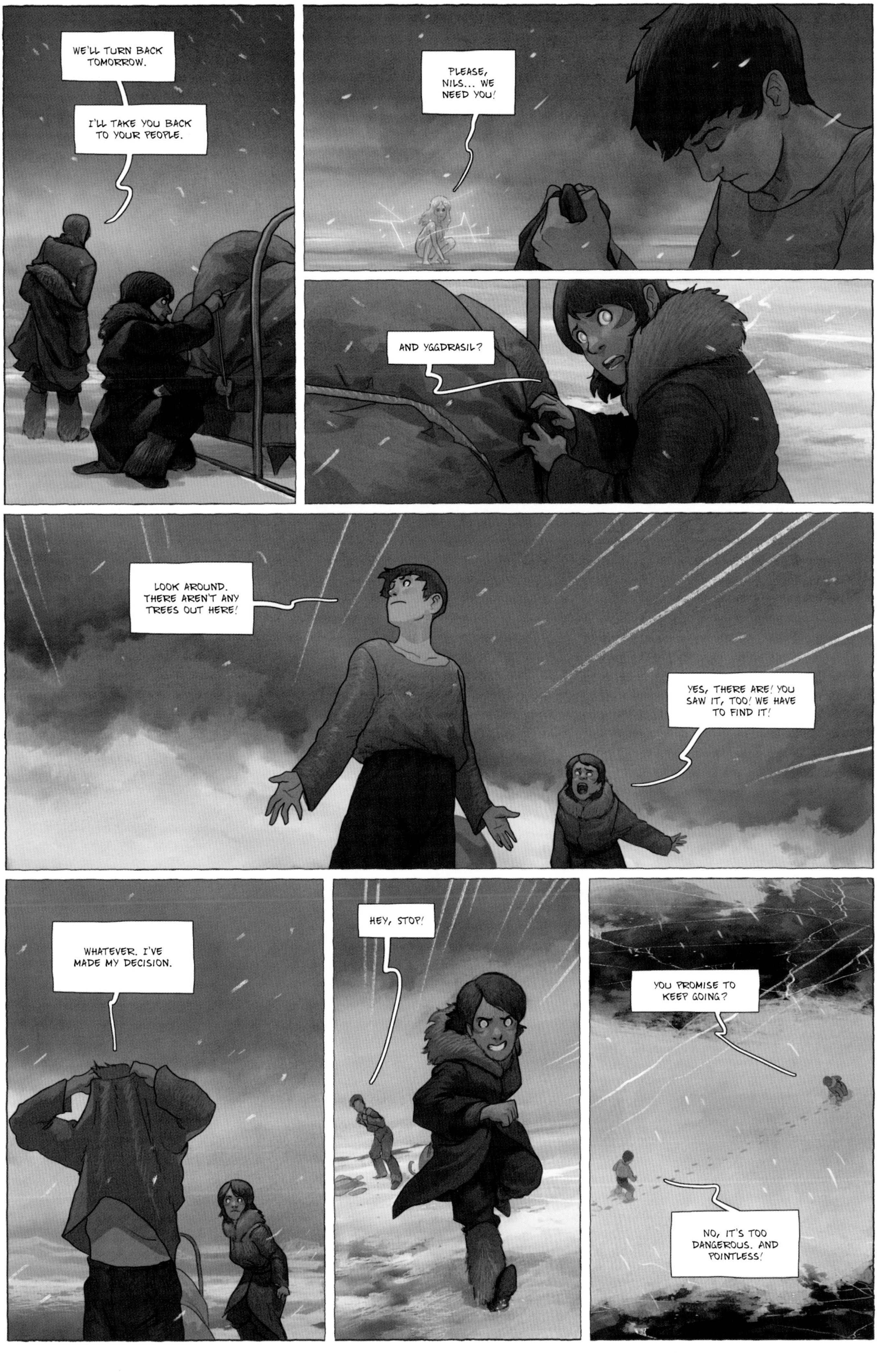
WE'LL TURN BACK TOMORROW.
I'LL TAKE YOU BACK TO YOUR PEOPLE.
PLEASE, NILS... WE NEED YOU!
AND YGGDRASIL?
LOOK AROUND. THERE AREN'T ANY TREES OUT HERE!
YES, THERE ARE! YOU SAW IT, TOO! WE HAVE TO FIND IT!
WHATEVER. I'VE MADE MY DECISION.
HEY, STOP!
YOU PROMISE TO KEEP GOING?
NO, IT'S TOO DANGEROUS. AND POINTLESS!

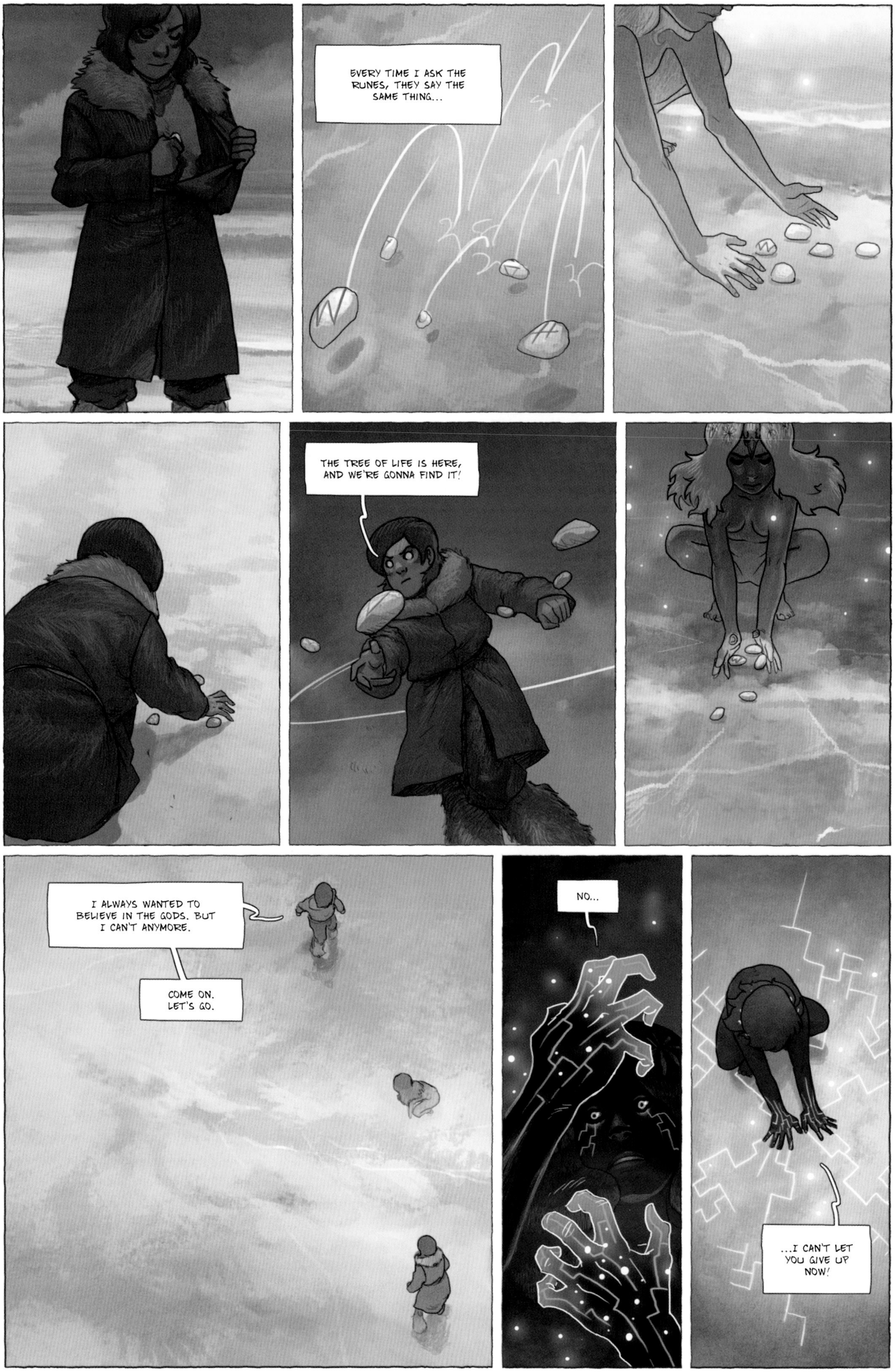

EVERY TIME I ASK THE RUNES, THEY SAY THE SAME THING...
THE TREE OF LIFE IS HERE, AND WE'RE GONNA FIND IT!
I ALWAYS WANTED TO BELIEVE IN THE GODS. BUT I CAN'T ANYMORE.
COME ON. LET'S GO.
NO...
...I CAN'T LET YOU GIVE UP NOW!

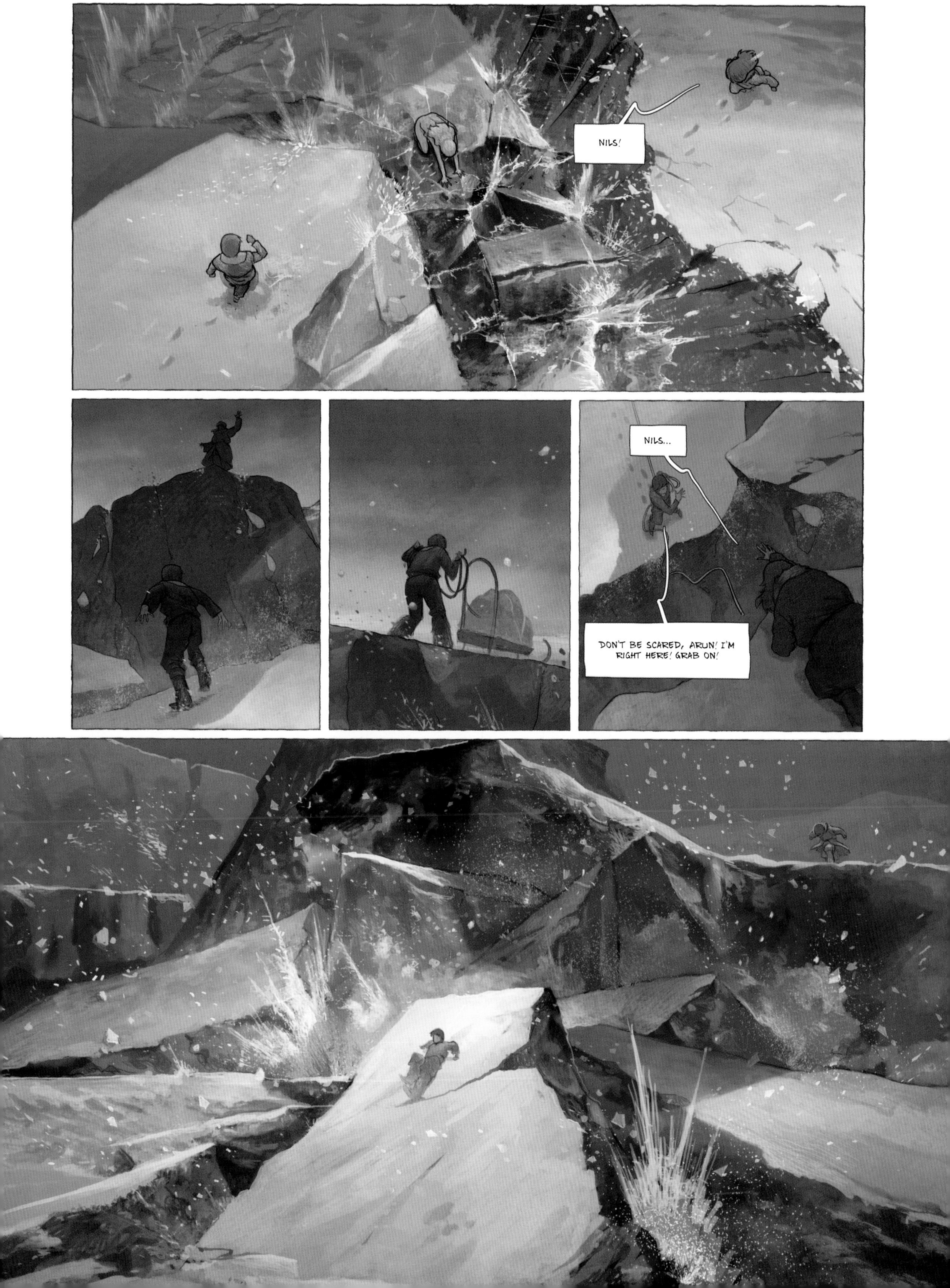
NILS!
NILS...
DON'T BE SCARED, ARUN! I'M RIGHT HERE! GRAB ON!

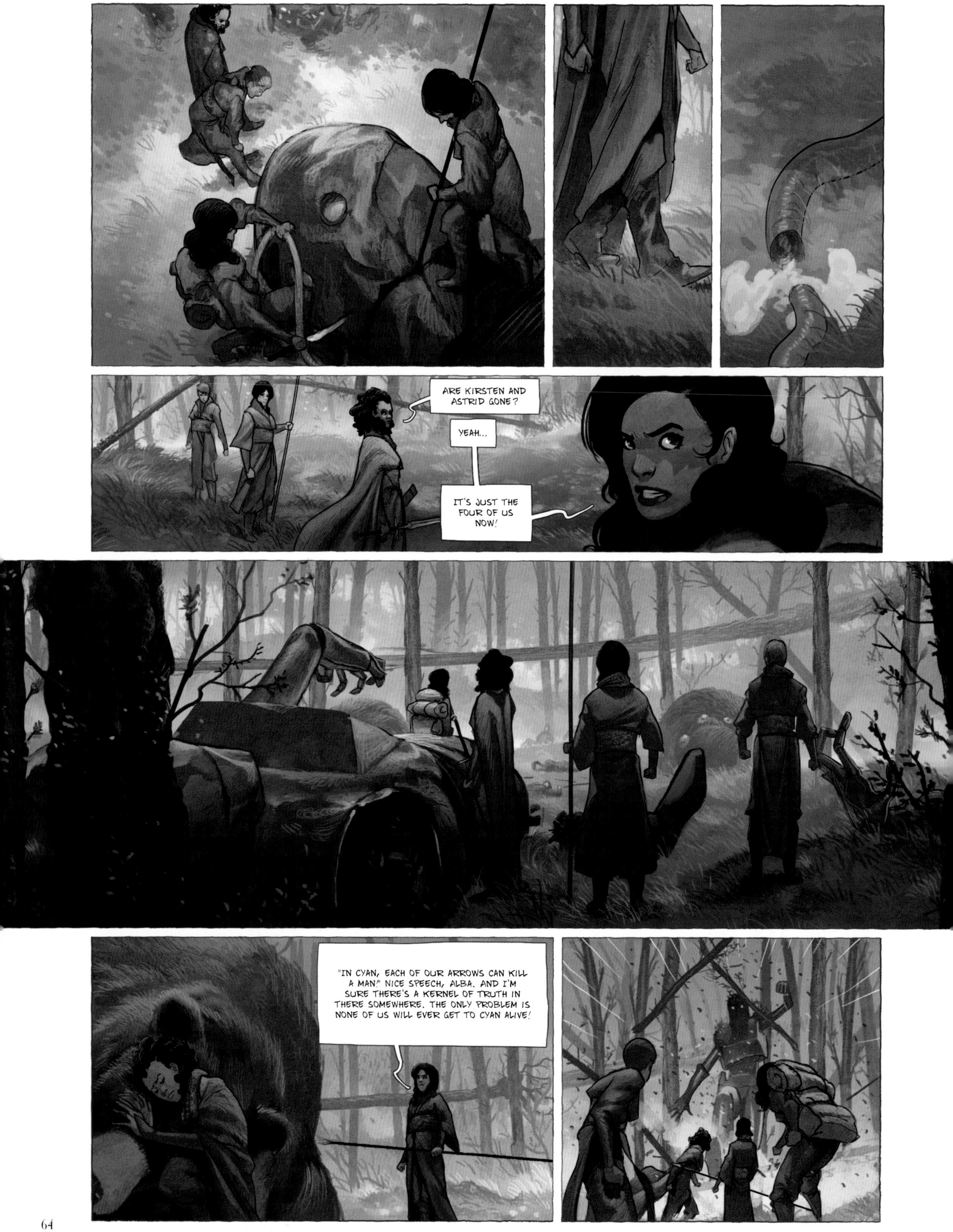
ARE KIRSTEN AND ASTRID GONE?
YEAH...
IT'S JUST THE FOUR OF US NOW!
"IN CYAN, EACH OF OUR ARROWS CAN KILL A MAN!" NICE SPEECH, ALBA. AND I'M SURE THERE'S A KERNEL OF TRUTH IN THERE SOMEWHERE. THE ONLY PROBLEM IS NONE OF US WILL EVER GET TO CYAN ALIVE!

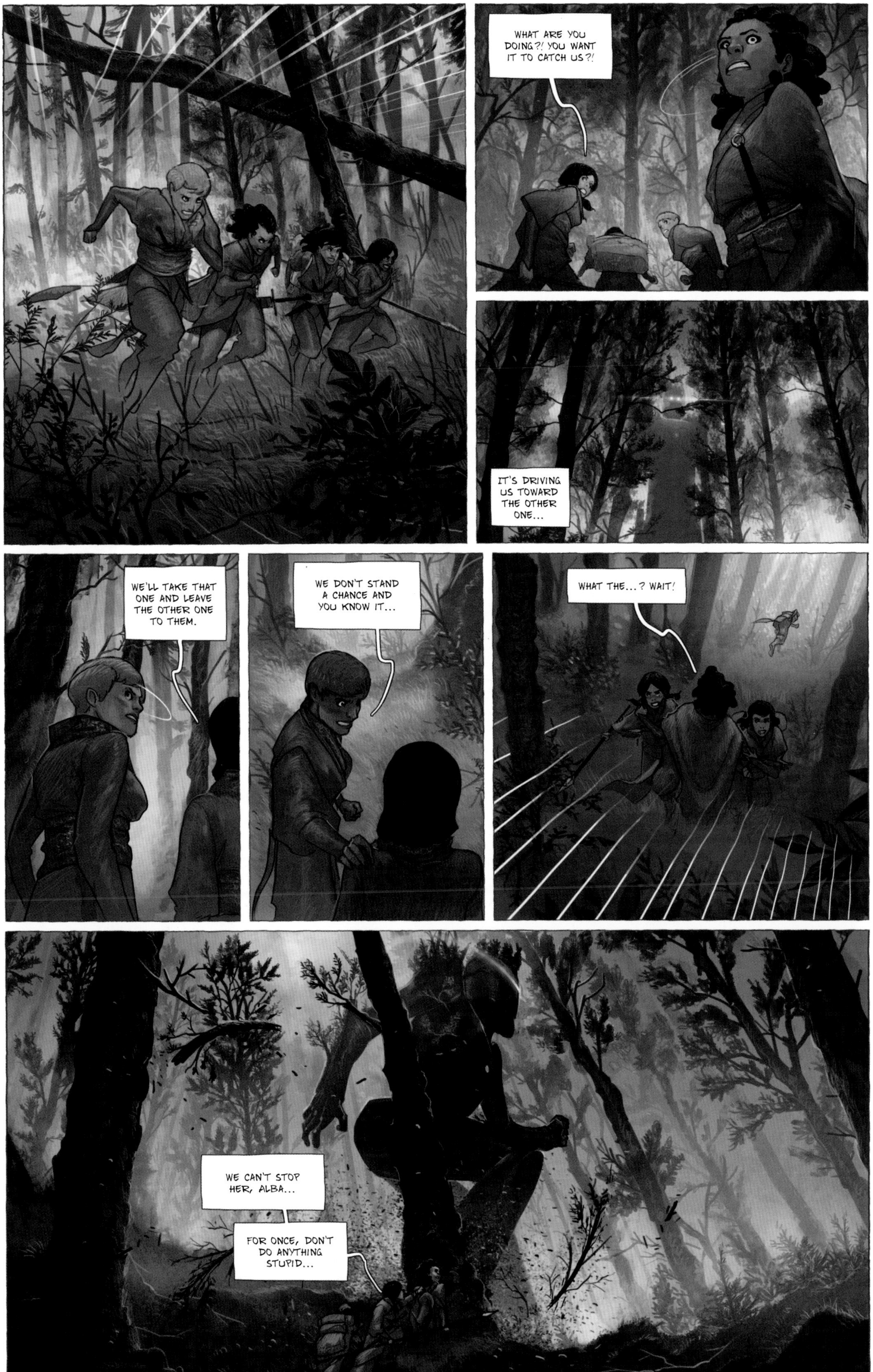
WHAT ARE YOU DOING?! YOU WANT IT TO CATCH US?!
IT'S DRIVING US TOWARD THE OTHER ONE...
WE'LL TAKE THAT ONE AND LEAVE THE OTHER ONE TO THEM.
WE DON'T STAND A CHANCE AND YOU KNOW IT...
WHAT THE...? WAIT!
WE CAN'T STOP HER, ALBA...
FOR ONCE, DON'T DO ANYTHING STUPID...

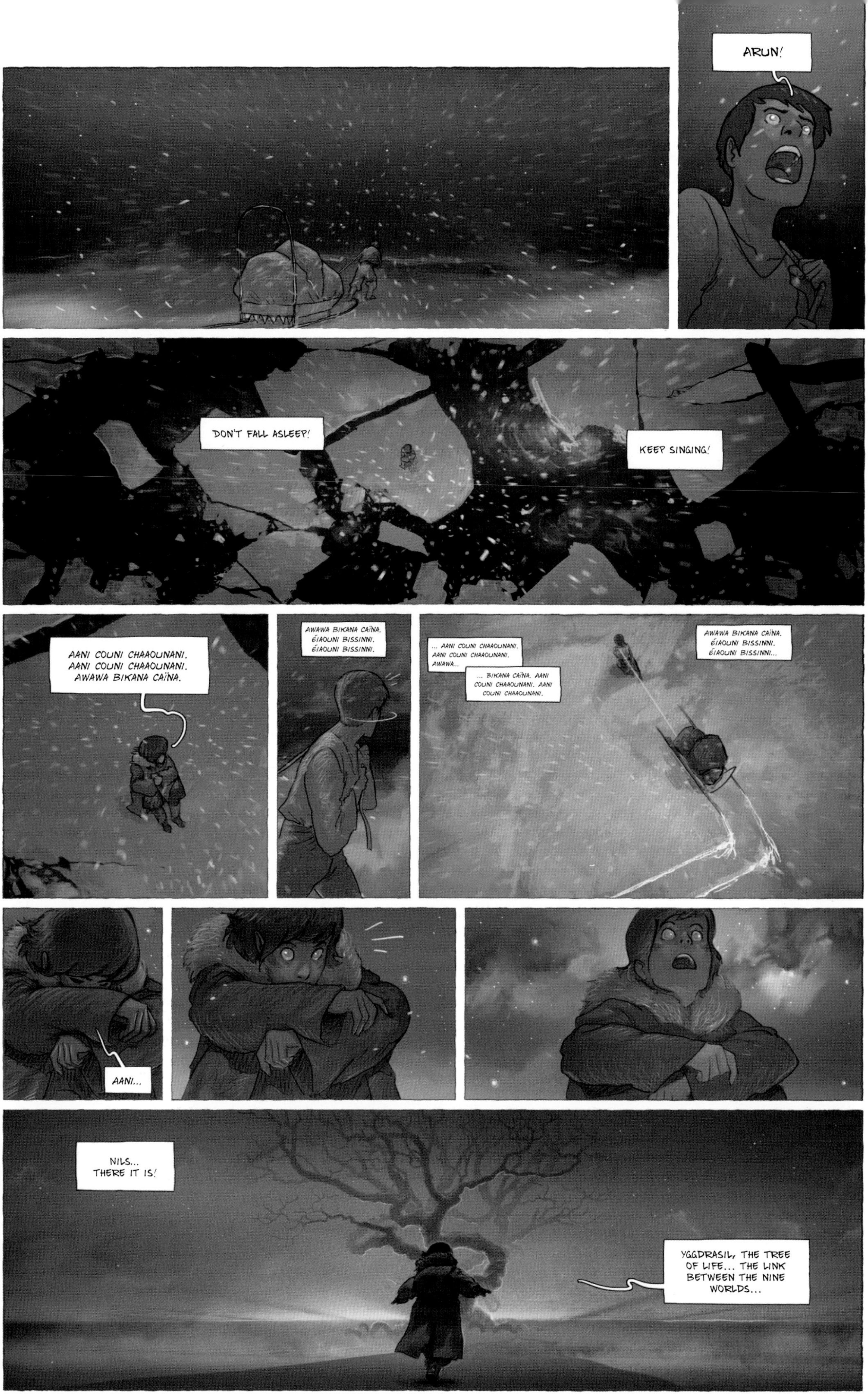
ARUN!
DON'T FALL ASLEEP!
KEEP SINGING!
AANI COUNI CHAAOUNANI.
AANI COUNI CHAAOUNANI.
AWAWA BIKANA CAÏNA.
AWAWA BIKANA CAÏNA.
ÉIAOUNI BISSINNI.
ÉIAOUNI BISSINNI.
... AANI COUNI CHAAOUNANI.
AANI COUNI CHAAOUNANI.
AWAWA...
... BIKANA CAÏNA. AANI
COUNI CHAAOUNANI. AANI
COUNI CHAAOUNANI.
AWAWA BIKANA CAÏNA.
ÉIAOUNI BISSINNI.
ÉIAOUNI BISSINNI...
AANI...
NILS...
THERE IT IS!
YGGDRASIL, THE TREE
OF LIFE... THE LINK
BETWEEN THE NINE
WORLDS...

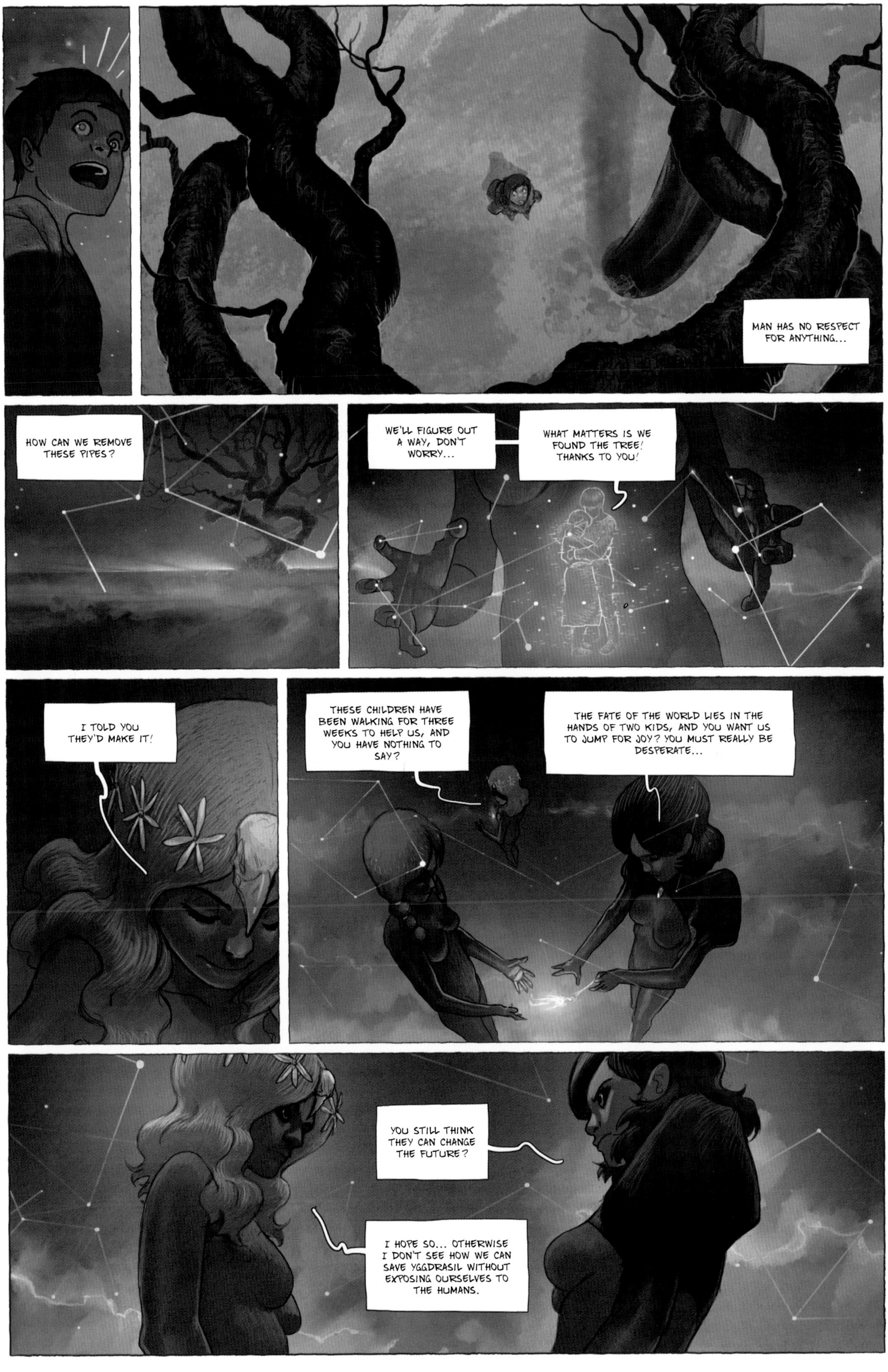
MAN HAS NO RESPECT FOR ANYTHING...
HOW CAN WE REMOVE THESE PIPES?
WE'LL FIGURE OUT A WAY, DON'T WORRY...
WHAT MATTERS IS WE FOUND THE TREE! THANKS TO YOU!
I TOLD YOU THEY'D MAKE IT!
THESE CHILDREN HAVE BEEN WALKING FOR THREE WEEKS TO HELP US, AND YOU HAVE NOTHING TO SAY?
THE FATE OF THE WORLD LIES IN THE HANDS OF TWO KIDS, AND YOU WANT US TO JUMP FOR JOY? YOU MUST REALLY BE DESPERATE...
YOU STILL THINK THEY CAN CHANGE THE FUTURE?
I HOPE SO... OTHERWISE I DON'T SEE HOW WE CAN SAVE YGGDRASIL WITHOUT EXPOSING OURSELVES TO THE HUMANS.

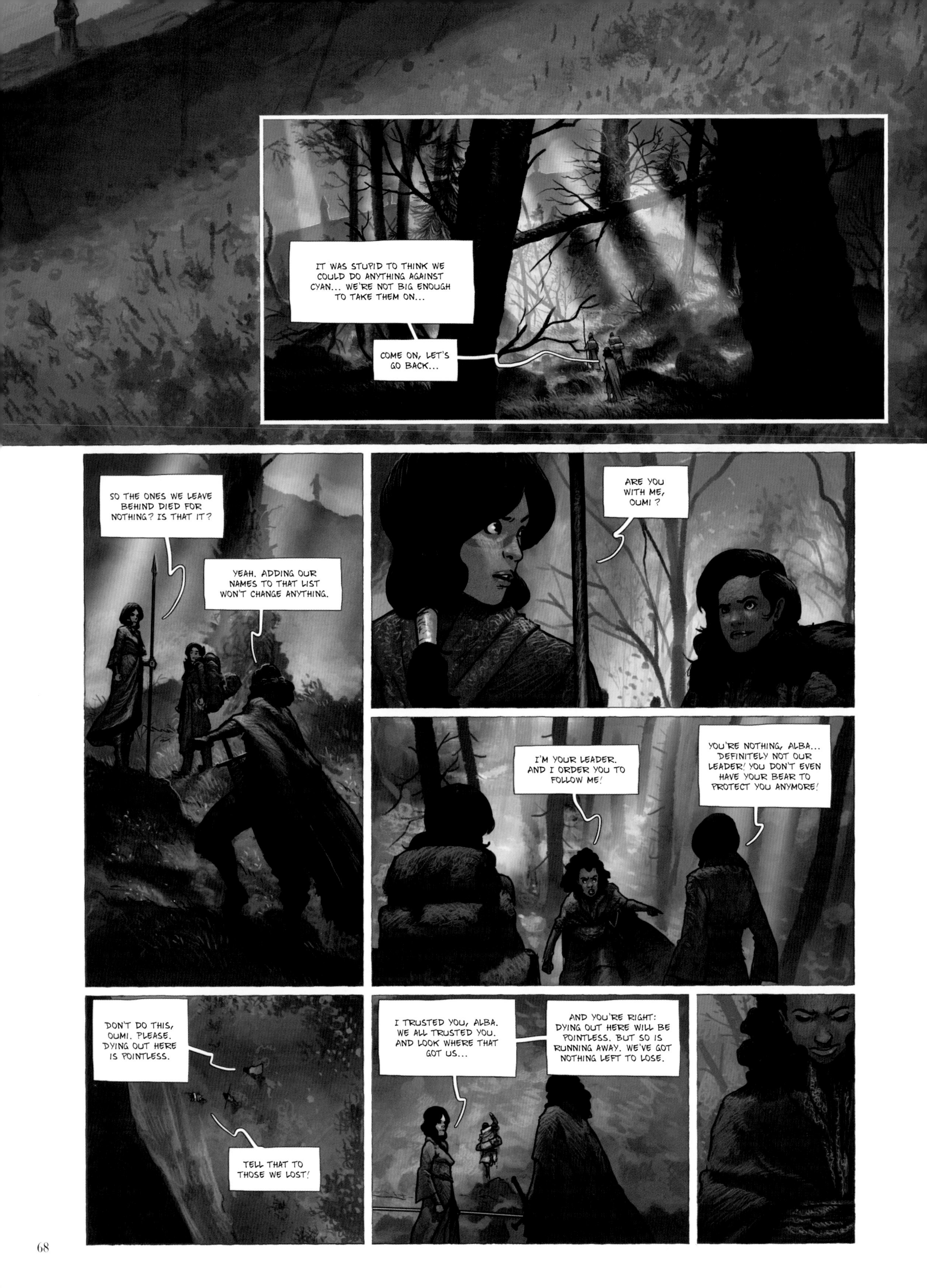
IT WAS STUPID TO THINK WE COULD DO ANYTHING AGAINST CYAN... WE'RE NOT BIG ENOUGH TO TAKE THEM ON...
COME ON, LET'S GO BACK...
SO THE ONES WE LEAVE BEHIND DIED FOR NOTHING? IS THAT IT?
YEAH. ADDING OUR NAMES TO THAT LIST WON'T CHANGE ANYTHING.
ARE YOU WITH ME, OUMI ?
I'M YOUR LEADER. AND I ORDER YOU TO FOLLOW ME!
YOU'RE NOTHING, ALBA... DEFINITELY NOT OUR LEADER! YOU DON'T EVEN HAVE YOUR BEAR TO PROTECT YOU ANYMORE!
DON'T DO THIS, OUMI. PLEASE. DYING OUT HERE IS POINTLESS.
TELL THAT TO THOSE WE LOST!
I TRUSTED YOU, ALBA. WE ALL TRUSTED YOU. AND LOOK WHERE THAT GOT US...
AND YOU'RE RIGHT: DYING OUT HERE WILL BE POINTLESS. BUT SO IS RUNNING AWAY. WE'VE GOT NOTHING LEFT TO LOSE.

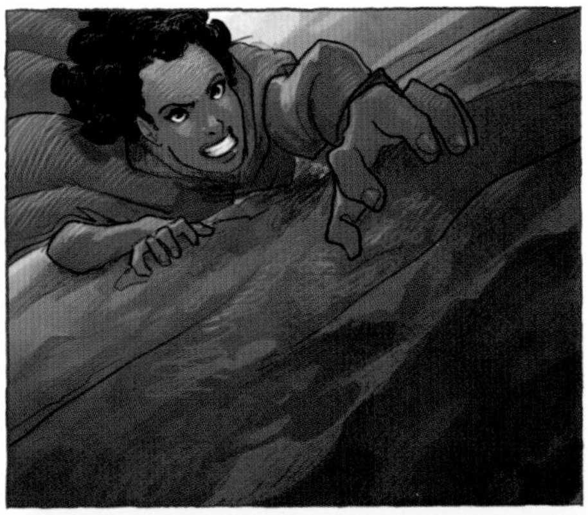

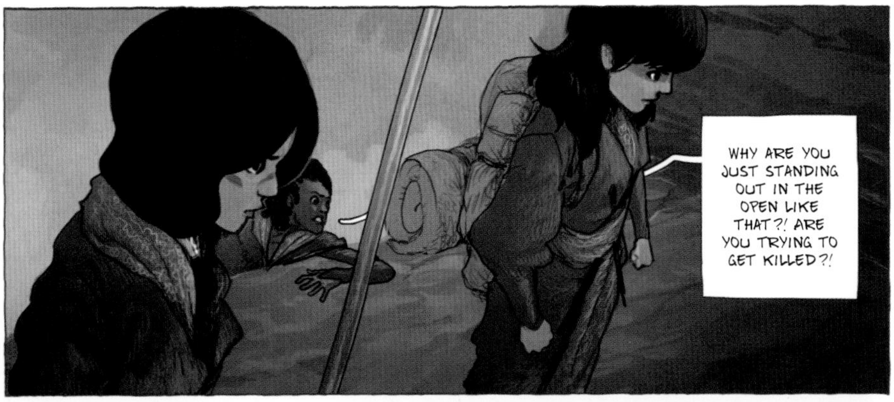
WHY ARE YOU JUST STANDING OUT IN THE OPEN LIKE THAT?! ARE YOU TRYING TO GET KILLED?!

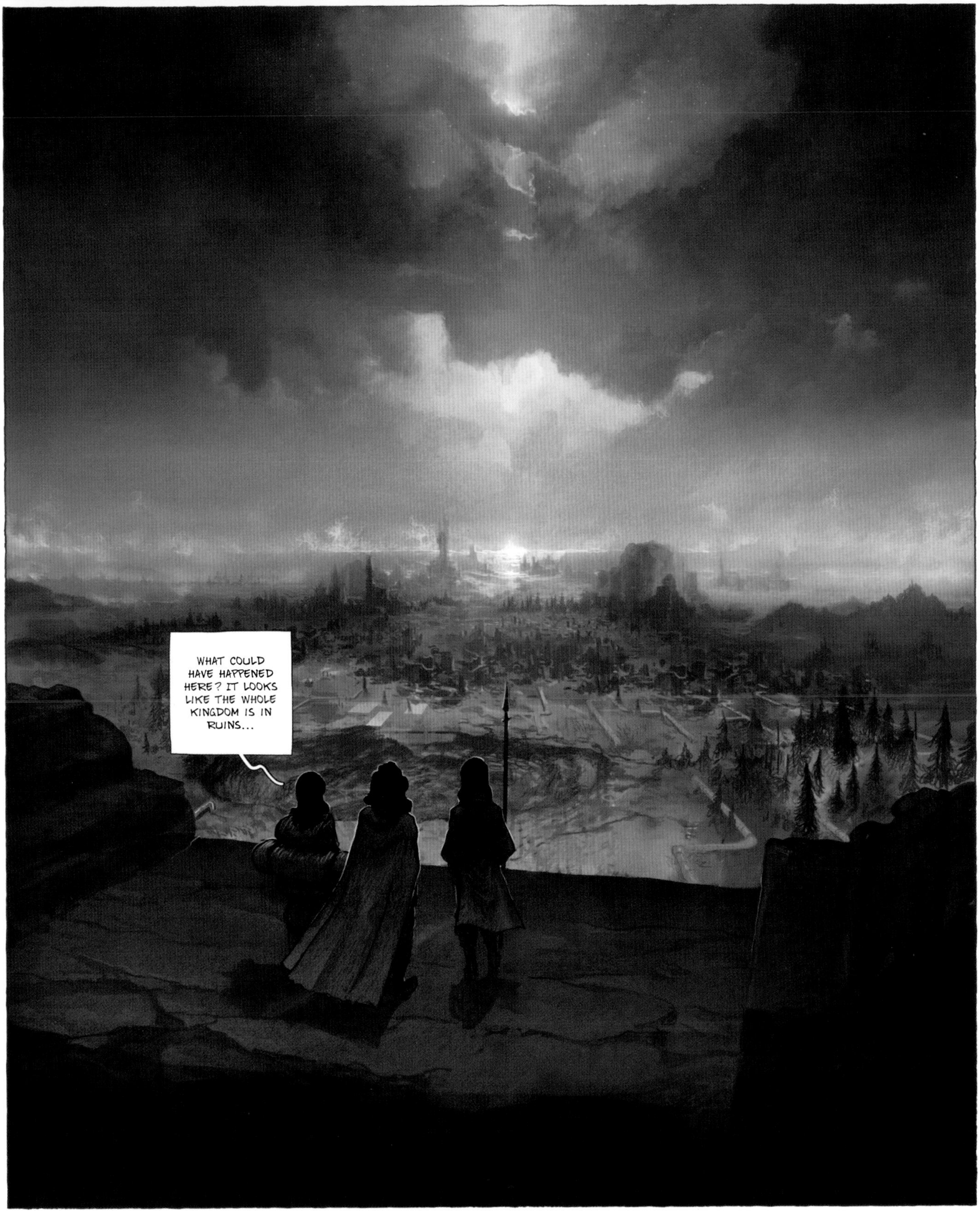
WHAT COULD HAVE HAPPENED HERE? IT LOOKS LIKE THE WHOLE KINGDOM IS IN RUINS...

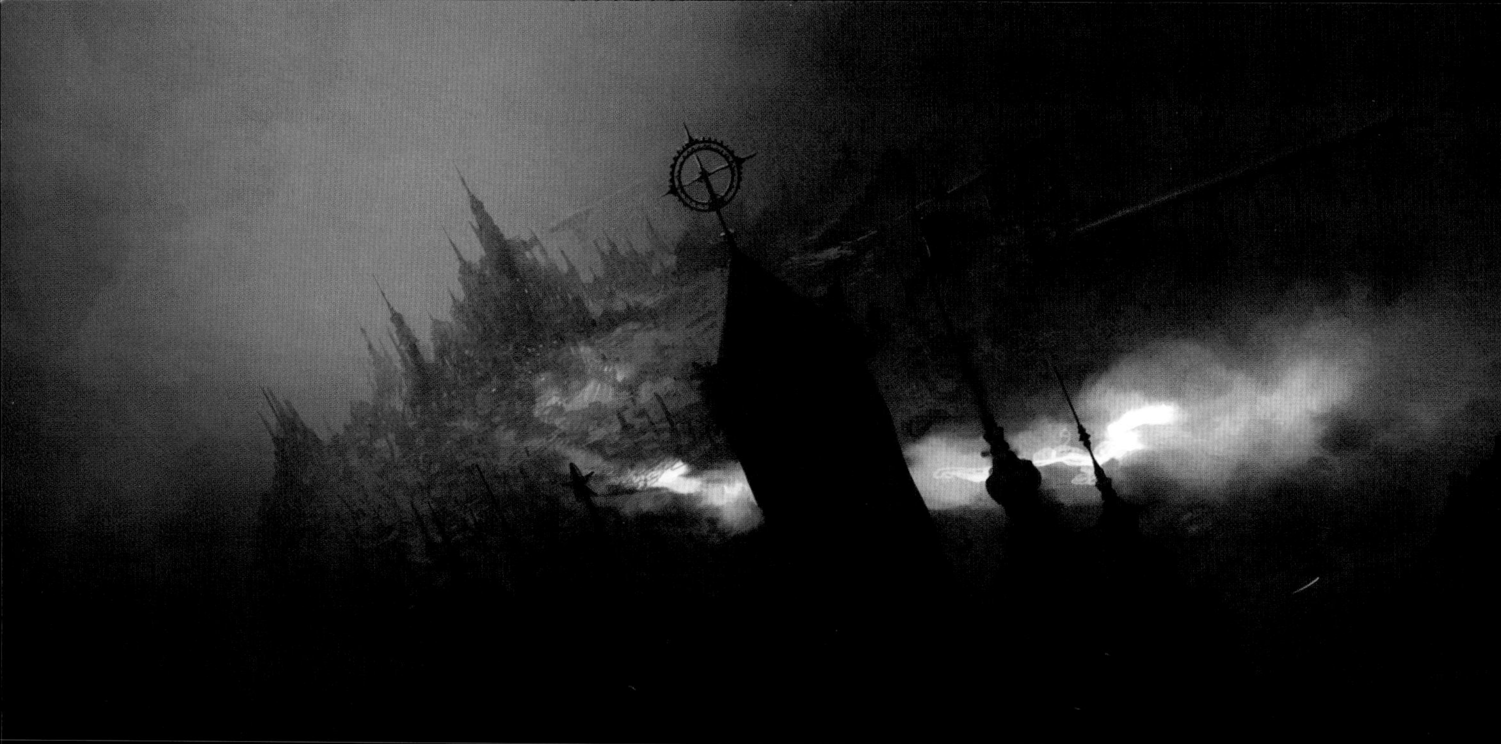

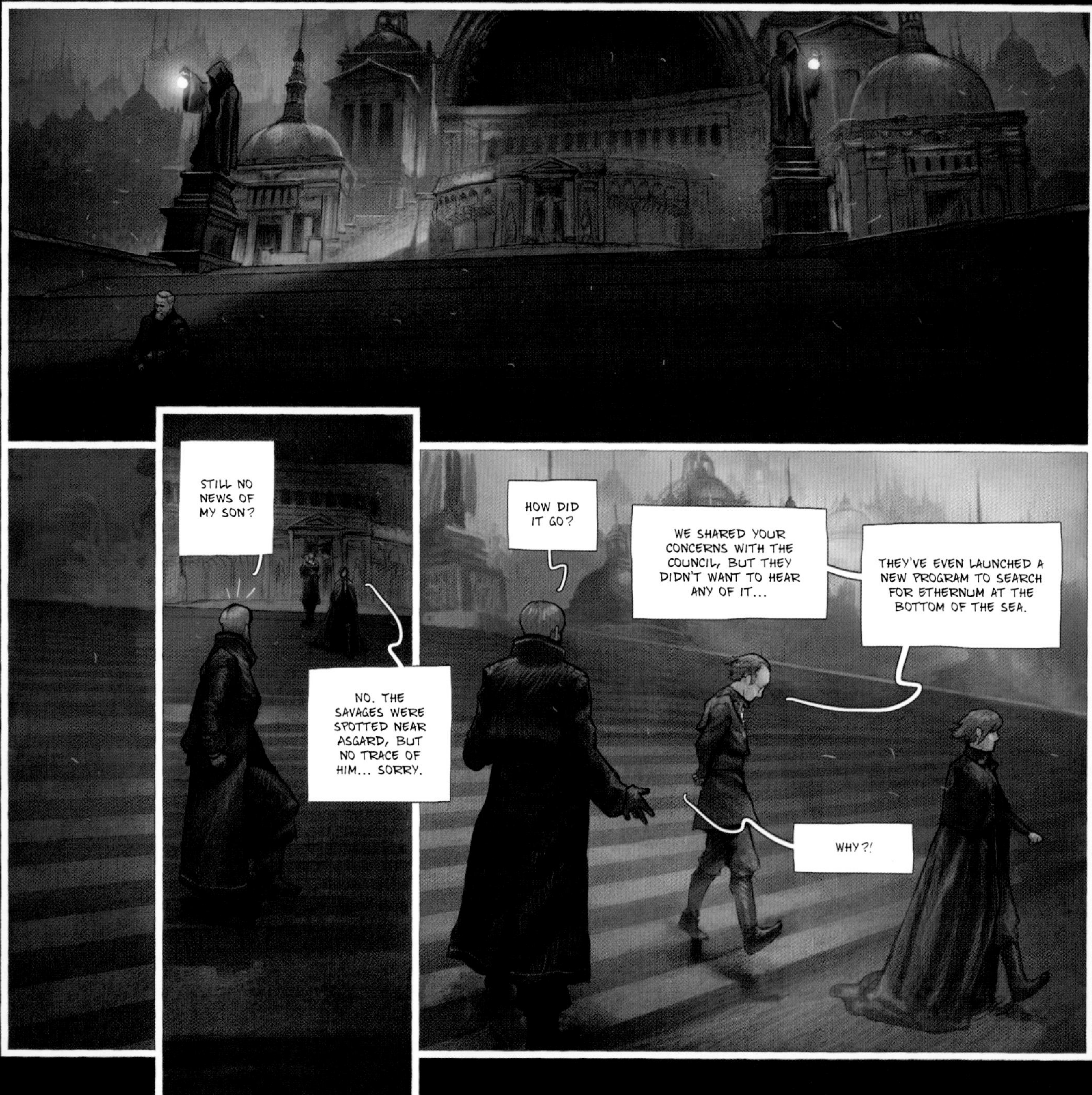
STILL NO NEWS OF MY SON?
NO. THE SAVAGES WERE SPOTTED NEAR ASGARD, BUT NO TRACE OF HIM... SORRY.
HOW DID IT GO?
WE SHARED YOUR CONCERNS WITH THE COUNCIL, BUT THEY DIDN'T WANT TO HEAR ANY OF IT...
THEY'VE EVEN LAUNCHED A NEW PROGRAM TO SEARCH FOR ETHERNUM AT THE BOTTOM OF THE SEA.
WHY?!

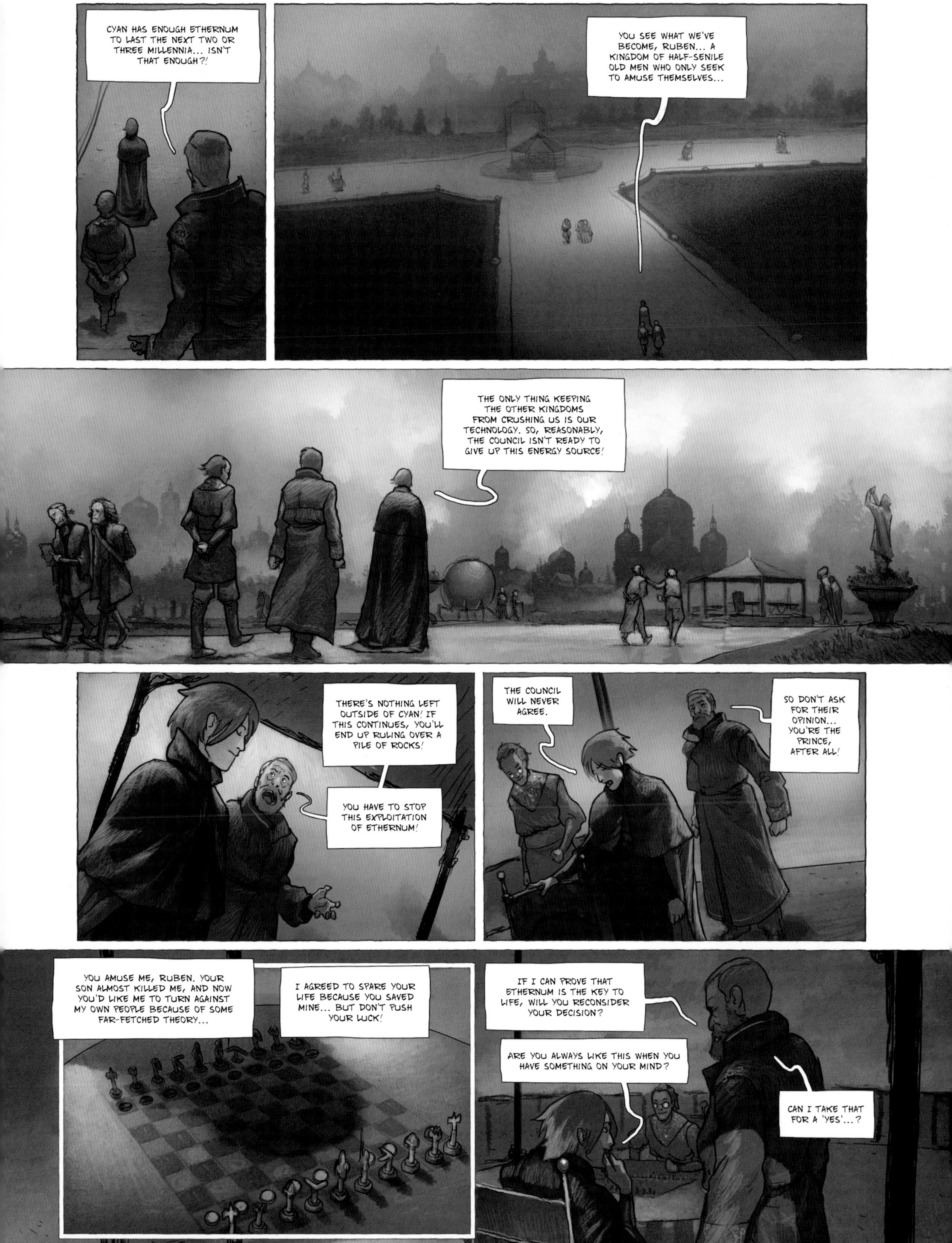
CYAN HAS ENOUGH ETHERNUM TO LAST THE NEXT TWO OR THREE MILLENNIA... ISN'T THAT ENOUGH?!
YOU SEE WHAT WE'VE BECOME, RUBEN... A KINGDOM OF HALF-SENILE OLD MEN WHO ONLY SEEK TO AMUSE THEMSELVES...
THE ONLY THING KEEPING THE OTHER KINGDOMS FROM CRUSHING US IS OUR TECHNOLOGY. SO, REASONABLY, THE COUNCIL ISN'T READY TO GIVE UP THIS ENERGY SOURCE!
THERE'S NOTHING LEFT OUTSIDE OF CYAN! IF THIS CONTINUES, YOU'LL END UP RULING OVER A PILE OF ROCKS!
YOU HAVE TO STOP THIS EXPLOITATION OF ETHERNUM!
THE COUNCIL WILL NEVER AGREE.
SO DON'T ASK FOR THEIR OPINION... YOU'RE THE PRINCE, AFTER ALL!
YOU AMUSE ME, RUBEN. YOUR SON ALMOST KILLED ME, AND NOW YOU'D LIKE ME TO TURN AGAINST MY OWN PEOPLE BECAUSE OF SOME FAR-FETCHED THEORY...
I AGREED TO SPARE YOUR LIFE BECAUSE YOU SAVED MINE... BUT DON'T PUSH YOUR LUCK!
IF I CAN PROVE THAT ETHERNUM IS THE KEY TO LIFE, WILL YOU RECONSIDER YOUR DECISION?
ARE YOU ALWAYS LIKE THIS WHEN YOU HAVE SOMETHING ON YOUR MIND?
CAN I TAKE THAT FOR A 'YES'...?

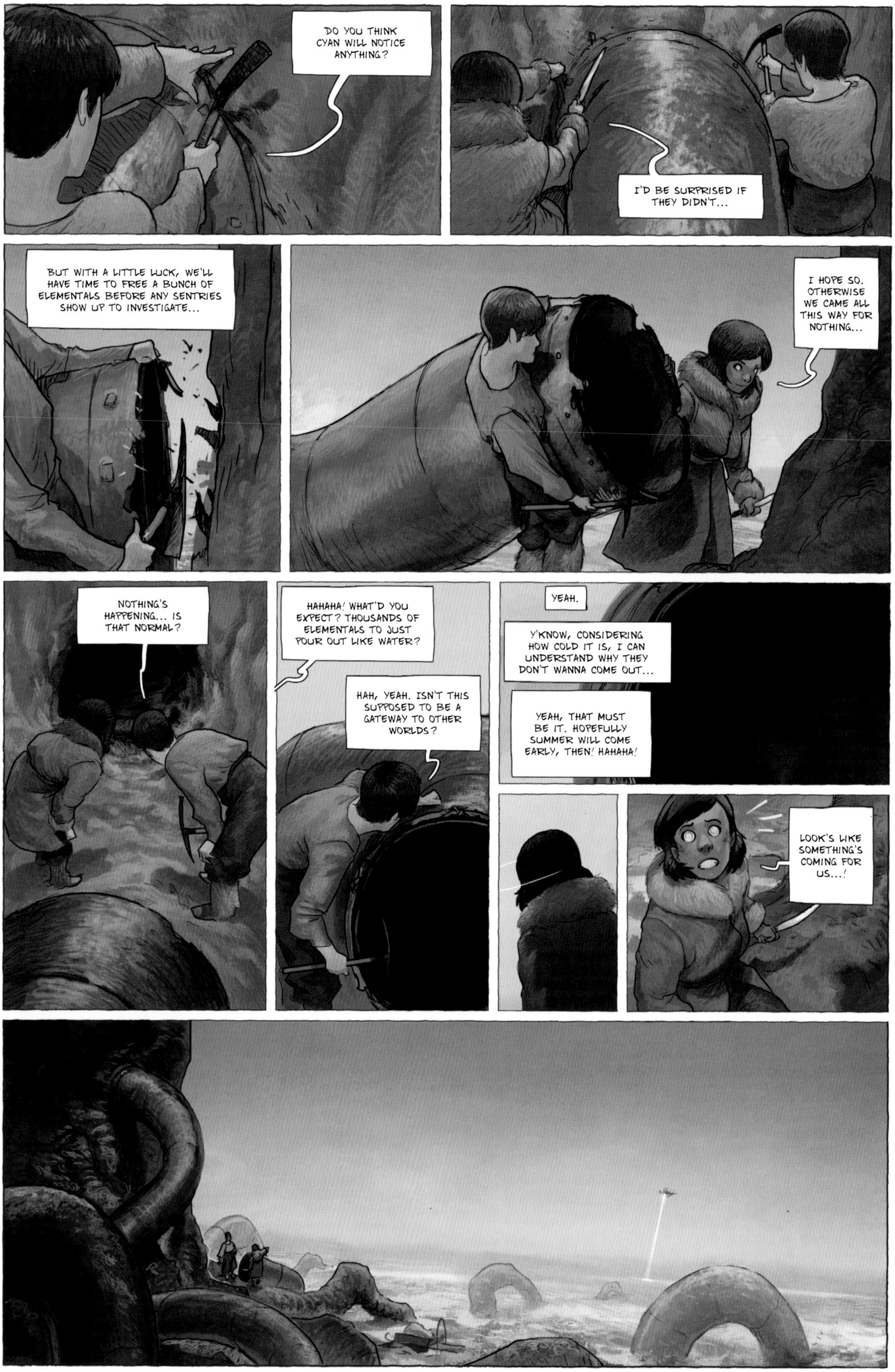
DO YOU THINK CYAN WILL NOTICE ANYTHING?
I'D BE SURPRISED IF THEY DIDN'T...
BUT WITH A LITTLE LUCK, WE'LL HAVE TIME TO FREE A BUNCH OF ELEMENTALS BEFORE ANY SENTRIES SHOW UP TO INVESTIGATE...
I HOPE SO. OTHERWISE WE CAME ALL THIS WAY FOR NOTHING...
NOTHING'S HAPPENING... IS THAT NORMAL?
HAHAHA! WHAT'D YOU EXPECT? THOUSANDS OF ELEMENTALS TO JUST POUR OUT LIKE WATER?
HAH, YEAH. ISN'T THIS SUPPOSED TO BE A GATEWAY TO OTHER WORLDS?
YEAH.
Y'KNOW, CONSIDERING HOW COLD IT IS, I CAN UNDERSTAND WHY THEY DON'T WANNA COME OUT...
YEAH, THAT MUST BE IT. HOPEFULLY SUMMER WILL COME EARLY, THEN! HAHAHA!
LOOK'S LIKE SOMETHING'S COMING FOR US...!

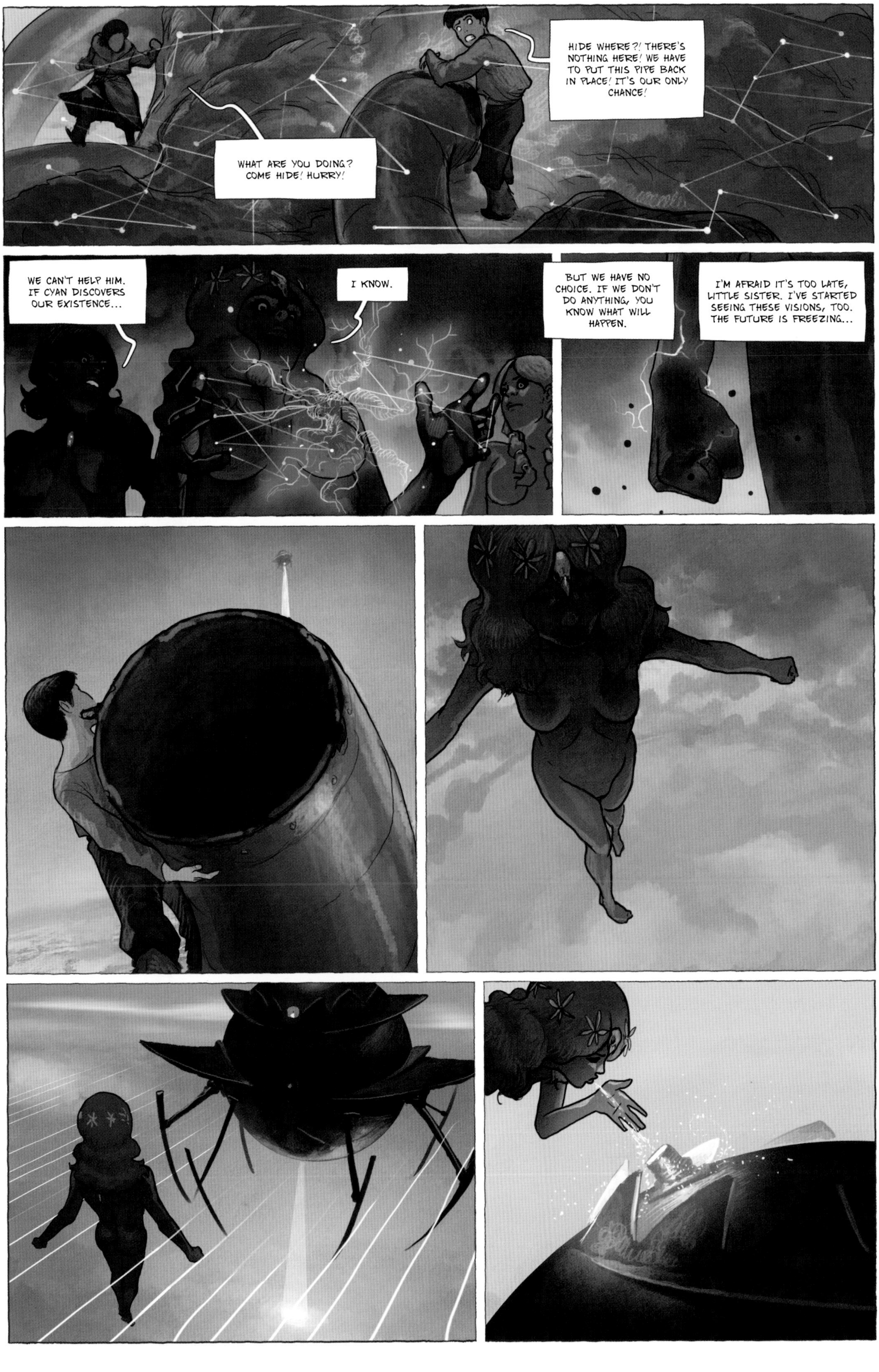
HIDE WHERE?! THERE'S NOTHING HERE! WE HAVE TO PUT THIS PIPE BACK IN PLACE! IT'S OUR ONLY CHANCE!
WHAT ARE YOU DOING? COME HIDE! HURRY!
WE CAN'T HELP HIM. IF CYAN DISCOVERS OUR EXISTENCE...
I KNOW.
BUT WE HAVE NO CHOICE. IF WE DON'T DO ANYTHING, YOU KNOW WHAT WILL HAPPEN.
I'M AFRAID IT'S TOO LATE, LITTLE SISTER. I'VE STARTED SEEING THESE VISIONS, TOO. THE FUTURE IS FREEZING...

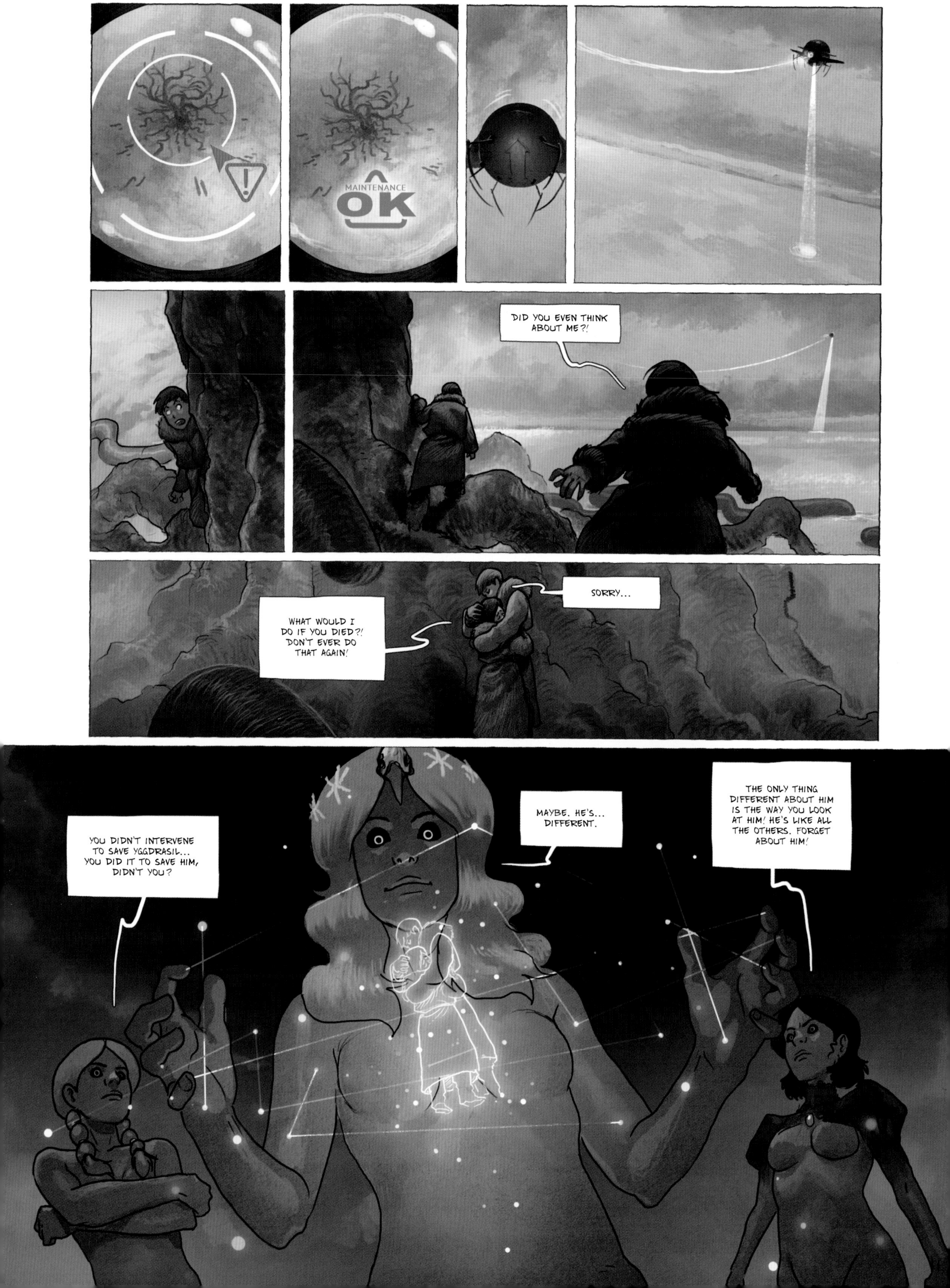
MAINTENANCE
OK
DID YOU EVEN THINK ABOUT ME?!
WHAT WOULD I DO IF YOU DIED?! DON'T EVER DO THAT AGAIN!
SORRY...
YOU DIDN'T INTERVENE TO SAVE YGGDRASIL... YOU DID IT TO SAVE HIM, DIDN'T YOU?
MAYBE. HE'S... DIFFERENT.
THE ONLY THING DIFFERENT ABOUT HIM IS THE WAY YOU LOOK AT HIM! HE'S LIKE ALL THE OTHERS. FORGET ABOUT HIM!

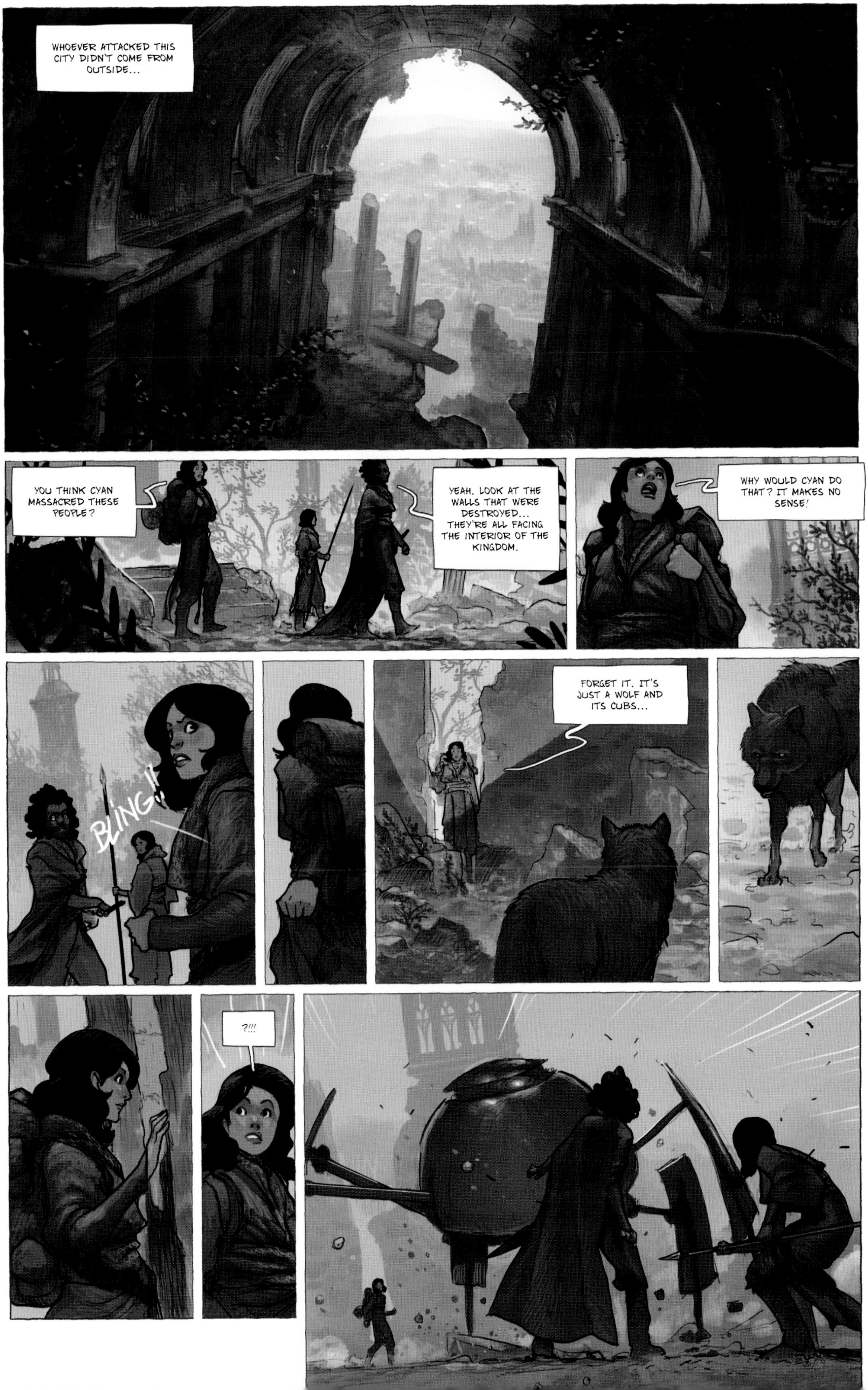
WHOEVER ATTACKED THIS CITY DIDN'T COME FROM OUTSIDE...
YOU THINK CYAN MASSACRED THESE PEOPLE?
YEAH. LOOK AT THE WALLS THAT WERE DESTROYED... THEY'RE ALL FACING THE INTERIOR OF THE KINGDOM.
WHY WOULD CYAN DO THAT? IT MAKES NO SENSE!
BLING!!
FORGET IT. IT'S JUST A WOLF AND ITS CUBS...
?!!!

SO?

THE VISION IS DIFFERENT.

BUT THE END IS THE SAME...

THE FUTURE IS SET, VERDANDI. THERE'S NOTHING YOU CAN DO.

FORGET THAT BOY. NOTHING GOOD HAS EVER COME FROM A UNION BETWEEN GODS AND MEN...

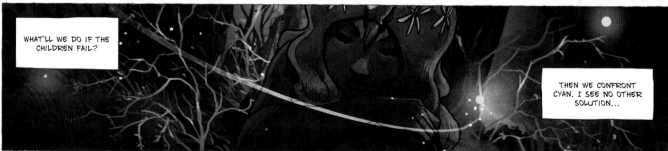

WHAT'LL WE DO IF THE CHILDREN FAIL?

THEN WE CONFRONT CYAN. I SEE NO OTHER SOLUTION...

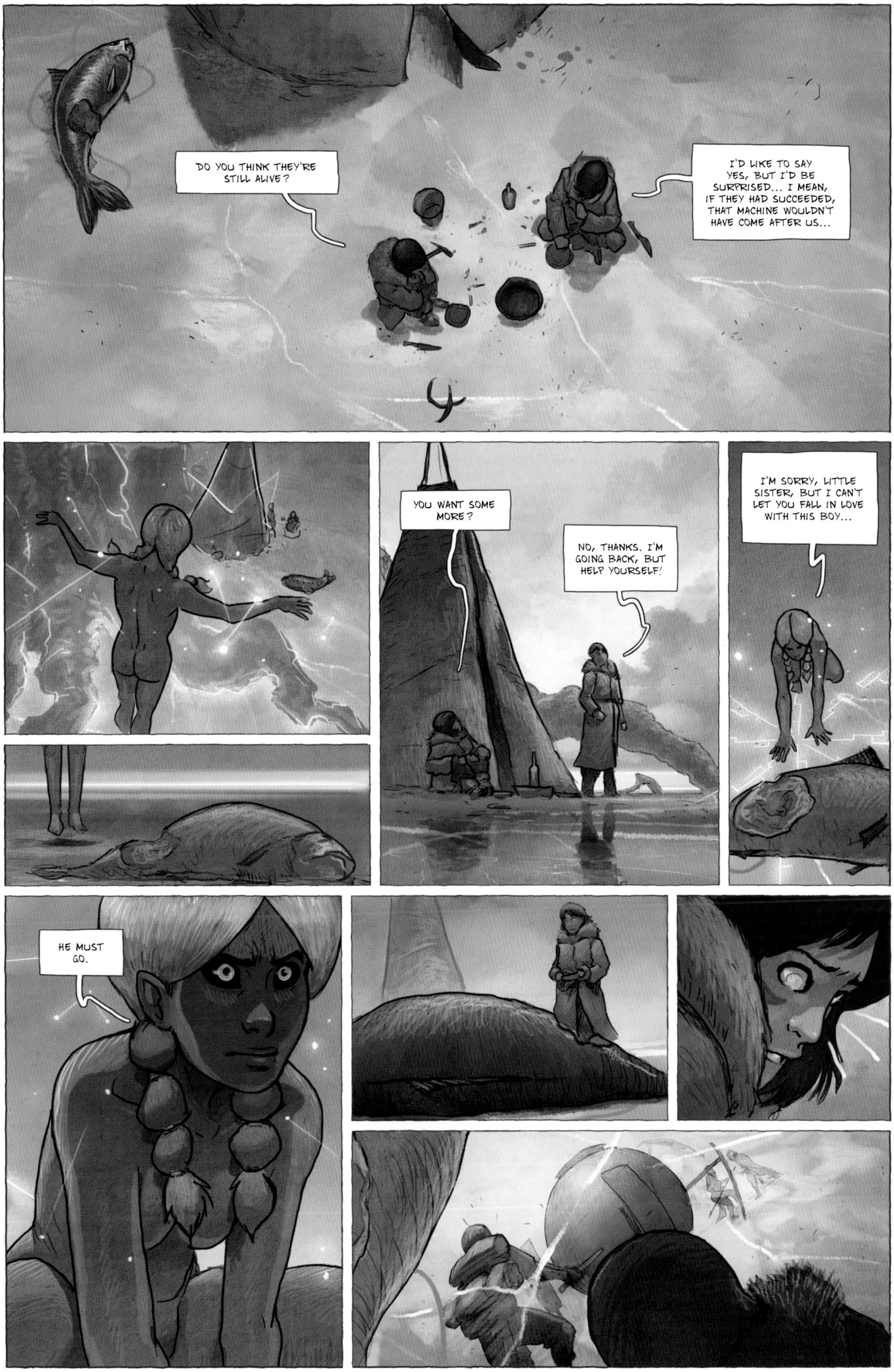
DO YOU THINK THEY'RE STILL ALIVE?
I'D LIKE TO SAY YES, BUT I'D BE SURPRISED... I MEAN, IF THEY HAD SUCCEEDED, THAT MACHINE WOULDN'T HAVE COME AFTER US...
YOU WANT SOME MORE?
NO, THANKS. I'M GOING BACK, BUT HELP YOURSELF!
I'M SORRY, LITTLE SISTER, BUT I CAN'T LET YOU FALL IN LOVE WITH THIS BOY...
HE MUST GO.

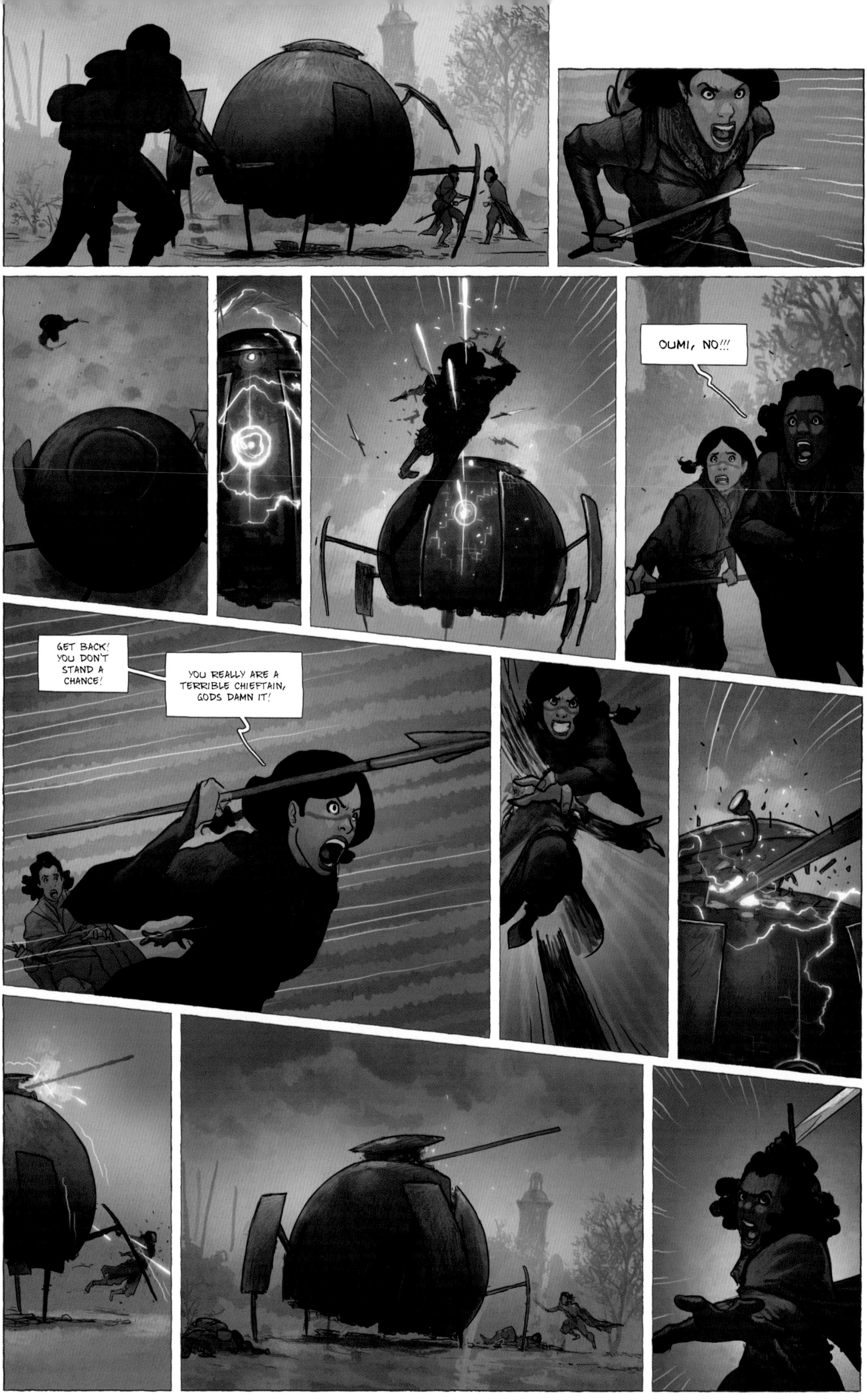
OUMI, NO!!!
GET BACK! YOU DON'T STAND A CHANCE!
YOU REALLY ARE A TERRIBLE CHIEFTAIN, GODS DAMN IT!

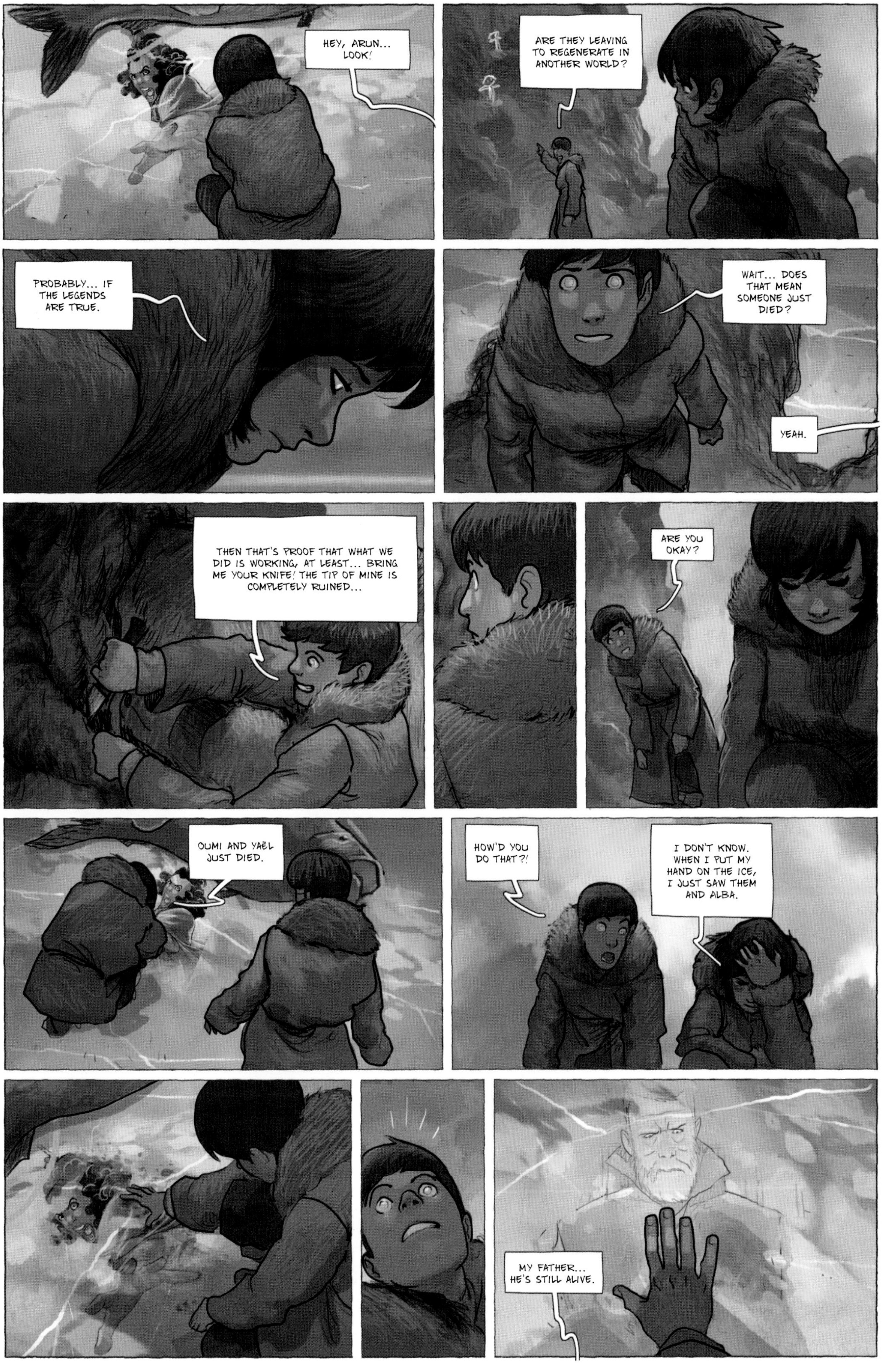
HEY, ARUN... LOOK!
ARE THEY LEAVING TO REGENERATE IN ANOTHER WORLD?
PROBABLY... IF THE LEGENDS ARE TRUE.
WAIT... DOES THAT MEAN SOMEONE JUST DIED?
YEAH.
THEN THAT'S PROOF THAT WHAT WE DID IS WORKING, AT LEAST... BRING ME YOUR KNIFE! THE TIP OF MINE IS COMPLETELY RUINED...
ARE YOU OKAY?
OUMI AND YAËL JUST DIED.
HOW'D YOU DO THAT?!
I DON'T KNOW. WHEN I PUT MY HAND ON THE ICE, I JUST SAW THEM AND ALBA.
MY FATHER... HE'S STILL ALIVE.

IF ETHERNUM CAN BIND ITSELF TO MATTER, THEN IT MUST BE ABLE TO COMMUNICATE WITH IT... BUT HOW?!

WE'LL SOON FIND OUT. I RELEASED THE ETHERNUM.

I BET IT'S VIBRATORY.

DOES MATTER EMIT VIBRATIONS?

OF COURSE. LOOK... THE RED FIELD IS EMITTED BY THE SEED, AND THE BLUE FIELD IS EMITTED BY THE ETHERNUM...

INCREDIBLE! IT LOOKS LIKE THE ETHERNUM'S FIELD FREQUENCY IS SHIFTING TO MATCH THE SEEDS...!

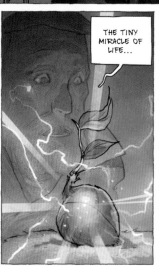

THE TINY MIRACLE OF LIFE...

WHAT'D YOU DO?! WHY DESTROY THE SEED?

TO SEE IF WE CAN REPRODUCE THE EXPERIMENT... NOW THAT WE'VE RECORDED THE FIELD EMITTED BY THE PLANT, WE CAN REPRODUCE IT WHENEVER WE WANT!

REVERSING THE PROCESS OF DEATH... THAT'D BE PRETTY INCREDIBLE, WOULDN'T IT?

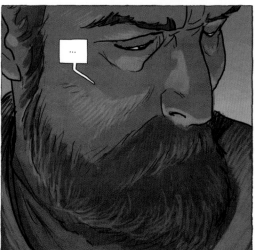

...

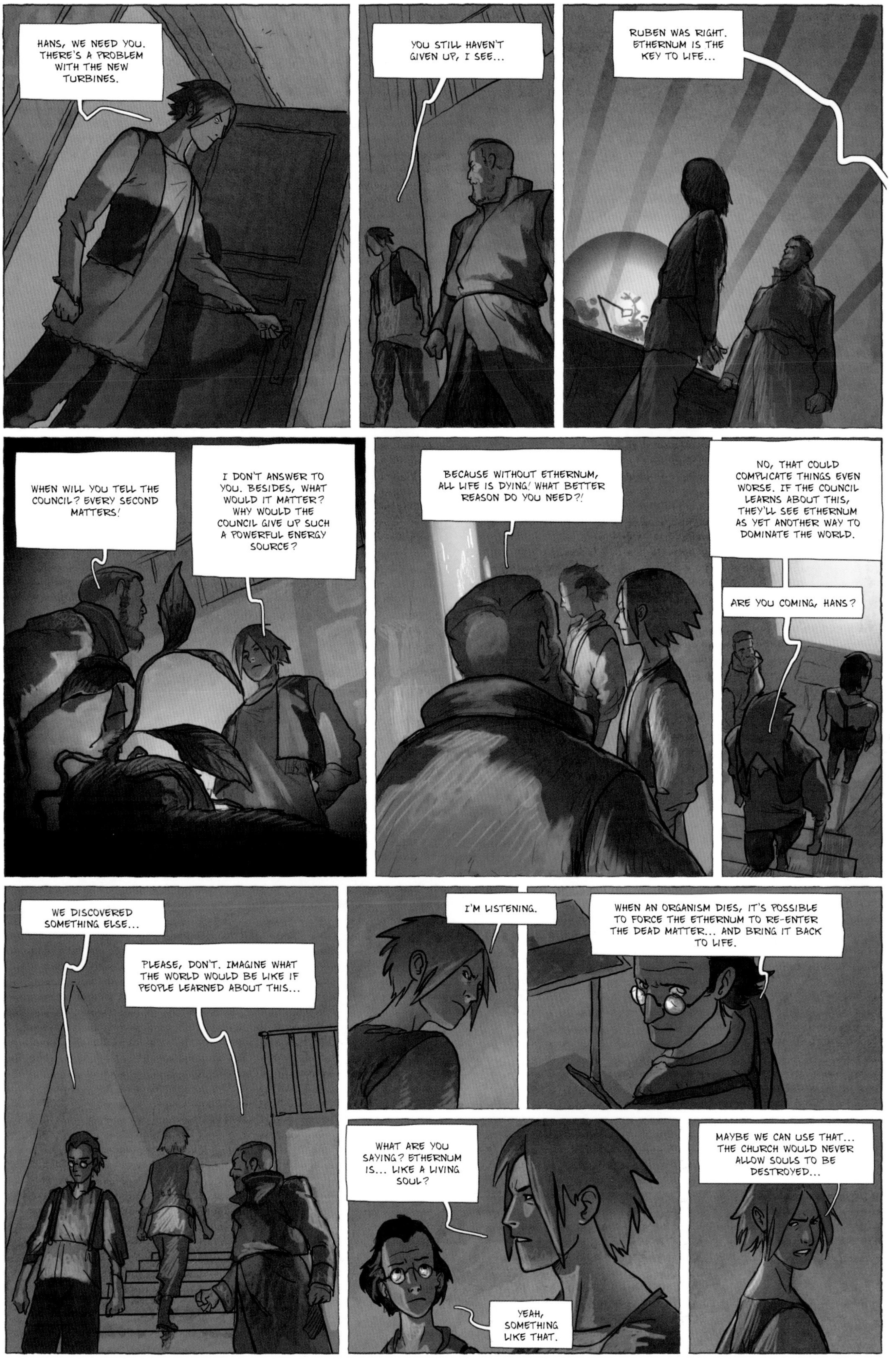
HANS, WE NEED YOU. THERE'S A PROBLEM WITH THE NEW TURBINES.
YOU STILL HAVEN'T GIVEN UP, I SEE...
RUBEN WAS RIGHT. ETHERNUM IS THE KEY TO LIFE...
WHEN WILL YOU TELL THE COUNCIL? EVERY SECOND MATTERS!
I DON'T ANSWER TO YOU. BESIDES, WHAT WOULD IT MATTER? WHY WOULD THE COUNCIL GIVE UP SUCH A POWERFUL ENERGY SOURCE?
BECAUSE WITHOUT ETHERNUM, ALL LIFE IS DYING! WHAT BETTER REASON DO YOU NEED?!
NO, THAT COULD COMPLICATE THINGS EVEN WORSE. IF THE COUNCIL LEARNS ABOUT THIS, THEY'LL SEE ETHERNUM AS YET ANOTHER WAY TO DOMINATE THE WORLD.
ARE YOU COMING, HANS?
WE DISCOVERED SOMETHING ELSE...
PLEASE, DON'T. IMAGINE WHAT THE WORLD WOULD BE LIKE IF PEOPLE LEARNED ABOUT THIS...
I'M LISTENING.
WHEN AN ORGANISM DIES, IT'S POSSIBLE TO FORCE THE ETHERNUM TO RE-ENTER THE DEAD MATTER... AND BRING IT BACK TO LIFE.
WHAT ARE YOU SAYING? ETHERNUM IS... LIKE A LIVING SOUL?
YEAH, SOMETHING LIKE THAT.
MAYBE WE CAN USE THAT... THE CHURCH WOULD NEVER ALLOW SOULS TO BE DESTROYED...

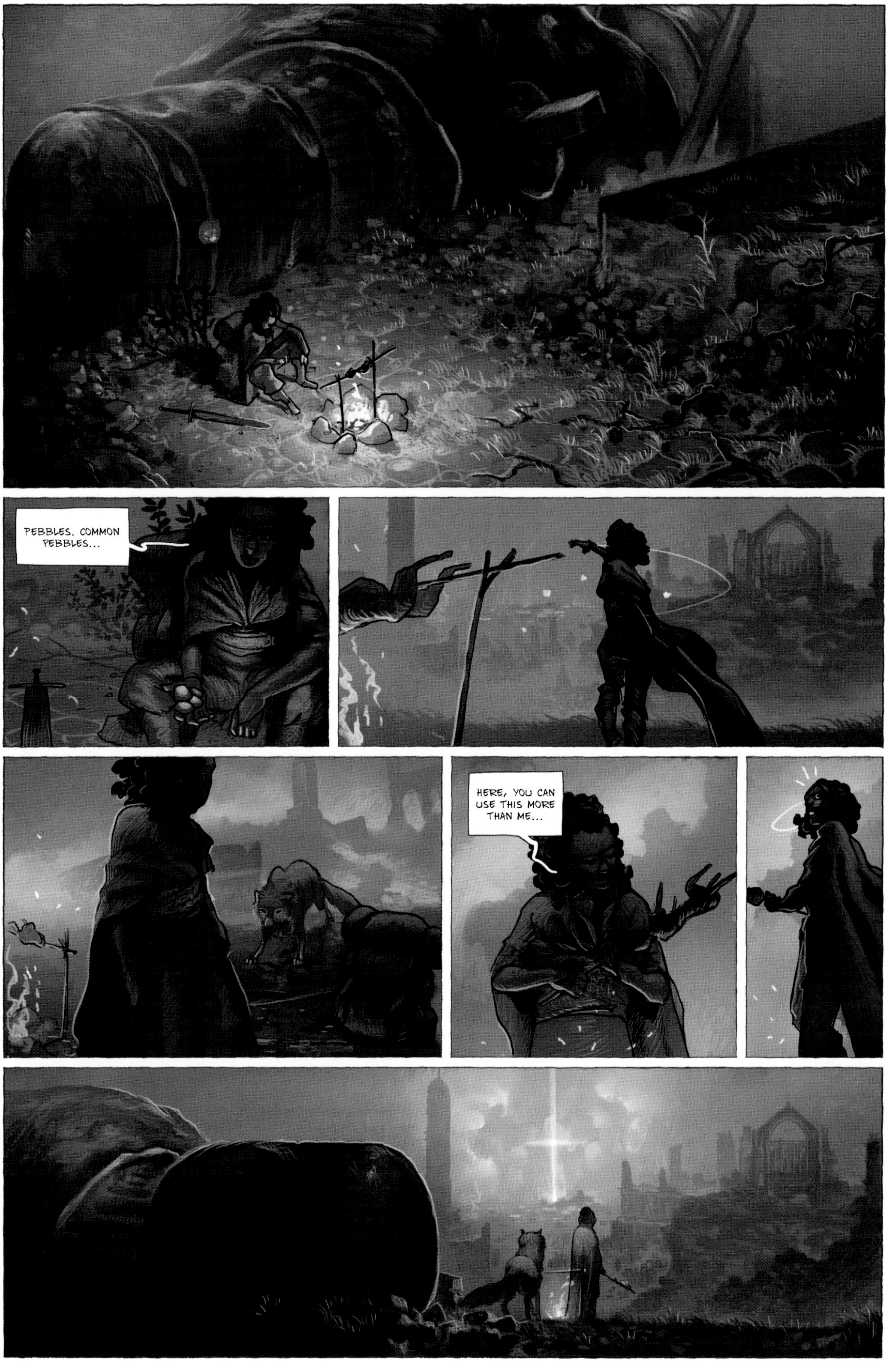
PEBBLES. COMMON PEBBLES...
HERE, YOU CAN USE THIS MORE THAN ME...

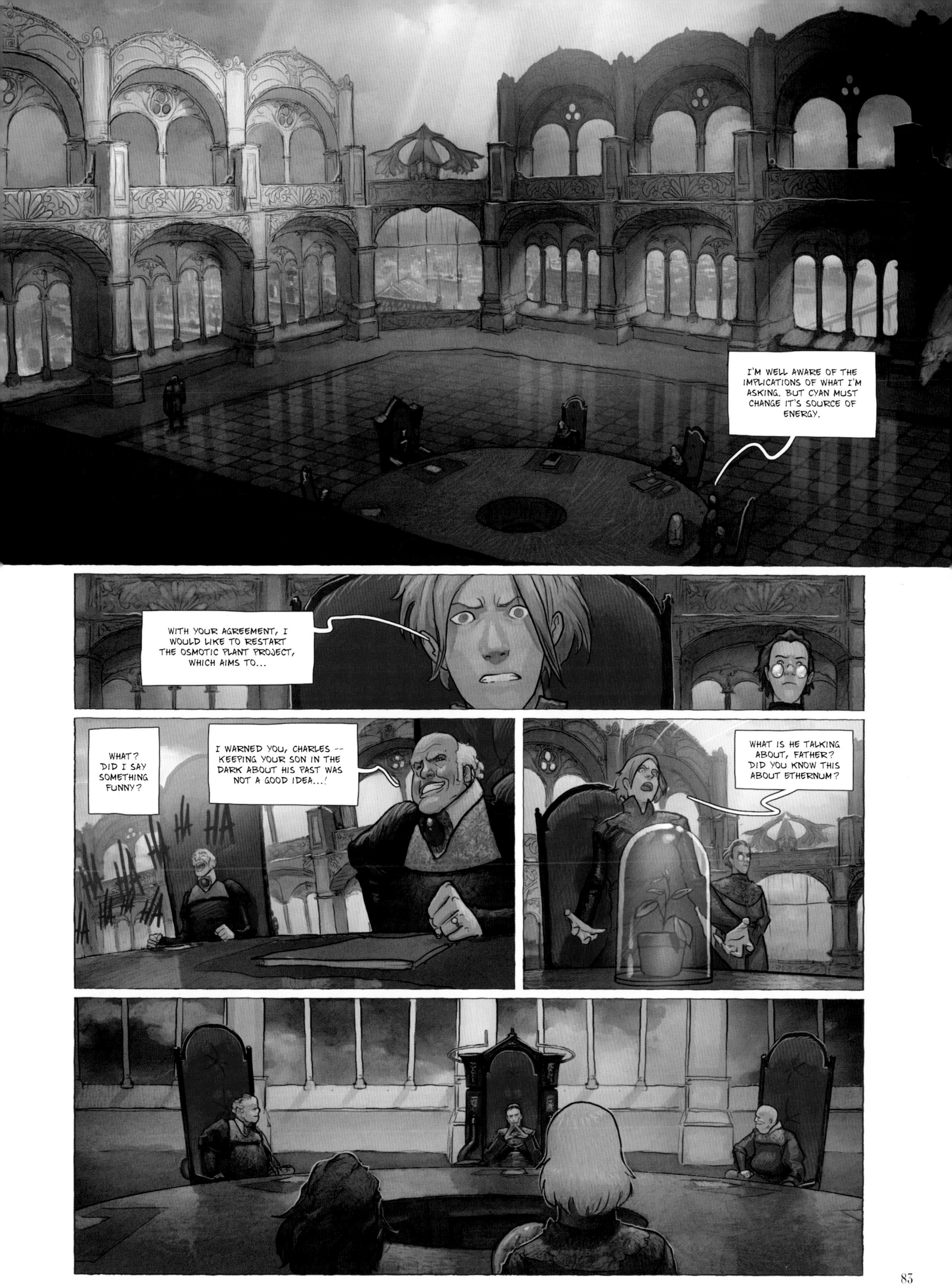
I'M WELL AWARE OF THE IMPLICATIONS OF WHAT I'M ASKING. BUT CYAN MUST CHANGE IT'S SOURCE OF ENERGY.
WITH YOUR AGREEMENT, I WOULD LIKE TO RESTART THE OSMOTIC PLANT PROJECT, WHICH AIMS TO...
WHAT? DID I SAY SOMETHING FUNNY?
I WARNED YOU, CHARLES -- KEEPING YOUR SON IN THE DARK ABOUT HIS PAST WAS NOT A GOOD IDEA...!
HA HA HA HA HA HA HA HA HA
WHAT IS HE TALKING ABOUT, FATHER? DID YOU KNOW THIS ABOUT ETHERNUM?

HOW COULD I BE SO NAIVE? THEY ALREADY KNOW WHAT THE PRINCE GOING TO SAY... IT'S OBVIOUS!

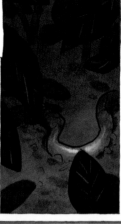

THAT'S WHY THEY SPEND SO MUCH MONEY TRACKING DOWN EVERY PARTICLE OF ETHERNUM...

THEY KNOW HOW PRECIOUS THEY ARE...!

OF COURSE WE KNOW!

WHY DO YOU KEEP USING ETHERNUM, THEN?

WHAT ARE YOU...

I'M NOT ADDRESSING YOU, OSLO. I'M ASKING MY FATHER!

YOU MAY BE THE PRINCE, SOREN. BUT SHOW RESPECT TO THE COUNCIL!

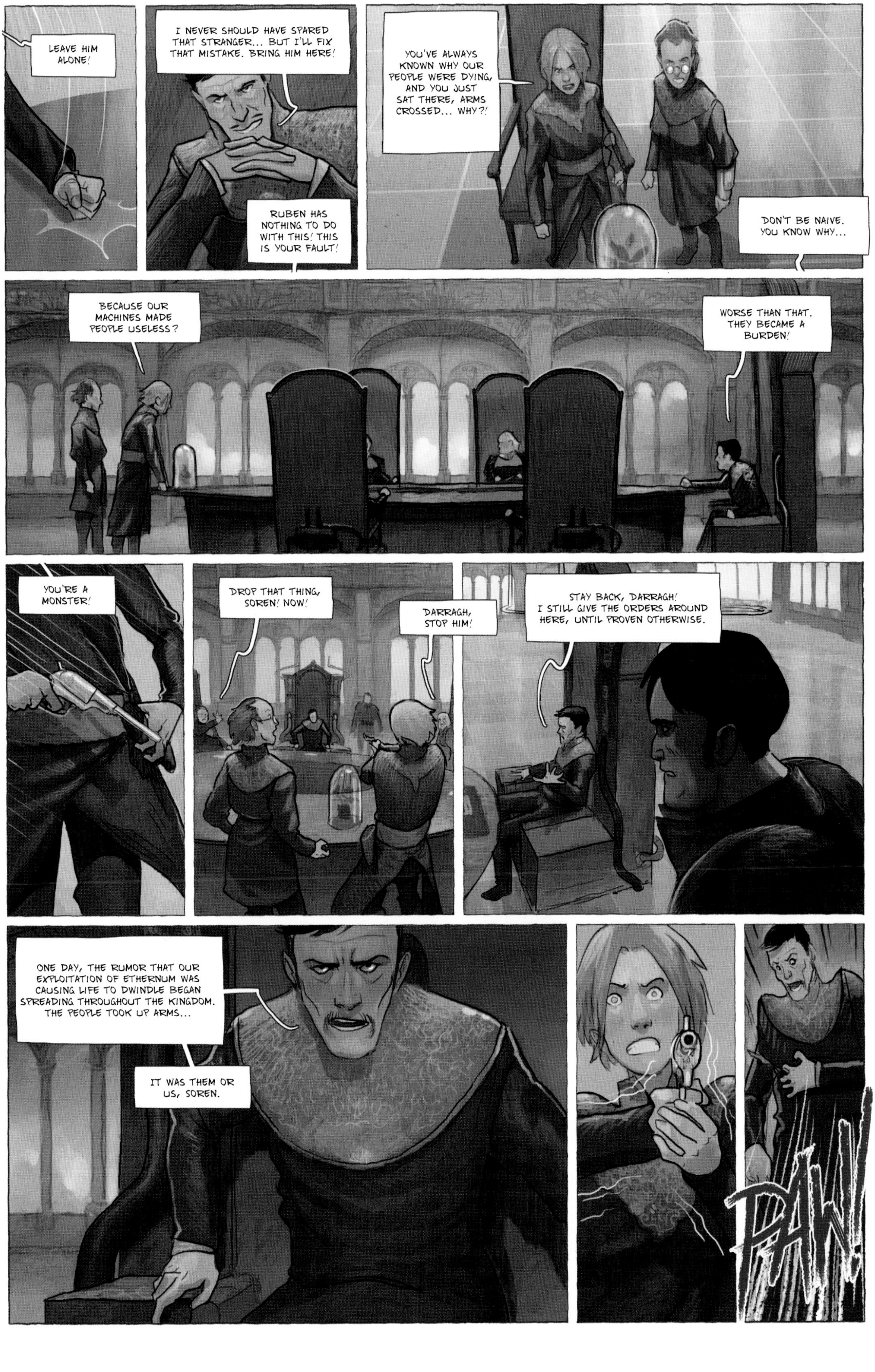
LEAVE HIM ALONE!
I NEVER SHOULD HAVE SPARED THAT STRANGER... BUT I'LL FIX THAT MISTAKE. BRING HIM HERE!
RUBEN HAS NOTHING TO DO WITH THIS! THIS IS YOUR FAULT!
YOU'VE ALWAYS KNOWN WHY OUR PEOPLE WERE DYING, AND YOU JUST SAT THERE, ARMS CROSSED... WHY?!
DON'T BE NAIVE. YOU KNOW WHY...
BECAUSE OUR MACHINES MADE PEOPLE USELESS?
WORSE THAN THAT. THEY BECAME A BURDEN!
YOU'RE A MONSTER!
DROP THAT THING, SOREN! NOW!
DARRAGH, STOP HIM!
STAY BACK, DARRAGH! I STILL GIVE THE ORDERS AROUND HERE, UNTIL PROVEN OTHERWISE.
ONE DAY, THE RUMOR THAT OUR EXPLOITATION OF ETHERNUM WAS CAUSING LIFE TO DWINDLE BEGAN SPREADING THROUGHOUT THE KINGDOM. THE PEOPLE TOOK UP ARMS...
IT WAS THEM OR US, SOREN.
PAW!

WHAT SHOULD I DO WITH HIM?

I DOUBT THE KING WOULD APPRECIATE THE FATE I'D CHOOSE FOR HIM... SO LET'S LET HIS FATHER DECIDE!

PULSE WEAKENING.

LEVEL THREE INTERNAL HEMORRHAGE DETECTED.

INITIATING SURGICAL PROTOCOL.

FOREIGN BODY REMOVED. BODY TISSUE HEALING.

PULSE WEAK.

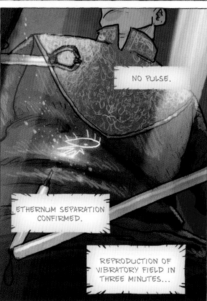

NO PULSE.

ETHERNUM SEPARATION CONFIRMED.

REPRODUCTION OF VIBRATORY FIELD IN THREE MINUTES...

YOU ALREADY KNEW ABOUT THIS...?

OF COURSE! THE PEOPLE SEATED AROUND THIS TABLE HAVEN'T FEARED DEATH IN YEARS... BUT DON'T WORRY, YOUR SEAT HAS BEEN READY FOR ALONG TIME.

THE FRUIT OF YOUR FATHER'S EDUCATION IS VERY IMPRESSIVE. YOU HAVE SUCH INTEGRITY, SOREN...

...BUT YOU'LL BECOME ONE OF US EVENTUALLY, YOU'LL SEE.

NEVER...

I'VE BEEN WAITING A LONG TIME FOR THIS, CHARLES...

IS THERE A PROBLEM?

YES. THE KING OF CYAN JUST DIED, BUT I CAN'T TAKE HIS SOUL...

DID YOU DO THIS?!

WHAT HAVE I DONE NOW?!

LOOK! THEY'RE GETTING READY TO LEAVE!

THAT'S GOOD NEWS, RIGHT?

I'M NOT JOKING. YOU KNOW WHAT WILL HAPPEN IF THEY DON'T FINISH REMOVING THOSE PIPES...

WE CAN'T CHANGE THE FUTURE. WHAT YOU SAW IN YOUR VISIONS WILL HAPPEN EVENTUALLY. AND THERE IS NOTHING YOU CAN DO TO STOP IT.

IF YOU CARE SO MUCH ABOUT HIM, NO ONE'S STOPPING YOU FROM FOLLOWING HIM!

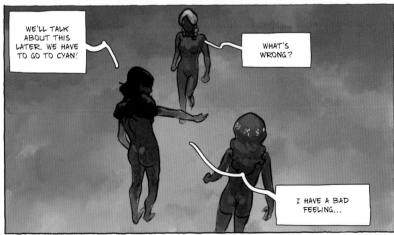

WE'LL TALK ABOUT THIS LATER. WE HAVE TO GO TO CYAN!

WHAT'S WRONG?

I HAVE A BAD FEELING...

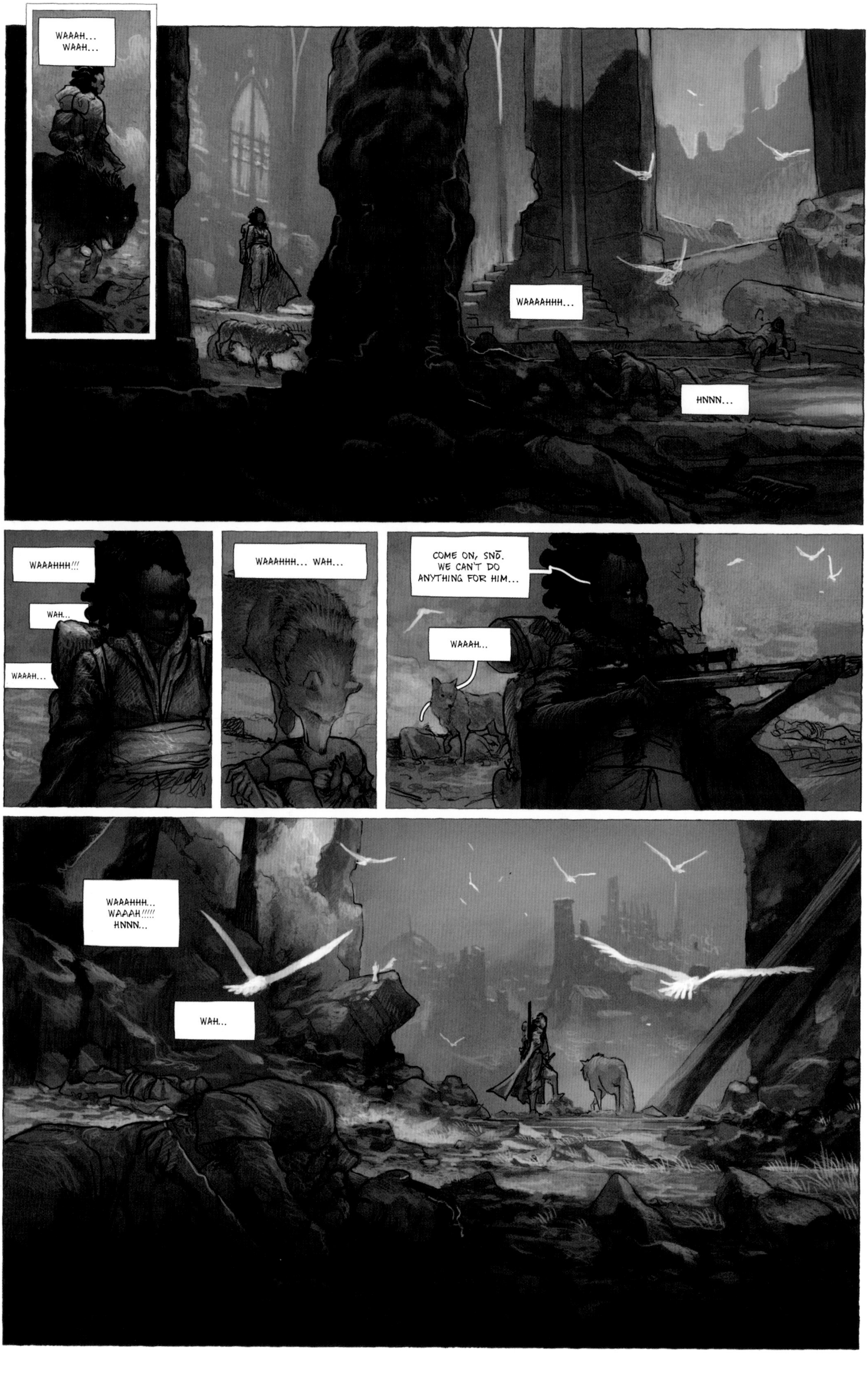
WAAAH... WAAH...
WAAAAHHH...
HNNN...
WAAAHHH!!!
WAH...
WAAAH...
WAAAHHH... WAH...
COME ON, SNŌ. WE CAN'T DO ANYTHING FOR HIM...
WAAAH...
WAAAHHH... WAAAH!!!!! HNNN...
WAH...

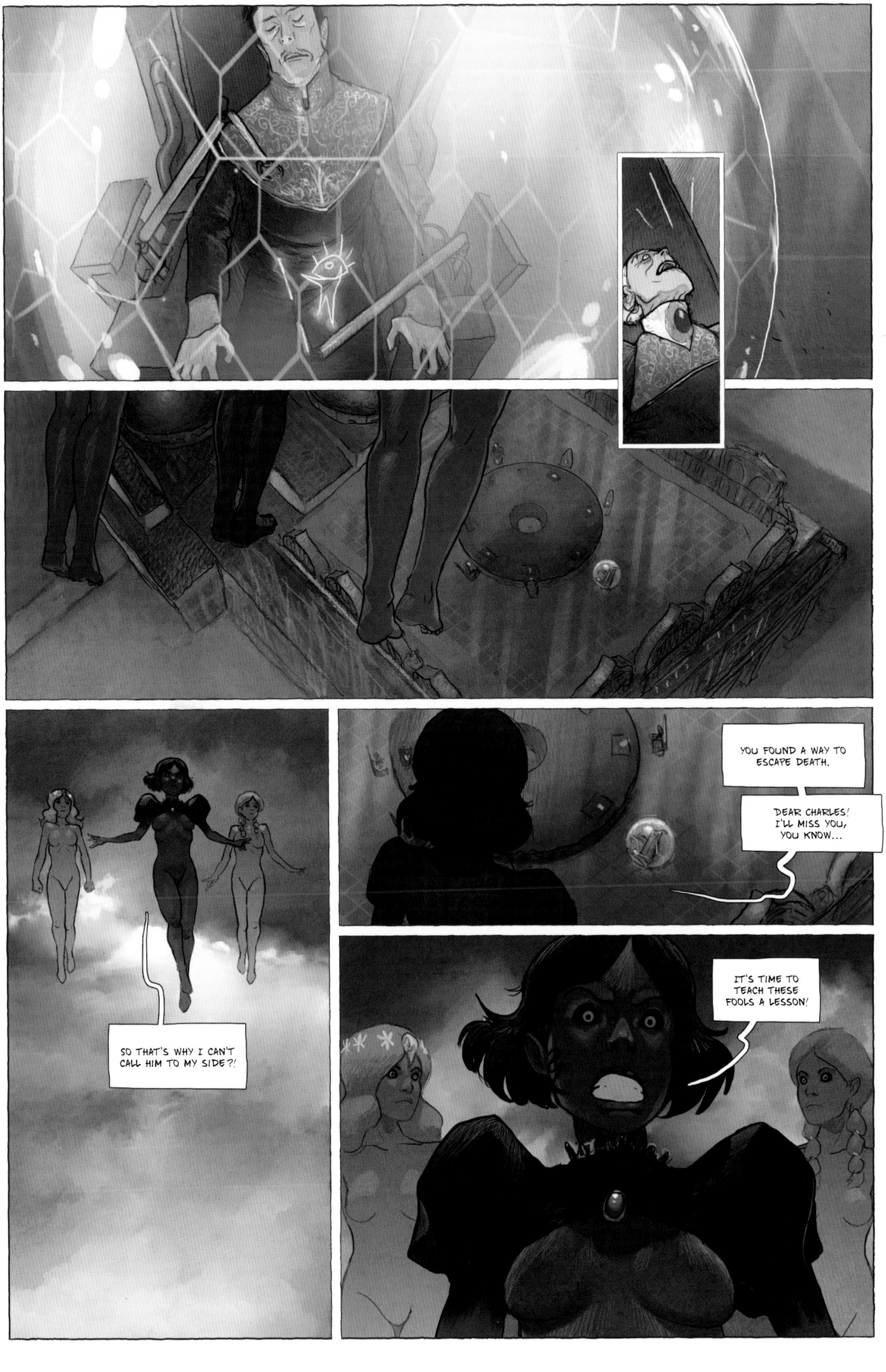
SO THAT'S WHY I CAN'T CALL HIM TO MY SIDE?!
YOU FOUND A WAY TO ESCAPE DEATH.
DEAR CHARLES! I'LL MISS YOU, YOU KNOW...
IT'S TIME TO TEACH THESE FOOLS A LESSON!

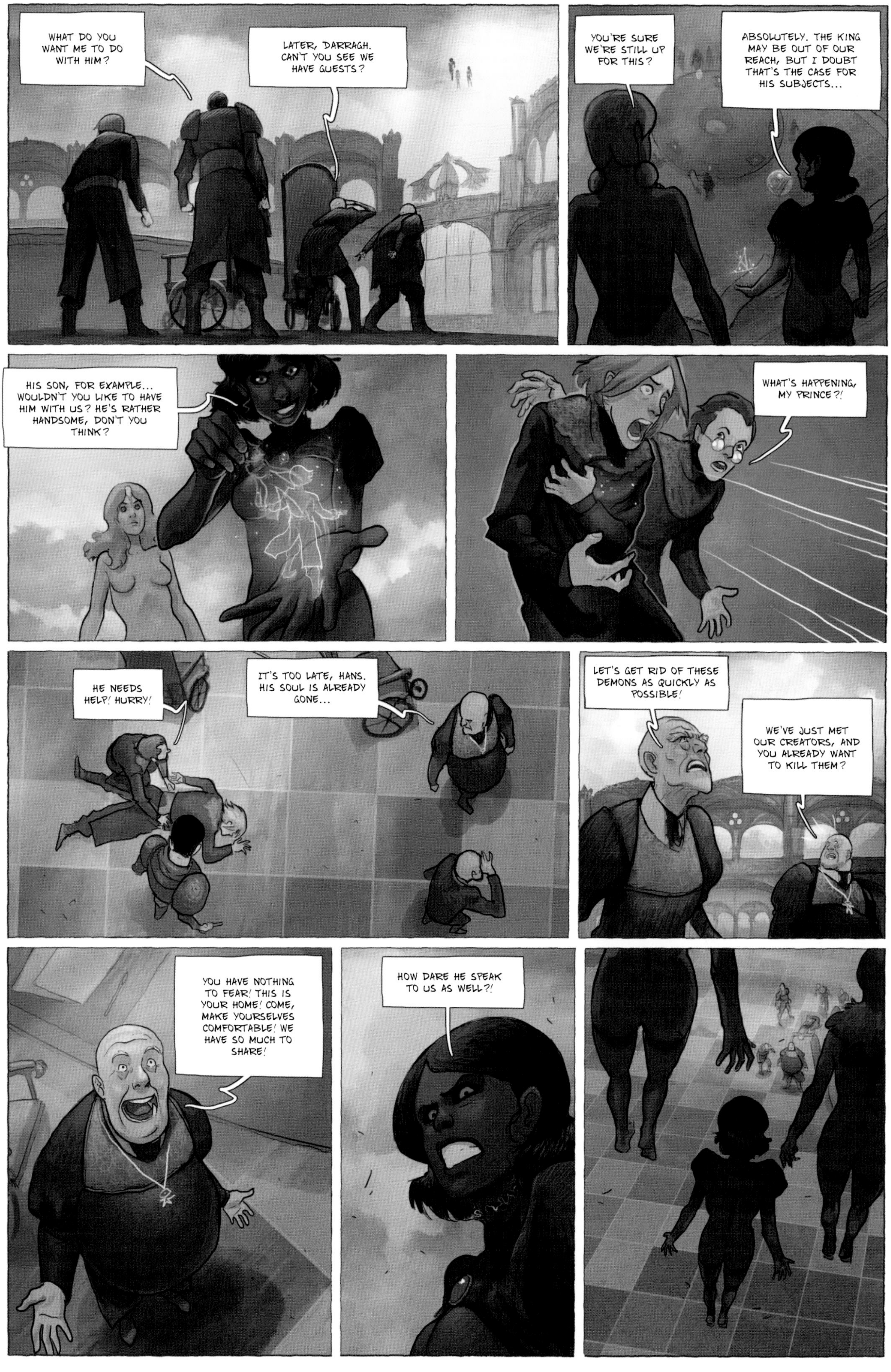
WHAT DO YOU WANT ME TO DO WITH HIM?
LATER, DARRAGH. CAN'T YOU SEE WE HAVE GUESTS?
YOU'RE SURE WE'RE STILL UP FOR THIS?
ABSOLUTELY. THE KING MAY BE OUT OF OUR REACH, BUT I DOUBT THAT'S THE CASE FOR HIS SUBJECTS...
HIS SON, FOR EXAMPLE... WOULDN'T YOU LIKE TO HAVE HIM WITH US? HE'S RATHER HANDSOME, DON'T YOU THINK?
WHAT'S HAPPENING, MY PRINCE?!
HE NEEDS HELP! HURRY!
IT'S TOO LATE, HANS. HIS SOUL IS ALREADY GONE...
LET'S GET RID OF THESE DEMONS AS QUICKLY AS POSSIBLE!
WE'VE JUST MET OUR CREATORS, AND YOU ALREADY WANT TO KILL THEM?
YOU HAVE NOTHING TO FEAR! THIS IS YOUR HOME! COME, MAKE YOURSELVES COMFORTABLE! WE HAVE SO MUCH TO SHARE!
HOW DARE HE SPEAK TO US AS WELL?!

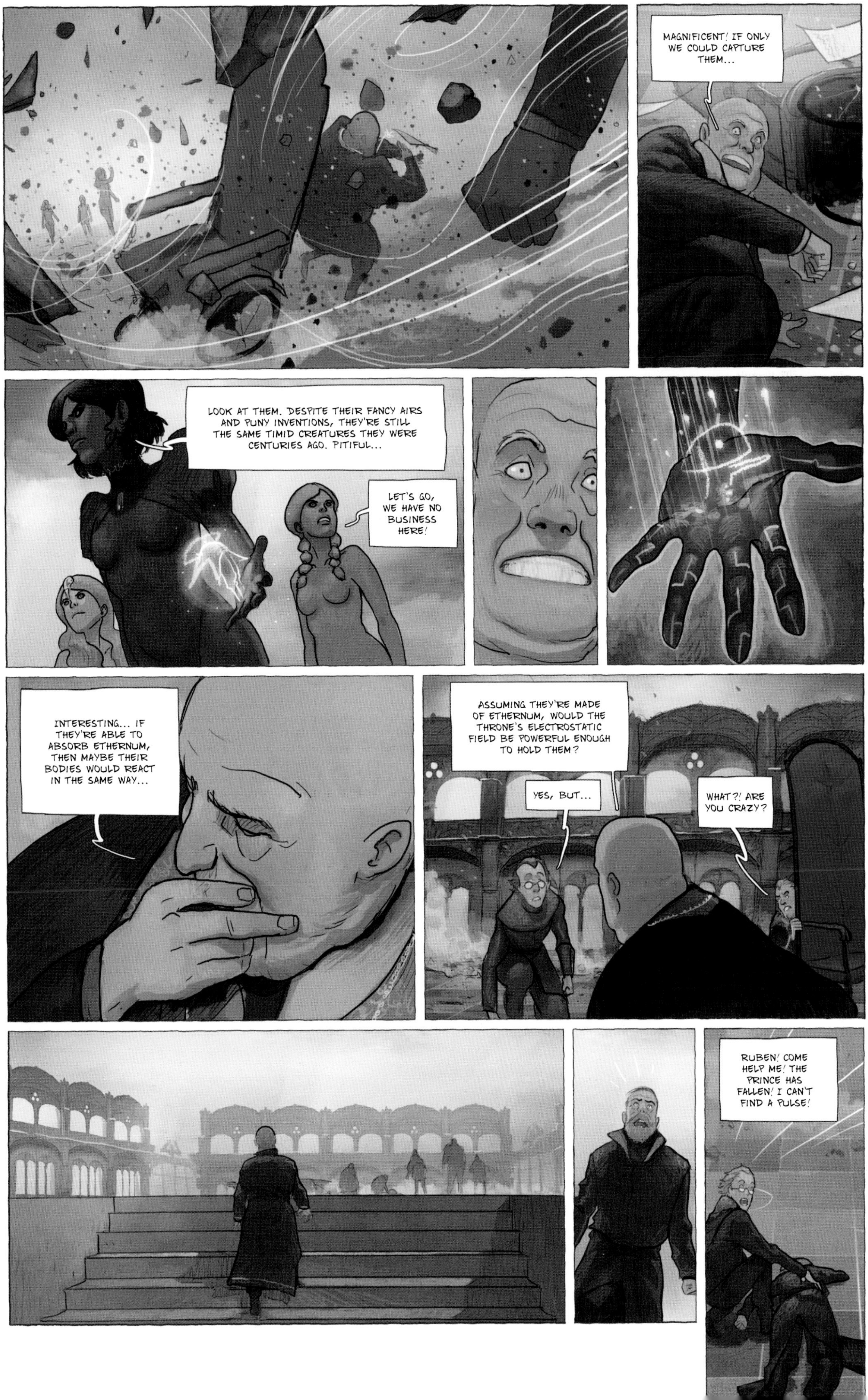
MAGNIFICENT! IF ONLY WE COULD CAPTURE THEM...
LOOK AT THEM. DESPITE THEIR FANCY AIRS AND PUNY INVENTIONS, THEY'RE STILL THE SAME TIMID CREATURES THEY WERE CENTURIES AGO. PITIFUL...
LET'S GO, WE HAVE NO BUSINESS HERE!
INTERESTING... IF THEY'RE ABLE TO ABSORB ETHERNUM, THEN MAYBE THEIR BODIES WOULD REACT IN THE SAME WAY...
ASSUMING THEY'RE MADE OF ETHERNUM, WOULD THE THRONE'S ELECTROSTATIC FIELD BE POWERFUL ENOUGH TO HOLD THEM?
YES, BUT...
WHAT?! ARE YOU CRAZY?
RUBEN! COME HELP ME! THE PRINCE HAS FALLEN! I CAN'T FIND A PULSE!

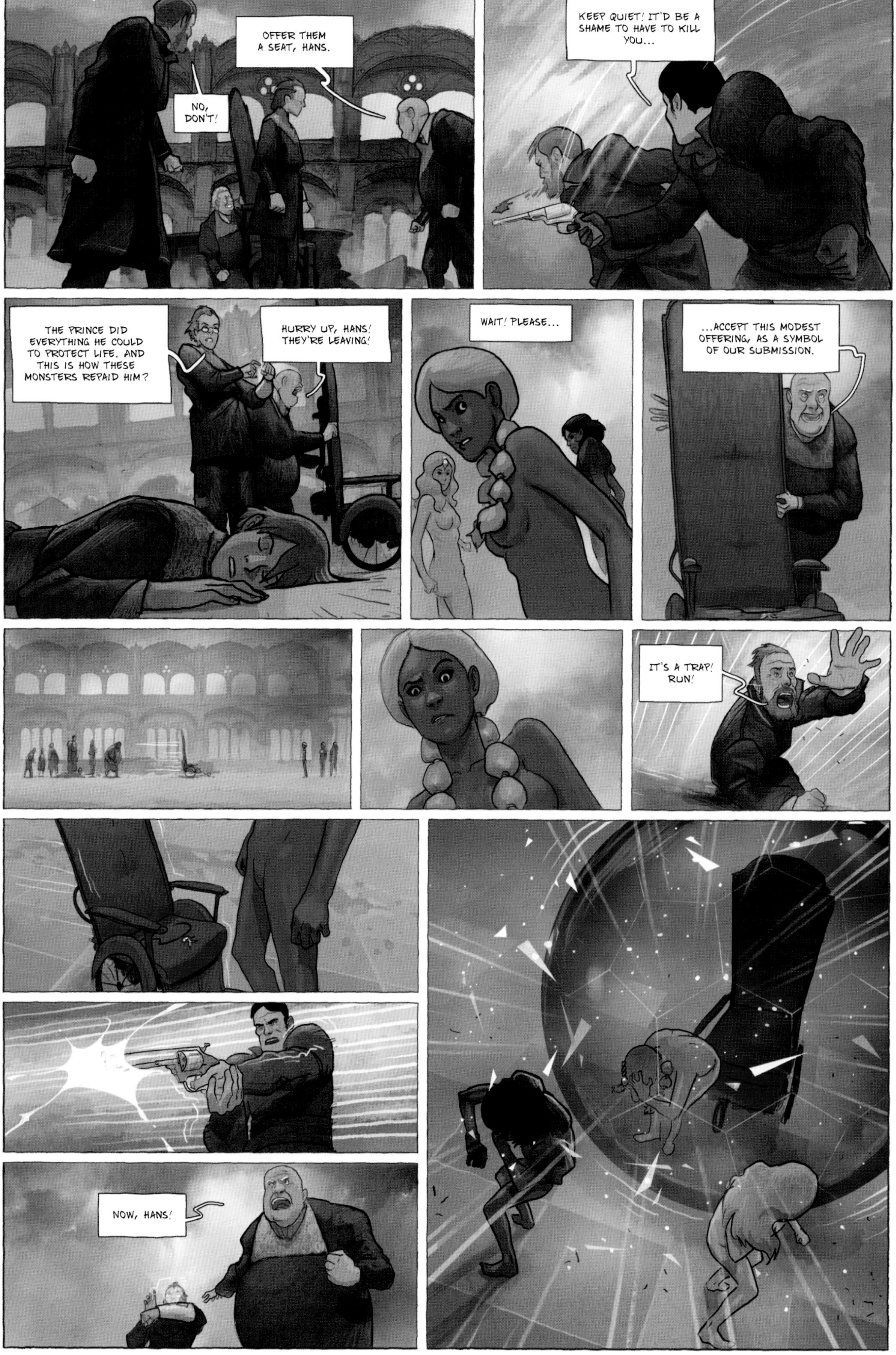
NO, DON'T!
OFFER THEM A SEAT, HANS.
KEEP QUIET! IT'D BE A SHAME TO HAVE TO KILL YOU...
THE PRINCE DID EVERYTHING HE COULD TO PROTECT LIFE. AND THIS IS HOW THESE MONSTERS REPAID HIM?
HURRY UP, HANS! THEY'RE LEAVING!
WAIT! PLEASE...
...ACCEPT THIS MODEST OFFERING, AS A SYMBOL OF OUR SUBMISSION.
IT'S A TRAP! RUN!
NOW, HANS!

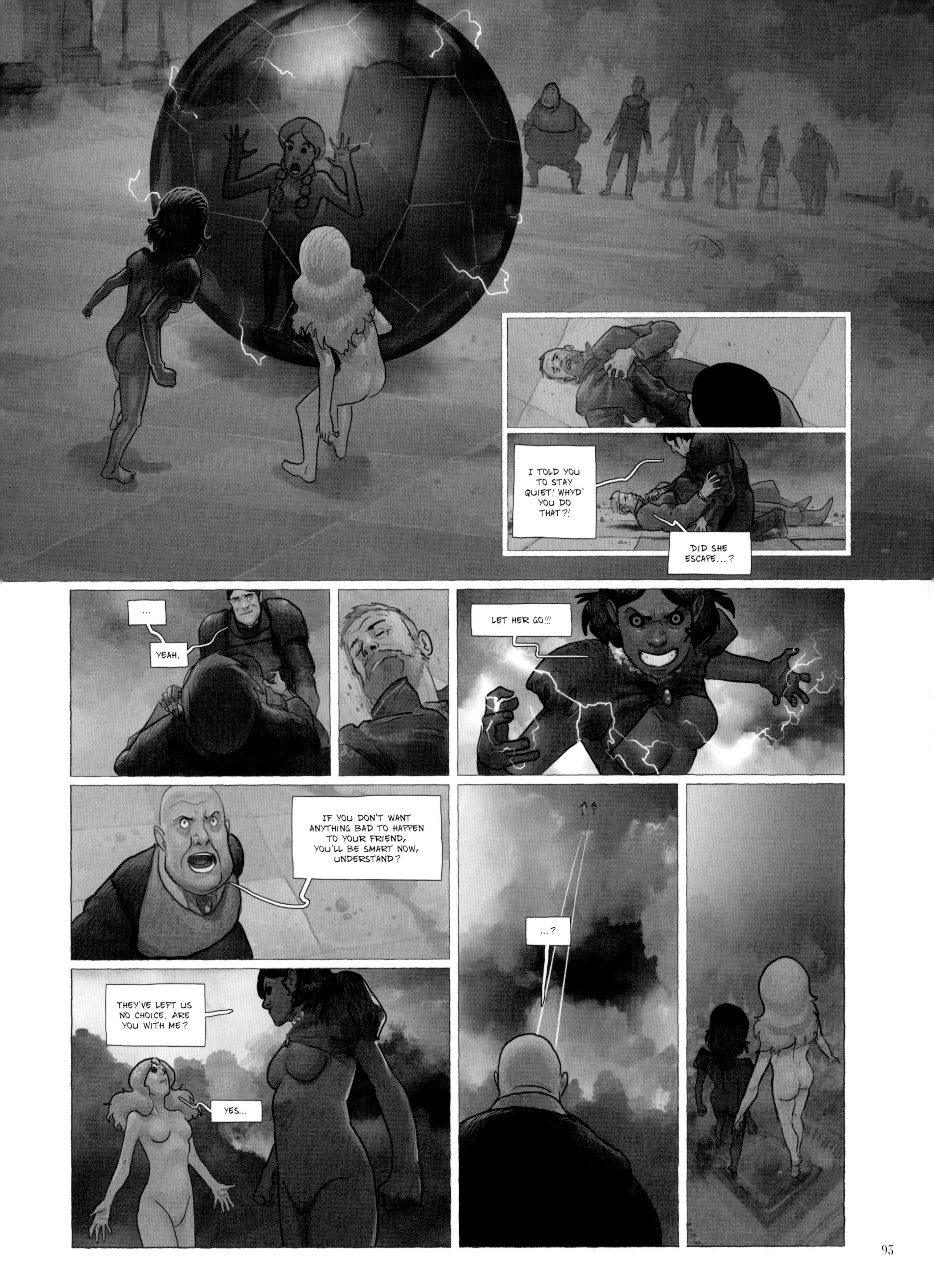
I TOLD YOU TO STAY QUIET! WHYD' YOU DO THAT?!
DID SHE ESCAPE...?
...
YEAH.
LET HER GO!!!
IF YOU DON'T WANT ANYTHING BAD TO HAPPEN TO YOUR FRIEND, YOU'LL BE SMART NOW, UNDERSTAND?
THEY'VE LEFT US NO CHOICE. ARE YOU WITH ME?
YES...
...?

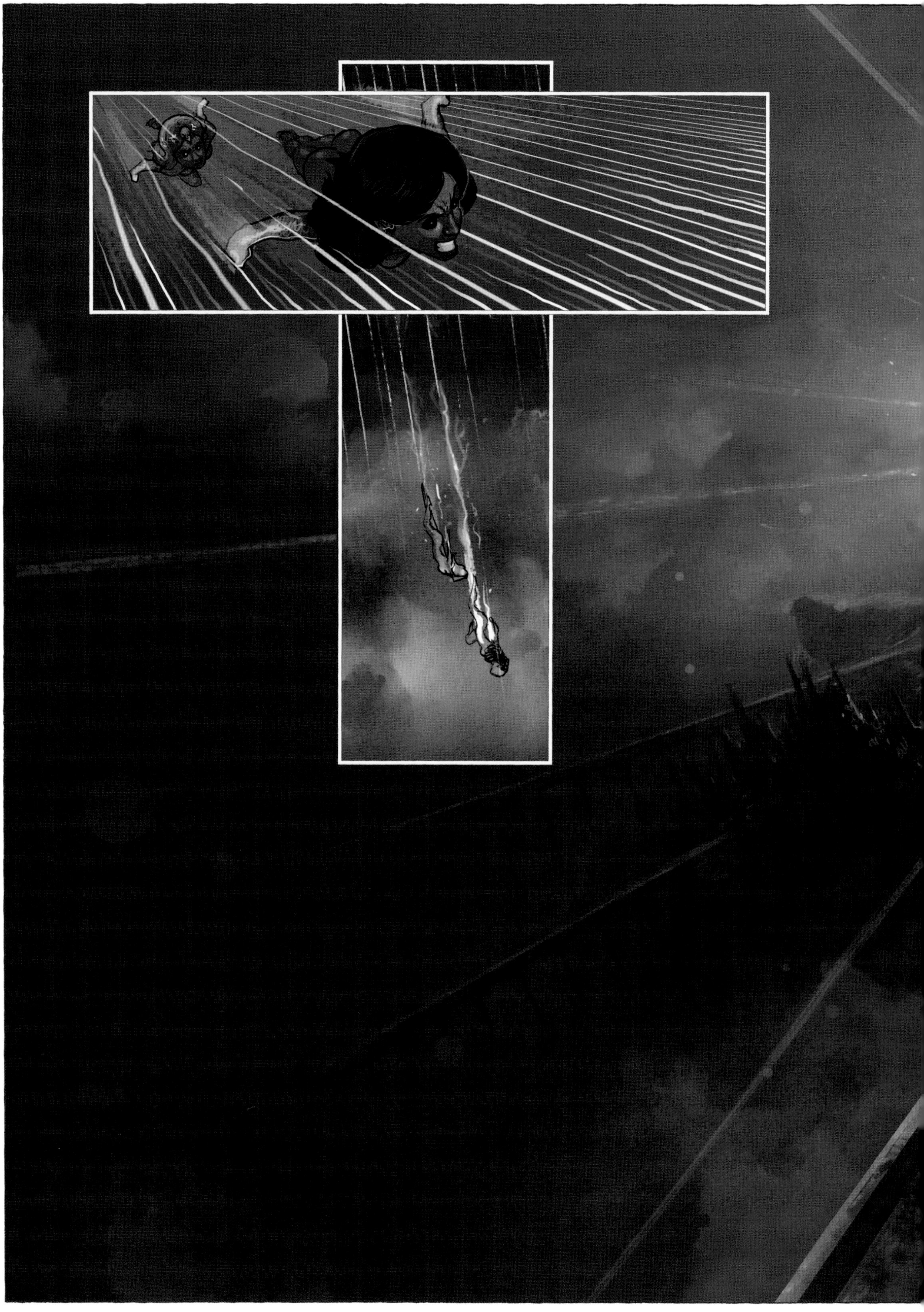

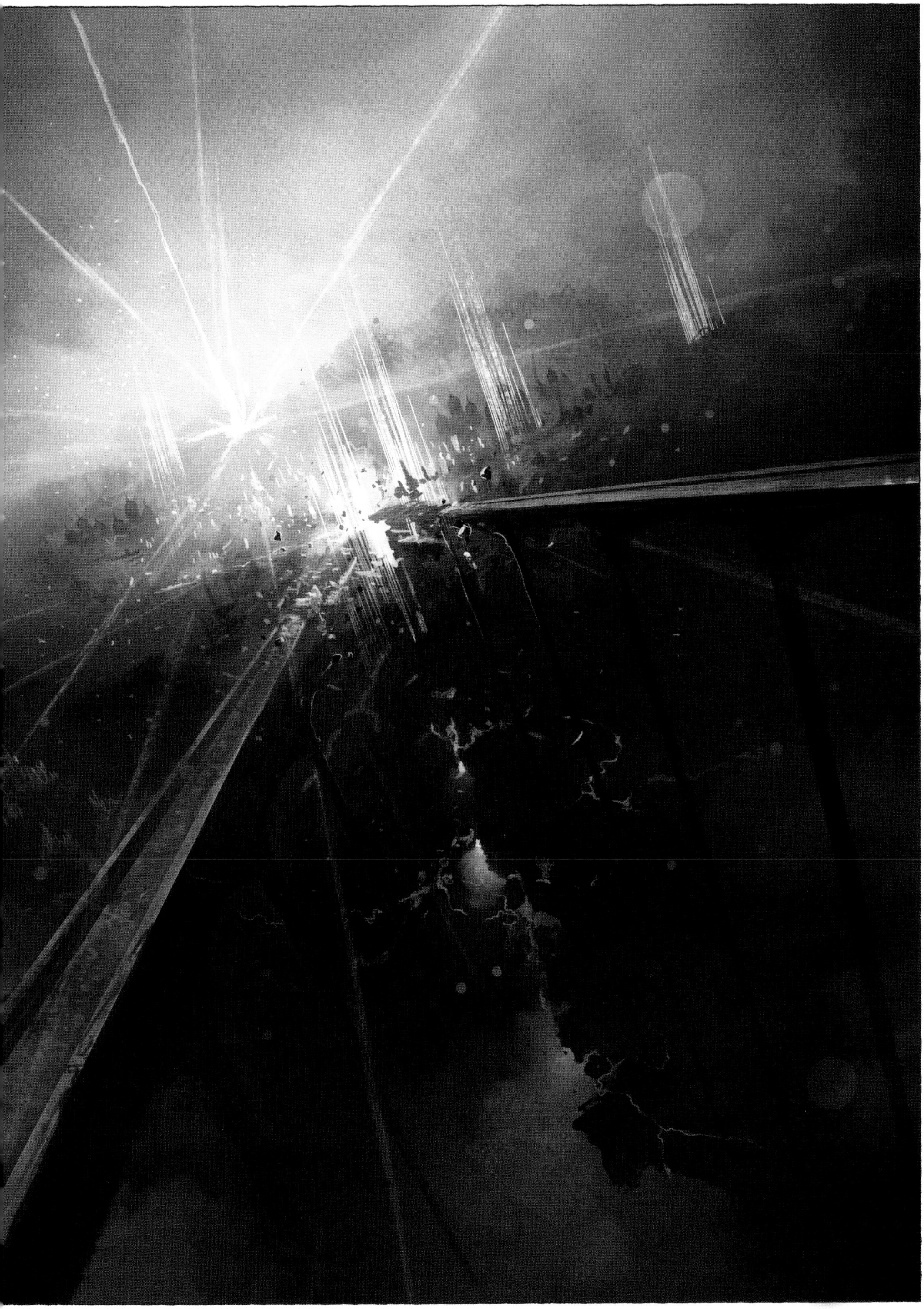

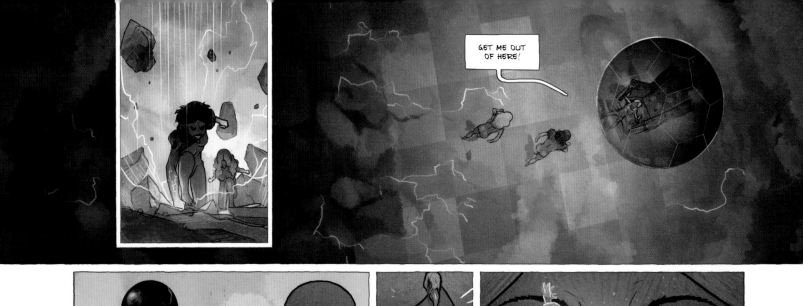

GET ME OUT OF HERE!

ANOMALY DETECTED NEAR THE MOTHER TREE.

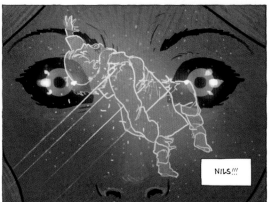

NILS!!!

URD IS TRAPPED AND ALL YOU CARE ABOUT IS THAT BOY?!

I'M SURE YOU CAN HANDLE THIS ALONE. BUT NILS HAS NO CHANCE WITHOUT ME...

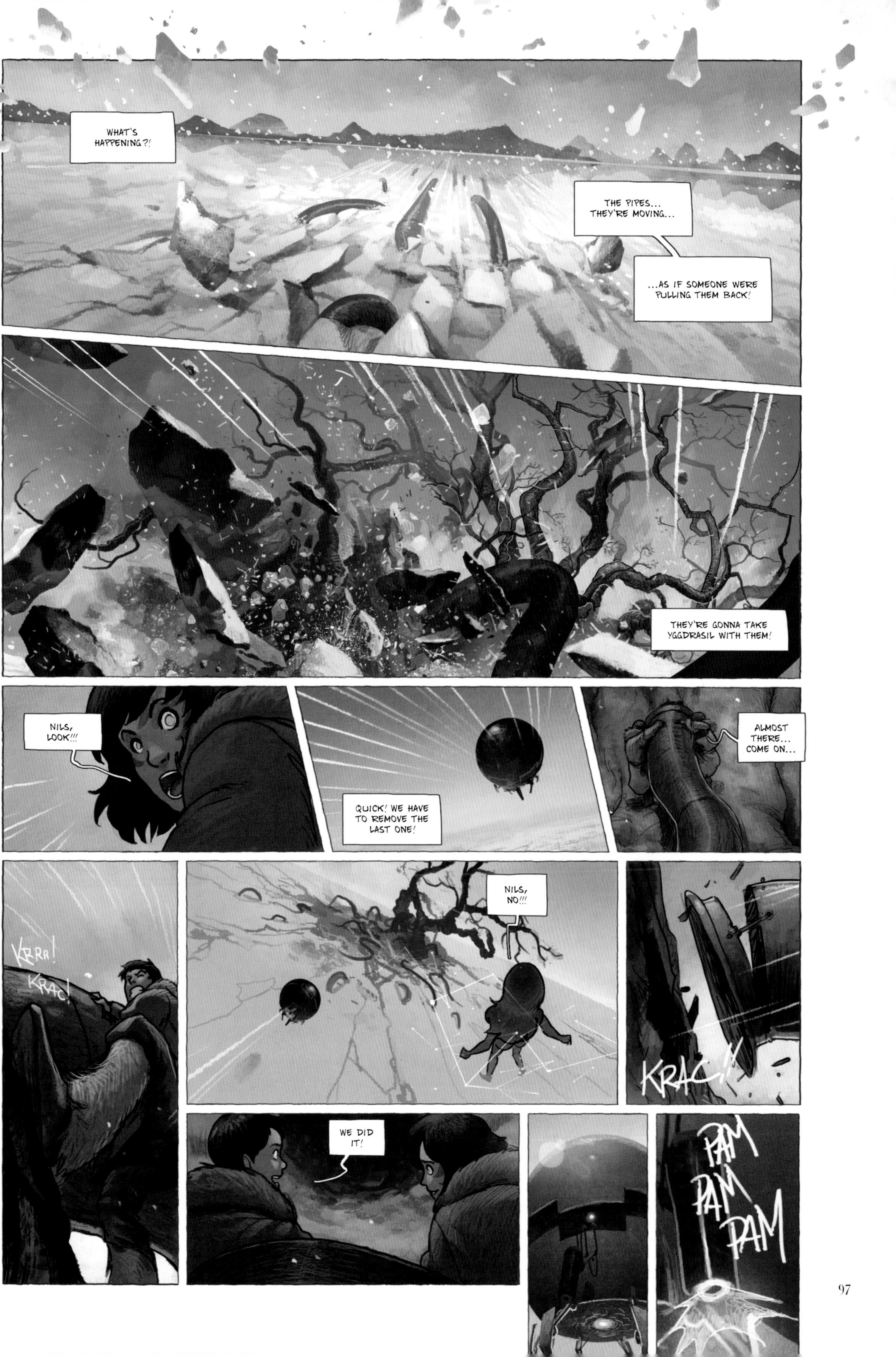
WHAT'S HAPPENING?!
THE PIPES... THEY'RE MOVING...
...AS IF SOMEONE WERE PULLING THEM BACK!
THEY'RE GONNA TAKE YGGDRASIL WITH THEM!
NILS, LOOK!!!
QUICK! WE HAVE TO REMOVE THE LAST ONE!
ALMOST THERE... COME ON...
KRRR!
KRAC!
NILS, NO!!!
KRAC!!
WE DID IT!
PAM PAM PAM PAM

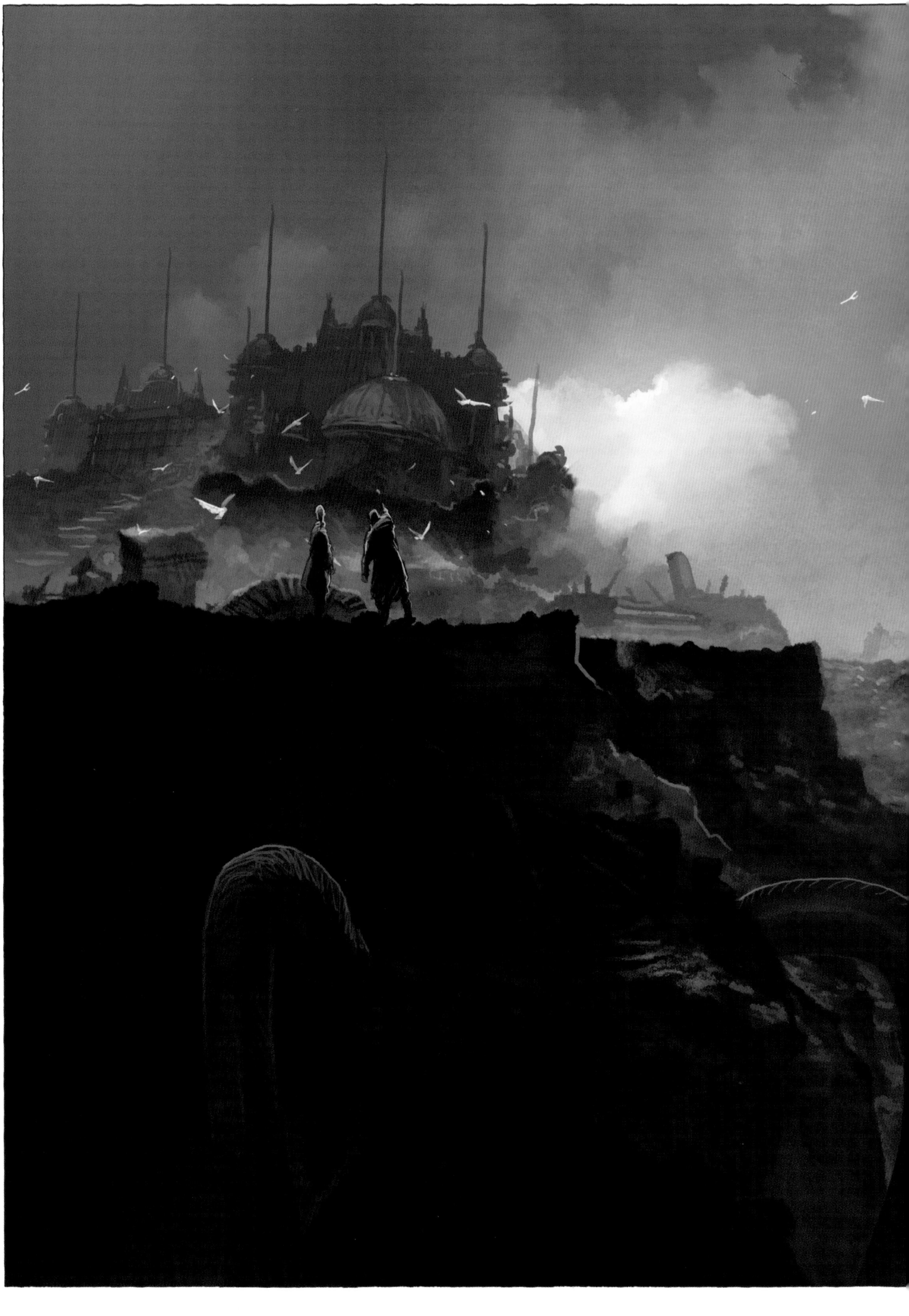

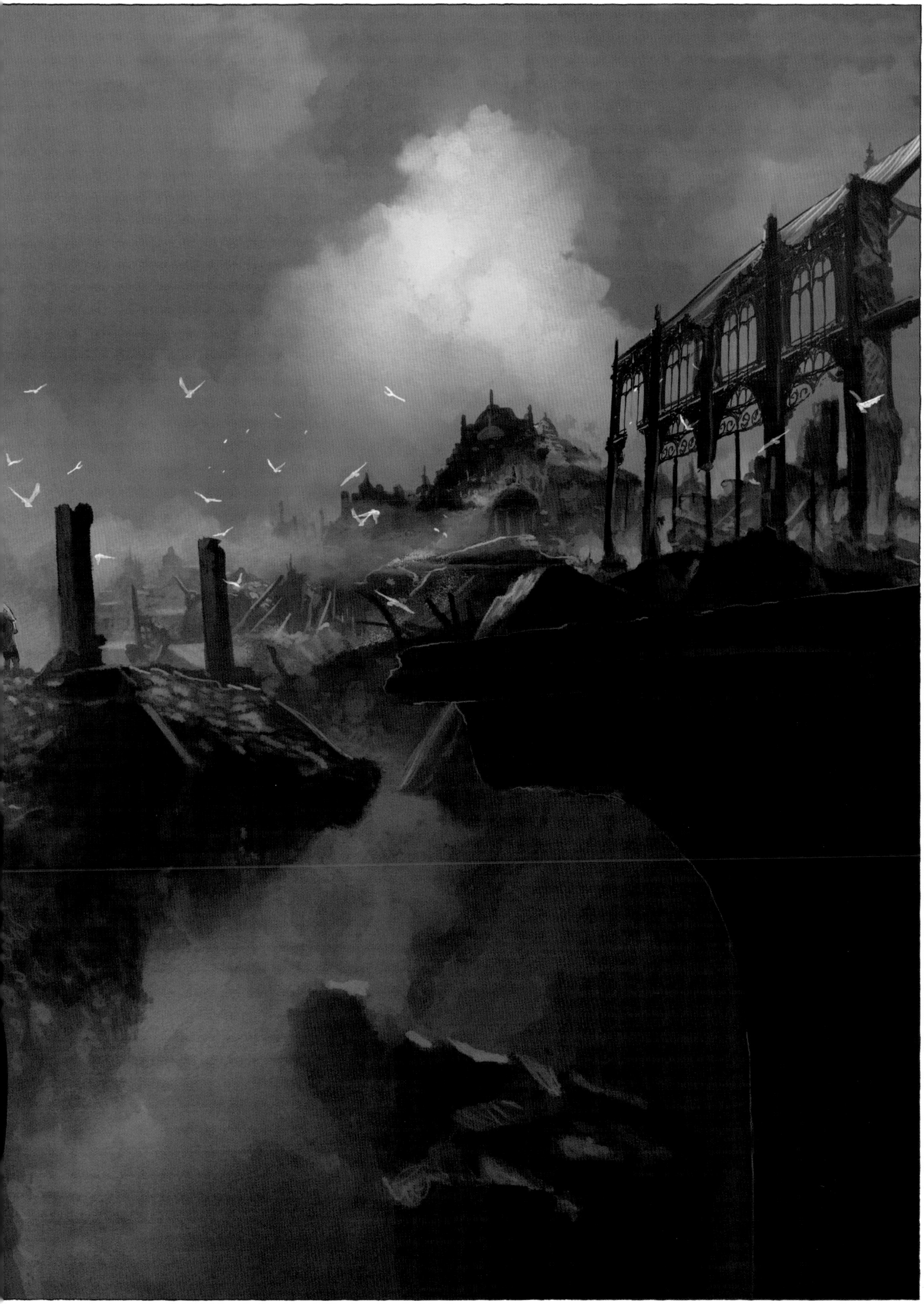

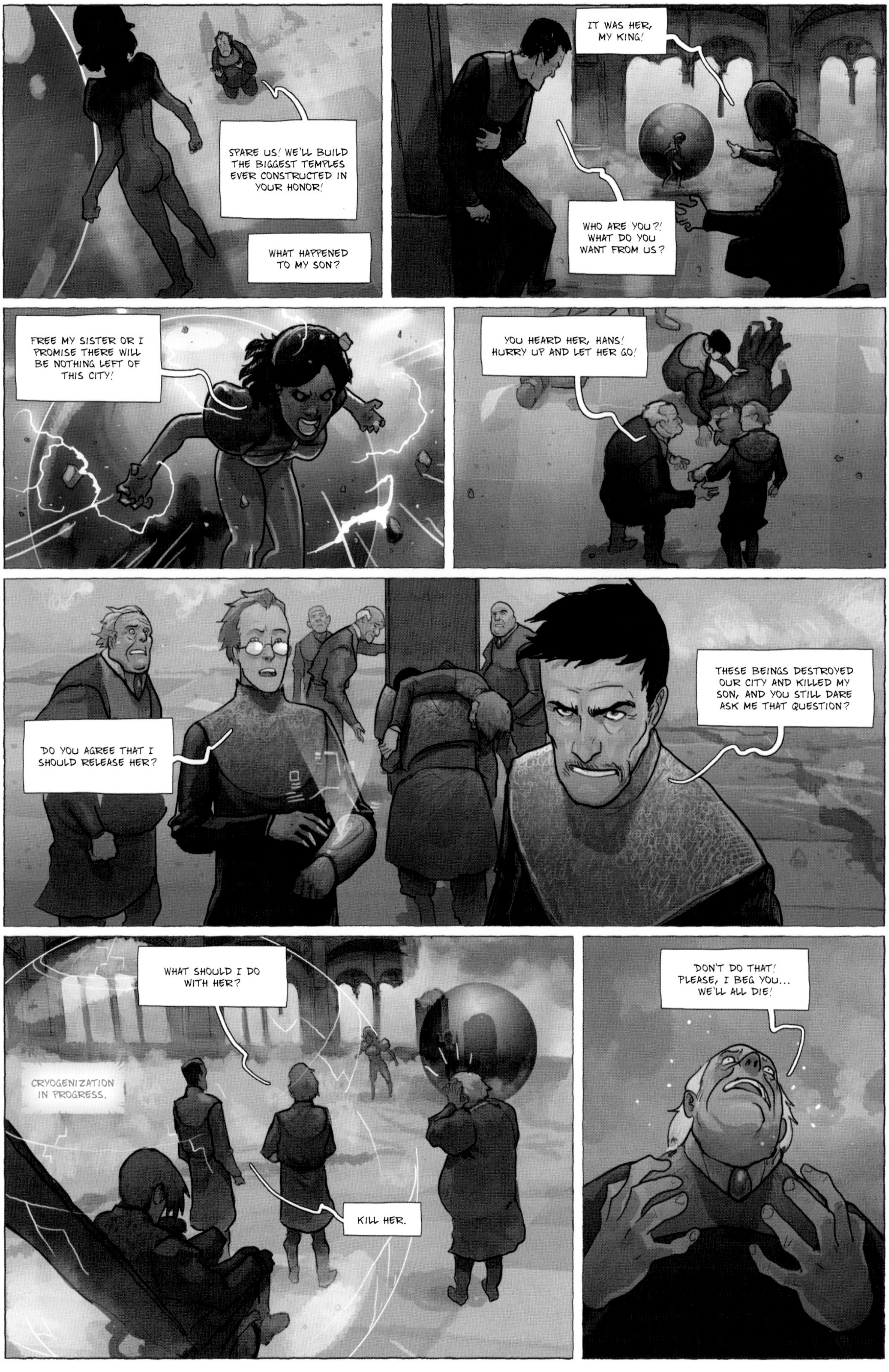
SPARE US! WE'LL BUILD THE BIGGEST TEMPLES EVER CONSTRUCTED IN YOUR HONOR!
WHAT HAPPENED TO MY SON?
IT WAS HER, MY KING!
WHO ARE YOU?! WHAT DO YOU WANT FROM US?
FREE MY SISTER OR I PROMISE THERE WILL BE NOTHING LEFT OF THIS CITY!
YOU HEARD HER, HANS! HURRY UP AND LET HER GO!
DO YOU AGREE THAT I SHOULD RELEASE HER?
THESE BEINGS DESTROYED OUR CITY AND KILLED MY SON, AND YOU STILL DARE ASK ME THAT QUESTION?
WHAT SHOULD I DO WITH HER?
CRYOGENIZATION IN PROGRESS.
KILL HER.
DON'T DO THAT! PLEASE, I BEG YOU... WE'LL ALL DIE!

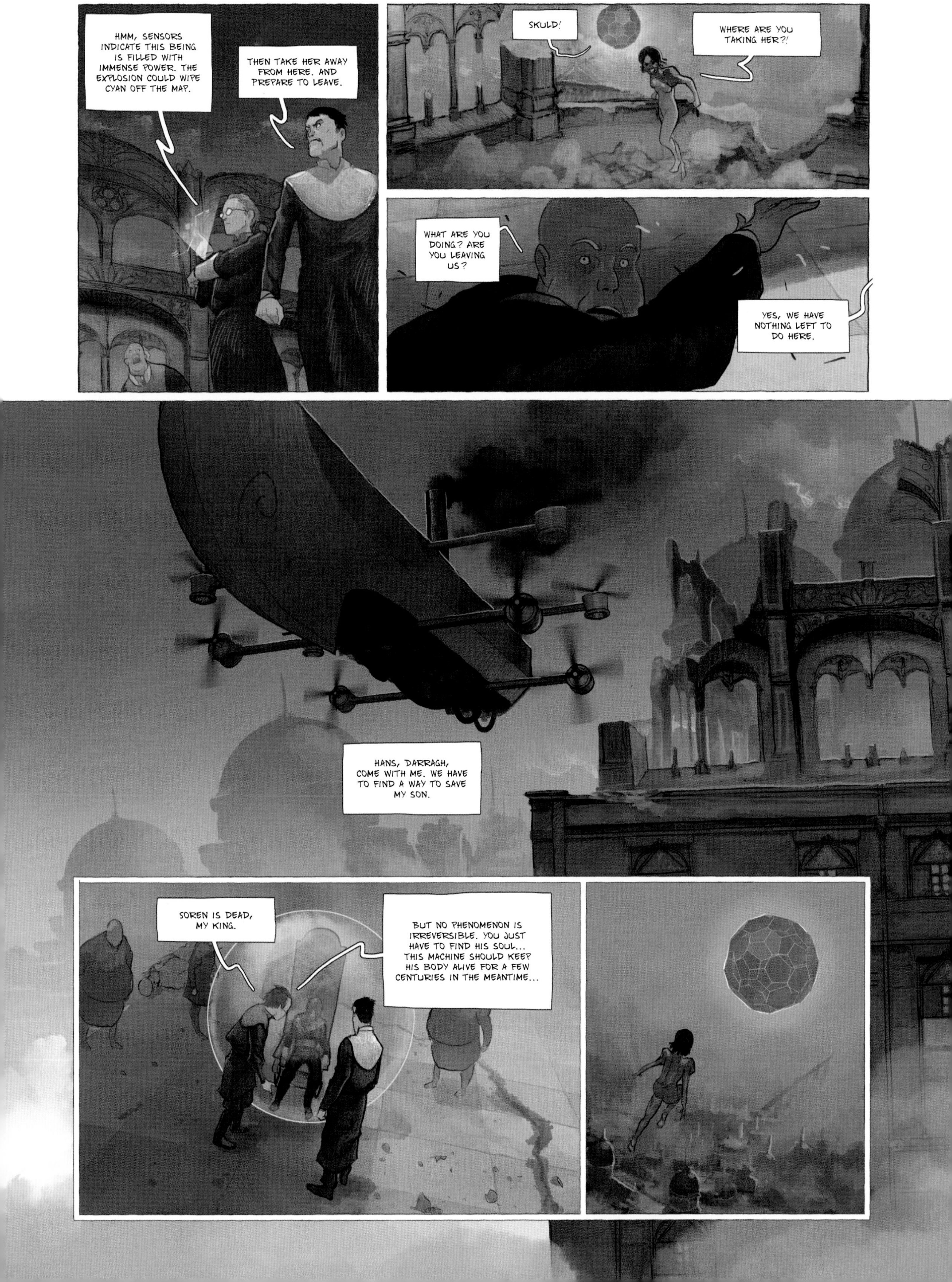
HMM, SENSORS INDICATE THIS BEING IS FILLED WITH IMMENSE POWER. THE EXPLOSION COULD WIPE CYAN OFF THE MAP.
THEN TAKE HER AWAY FROM HERE. AND PREPARE TO LEAVE.
SKULD!
WHERE ARE YOU TAKING HER?!
WHAT ARE YOU DOING? ARE YOU LEAVING US?
YES, WE HAVE NOTHING LEFT TO DO HERE.
HANS, DARRAGH, COME WITH ME. WE HAVE TO FIND A WAY TO SAVE MY SON.
SOREN IS DEAD, MY KING.
BUT NO PHENOMENON IS IRREVERSIBLE. YOU JUST HAVE TO FIND HIS SOUL... THIS MACHINE SHOULD KEEP HIS BODY ALIVE FOR A FEW CENTURIES IN THE MEANTIME...

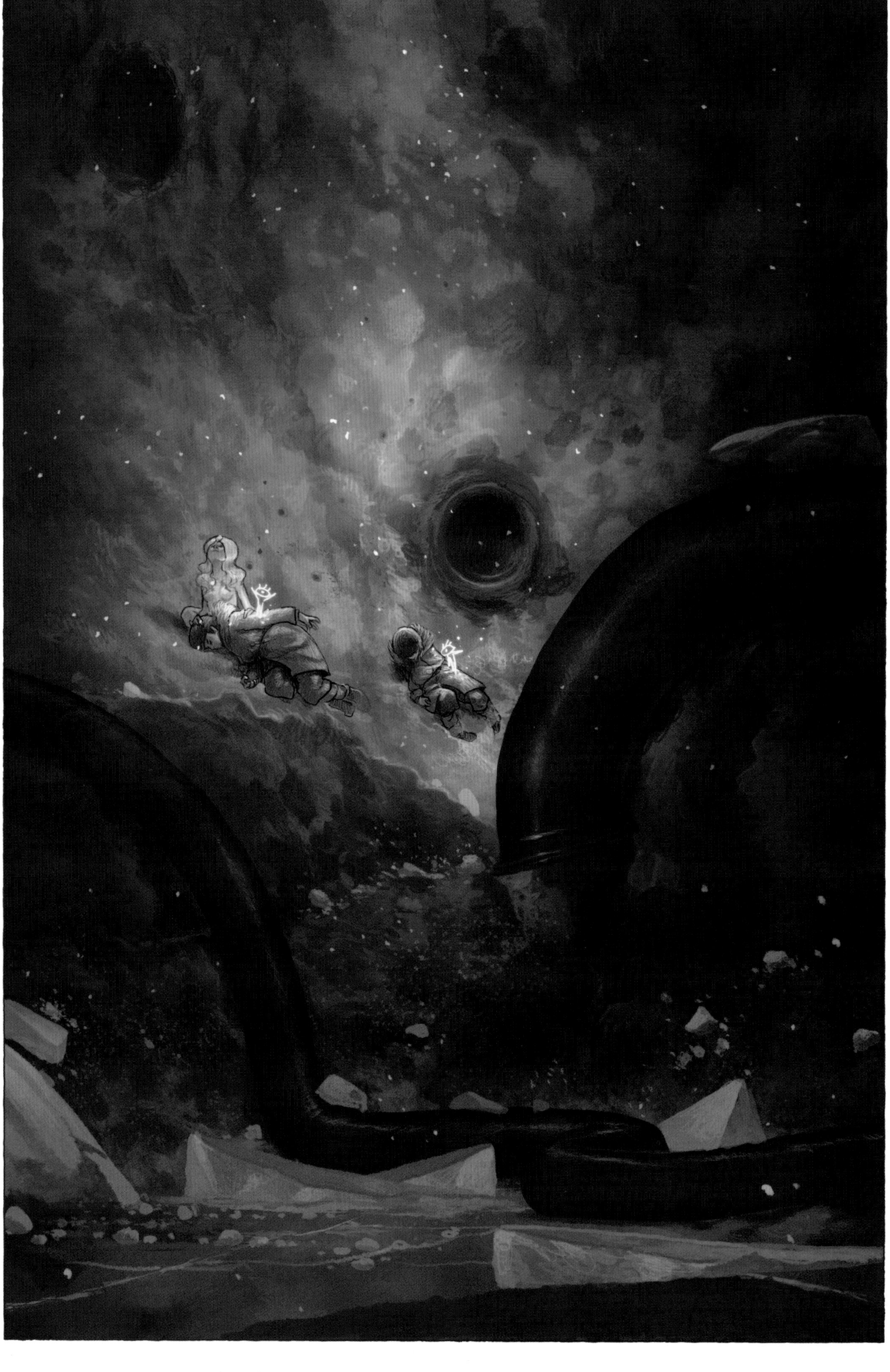

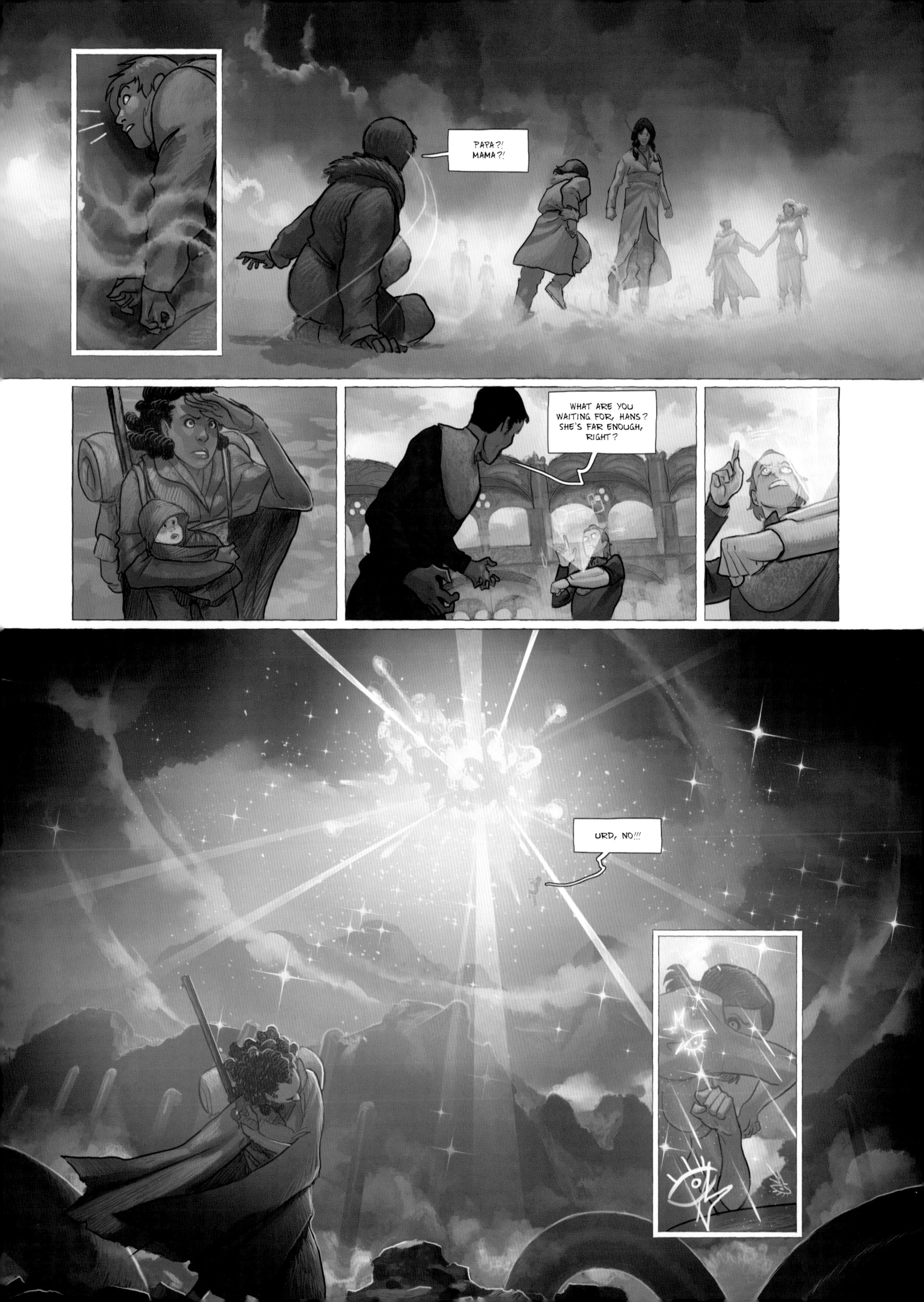
PAPA?! MAMA?!
WHAT ARE YOU WAITING FOR, HANS? SHE'S FAR ENOUGH, RIGHT?
URD, NO!!!

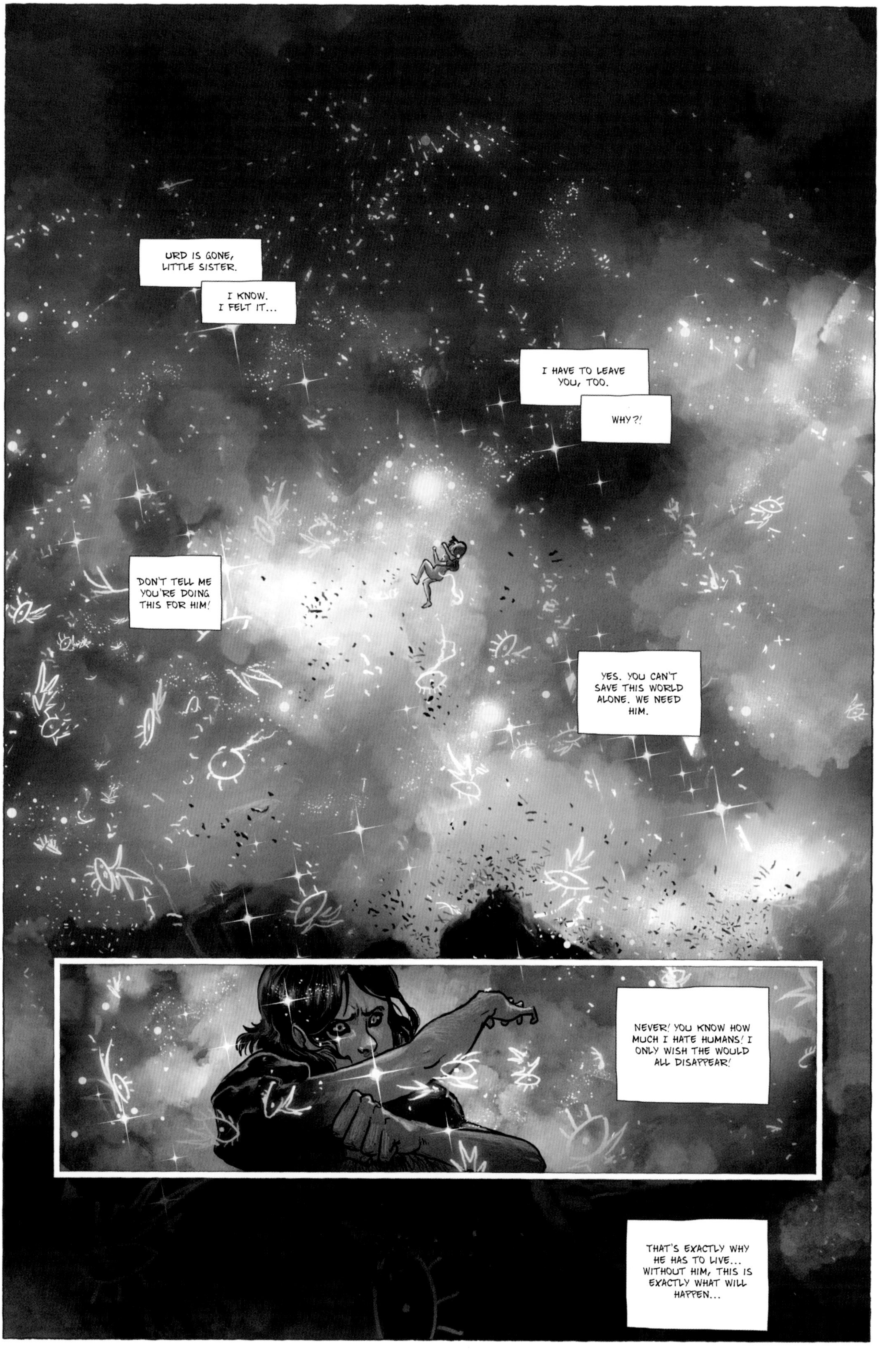
URD IS GONE, LITTLE SISTER.
I KNOW. I FELT IT...
I HAVE TO LEAVE YOU, TOO.
WHY?!
DON'T TELL ME YOU'RE DOING THIS FOR HIM!
YES. YOU CAN'T SAVE THIS WORLD ALONE. WE NEED HIM.
NEVER! YOU KNOW HOW MUCH I HATE HUMANS! I ONLY WISH THE WOULD ALL DISAPPEAR!
THAT'S EXACTLY WHY HE HAS TO LIVE... WITHOUT HIM, THIS IS EXACTLY WHAT WILL HAPPEN...

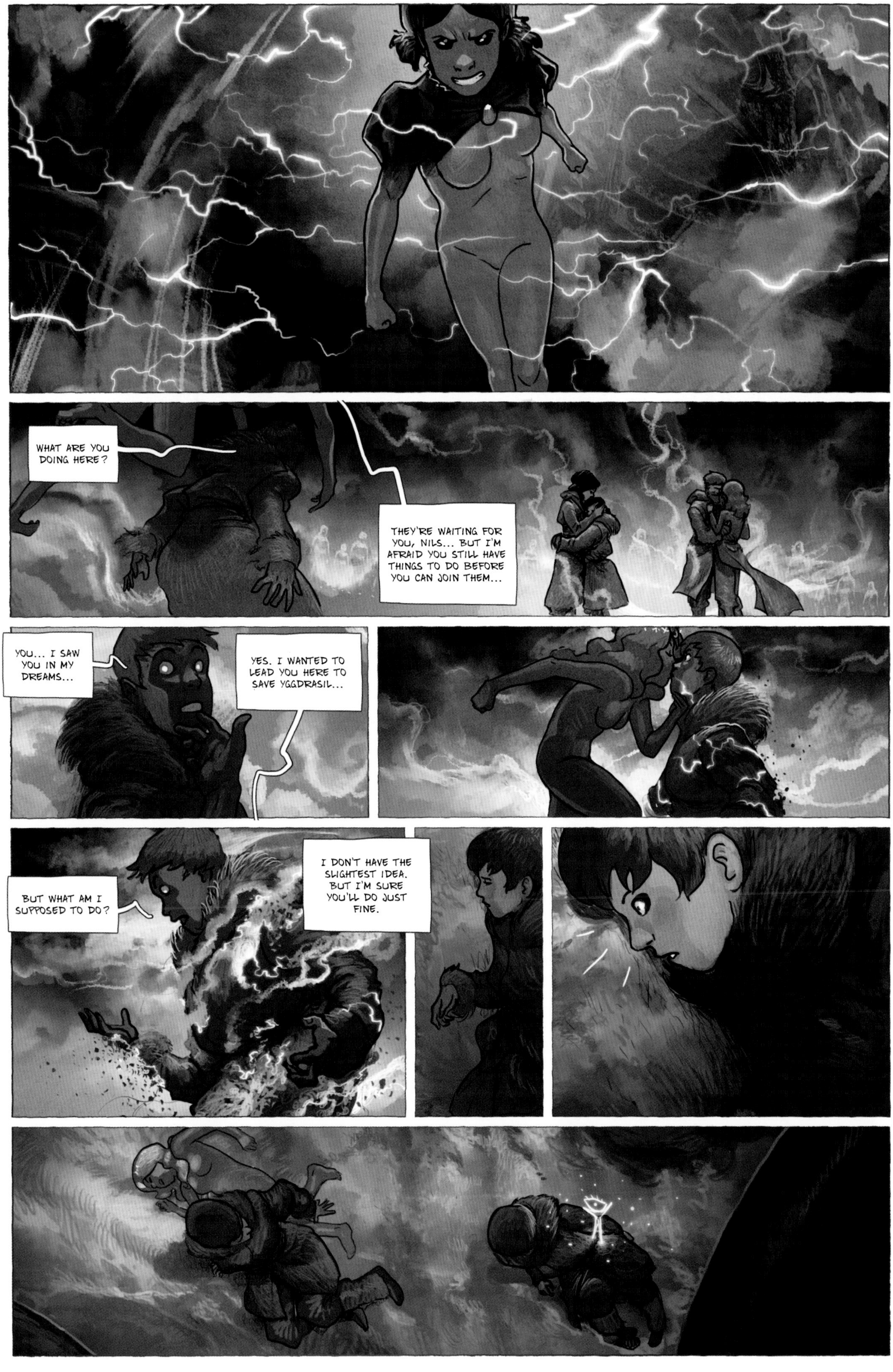

WHAT ARE YOU DOING HERE?
THEY'RE WAITING FOR YOU, NILS... BUT I'M AFRAID YOU STILL HAVE THINGS TO DO BEFORE YOU CAN JOIN THEM...
YOU... I SAW YOU IN MY DREAMS...
YES. I WANTED TO LEAD YOU HERE TO SAVE YGGDRASIL...
BUT WHAT AM I SUPPOSED TO DO?
I DON'T HAVE THE SLIGHTEST IDEA. BUT I'M SURE YOU'LL DO JUST FINE.

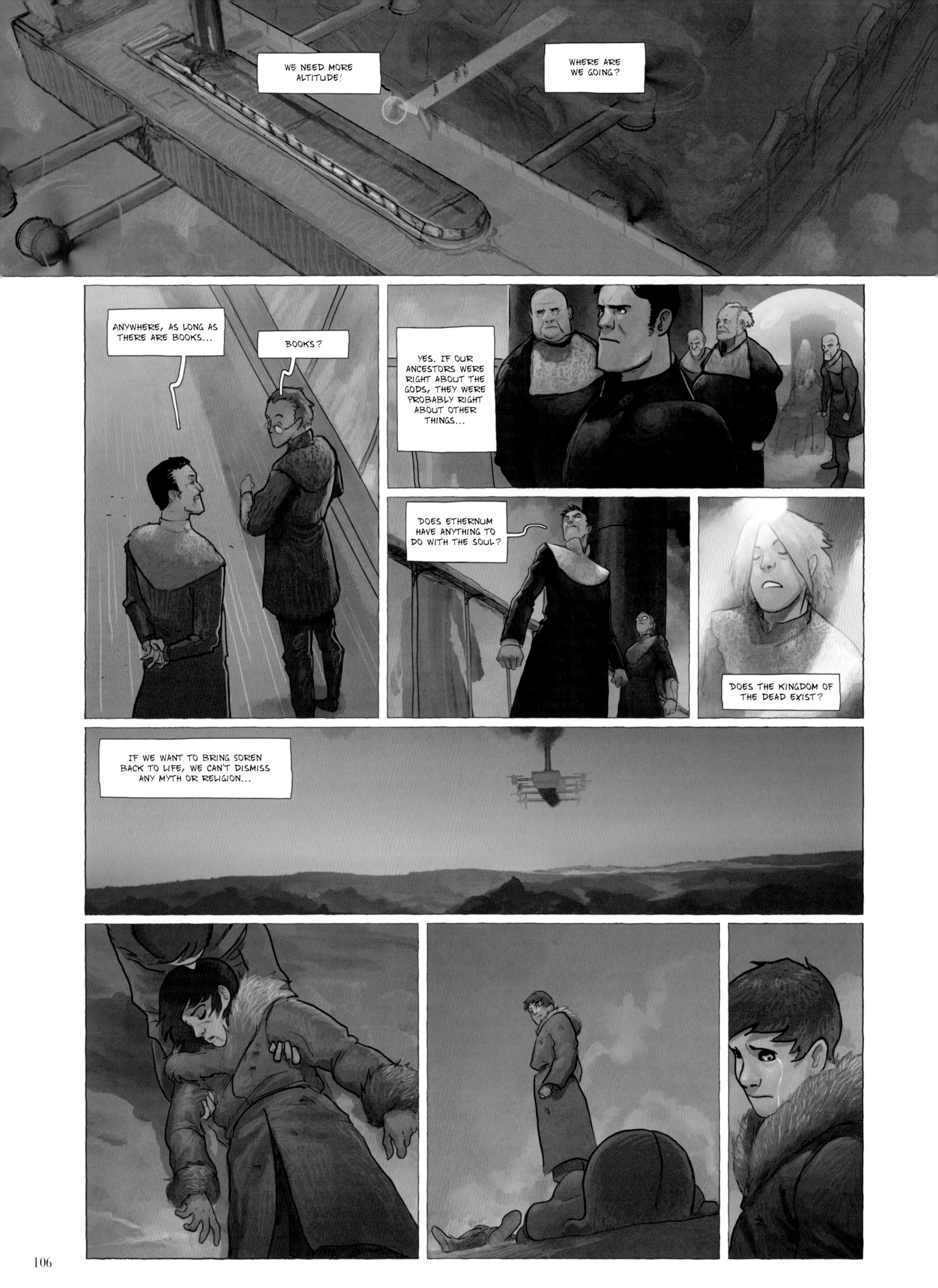
WE NEED MORE ALTITUDE!
WHERE ARE WE GOING?
ANYWHERE, AS LONG AS THERE ARE BOOKS...
BOOKS?
YES. IF OUR ANCESTORS WERE RIGHT ABOUT THE GODS, THEY WERE PROBABLY RIGHT ABOUT OTHER THINGS...
DOES ETHERNUM HAVE ANYTHING TO DO WITH THE SOUL?
DOES THE KINGDOM OF THE DEAD EXIST?
IF WE WANT TO BRING SOREN BACK TO LIFE, WE CAN'T DISMISS ANY MYTH OR RELIGION...

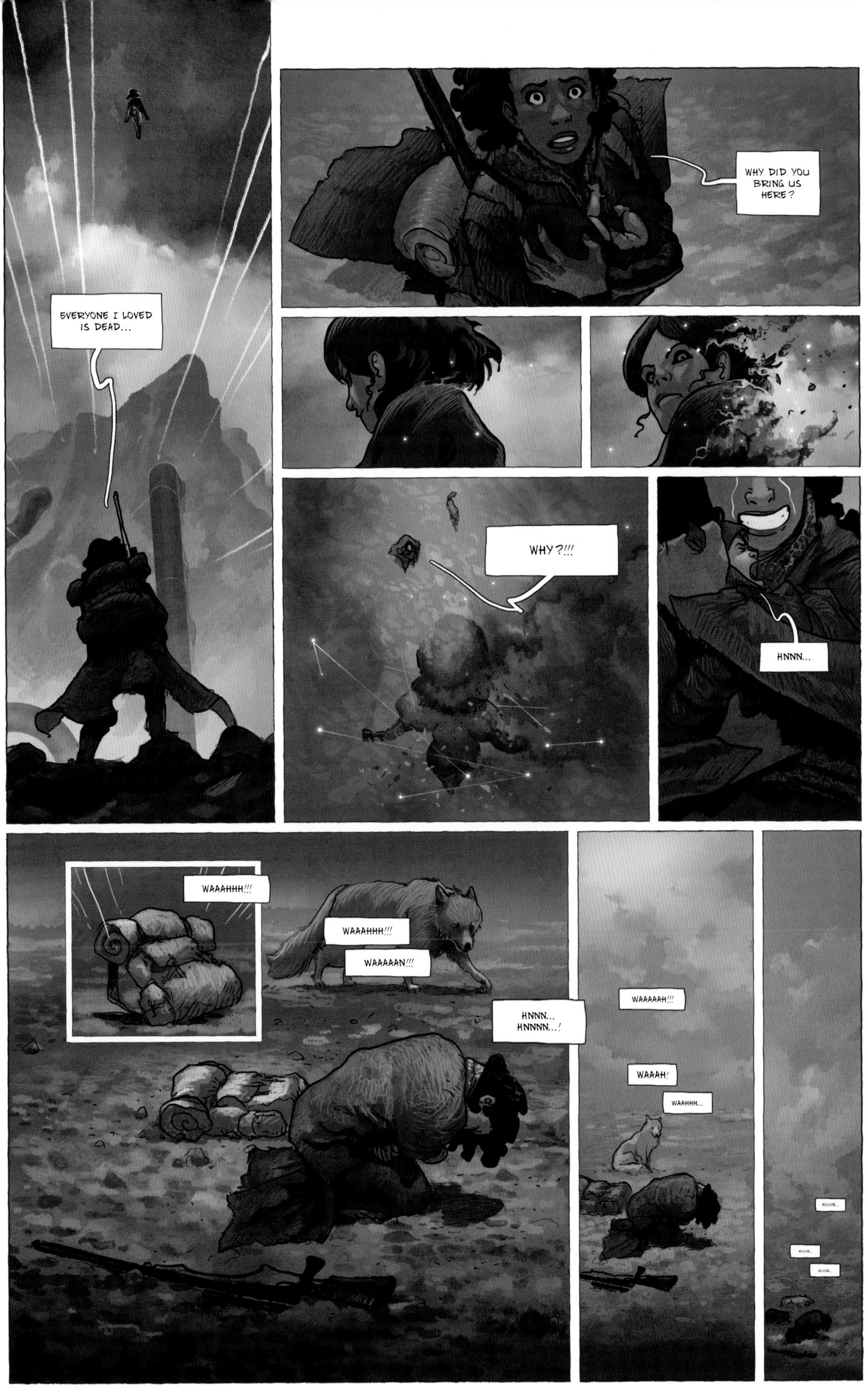
EVERYONE I LOVED IS DEAD...
WHY DID YOU BRING US HERE?
WHY?!!!
HNNN...
WAAAHHH!!!
WAAAHHH!!!
WAAAAAN!!!
HNNN... HNNNN...!
WAAAAAH!!!
WAAAH!
WAAHHH...
HIIIIN...
HIIIIN...
HIIIIN...

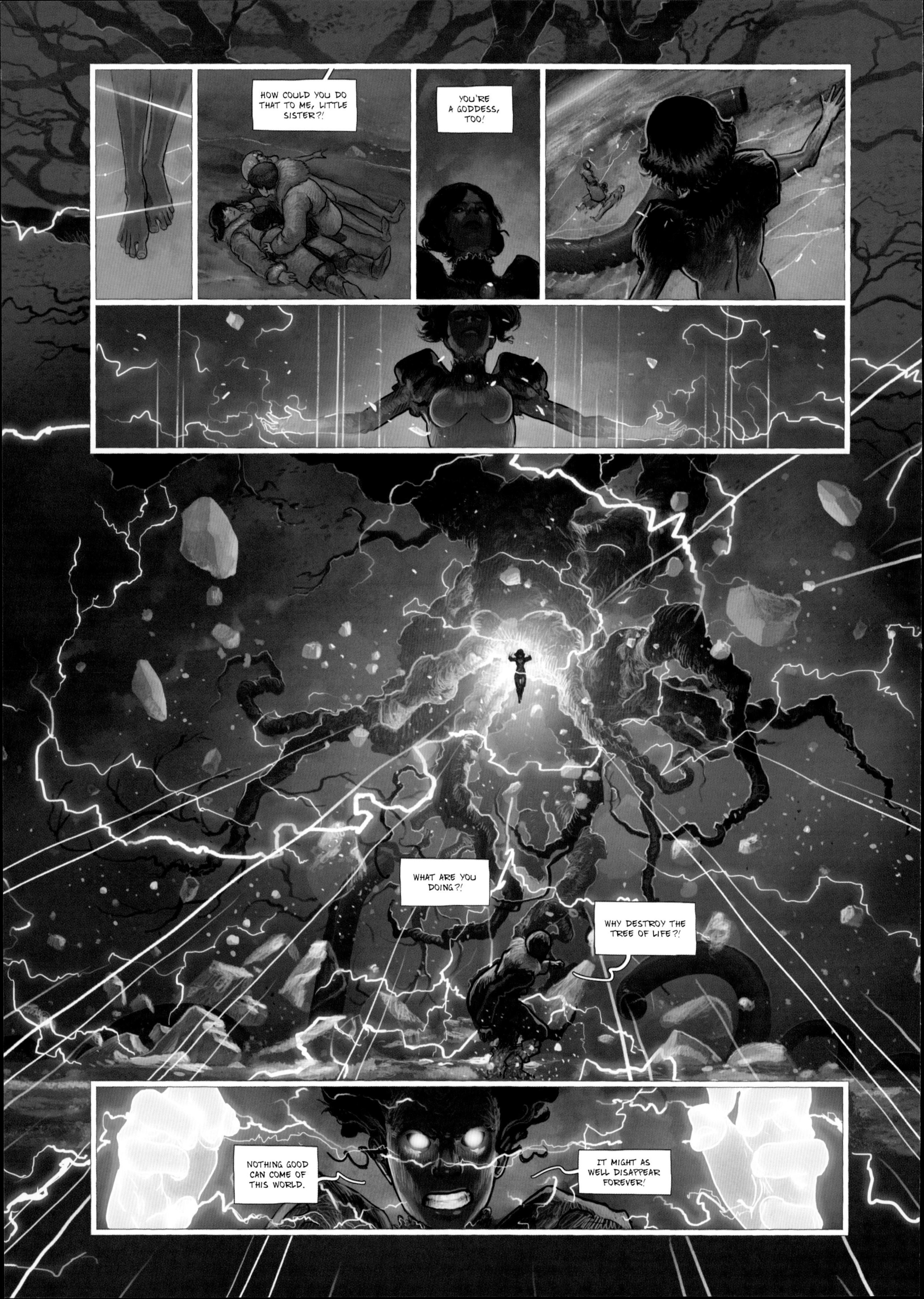
HOW COULD YOU DO THAT TO ME, LITTLE SISTER?!
YOU'RE A GODDESS, TOO!
WHAT ARE YOU DOING?!
WHY DESTROY THE TREE OF LIFE?!
NOTHING GOOD CAN COME OF THIS WORLD.
IT MIGHT AS WELL DISAPPEAR FOREVER!

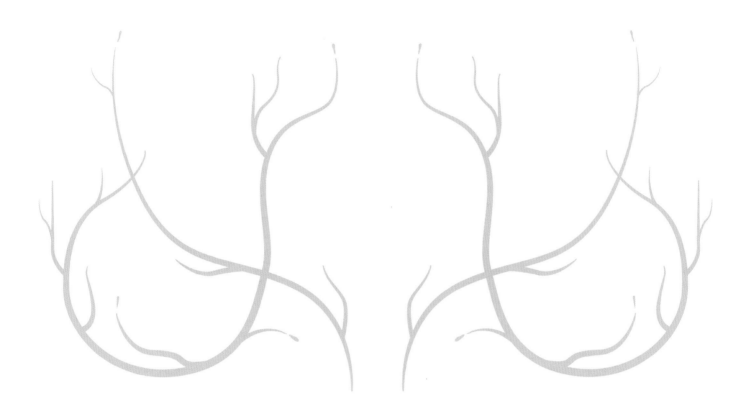

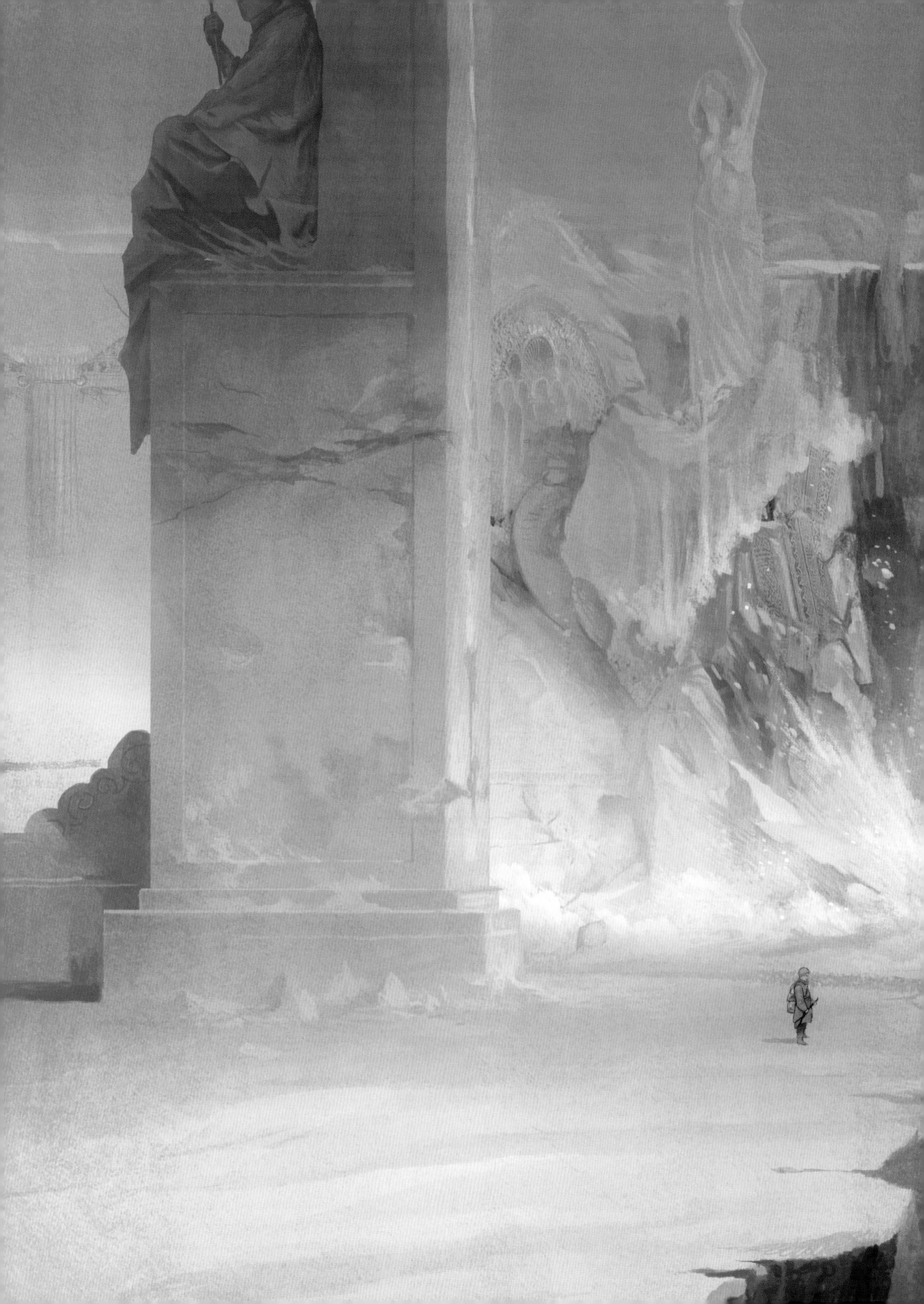

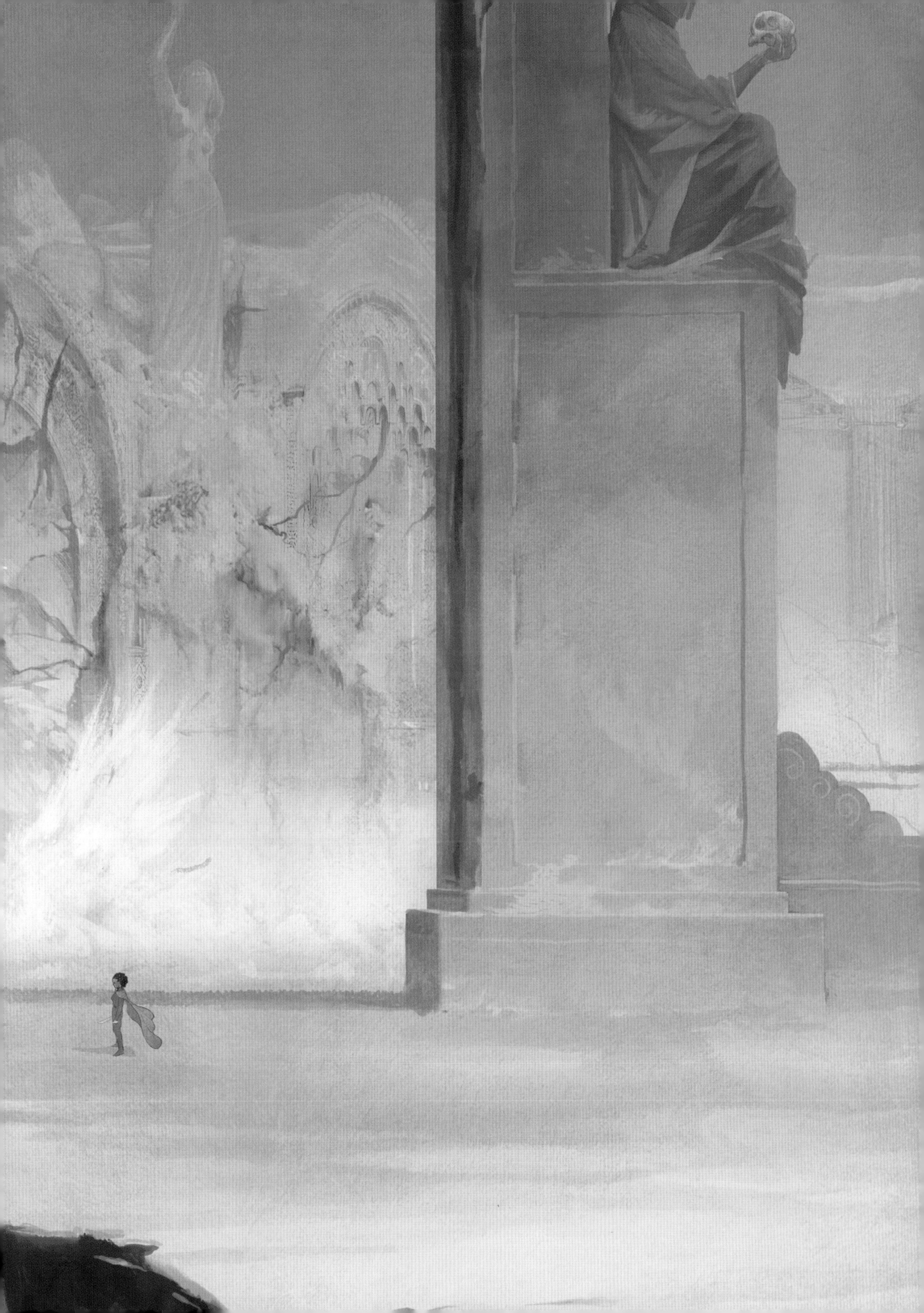

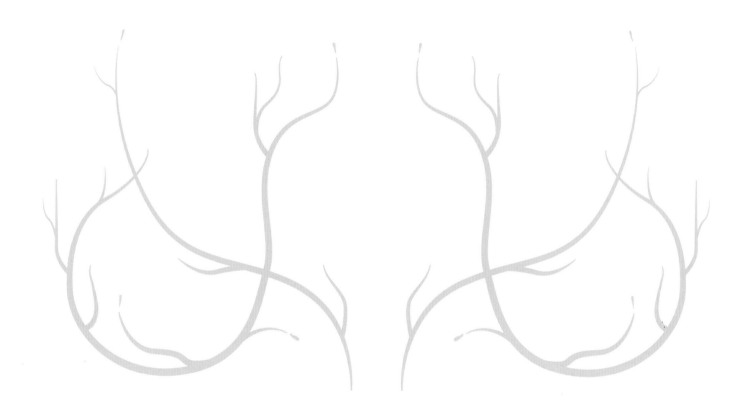

Chapter Three
THE TREE OF LIFE

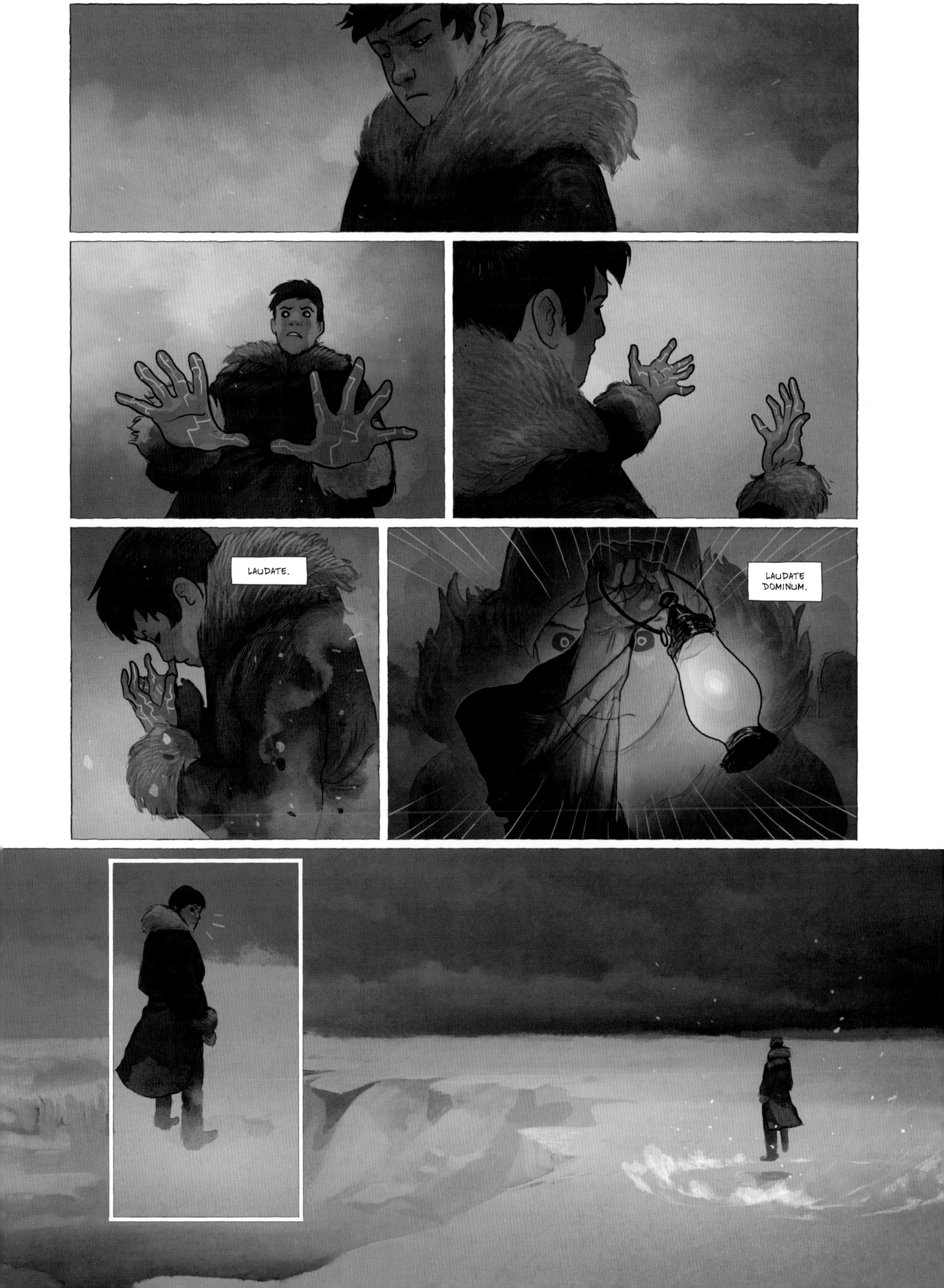
LAUDATE.
LAUDATE DOMINUM.

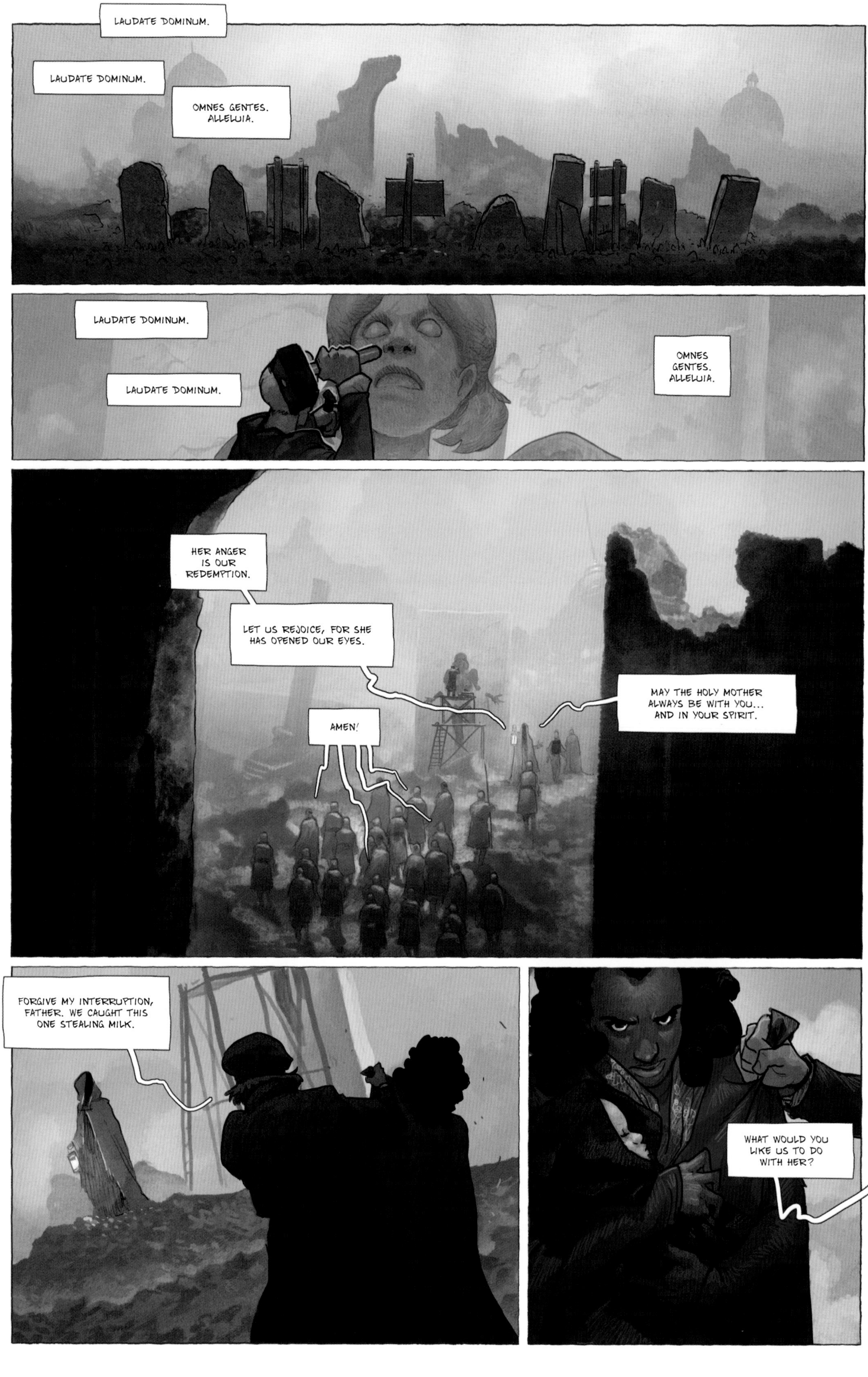

LAUDATE DOMINUM.
LAUDATE DOMINUM.
OMNES GENTES. ALLELUIA.
LAUDATE DOMINUM.
LAUDATE DOMINUM.
OMNES GENTES. ALLELUIA.
HER ANGER IS OUR REDEMPTION.
LET US REJOICE, FOR SHE HAS OPENED OUR EYES.
MAY THE HOLY MOTHER ALWAYS BE WITH YOU... AND IN YOUR SPIRIT.
AMEN!
FORGIVE MY INTERRUPTION, FATHER. WE CAUGHT THIS ONE STEALING MILK.
WHAT WOULD YOU LIKE US TO DO WITH HER?

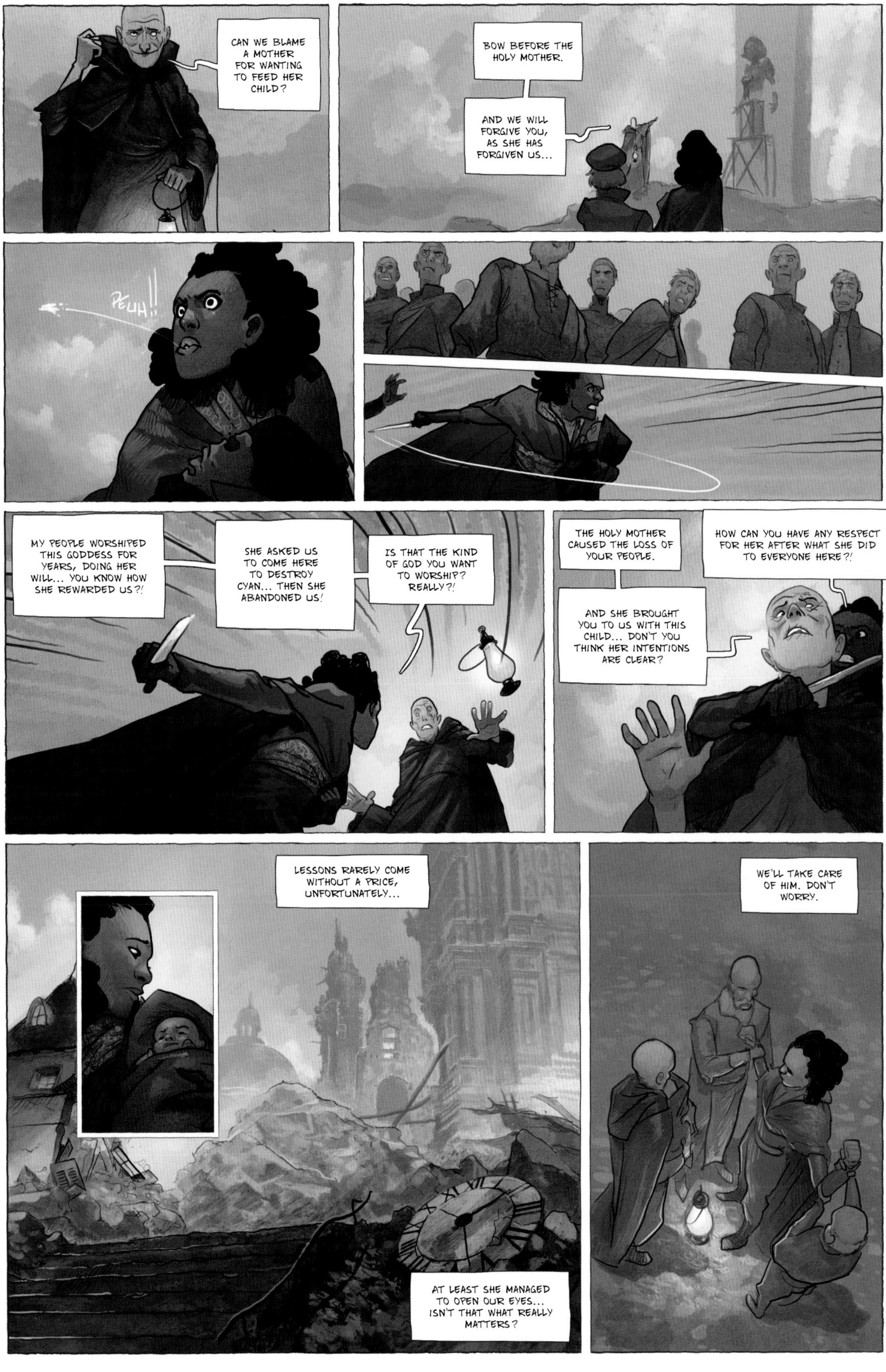
CAN WE BLAME A MOTHER FOR WANTING TO FEED HER CHILD?
BOW BEFORE THE HOLY MOTHER.
AND WE WILL FORGIVE YOU, AS SHE HAS FORGIVEN US...
PEUH!!
MY PEOPLE WORSHIPED THIS GODDESS FOR YEARS, DOING HER WILL... YOU KNOW HOW SHE REWARDED US?!
SHE ASKED US TO COME HERE TO DESTROY CYAN... THEN SHE ABANDONED US!
IS THAT THE KIND OF GOD YOU WANT TO WORSHIP? REALLY?!
THE HOLY MOTHER CAUSED THE LOSS OF YOUR PEOPLE.
HOW CAN YOU HAVE ANY RESPECT FOR HER AFTER WHAT SHE DID TO EVERYONE HERE?!
AND SHE BROUGHT YOU TO US WITH THIS CHILD... DON'T YOU THINK HER INTENTIONS ARE CLEAR?
LESSONS RARELY COME WITHOUT A PRICE, UNFORTUNATELY...
AT LEAST SHE MANAGED TO OPEN OUR EYES... ISN'T THAT WHAT REALLY MATTERS?
WE'LL TAKE CARE OF HIM. DON'T WORRY.

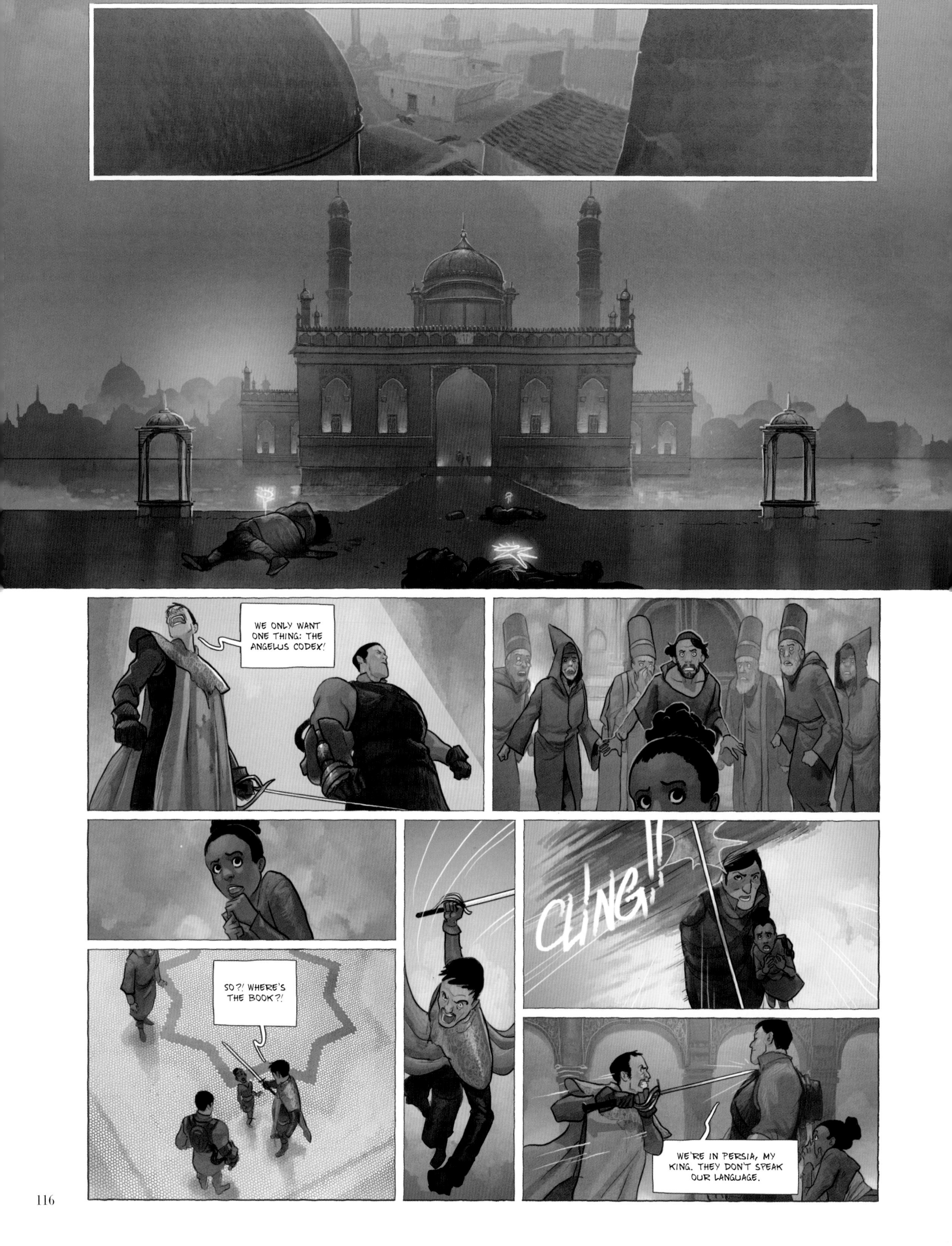
WE ONLY WANT ONE THING: THE ANGELUS CODEX!
SO?! WHERE'S THE BOOK?!
CLING!!
WE'RE IN PERSIA, MY KING. THEY DON'T SPEAK OUR LANGUAGE.

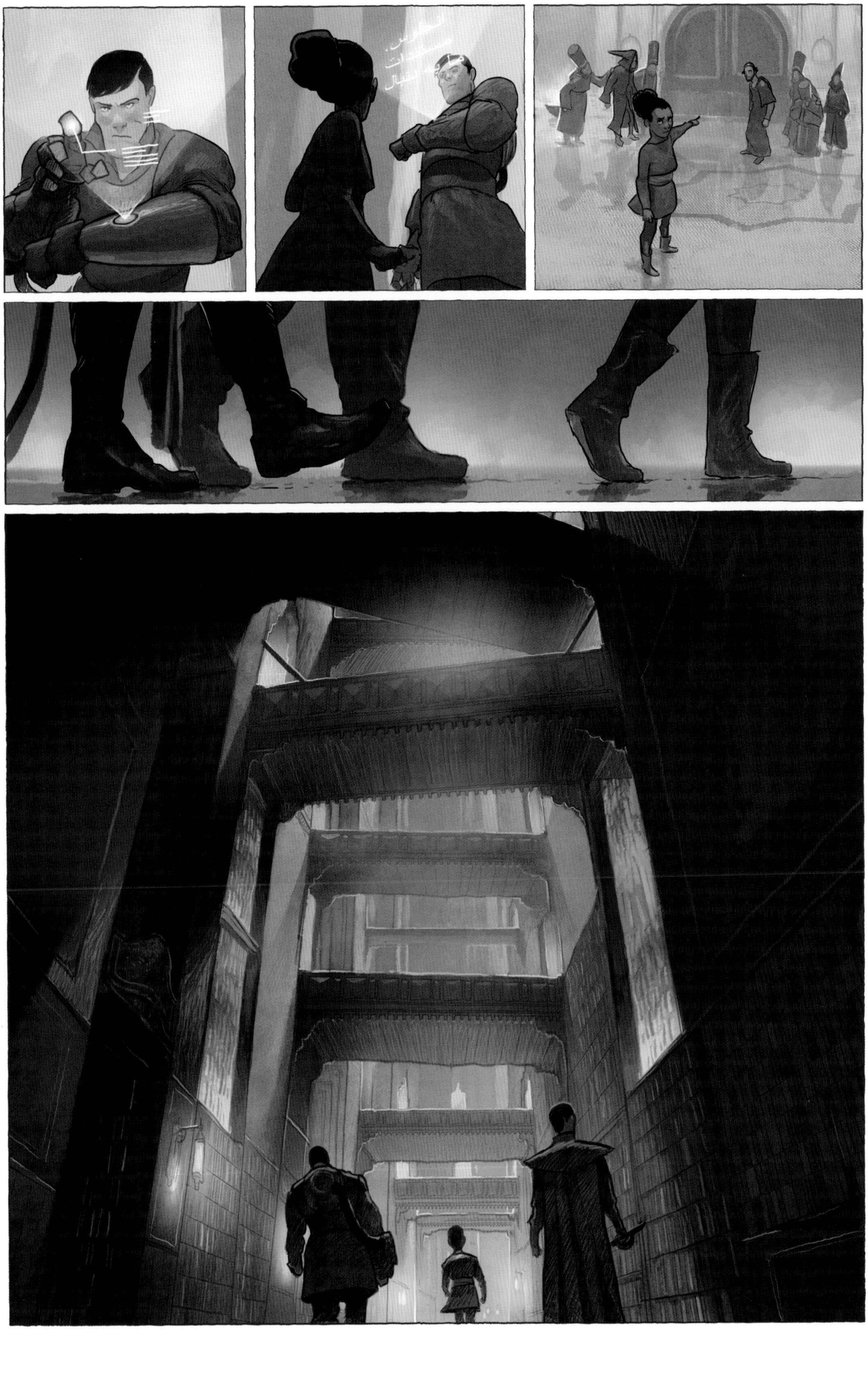

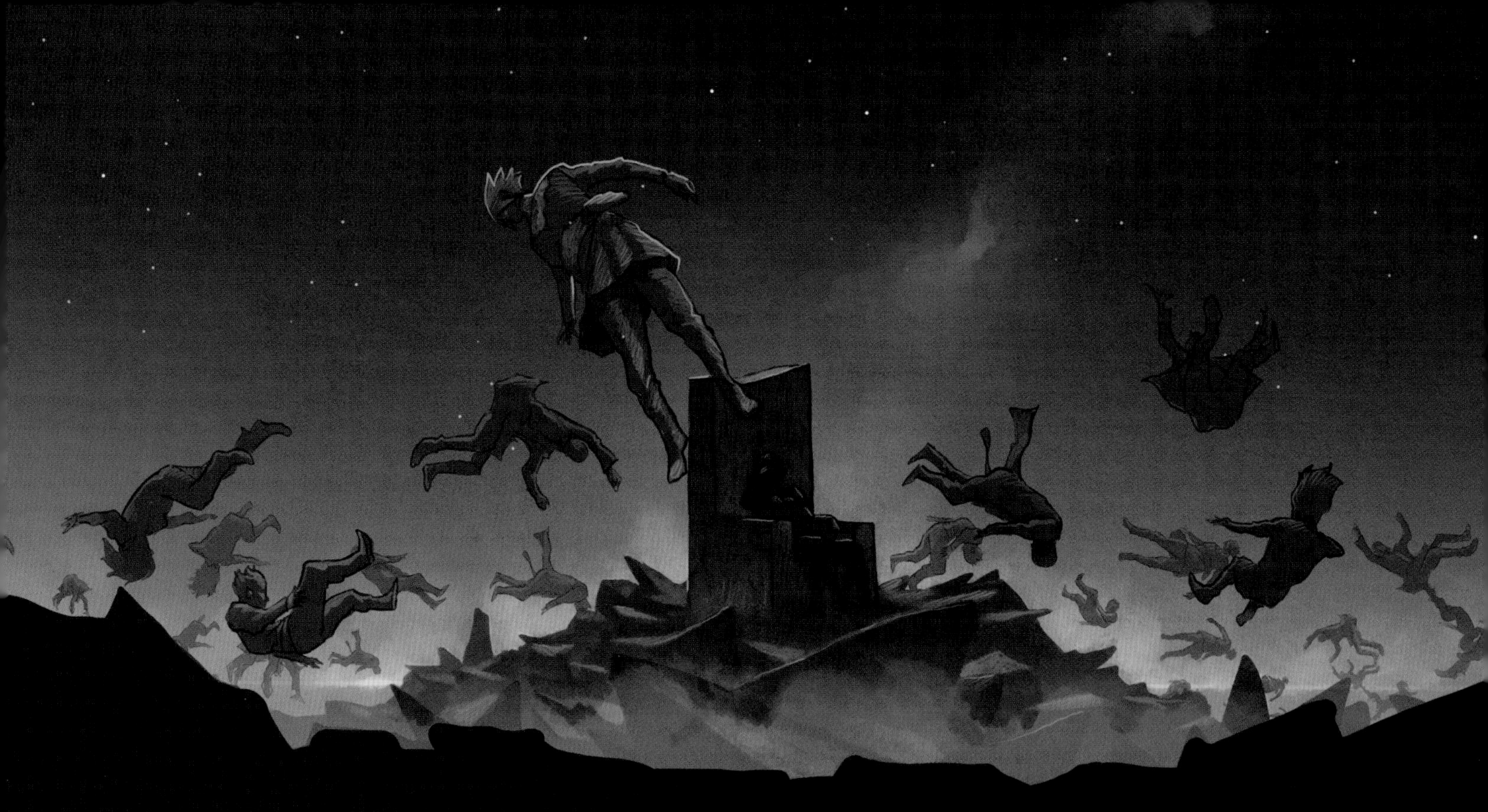
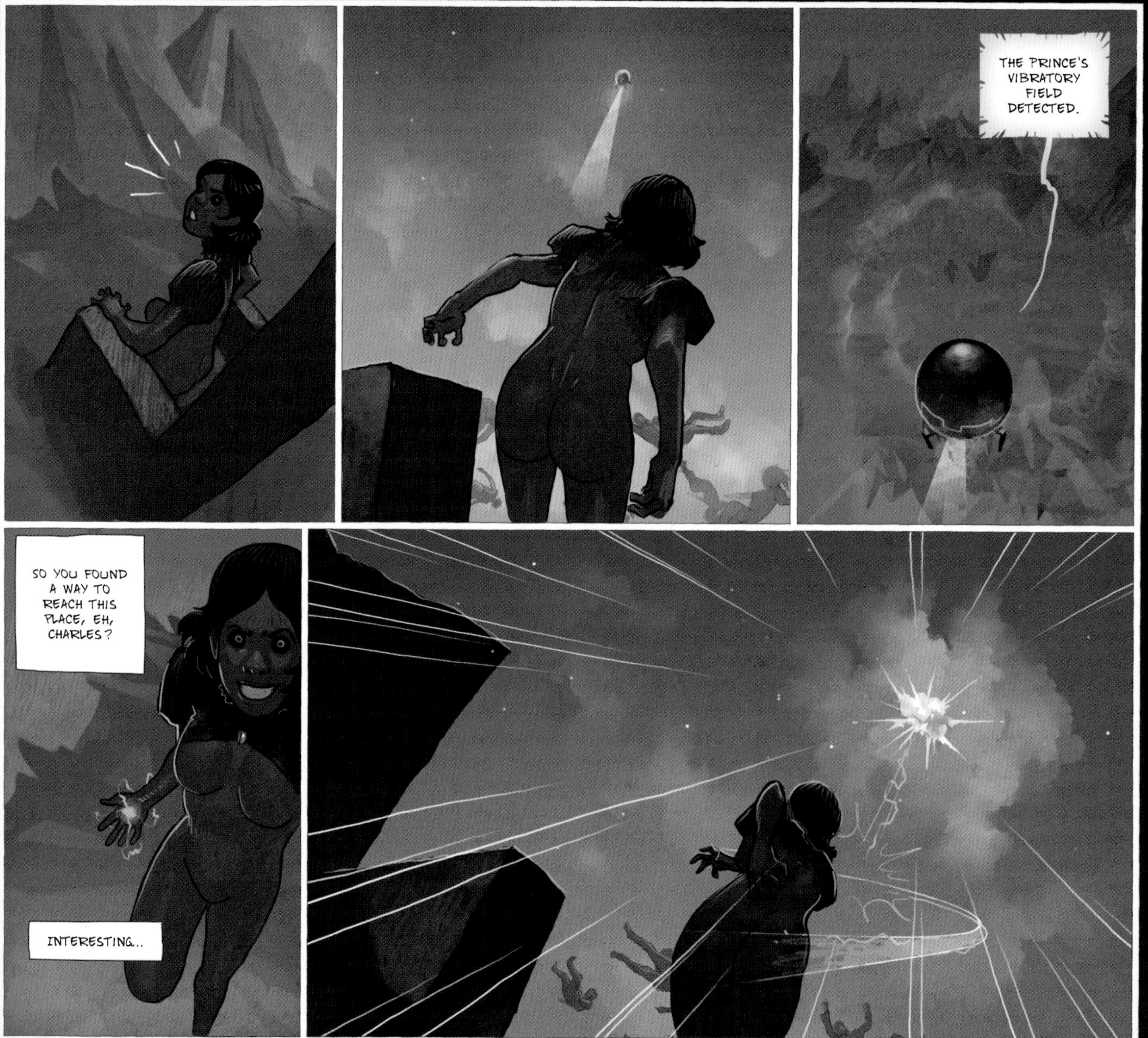
THE PRINCE'S VIBRATORY FIELD DETECTED.
SO YOU FOUND A WAY TO REACH THIS PLACE, EH, CHARLES?
INTERESTING...

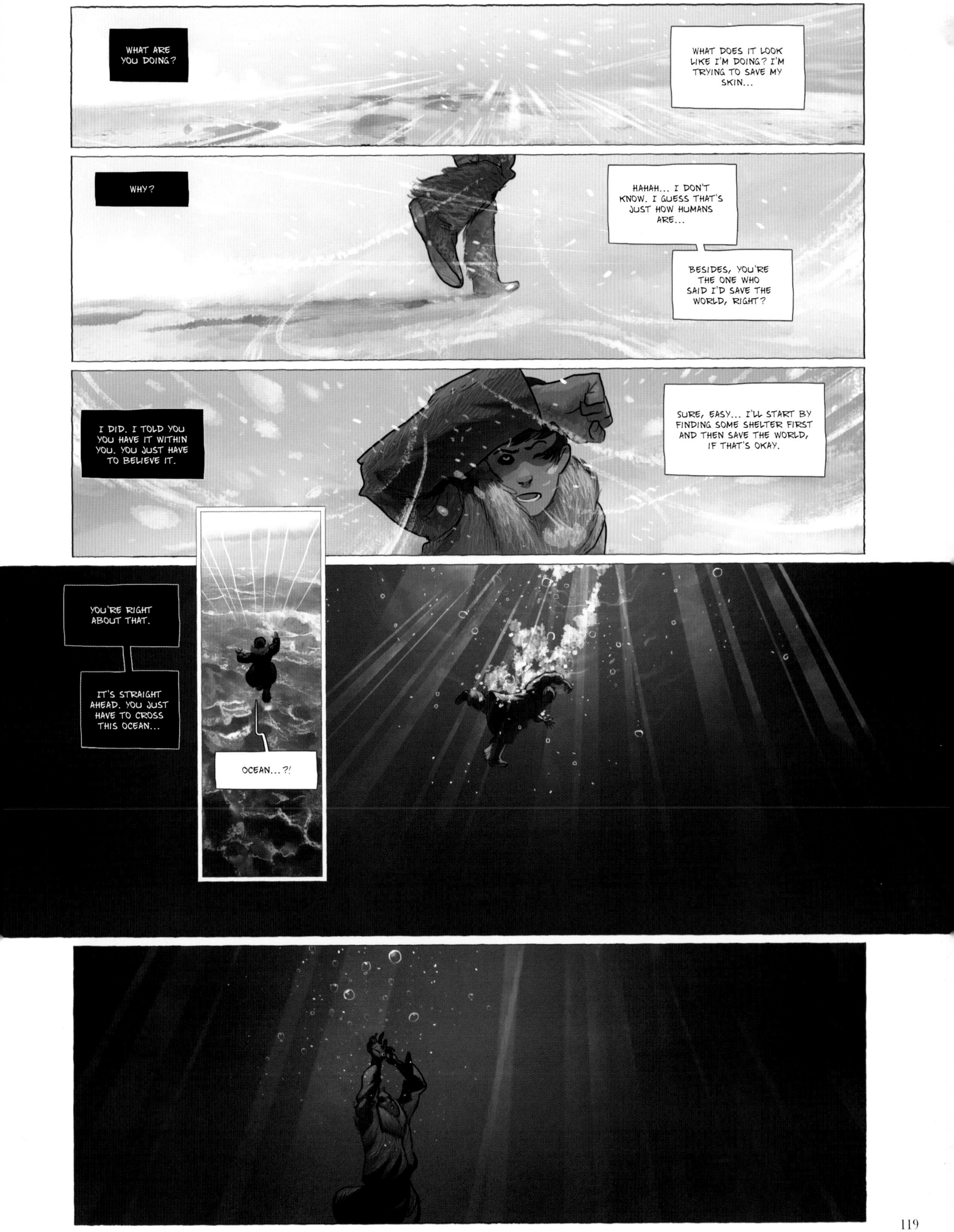

WHAT ARE YOU DOING?
WHAT DOES IT LOOK LIKE I'M DOING? I'M TRYING TO SAVE MY SKIN...
WHY?
HAHAH... I DON'T KNOW. I GUESS THAT'S JUST HOW HUMANS ARE...
BESIDES, YOU'RE THE ONE WHO SAID I'D SAVE THE WORLD, RIGHT?
I DID. I TOLD YOU YOU HAVE IT WITHIN YOU. YOU JUST HAVE TO BELIEVE IT.
SURE, EASY... I'LL START BY FINDING SOME SHELTER FIRST AND THEN SAVE THE WORLD, IF THAT'S OKAY.
YOU'RE RIGHT ABOUT THAT.
IT'S STRAIGHT AHEAD. YOU JUST HAVE TO CROSS THIS OCEAN...
OCEAN...?!

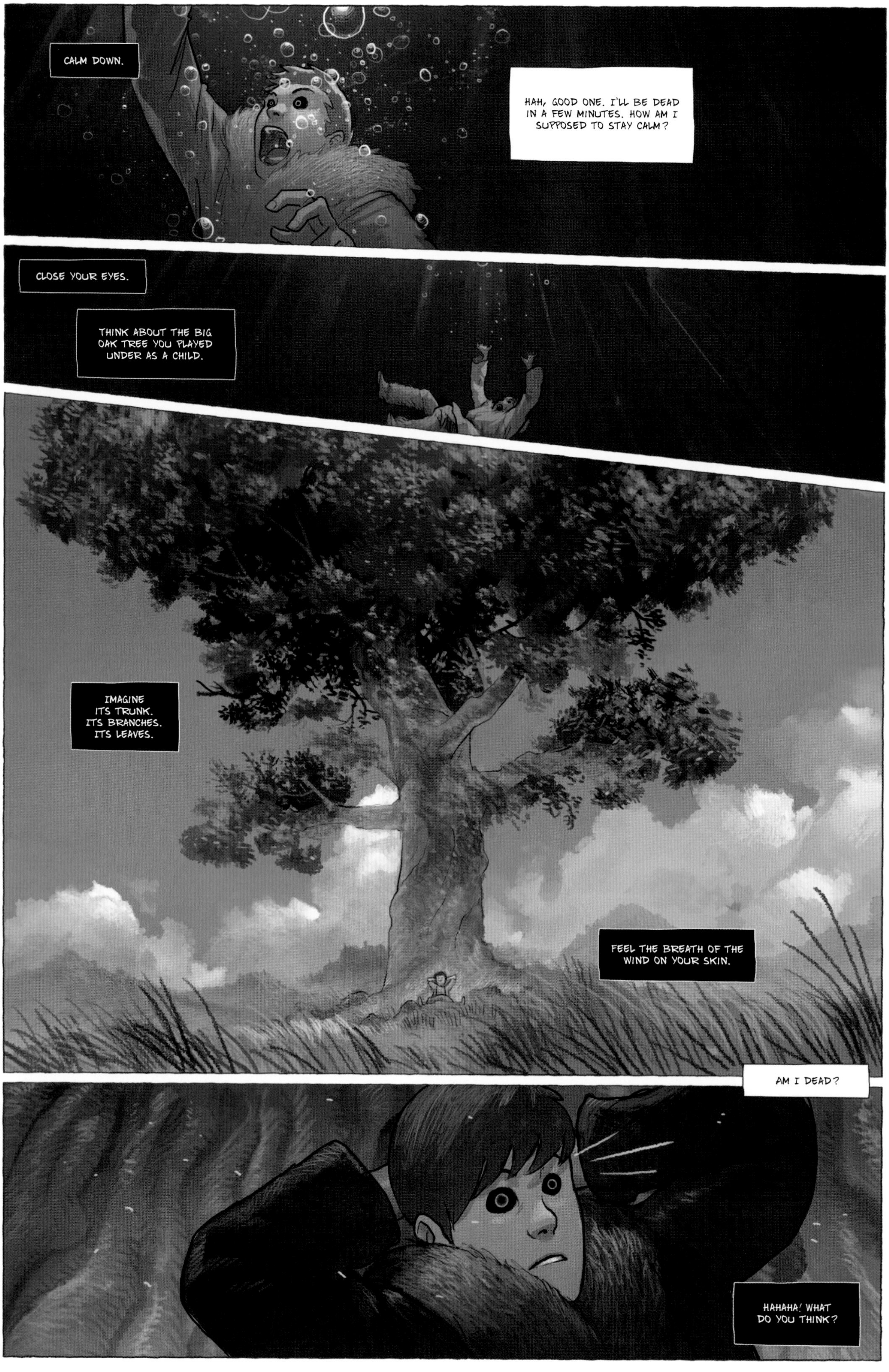
CALM DOWN.
HAH, GOOD ONE. I'LL BE DEAD IN A FEW MINUTES. HOW AM I SUPPOSED TO STAY CALM?
CLOSE YOUR EYES.
THINK ABOUT THE BIG OAK TREE YOU PLAYED UNDER AS A CHILD.
IMAGINE ITS TRUNK. ITS BRANCHES. ITS LEAVES.
FEEL THE BREATH OF THE WIND ON YOUR SKIN.
AM I DEAD?
HAHAHA! WHAT DO YOU THINK?

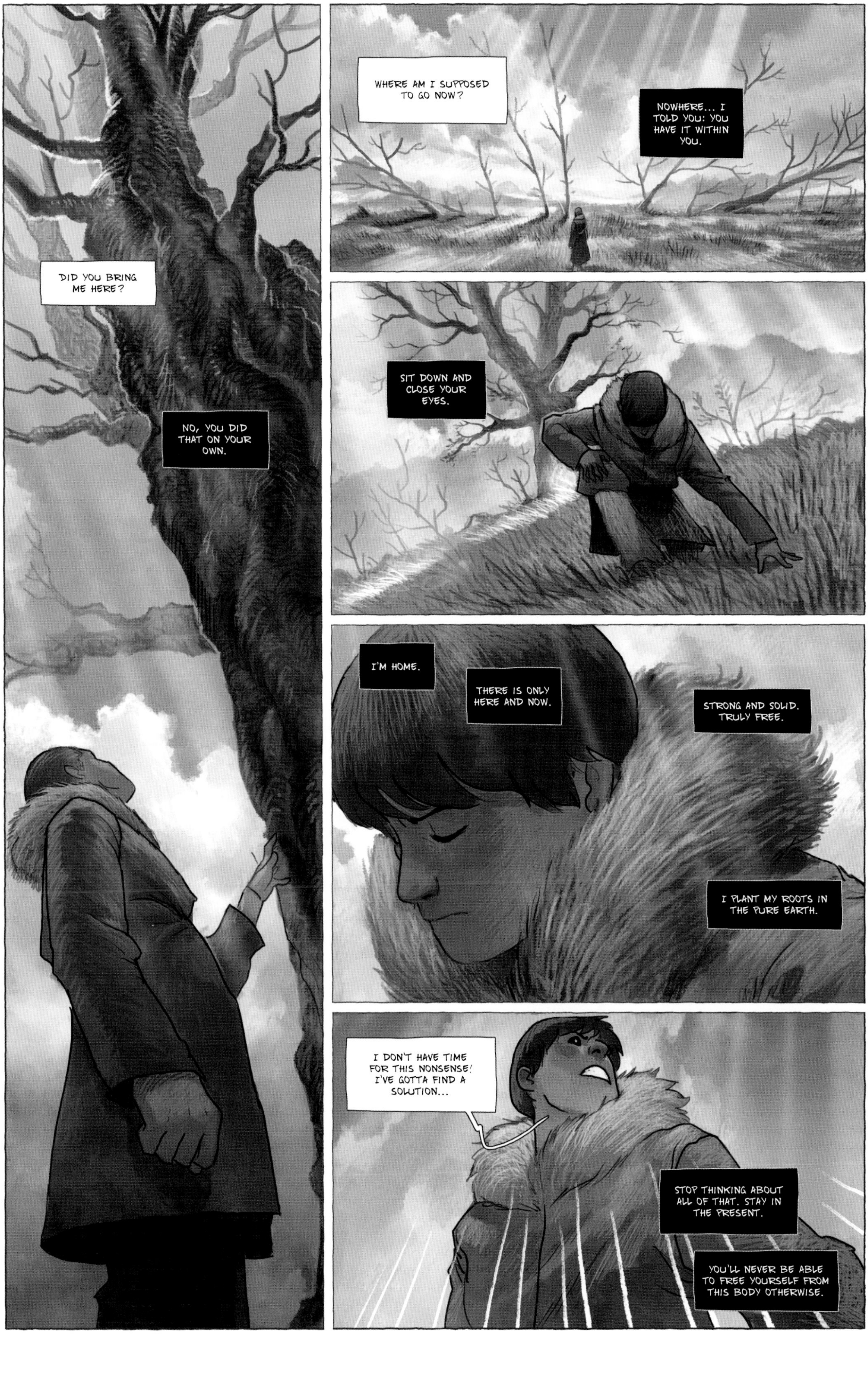

DID YOU BRING ME HERE?
NO, YOU DID THAT ON YOUR OWN.
WHERE AM I SUPPOSED TO GO NOW?
NOWHERE... I TOLD YOU: YOU HAVE IT WITHIN YOU.
SIT DOWN AND CLOSE YOUR EYES.
I'M HOME.
THERE IS ONLY HERE AND NOW.
STRONG AND SOLID. TRULY FREE.
I PLANT MY ROOTS IN THE PURE EARTH.
I DON'T HAVE TIME FOR THIS NONSENSE! I'VE GOTTA FIND A SOLUTION...
STOP THINKING ABOUT ALL OF THAT. STAY IN THE PRESENT.
YOU'LL NEVER BE ABLE TO FREE YOURSELF FROM THIS BODY OTHERWISE.

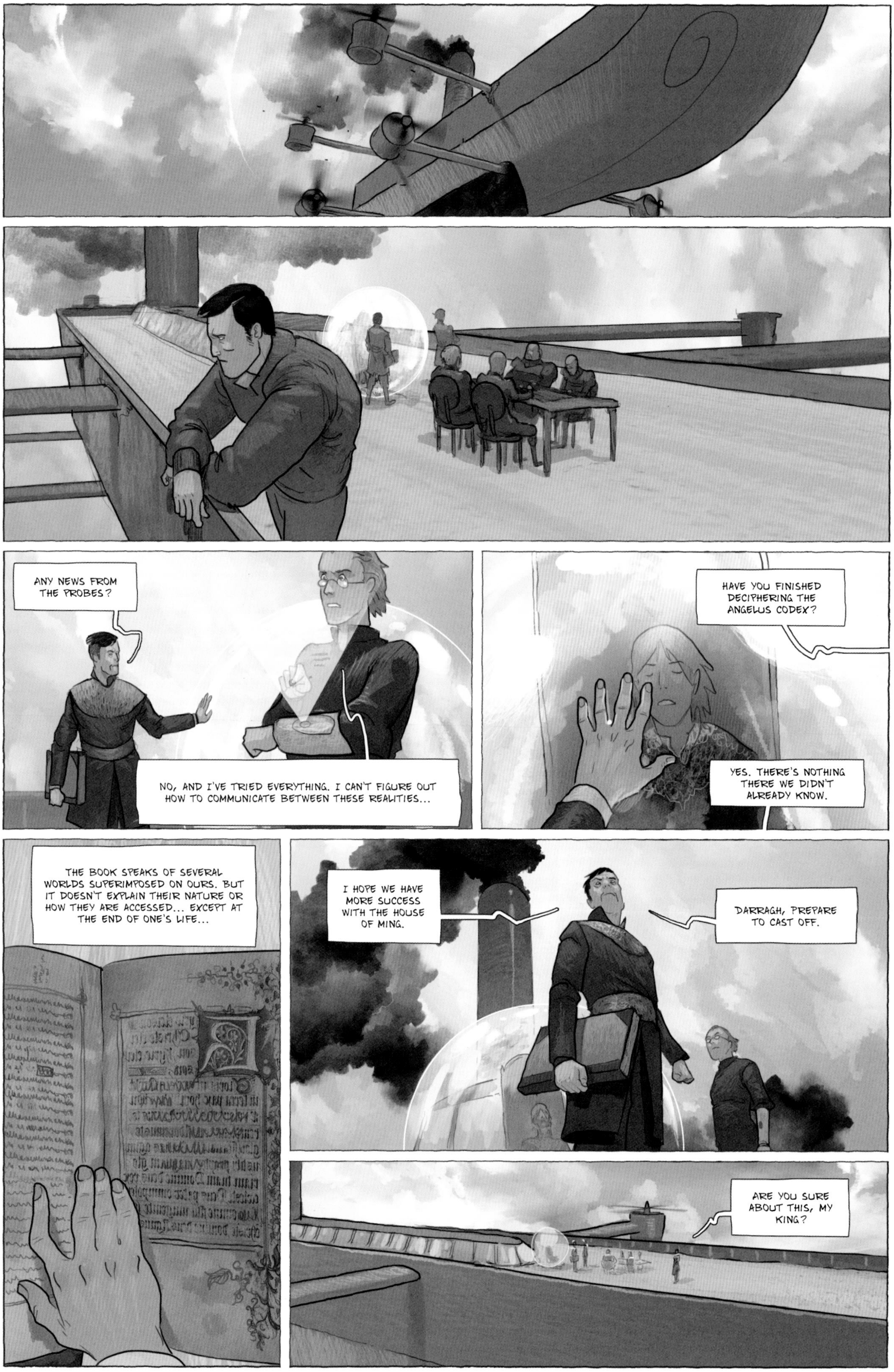

ANY NEWS FROM THE PROBES?
NO, AND I'VE TRIED EVERYTHING. I CAN'T FIGURE OUT HOW TO COMMUNICATE BETWEEN THESE REALITIES...
HAVE YOU FINISHED DECIPHERING THE ANGELUS CODEX?
YES. THERE'S NOTHING THERE WE DIDN'T ALREADY KNOW.
THE BOOK SPEAKS OF SEVERAL WORLDS SUPERIMPOSED ON OURS. BUT IT DOESN'T EXPLAIN THEIR NATURE OR HOW THEY ARE ACCESSED... EXCEPT AT THE END OF ONE'S LIFE...
I HOPE WE HAVE MORE SUCCESS WITH THE HOUSE OF MING.
DARRAGH, PREPARE TO CAST OFF.
ARE YOU SURE ABOUT THIS, MY KING?

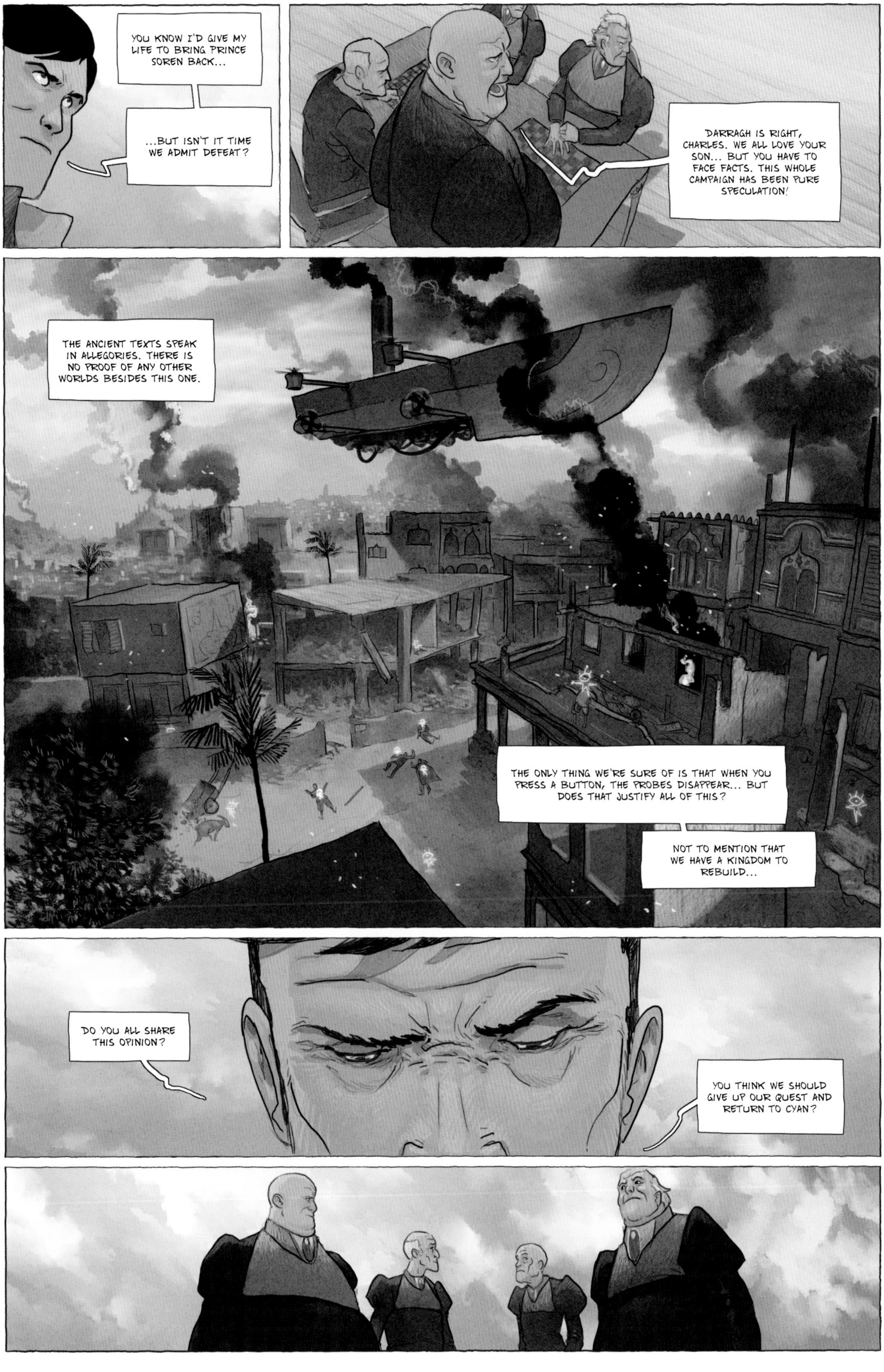

YOU KNOW I'D GIVE MY LIFE TO BRING PRINCE SOREN BACK...
...BUT ISN'T IT TIME WE ADMIT DEFEAT?
DARRAGH IS RIGHT, CHARLES. WE ALL LOVE YOUR SON... BUT YOU HAVE TO FACE FACTS. THIS WHOLE CAMPAIGN HAS BEEN PURE SPECULATION!
THE ANCIENT TEXTS SPEAK IN ALLEGORIES. THERE IS NO PROOF OF ANY OTHER WORLDS BESIDES THIS ONE.
THE ONLY THING WE'RE SURE OF IS THAT WHEN YOU PRESS A BUTTON, THE PROBES DISAPPEAR... BUT DOES THAT JUSTIFY ALL OF THIS?
NOT TO MENTION THAT WE HAVE A KINGDOM TO REBUILD...
DO YOU ALL SHARE THIS OPINION?
YOU THINK WE SHOULD GIVE UP OUR QUEST AND RETURN TO CYAN?

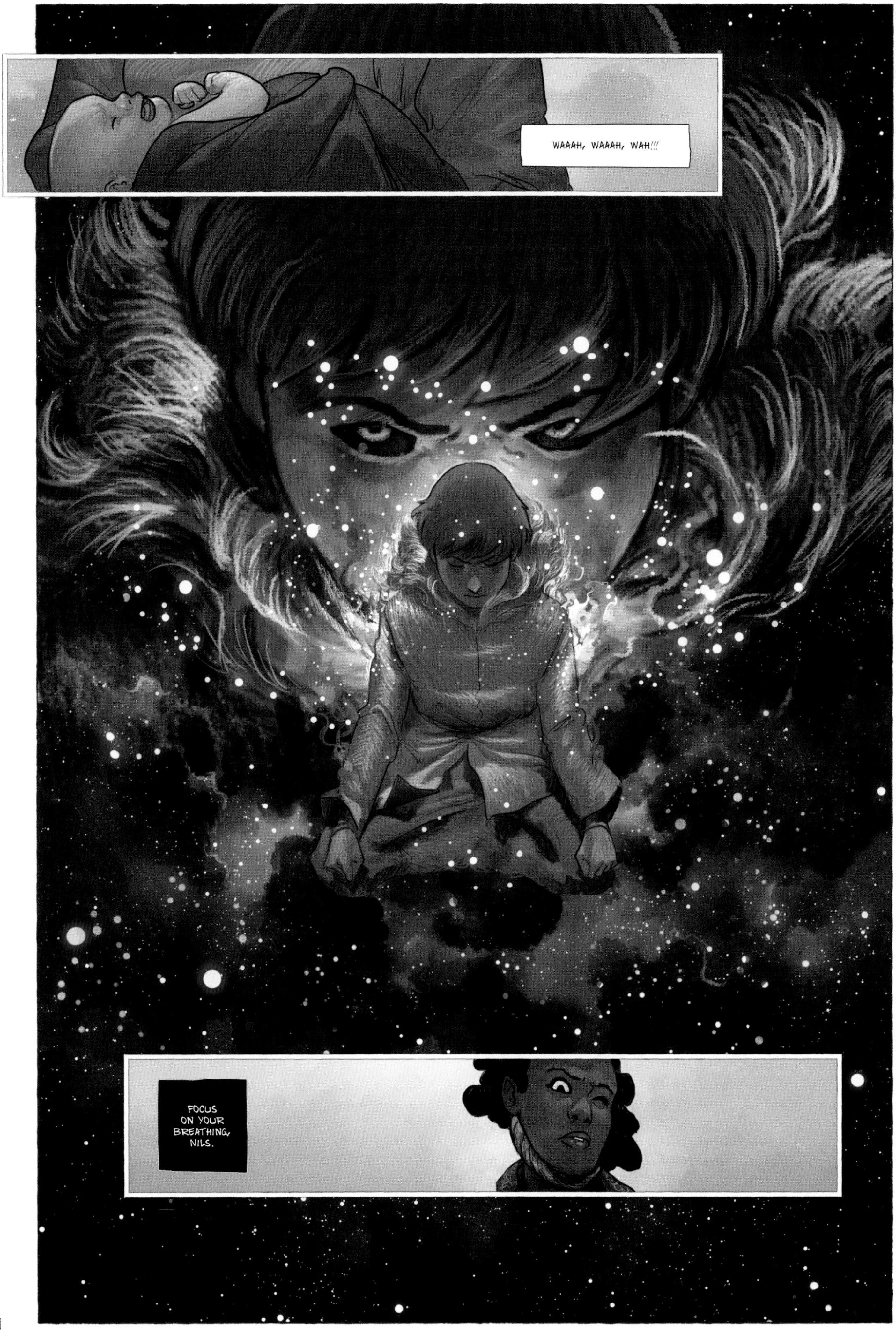
WAAAH, WAAAH, WAH!!!
FOCUS ON YOUR BREATHING, NILS.

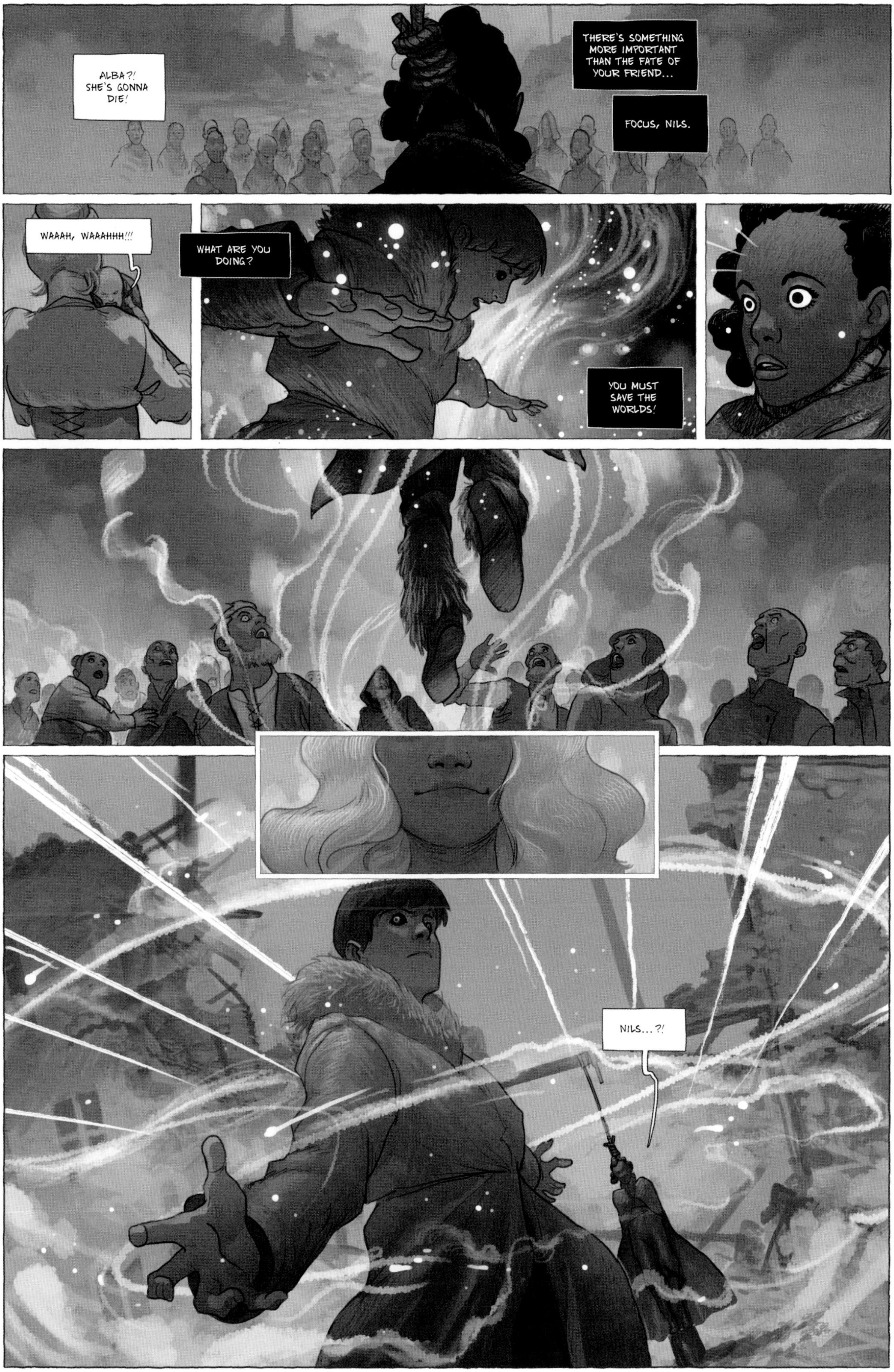
ALBA?! SHE'S GONNA DIE!
THERE'S SOMETHING MORE IMPORTANT THAN THE FATE OF YOUR FRIEND...
FOCUS, NILS.
WAAAH, WAAAHHH!!!
WHAT ARE YOU DOING?
YOU MUST SAVE THE WORLDS!
NILS...?!

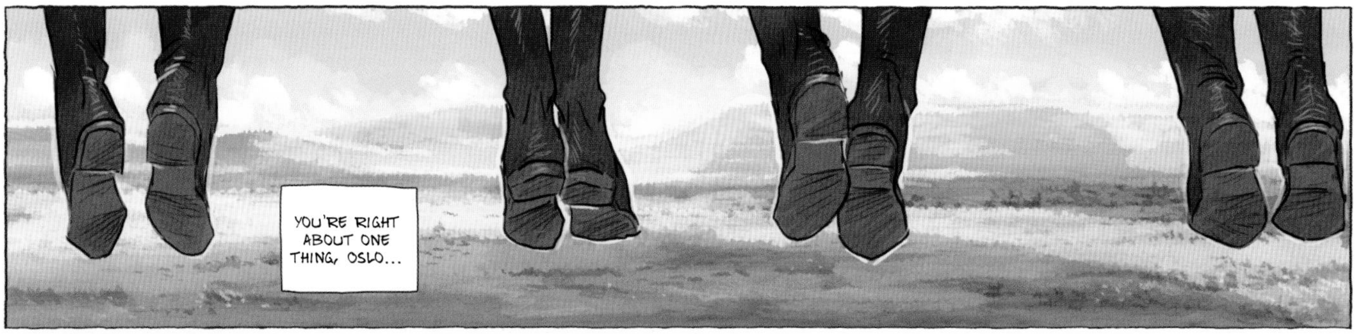
YOU'RE RIGHT ABOUT ONE THING, OSLO...
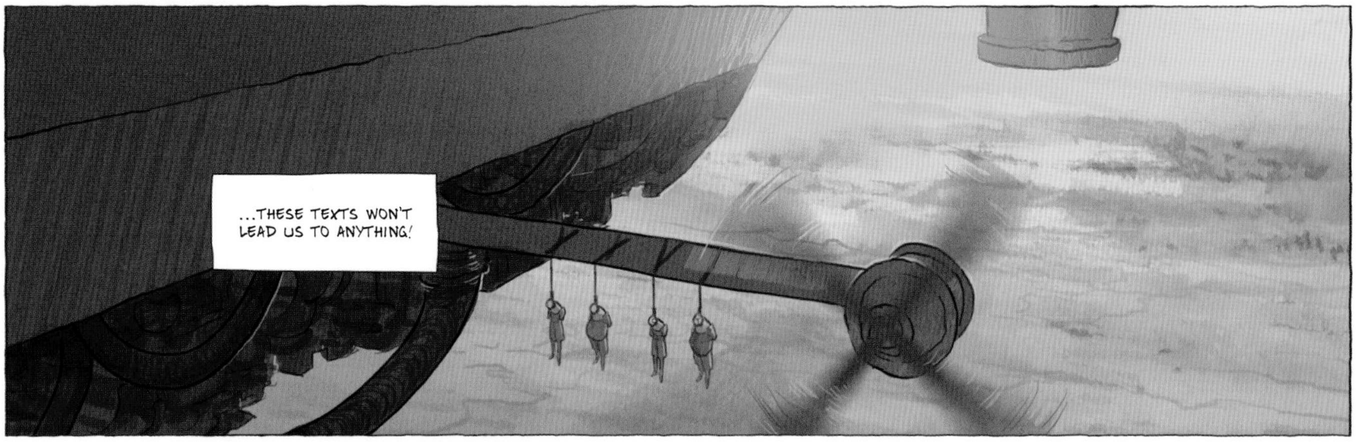
...THESE TEXTS WON'T LEAD US TO ANYTHING!
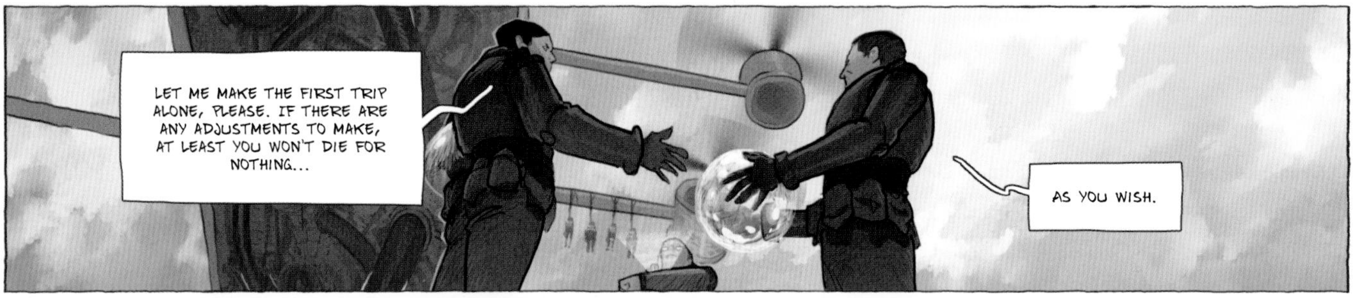
LET ME MAKE THE FIRST TRIP ALONE, PLEASE. IF THERE ARE ANY ADJUSTMENTS TO MAKE, AT LEAST YOU WON'T DIE FOR NOTHING...
AS YOU WISH.
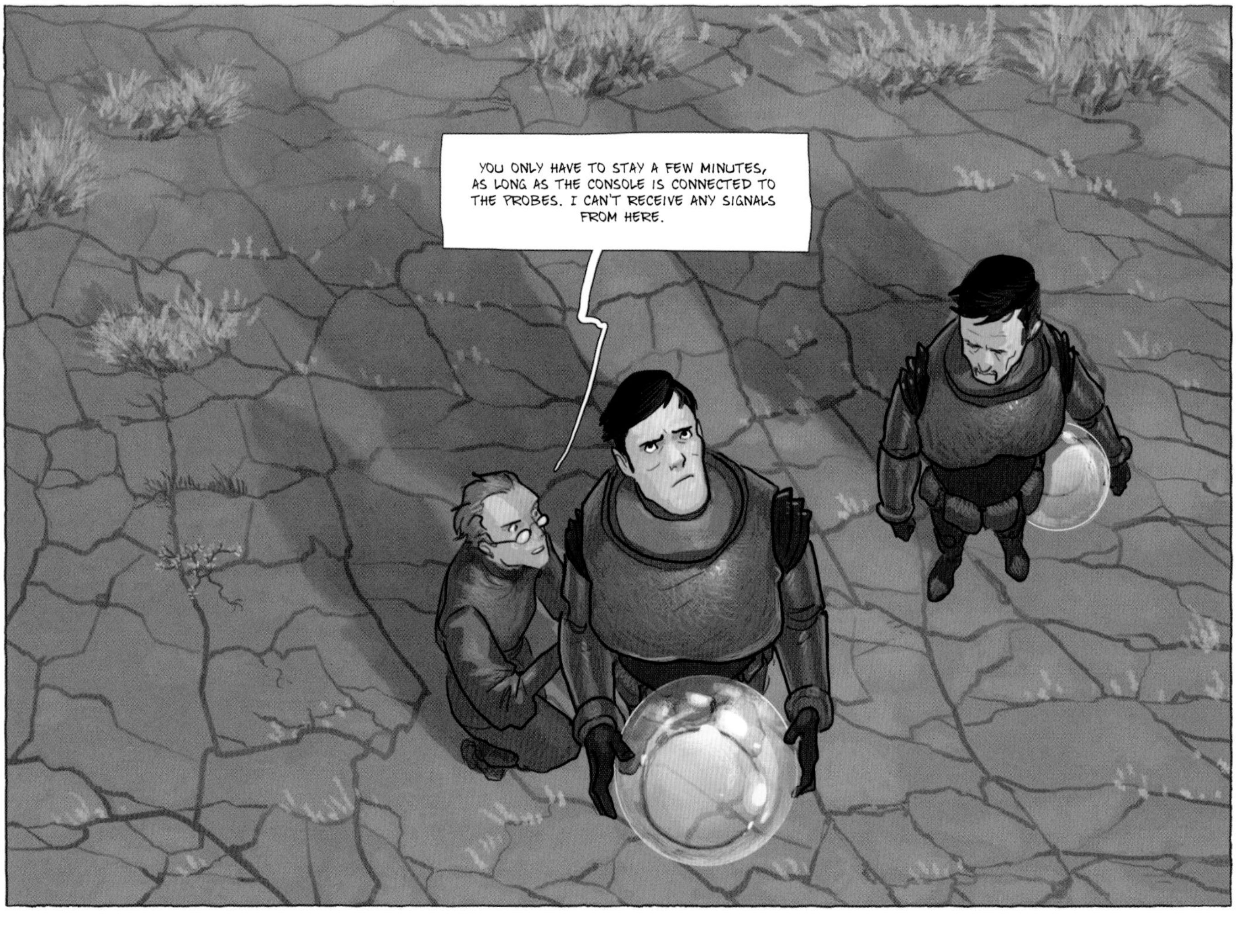
YOU ONLY HAVE TO STAY A FEW MINUTES, AS LONG AS THE CONSOLE IS CONNECTED TO THE PROBES. I CAN'T RECEIVE ANY SIGNALS FROM HERE.

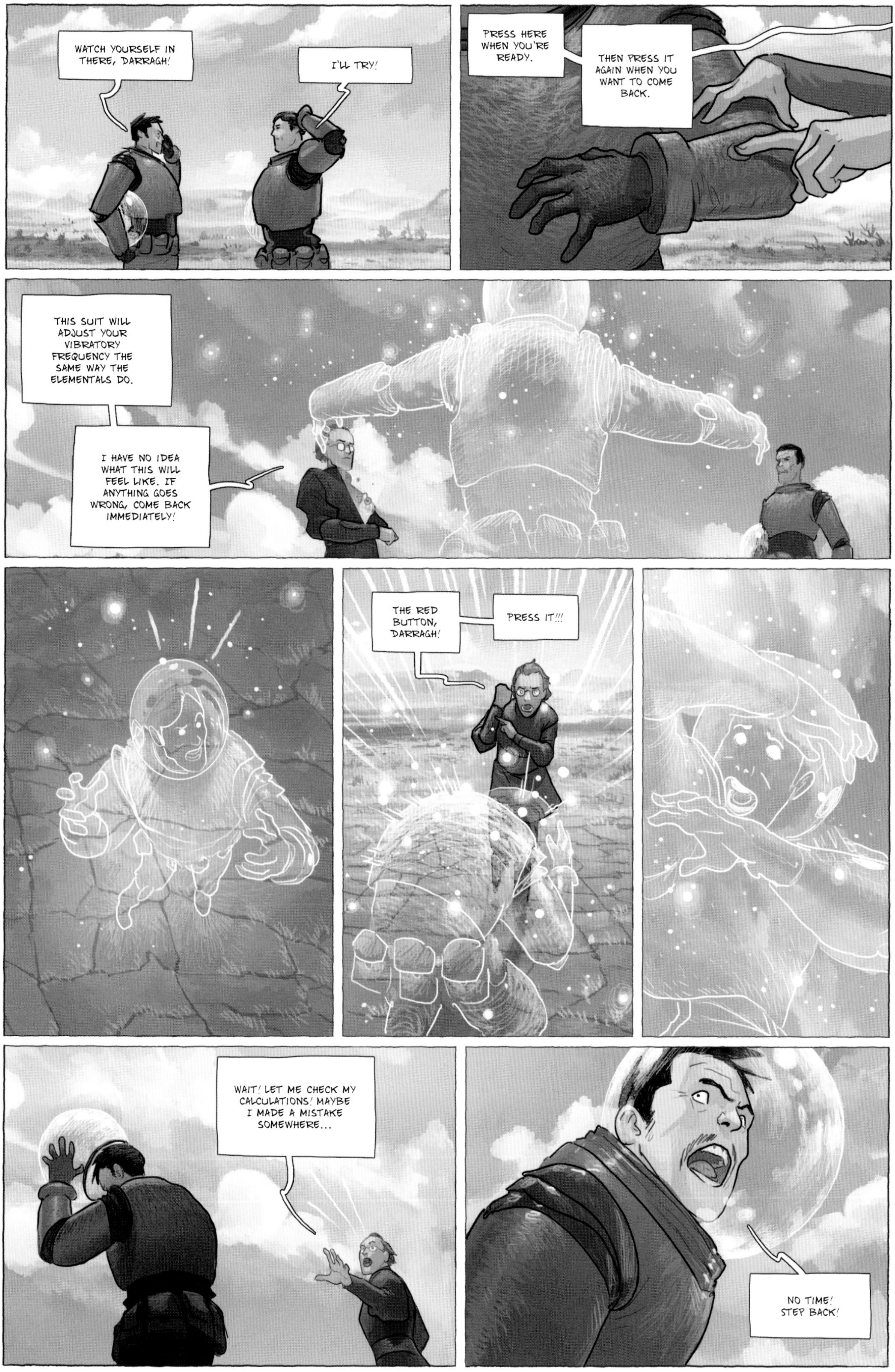
WATCH YOURSELF IN THERE, DARRAGH!
I'LL TRY!
PRESS HERE WHEN YOU'RE READY.
THEN PRESS IT AGAIN WHEN YOU WANT TO COME BACK.
THIS SUIT WILL ADJUST YOUR VIBRATORY FREQUENCY THE SAME WAY THE ELEMENTALS DO.
I HAVE NO IDEA WHAT THIS WILL FEEL LIKE. IF ANYTHING GOES WRONG, COME BACK IMMEDIATELY!
THE RED BUTTON, DARRAGH!
PRESS IT!!!
WAIT! LET ME CHECK MY CALCULATIONS! MAYBE I MADE A MISTAKE SOMEWHERE...
NO TIME! STEP BACK!

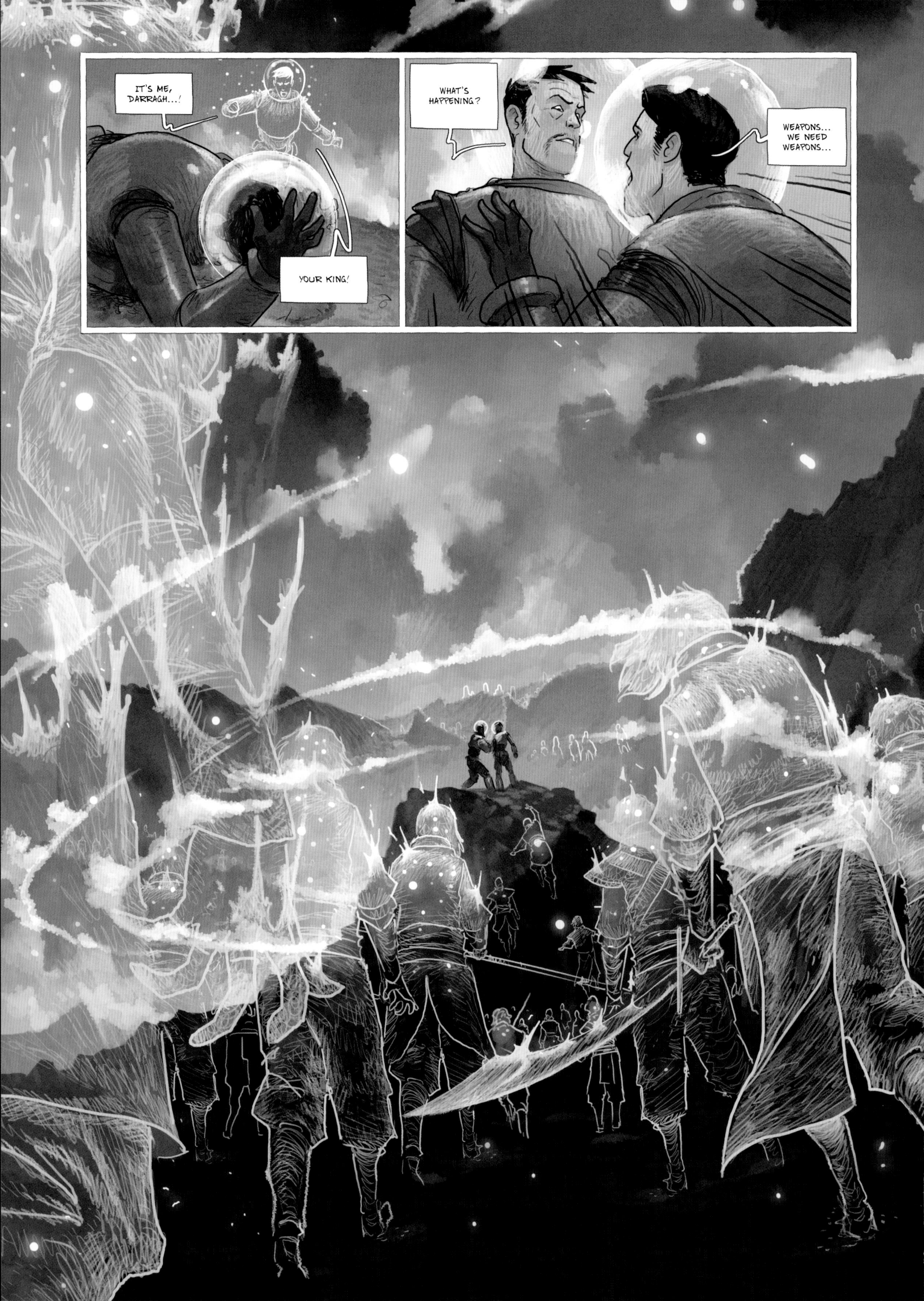
IT'S ME, DARRAGH...!
YOUR KING!
WHAT'S HAPPENING?
WEAPONS... WE NEED WEAPONS...

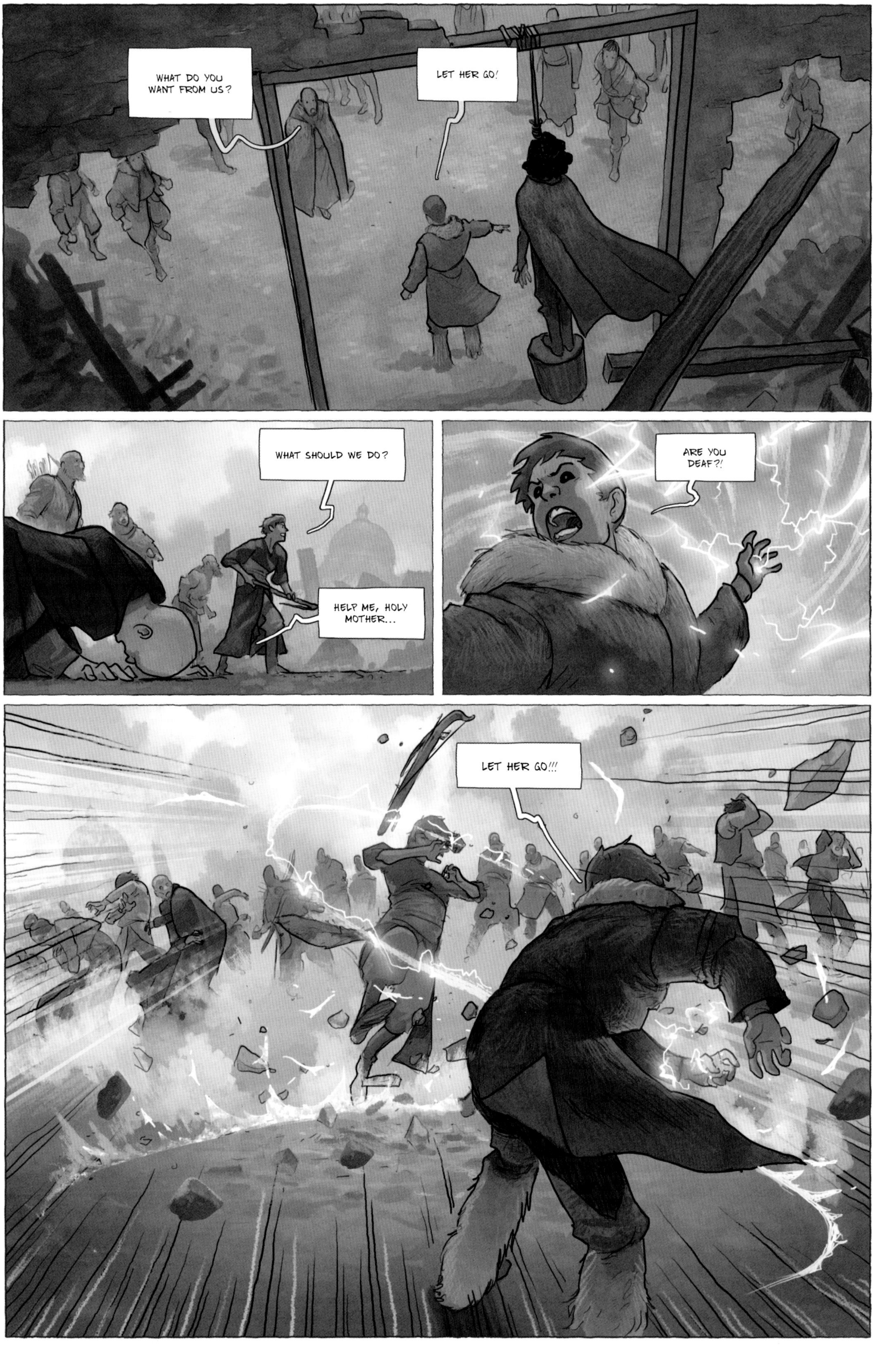
WHAT DO YOU WANT FROM US?
LET HER GO!
WHAT SHOULD WE DO?
HELP ME, HOLY MOTHER...
ARE YOU DEAF?!
LET HER GO!!!

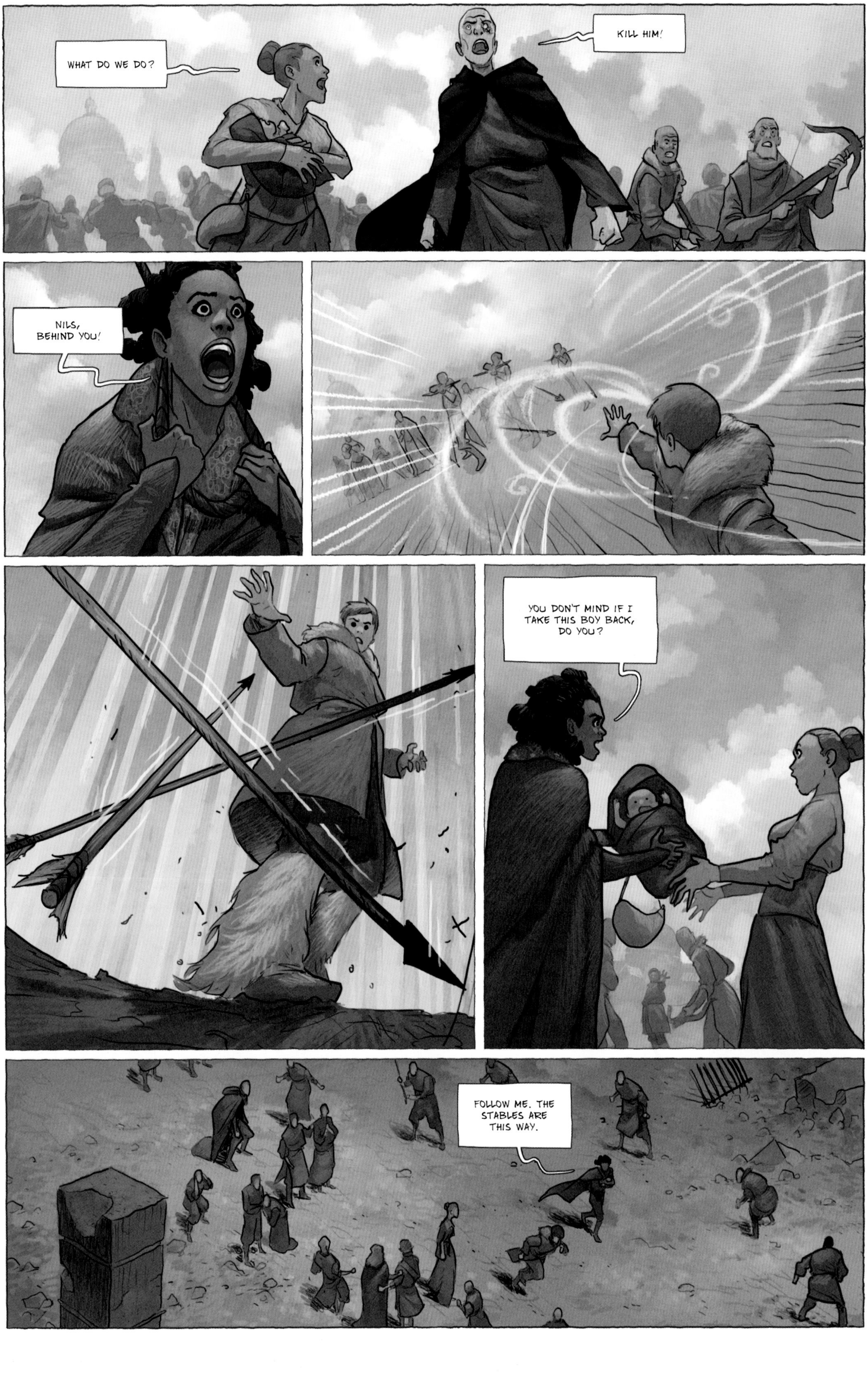
WHAT DO WE DO?
KILL HIM!
NILS, BEHIND YOU!
YOU DON'T MIND IF I TAKE THIS BOY BACK, DO YOU?
FOLLOW ME. THE STABLES ARE THIS WAY.

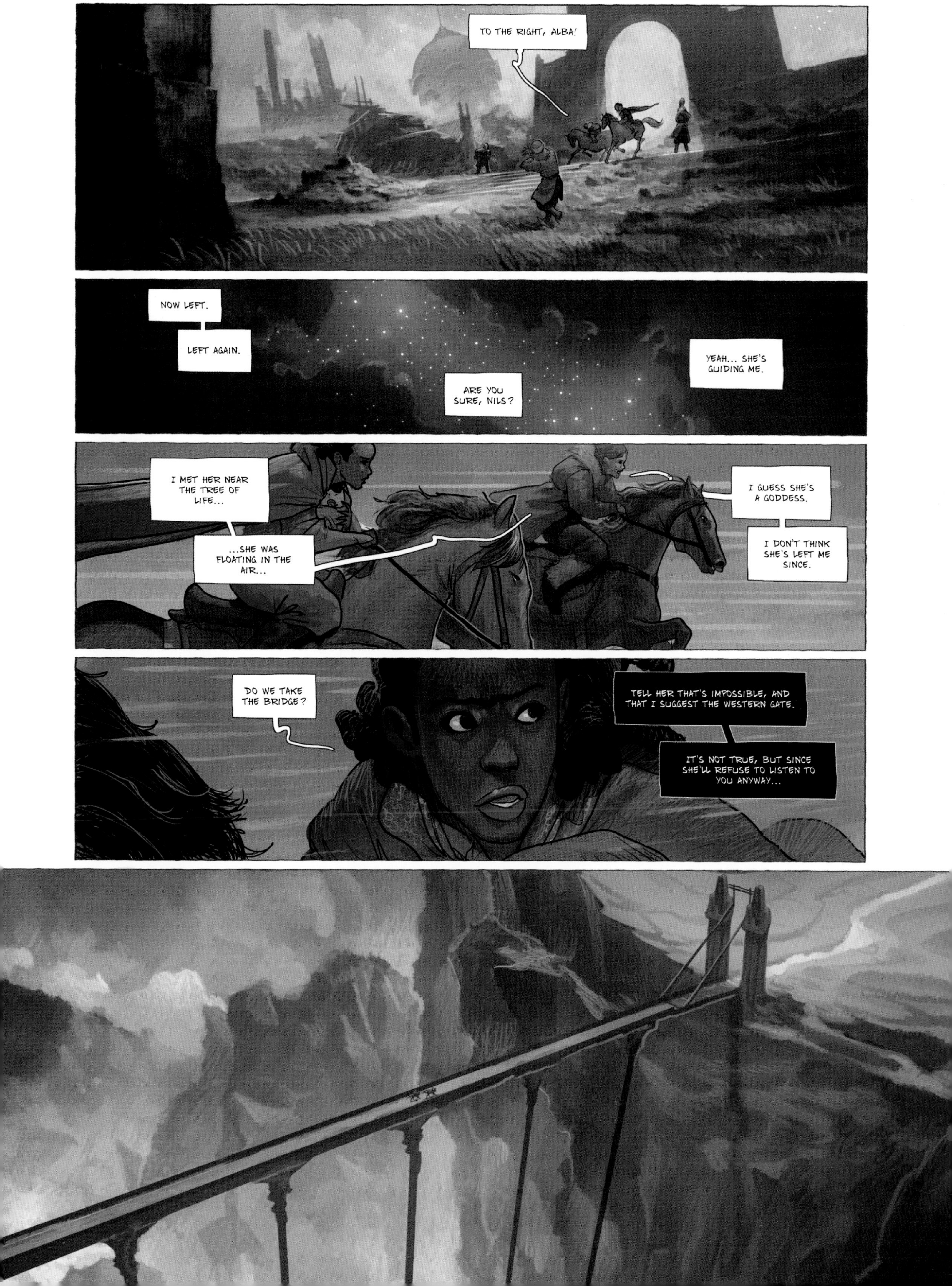

TO THE RIGHT, ALBA!
NOW LEFT.
LEFT AGAIN.
ARE YOU SURE, NILS?
YEAH... SHE'S GUIDING ME.
I MET HER NEAR THE TREE OF LIFE...
...SHE WAS FLOATING IN THE AIR...
I GUESS SHE'S A GODDESS.
I DON'T THINK SHE'S LEFT ME SINCE.
DO WE TAKE THE BRIDGE?
TELL HER THAT'S IMPOSSIBLE, AND THAT I SUGGEST THE WESTERN GATE.
IT'S NOT TRUE, BUT SINCE SHE'LL REFUSE TO LISTEN TO YOU ANYWAY...

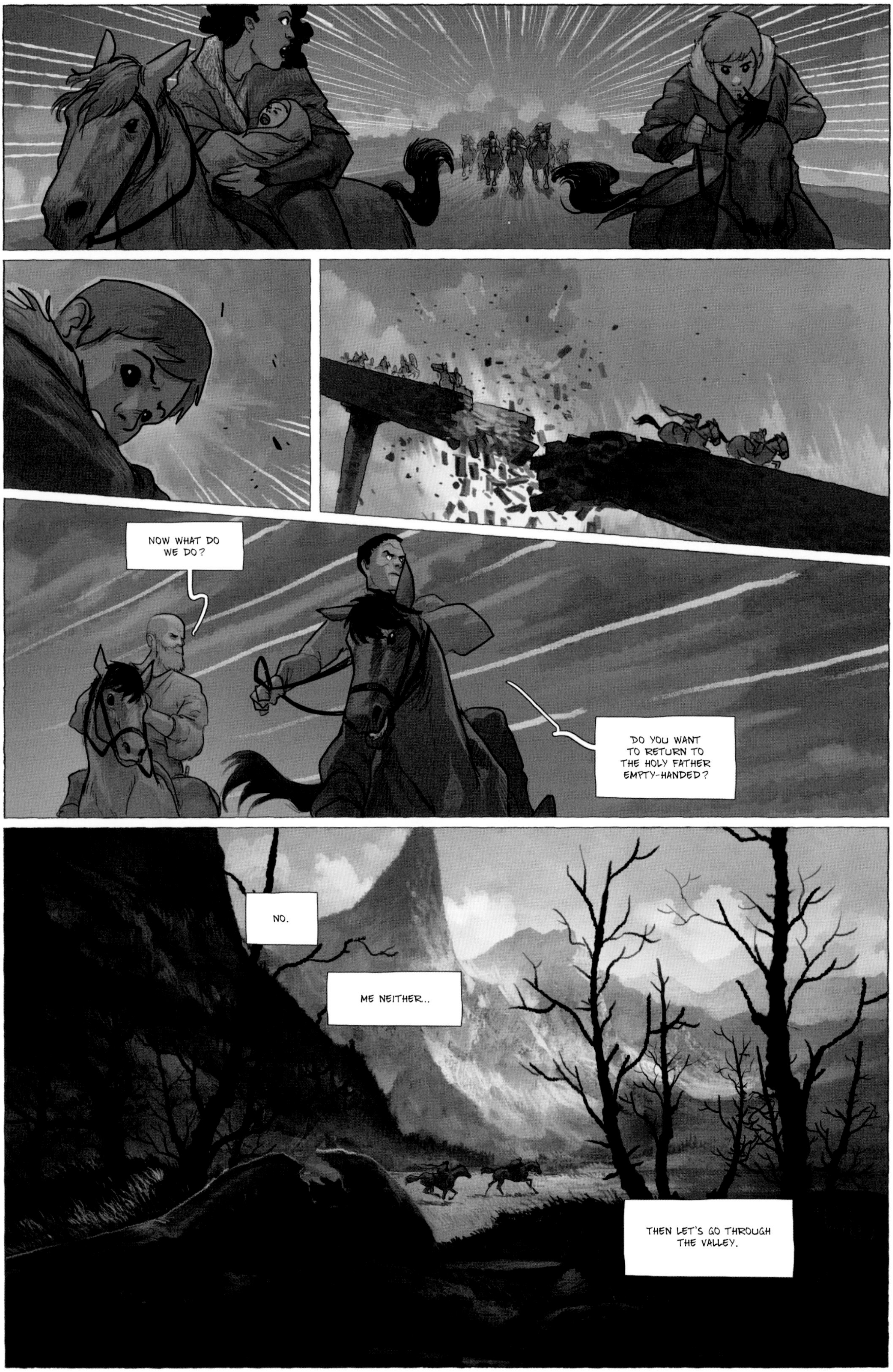
NOW WHAT DO WE DO?
DO YOU WANT TO RETURN TO THE HOLY FATHER EMPTY-HANDED?
NO.
ME NEITHER..
THEN LET'S GO THROUGH THE VALLEY.

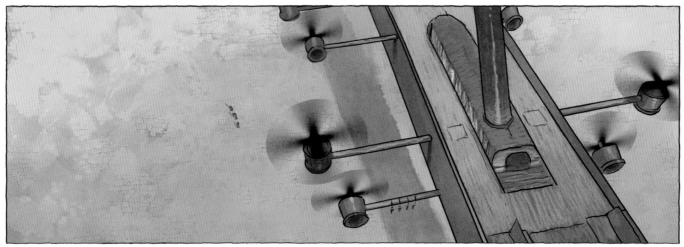

ALL THOSE DEAD... HOW CAN WE EVER FORGIVE OURSELVES?!

HE'S THERE, MY KING.

WHAT?

YOUR SON. HE'S THERE! A PROBE DETECTED HIS PRESENCE TWO THOUSAND KILOMETERS FROM YOUR ARRIVAL POINT!

EVERYONE WE KILLED... THEY WERE THERE!

DO YOU THINK WE CAN FIGHT THE DEAD?!

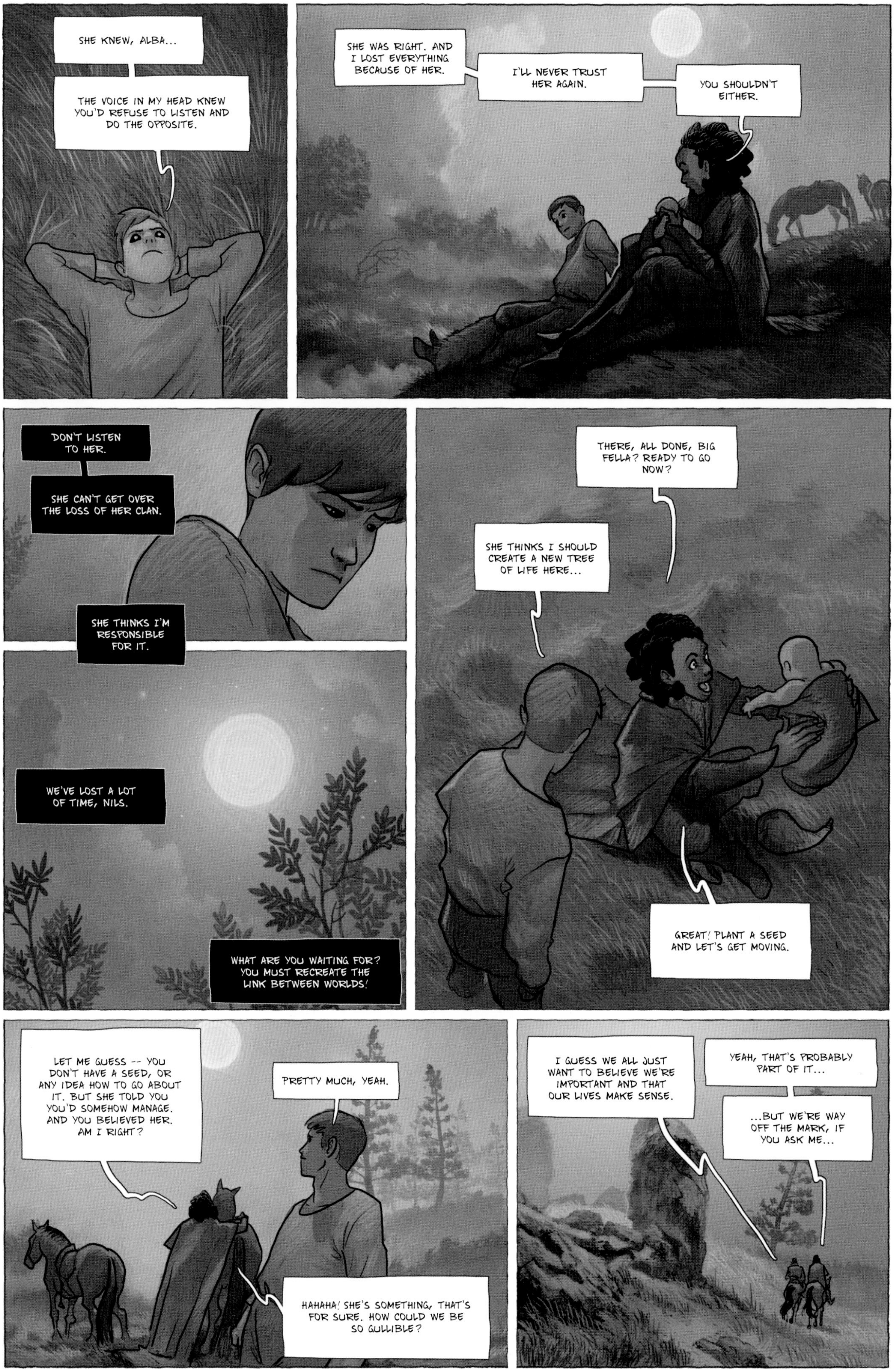

SHE KNEW, ALBA...
THE VOICE IN MY HEAD KNEW YOU'D REFUSE TO LISTEN AND DO THE OPPOSITE.
SHE WAS RIGHT. AND I LOST EVERYTHING BECAUSE OF HER.
I'LL NEVER TRUST HER AGAIN.
YOU SHOULDN'T EITHER.
DON'T LISTEN TO HER.
SHE CAN'T GET OVER THE LOSS OF HER CLAN.
SHE THINKS I'M RESPONSIBLE FOR IT.
WE'VE LOST A LOT OF TIME, NILS.
WHAT ARE YOU WAITING FOR? YOU MUST RECREATE THE LINK BETWEEN WORLDS!
THERE, ALL DONE, BIG FELLA? READY TO GO NOW?
SHE THINKS I SHOULD CREATE A NEW TREE OF LIFE HERE...
GREAT! PLANT A SEED AND LET'S GET MOVING.
LET ME GUESS -- YOU DON'T HAVE A SEED, OR ANY IDEA HOW TO GO ABOUT IT. BUT SHE TOLD YOU YOU'D SOMEHOW MANAGE. AND YOU BELIEVED HER. AM I RIGHT?
PRETTY MUCH, YEAH.
HAHAHA! SHE'S SOMETHING, THAT'S FOR SURE. HOW COULD WE BE SO GULLIBLE?
I GUESS WE ALL JUST WANT TO BELIEVE WE'RE IMPORTANT AND THAT OUR LIVES MAKE SENSE.
YEAH, THAT'S PROBABLY PART OF IT...
...BUT WE'RE WAY OFF THE MARK, IF YOU ASK ME...

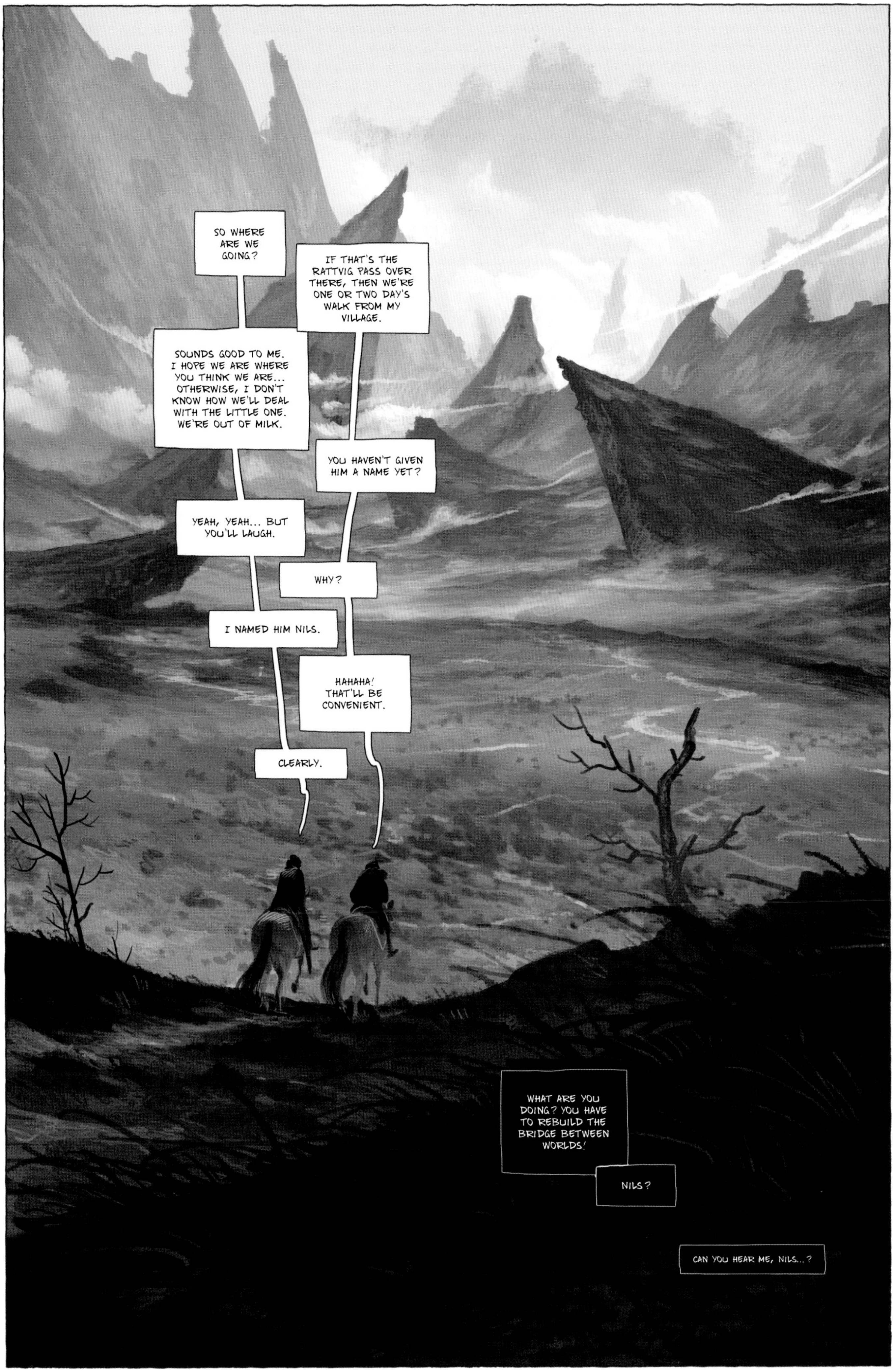
SO WHERE ARE WE GOING?
IF THAT'S THE RATTVIG PASS OVER THERE, THEN WE'RE ONE OR TWO DAY'S WALK FROM MY VILLAGE.
SOUNDS GOOD TO ME. I HOPE WE ARE WHERE YOU THINK WE ARE... OTHERWISE, I DON'T KNOW HOW WE'LL DEAL WITH THE LITTLE ONE. WE'RE OUT OF MILK.
YOU HAVEN'T GIVEN HIM A NAME YET?
YEAH, YEAH... BUT YOU'LL LAUGH.
WHY?
I NAMED HIM NILS.
HAHAHA! THAT'LL BE CONVENIENT.
CLEARLY.
WHAT ARE YOU DOING? YOU HAVE TO REBUILD THE BRIDGE BETWEEN WORLDS!
NILS?
CAN YOU HEAR ME, NILS...?

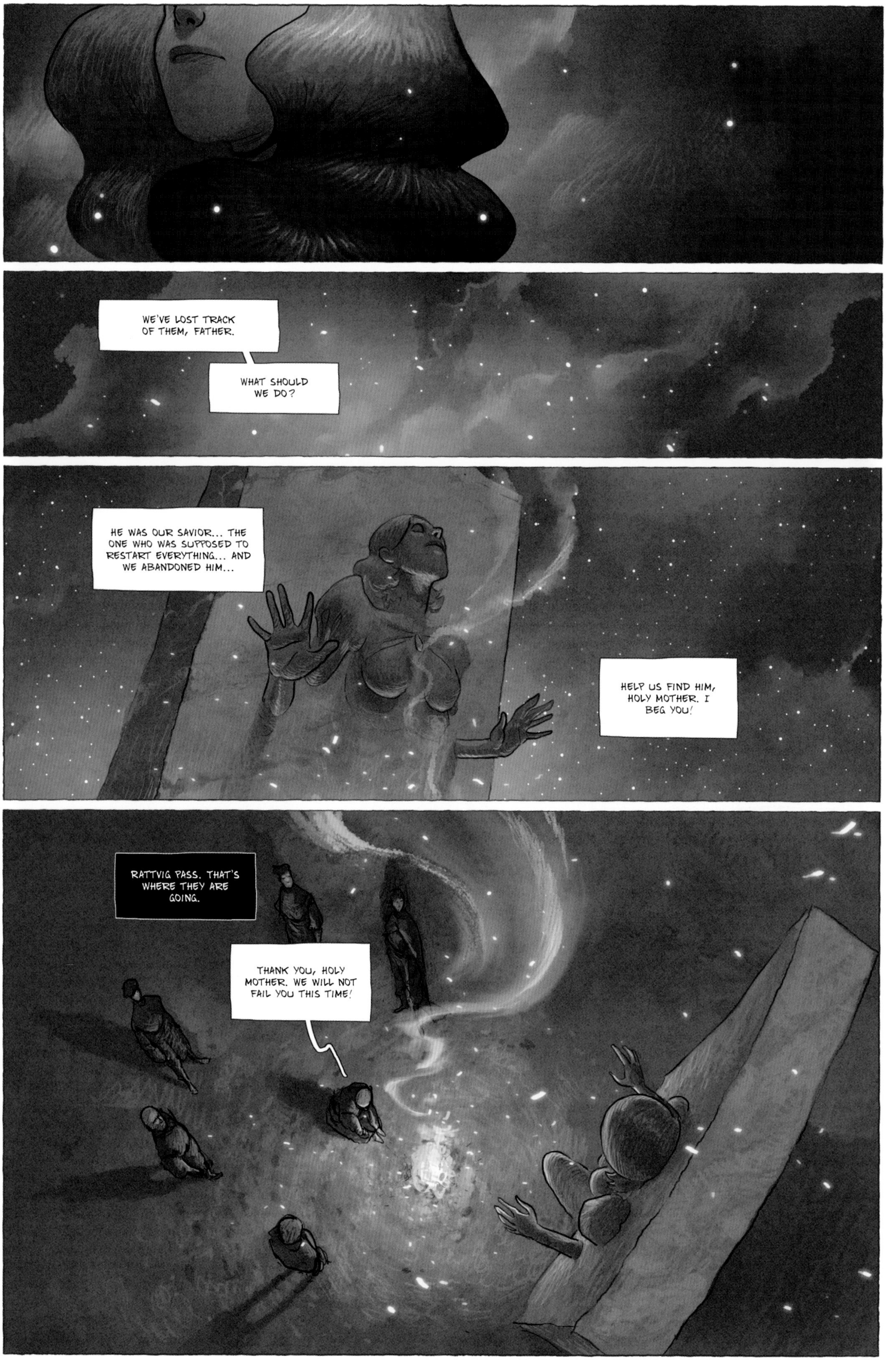
WE'VE LOST TRACK OF THEM, FATHER.
WHAT SHOULD WE DO?
HE WAS OUR SAVIOR... THE ONE WHO WAS SUPPOSED TO RESTART EVERYTHING... AND WE ABANDONED HIM...
HELP US FIND HIM, HOLY MOTHER. I BEG YOU!
RATTVIG PASS. THAT'S WHERE THEY ARE GOING.
THANK YOU, HOLY MOTHER. WE WILL NOT FAIL YOU THIS TIME!

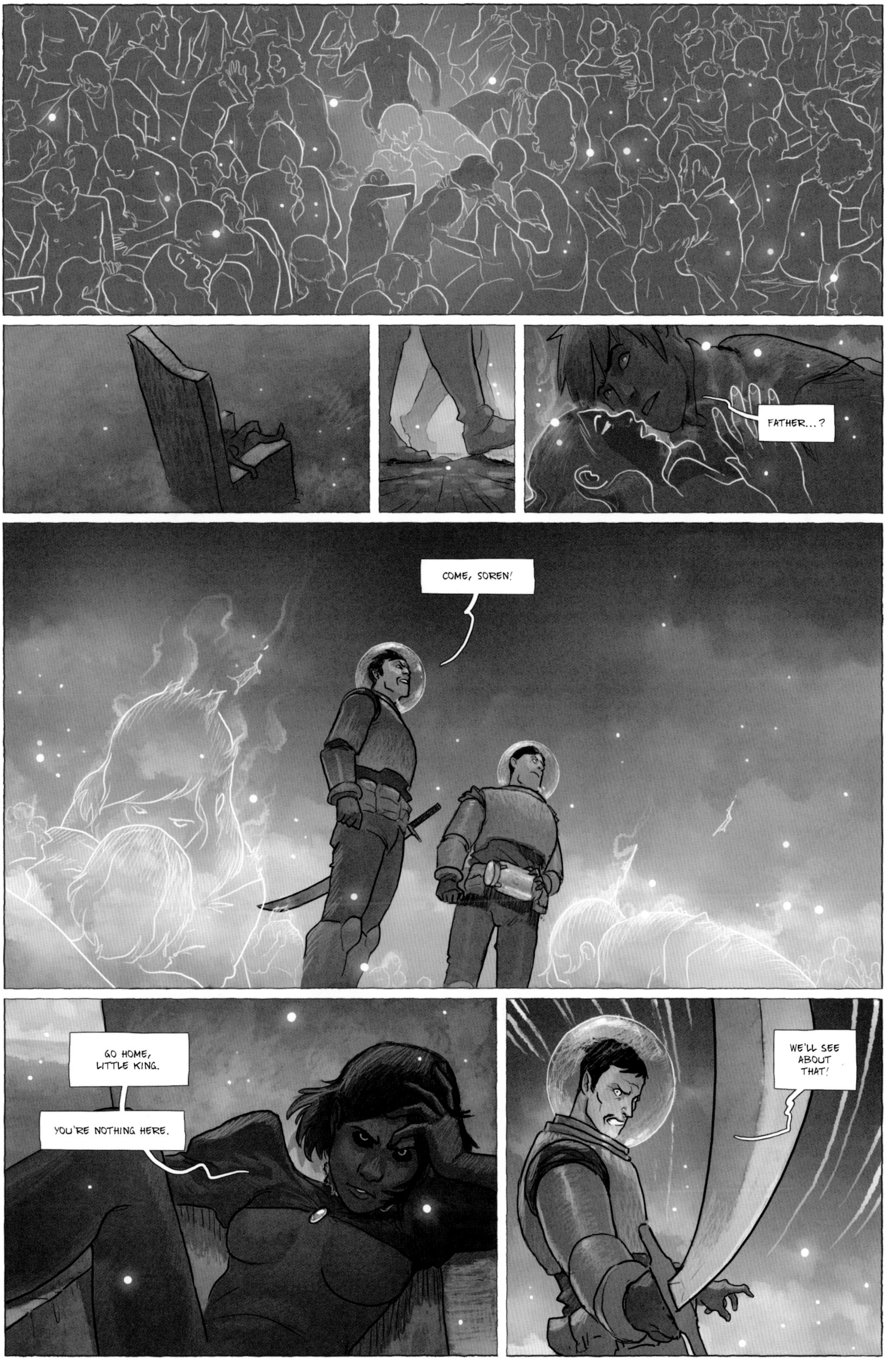
FATHER...?
COME, SOREN!
GO HOME, LITTLE KING.
YOU'RE NOTHING HERE.
WE'LL SEE ABOUT THAT!

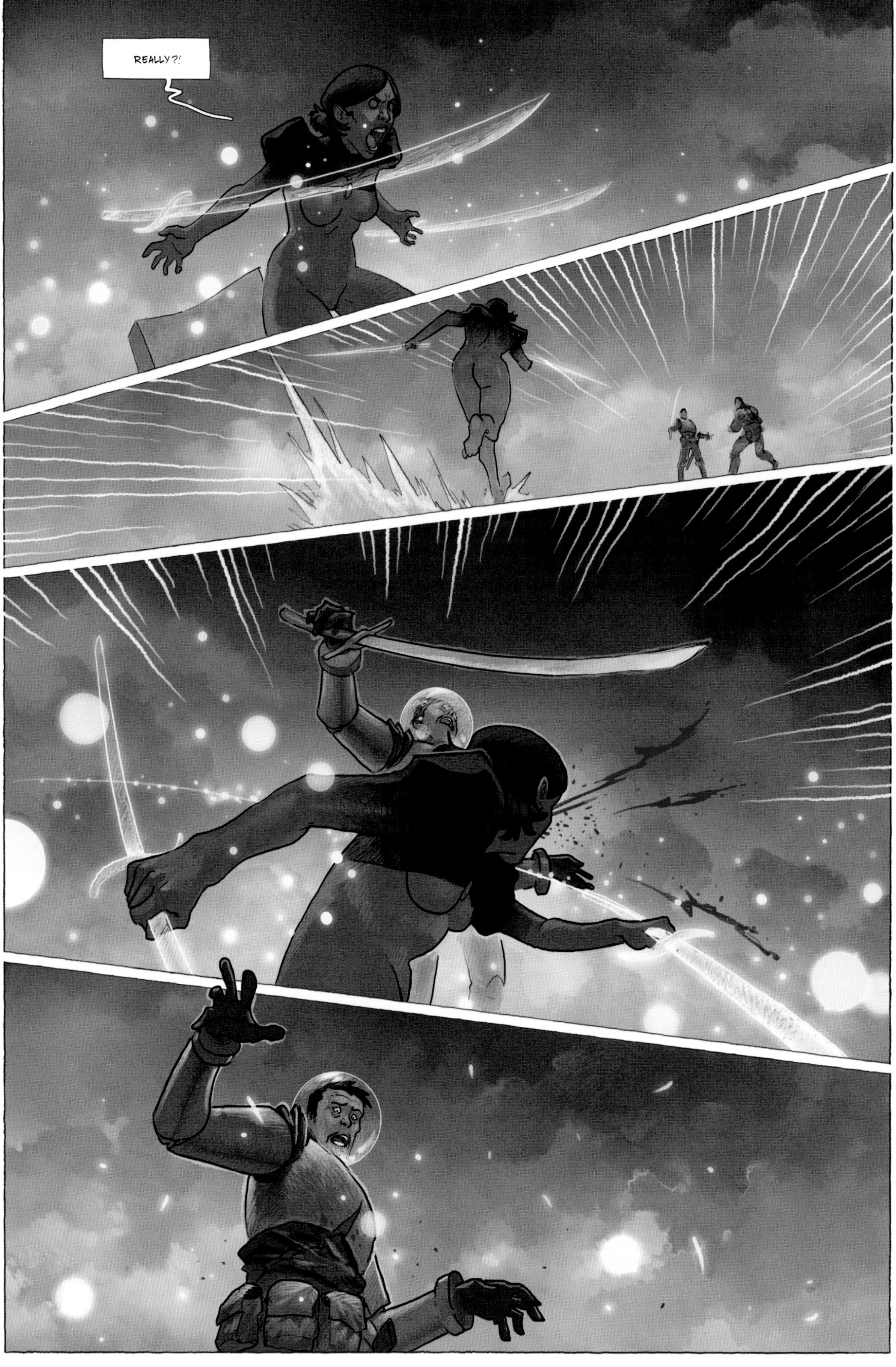
REALLY?!

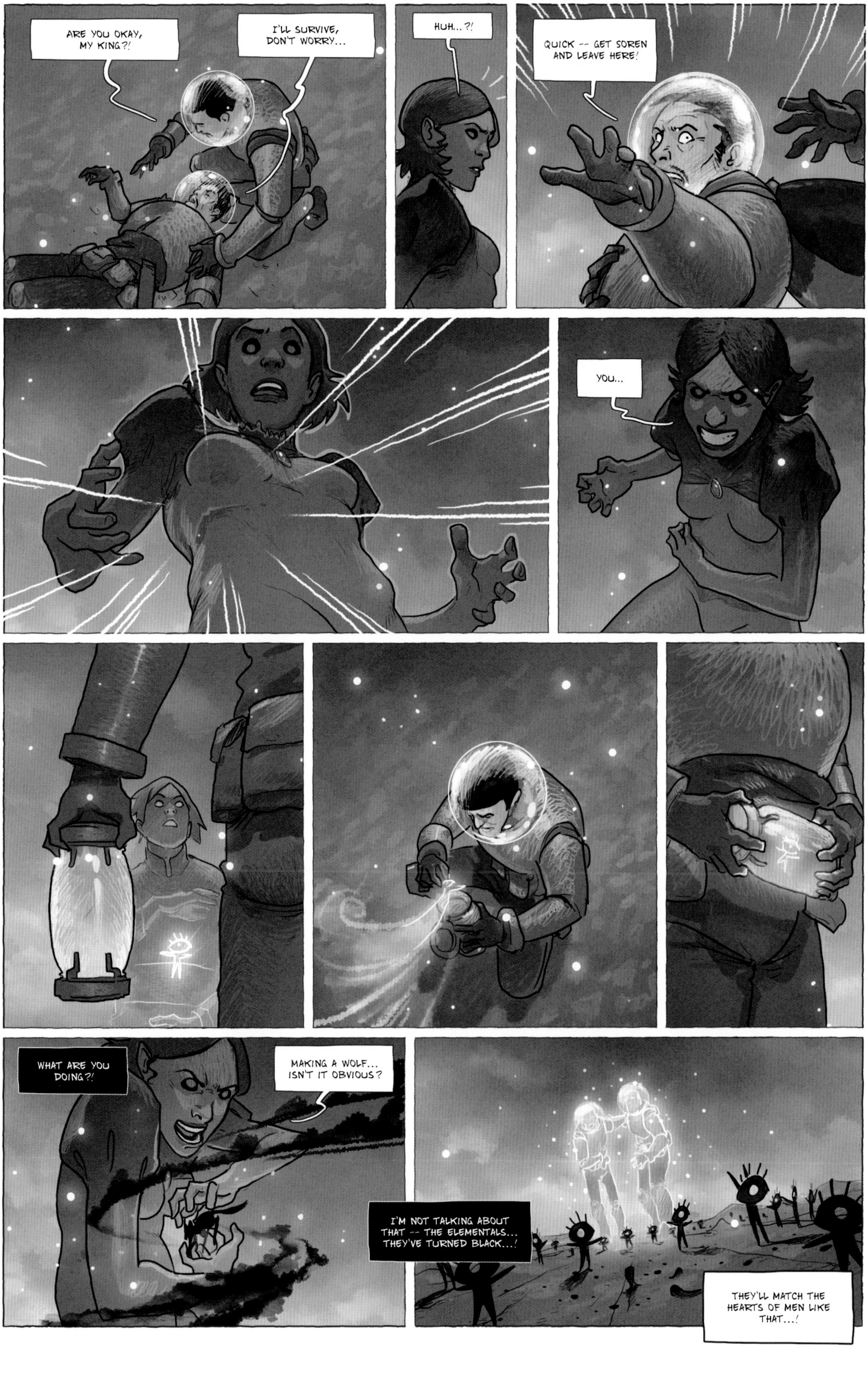

ARE YOU OKAY, MY KING?!
I'LL SURVIVE, DON'T WORRY...
HUH...?!
QUICK -- GET SOREN AND LEAVE HERE!
YOU...
WHAT ARE YOU DOING?!
MAKING A WOLF... ISN'T IT OBVIOUS?
I'M NOT TALKING ABOUT THAT -- THE ELEMENTALS... THEY'VE TURNED BLACK...!
THEY'LL MATCH THE HEARTS OF MEN LIKE THAT...!

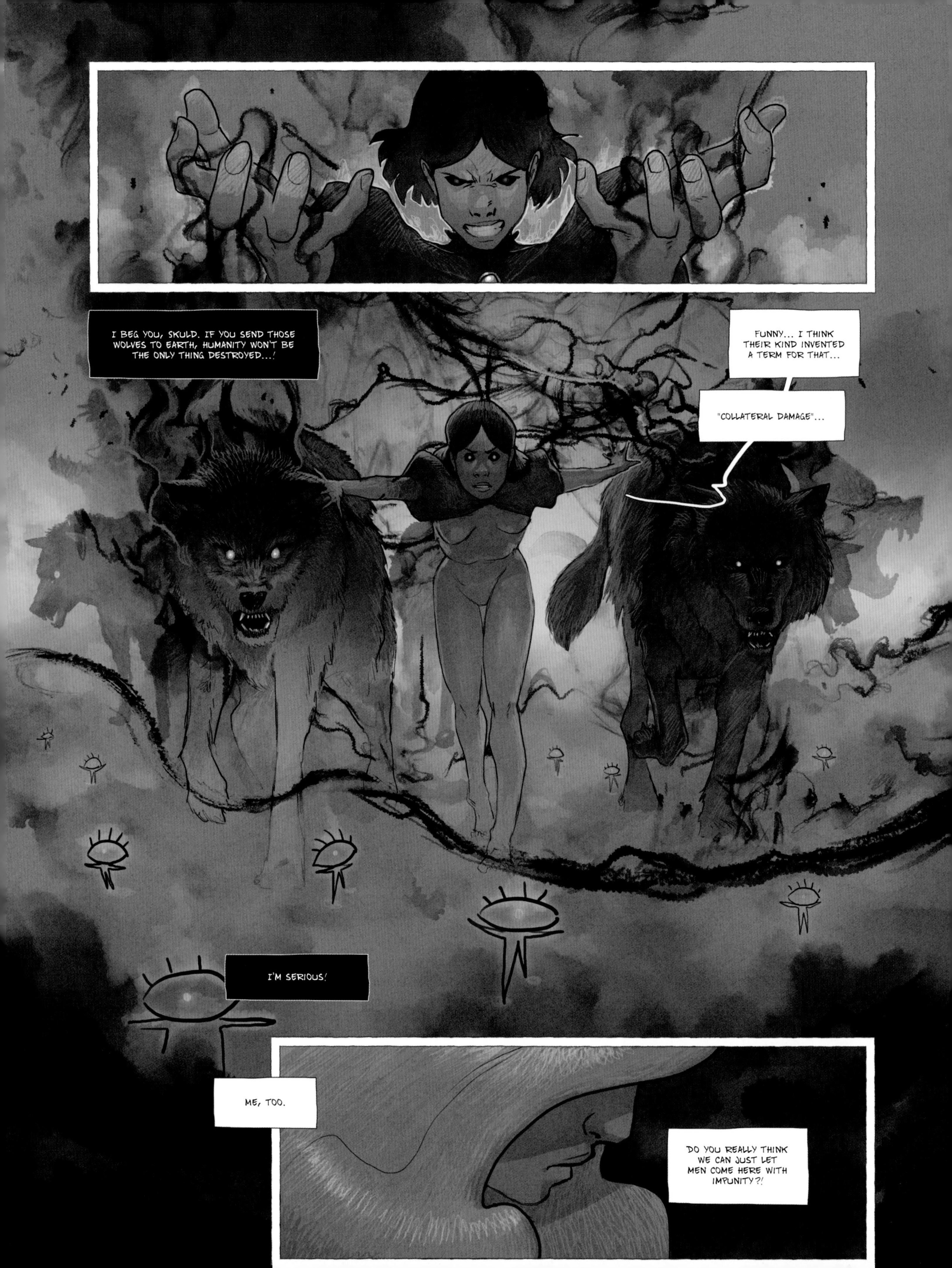
I BEG YOU, SKULD. IF YOU SEND THOSE WOLVES TO EARTH, HUMANITY WON'T BE THE ONLY THING DESTROYED...!
FUNNY... I THINK THEIR KIND INVENTED A TERM FOR THAT...
"COLLATERAL DAMAGE"...
I'M SERIOUS!
ME, TOO.
DO YOU REALLY THINK WE CAN JUST LET MEN COME HERE WITH IMPUNITY?!

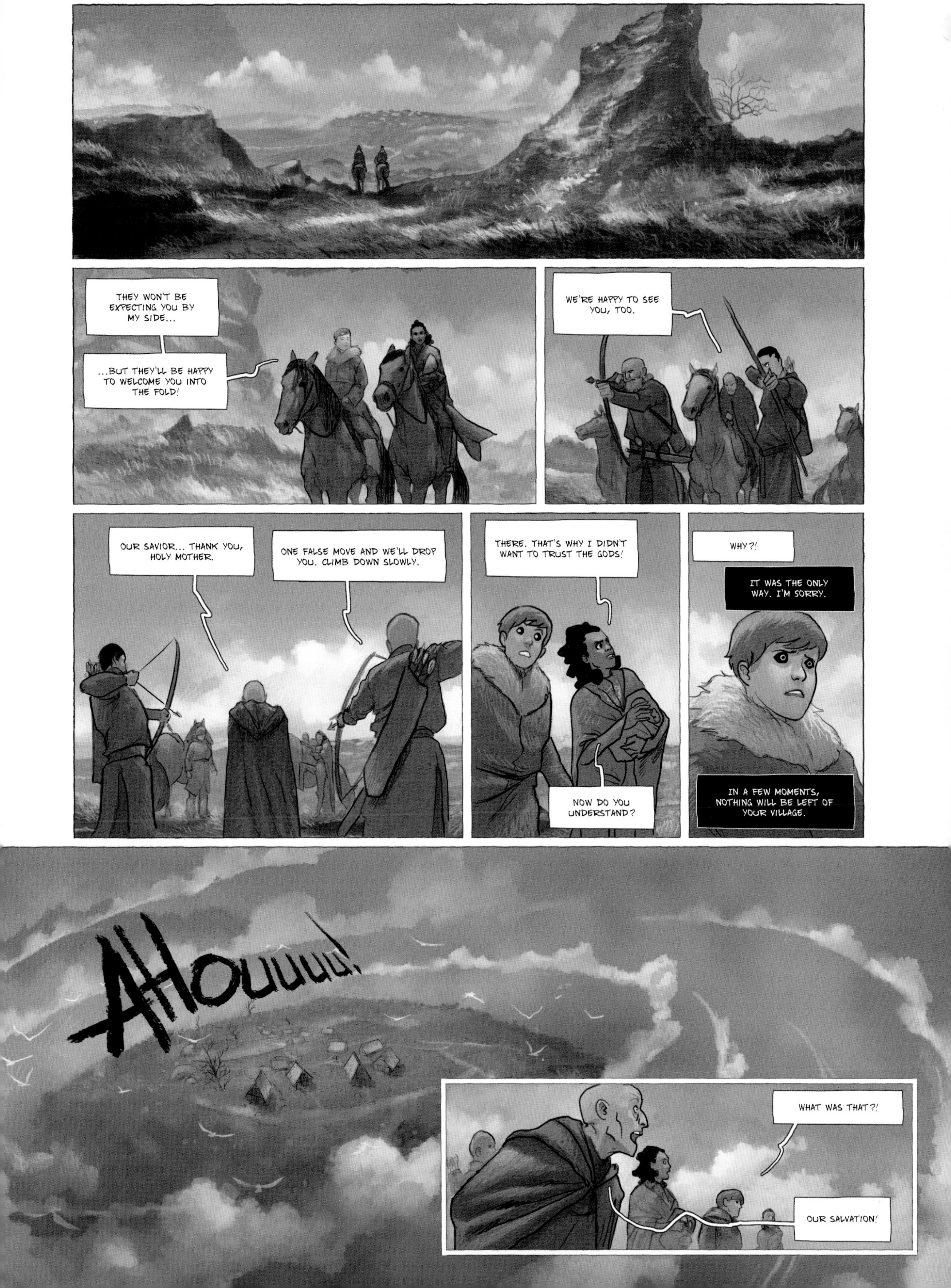
THEY WON'T BE EXPECTING YOU BY MY SIDE...
...BUT THEY'LL BE HAPPY TO WELCOME YOU INTO THE FOLD!
WE'RE HAPPY TO SEE YOU, TOO.
OUR SAVIOR... THANK YOU, HOLY MOTHER.
ONE FALSE MOVE AND WE'LL DROP YOU. CLIMB DOWN SLOWLY.
THERE. THAT'S WHY I DIDN'T WANT TO TRUST THE GODS!
NOW DO YOU UNDERSTAND?
WHY?!
IT WAS THE ONLY WAY. I'M SORRY.
IN A FEW MOMENTS, NOTHING WILL BE LEFT OF YOUR VILLAGE.
AHouuuu!
WHAT WAS THAT?!
OUR SALVATION!

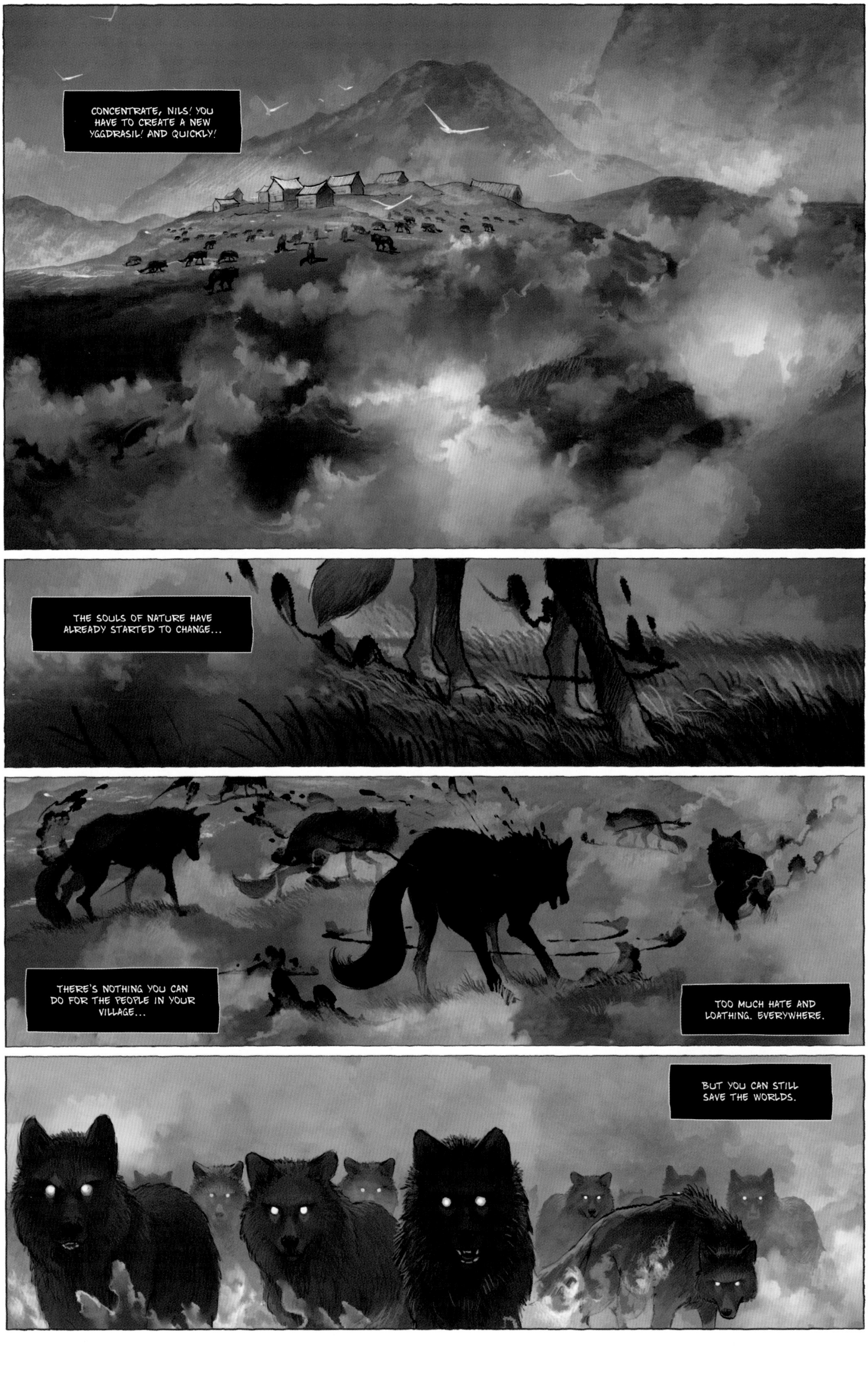
CONCENTRATE, NILS! YOU HAVE TO CREATE A NEW YGGDRASIL! AND QUICKLY!
THE SOULS OF NATURE HAVE ALREADY STARTED TO CHANGE...
THERE'S NOTHING YOU CAN DO FOR THE PEOPLE IN YOUR VILLAGE...
TOO MUCH HATE AND LOATHING. EVERYWHERE.
BUT YOU CAN STILL SAVE THE WORLDS.

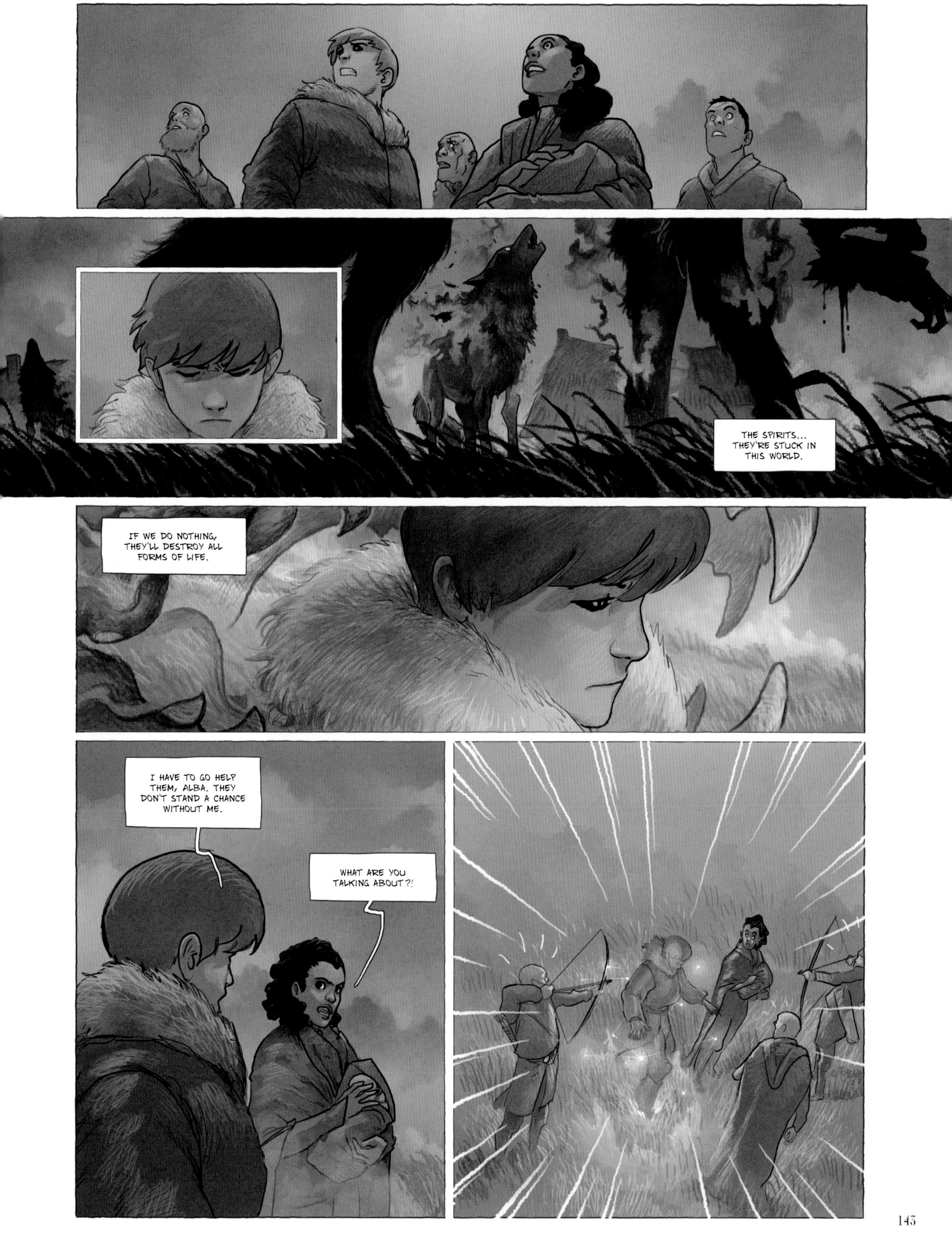
THE SPIRITS... THEY'RE STUCK IN THIS WORLD.
IF WE DO NOTHING, THEY'LL DESTROY ALL FORMS OF LIFE.
I HAVE TO GO HELP THEM, ALBA. THEY DON'T STAND A CHANCE WITHOUT ME.
WHAT ARE YOU TALKING ABOUT?!

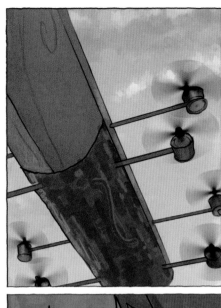

I DON'T UNDERSTAND WHY IT'S NOT WORKING...

MAYBE THE PRINCE WAS UNCONSCIOUS FOR TOO LONG...?

...I'M SORRY, MY KING.

IT'S NOT YOUR FAULT... THIS IS ALL BECAUSE OF THOSE CREATURES... DO YOU THINK IT'S POSSIBLE TO SEND THE REMAINING ELEMENTALS BACK TO THEIR WORLD?

YOU WANT TO DESTROY THEM?

YES... AS LONG AS THE GODS EXIST, MAN WILL NEVER BE FREE.

WILL THIS NEVER END...?

WHAT'S HAPPENED TO YOU, DARRAGH? CAN'T YOU SEE THEY'RE OUR ENEMIES?

YOU'RE RIGHT.

I'M SORRY, MY KING.

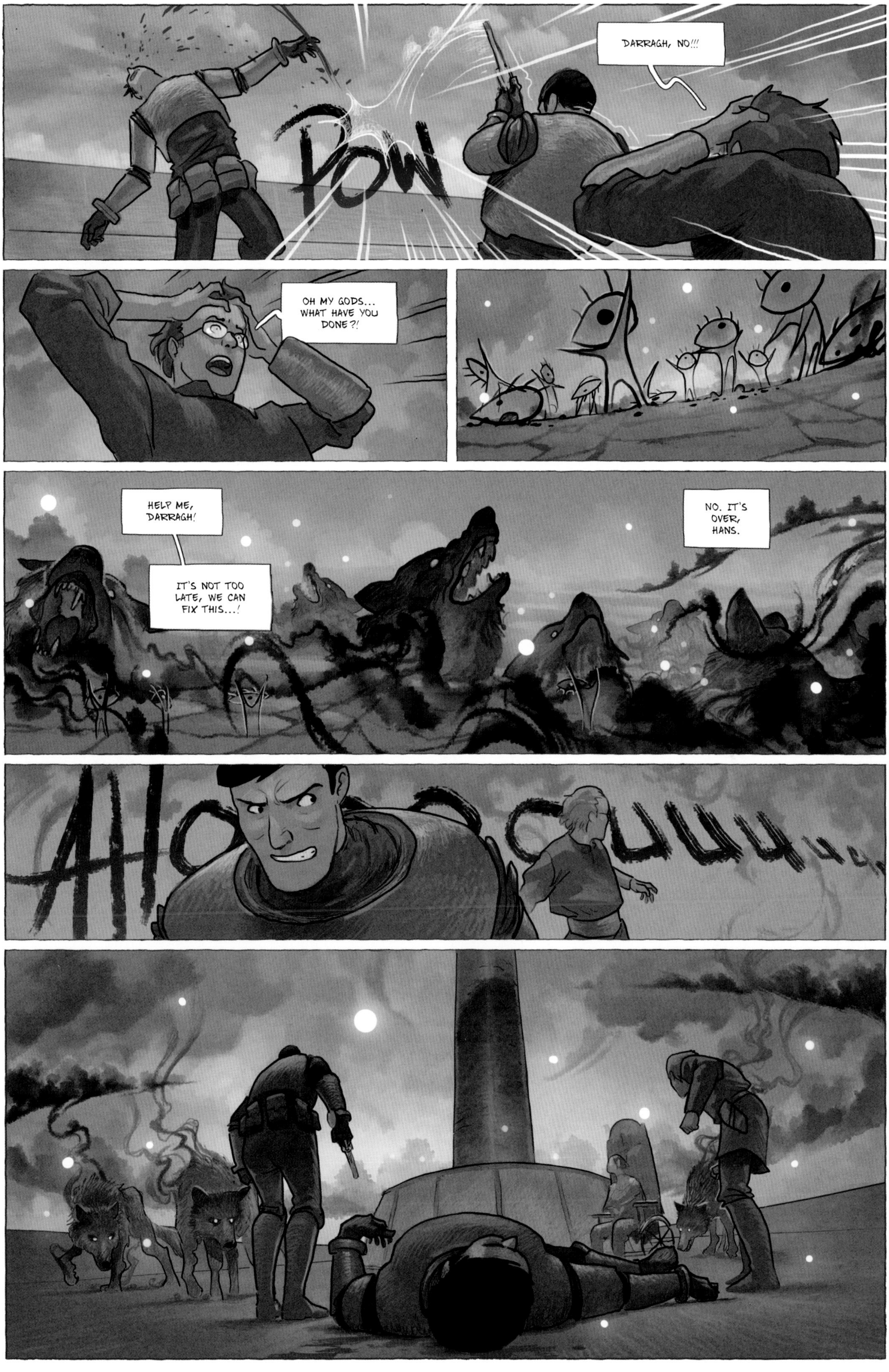
DARRAGH, NO!!!
POW
OH MY GODS... WHAT HAVE YOU DONE?!
HELP ME, DARRAGH!
IT'S NOT TOO LATE, WE CAN FIX THIS...!
NO. IT'S OVER, HANS.
AHOOOUUUU...

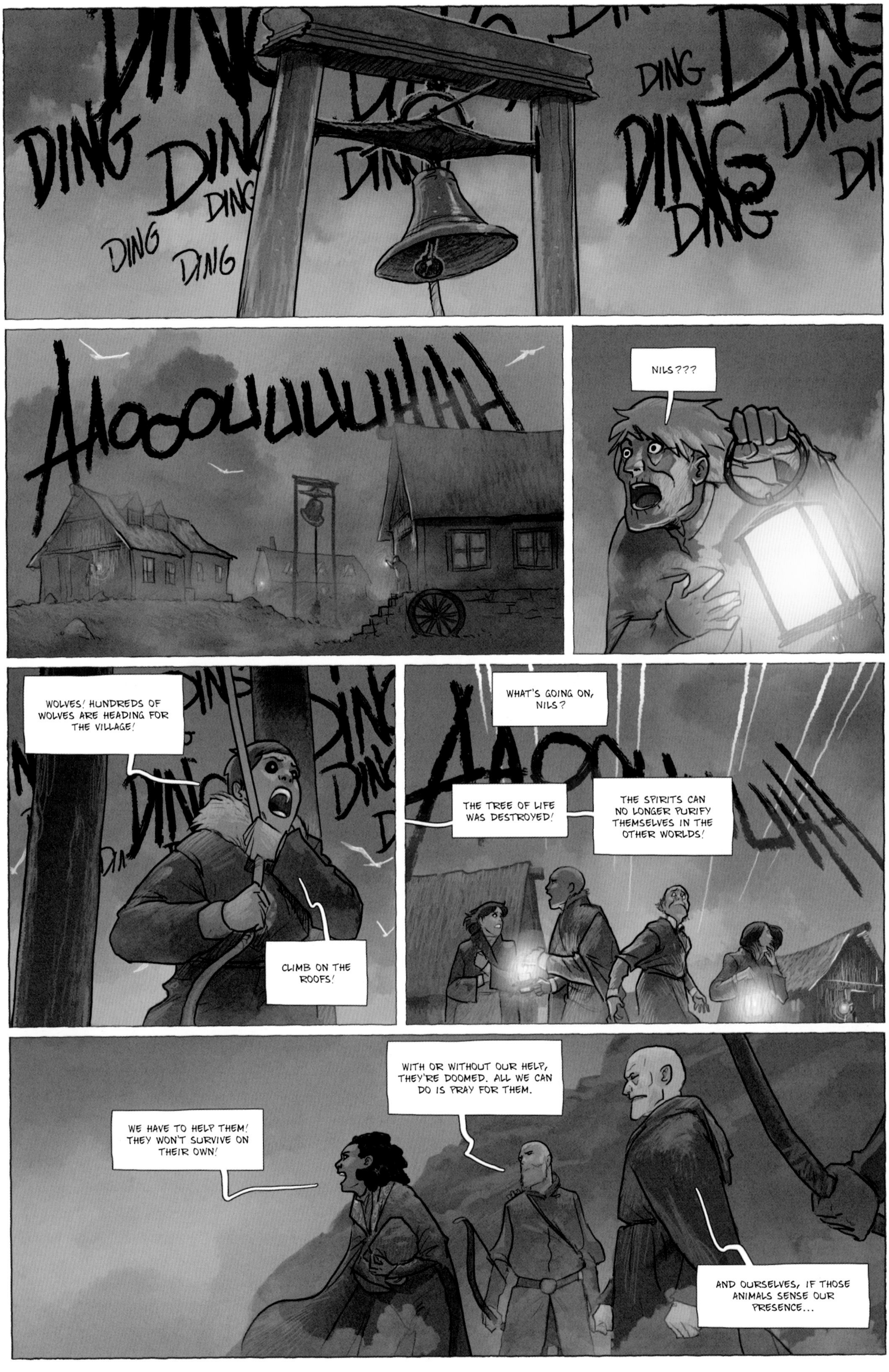
DING DING DING DING DING DING
DING DING DING DING DING DING
AAOOOUUUUHHH
NILS???
WOLVES! HUNDREDS OF WOLVES ARE HEADING FOR THE VILLAGE!
CLIMB ON THE ROOFS!
WHAT'S GOING ON, NILS?
THE TREE OF LIFE WAS DESTROYED!
THE SPIRITS CAN NO LONGER PURIFY THEMSELVES IN THE OTHER WORLDS!
WE HAVE TO HELP THEM! THEY WON'T SURVIVE ON THEIR OWN!
WITH OR WITHOUT OUR HELP, THEY'RE DOOMED. ALL WE CAN DO IS PRAY FOR THEM.
AND OURSELVES, IF THOSE ANIMALS SENSE OUR PRESENCE...

I TOLD YOU... YOU CAN'T DO ANYTHING FOR THEM...

...BUT YOU CAN STILL SAVE THIS WORLD! COME ON!

NO.

NOW I UNDERSTAND WHY YOU WERE SO AFRAID I'D BREAK MY NECK UP HERE, POP...

...THIS CLIFF IS PRETTY IMPRESSIVE FROM UP HERE!

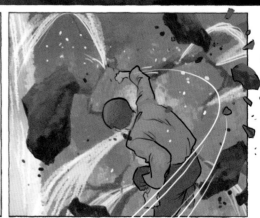

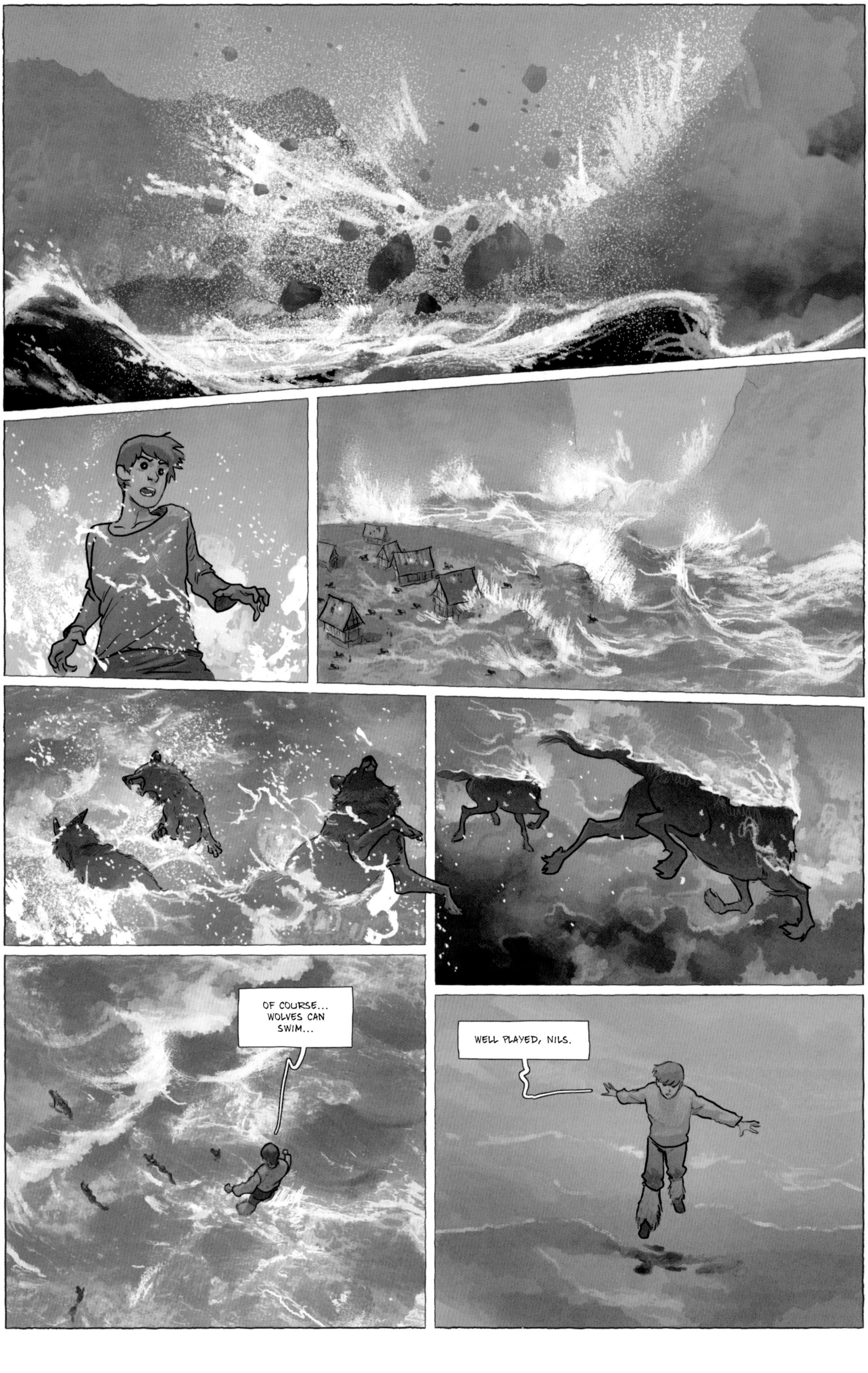
OF COURSE... WOLVES CAN SWIM...
WELL PLAYED, NILS.

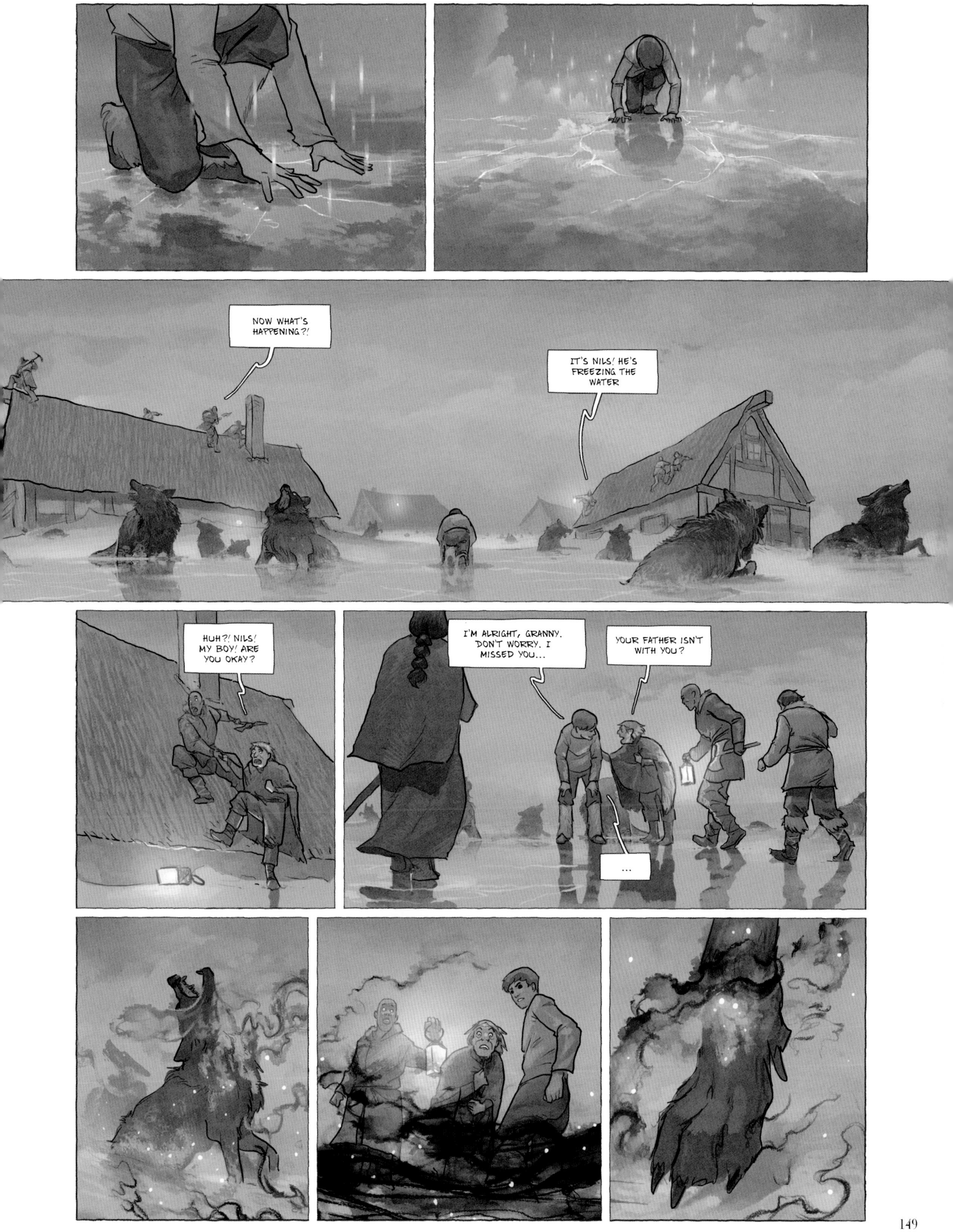
NOW WHAT'S HAPPENING?!
IT'S NILS! HE'S FREEZING THE WATER
HUH?! NILS! MY BOY! ARE YOU OKAY?
I'M ALRIGHT, GRANNY. DON'T WORRY. I MISSED YOU...
YOUR FATHER ISN'T WITH YOU?
...

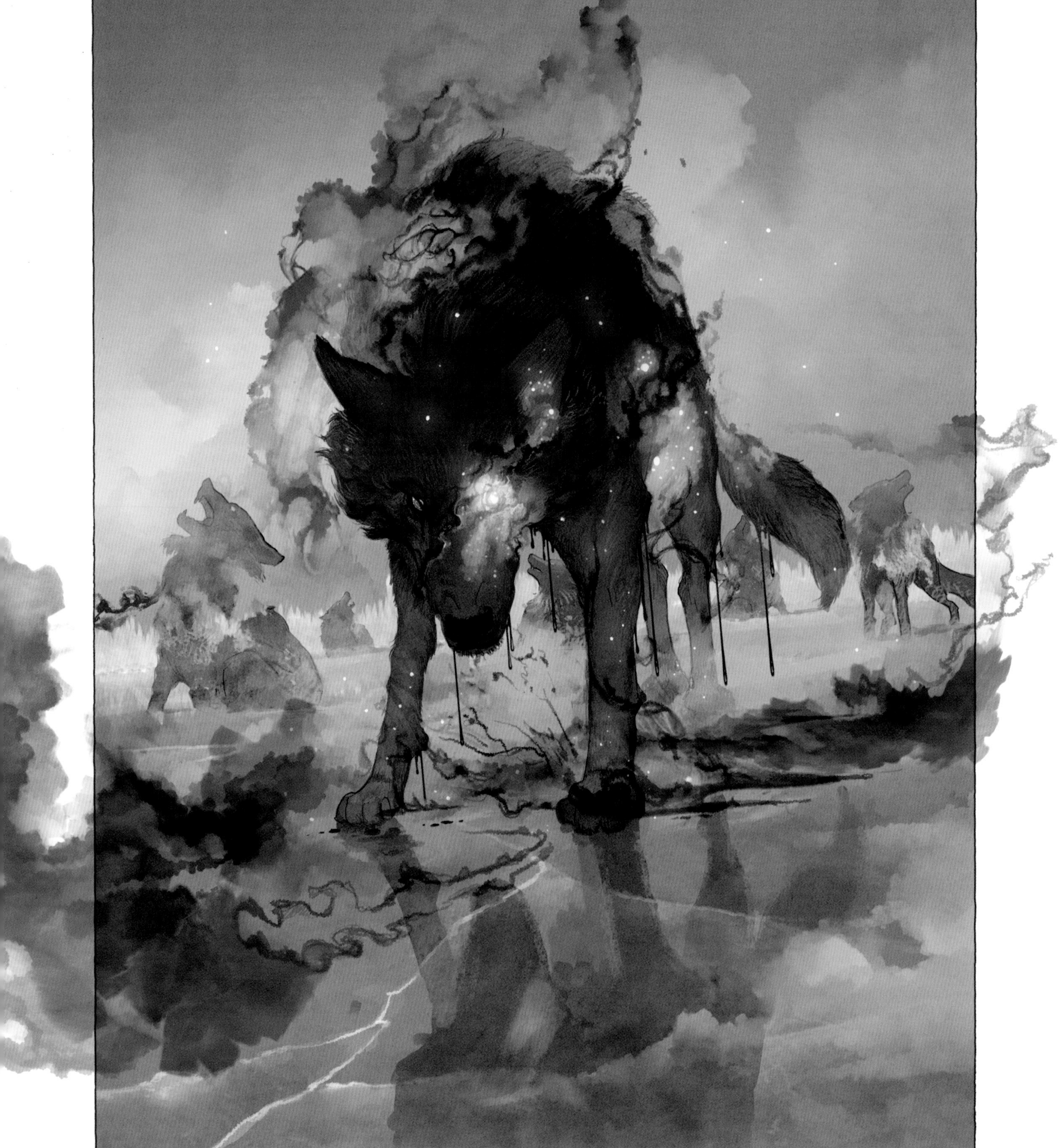

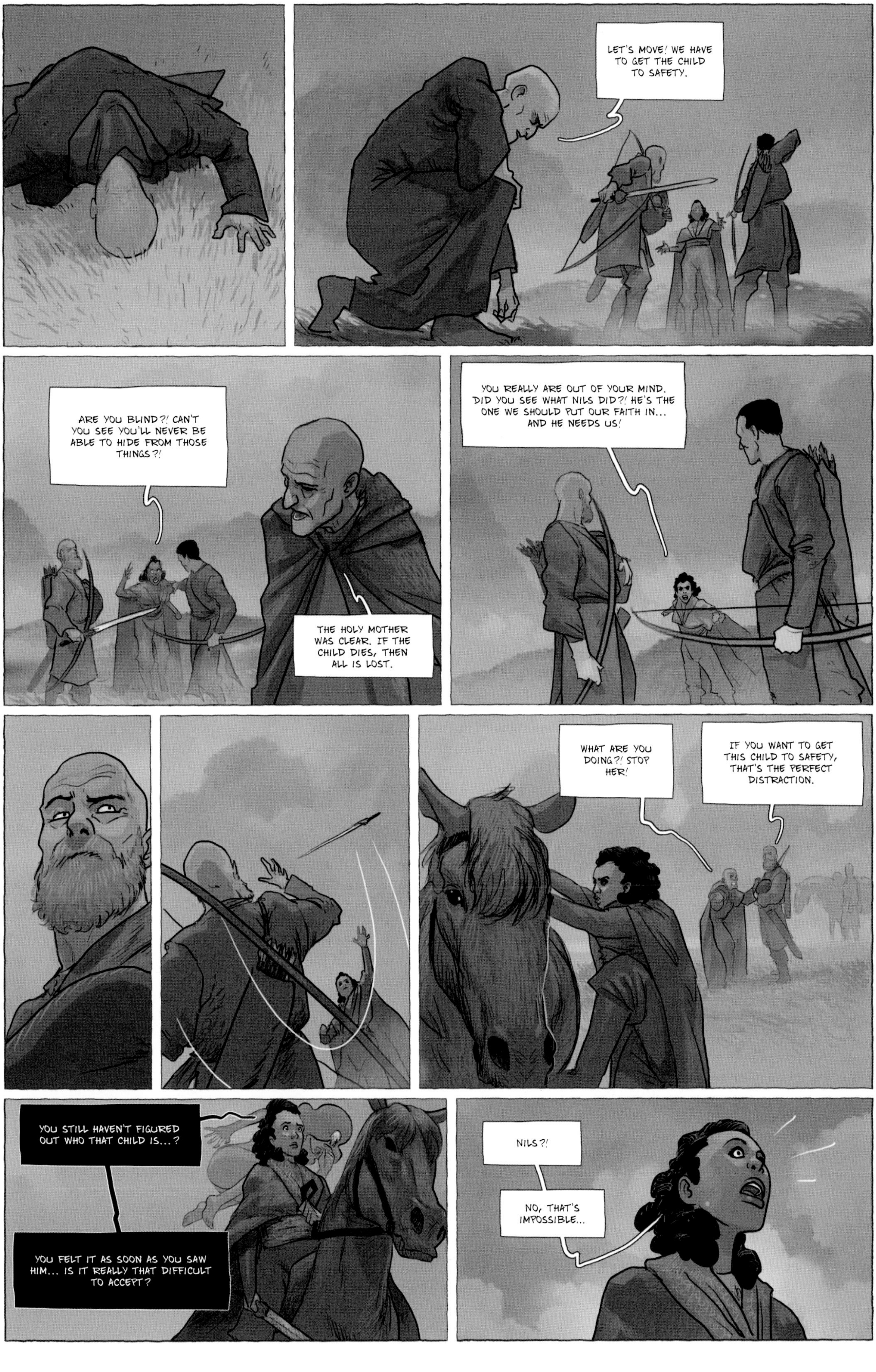
LET'S MOVE! WE HAVE TO GET THE CHILD TO SAFETY.
ARE YOU BLIND?! CAN'T YOU SEE YOU'LL NEVER BE ABLE TO HIDE FROM THOSE THINGS?!
THE HOLY MOTHER WAS CLEAR. IF THE CHILD DIES, THEN ALL IS LOST.
YOU REALLY ARE OUT OF YOUR MIND. DID YOU SEE WHAT NILS DID?! HE'S THE ONE WE SHOULD PUT OUR FAITH IN... AND HE NEEDS US!
WHAT ARE YOU DOING?! STOP HER!
IF YOU WANT TO GET THIS CHILD TO SAFETY, THAT'S THE PERFECT DISTRACTION.
YOU STILL HAVEN'T FIGURED OUT WHO THAT CHILD IS...?
YOU FELT IT AS SOON AS YOU SAW HIM... IS IT REALLY THAT DIFFICULT TO ACCEPT?
NILS?!
NO, THAT'S IMPOSSIBLE...

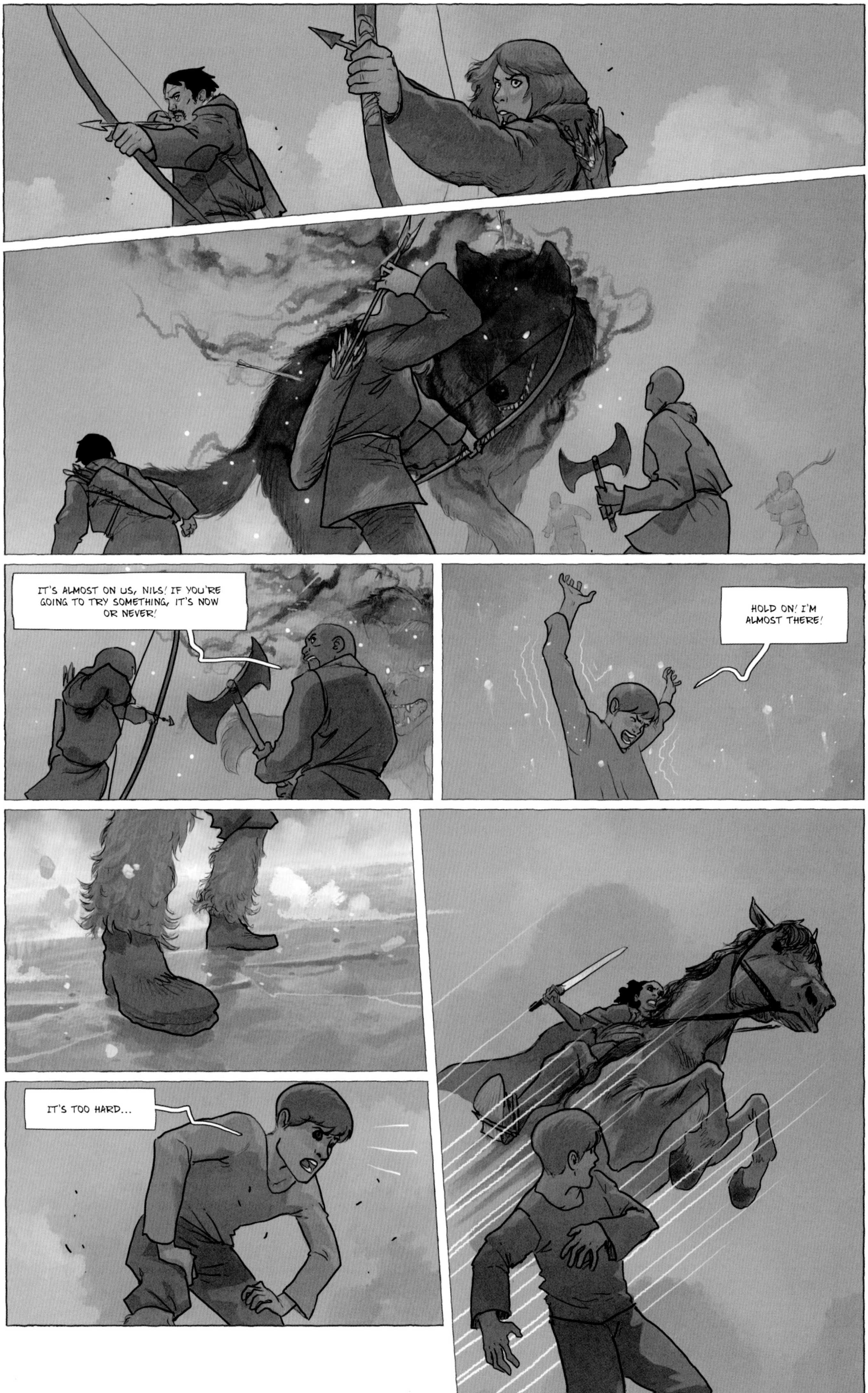
IT'S ALMOST ON US, NILS! IF YOU'RE GOING TO TRY SOMETHING, IT'S NOW OR NEVER!
HOLD ON! I'M ALMOST THERE!
IT'S TOO HARD...

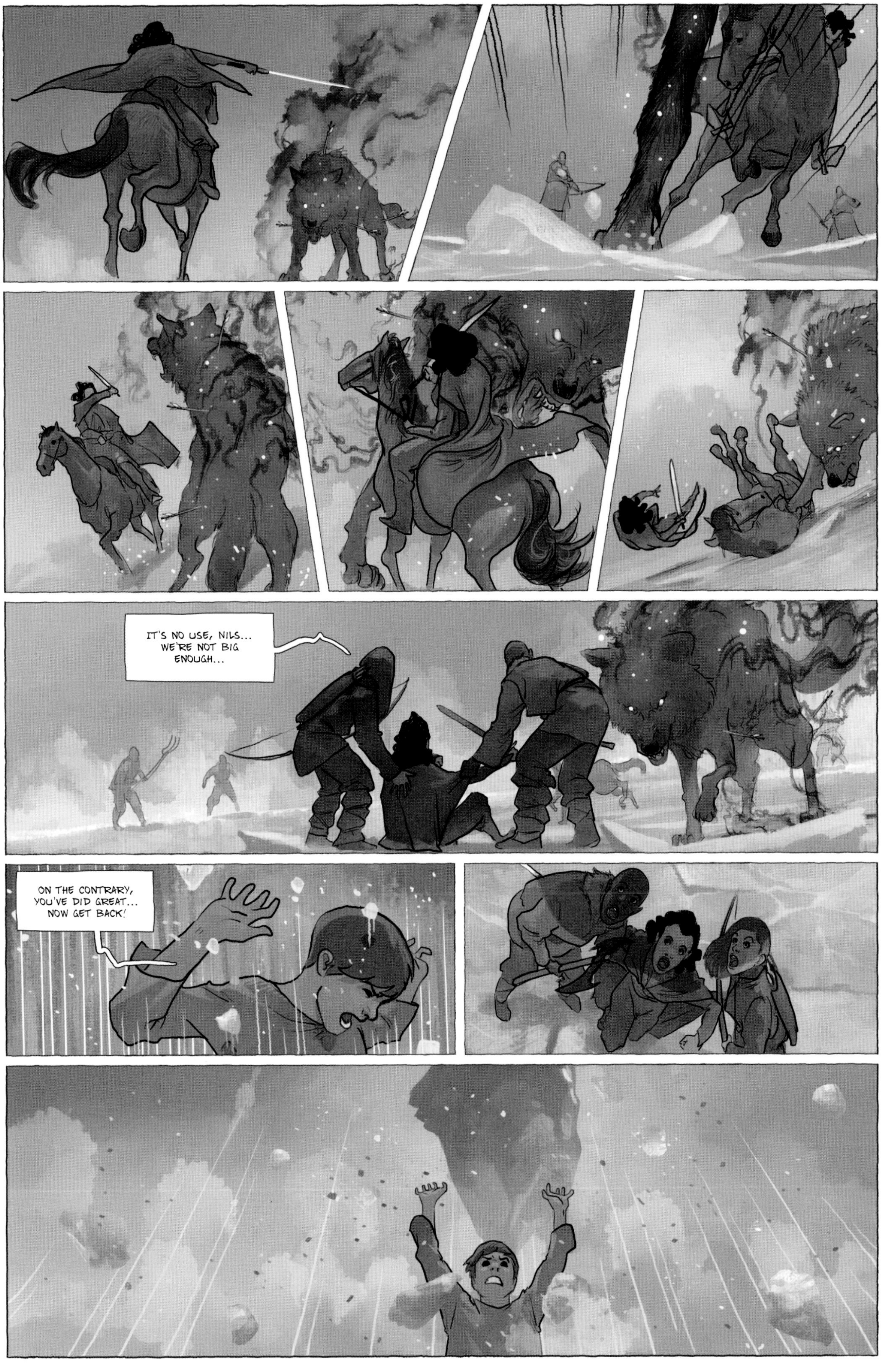
IT'S NO USE, NILS... WE'RE NOT BIG ENOUGH...
ON THE CONTRARY, YOU'VE DID GREAT... NOW GET BACK!

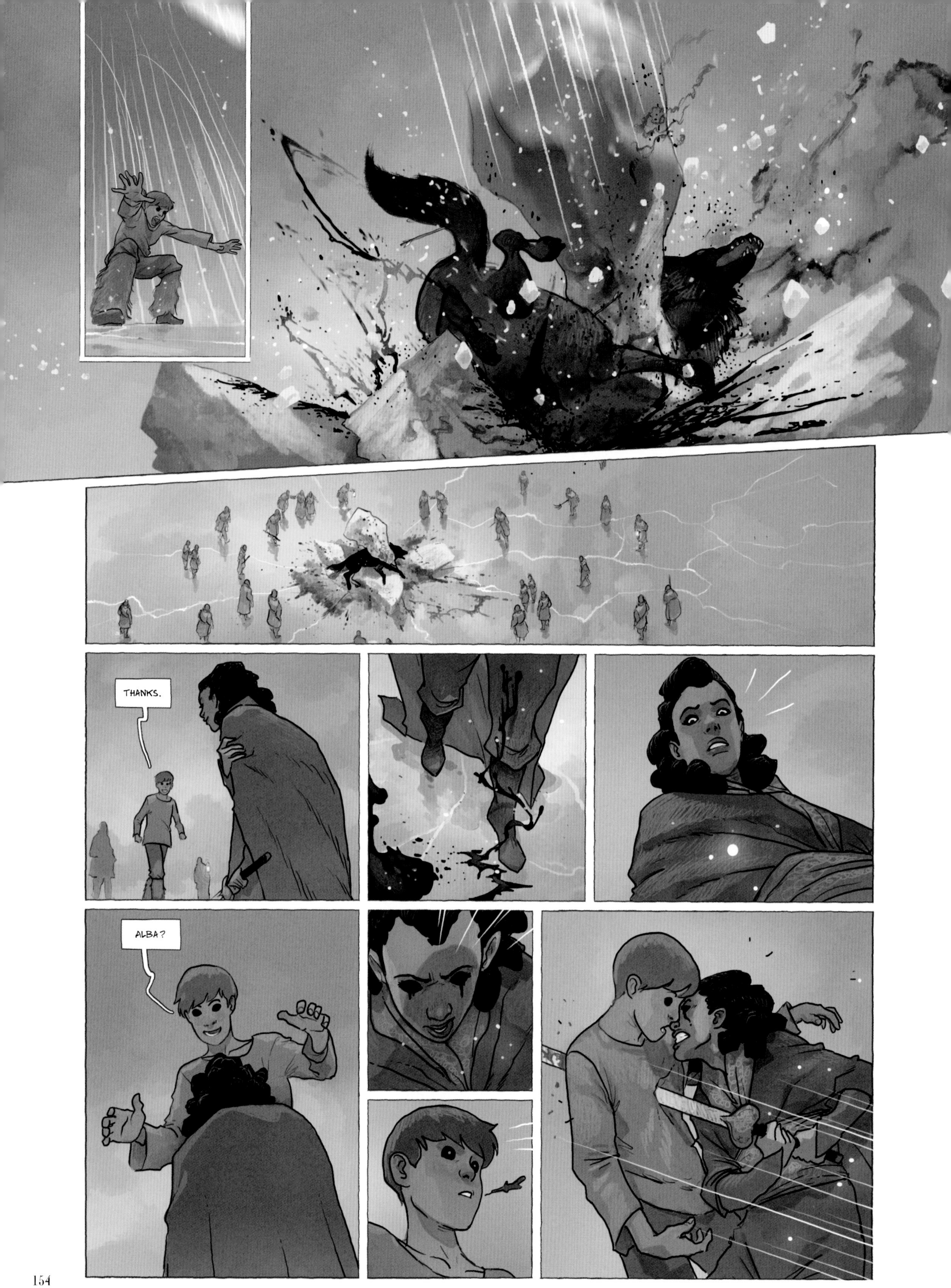
THANKS.
ALBA?

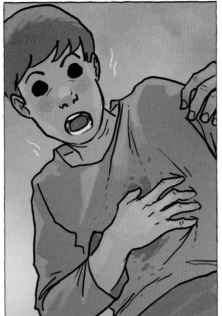

NILS, NO!!!

WE CAN'T DO ANYTHING FOR HIM... RUN!

NO, NO... THIS IS IMPOSSIBLE.

YOU CAN'T BE DEAD...

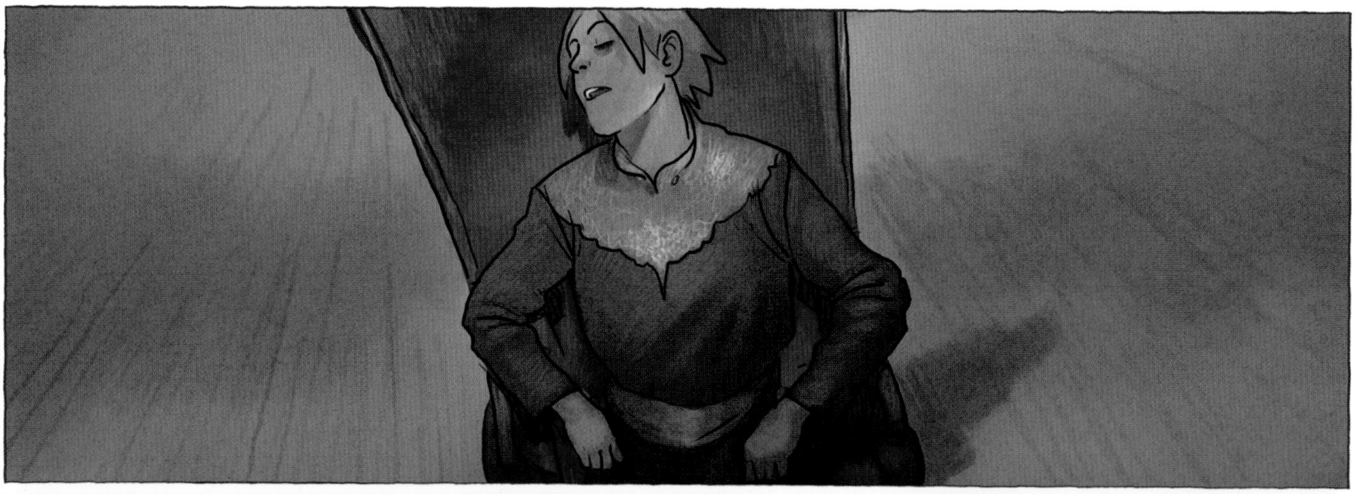
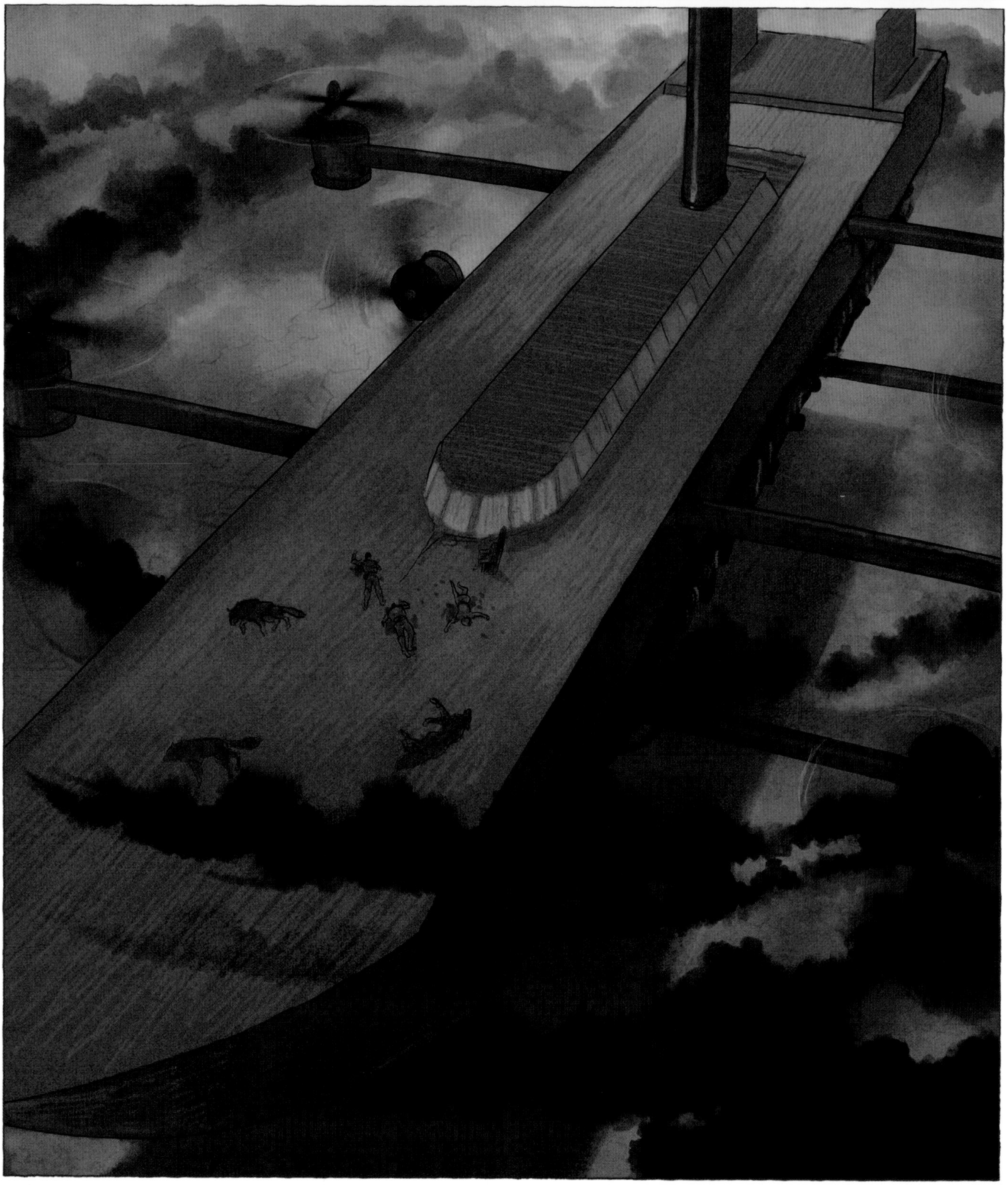

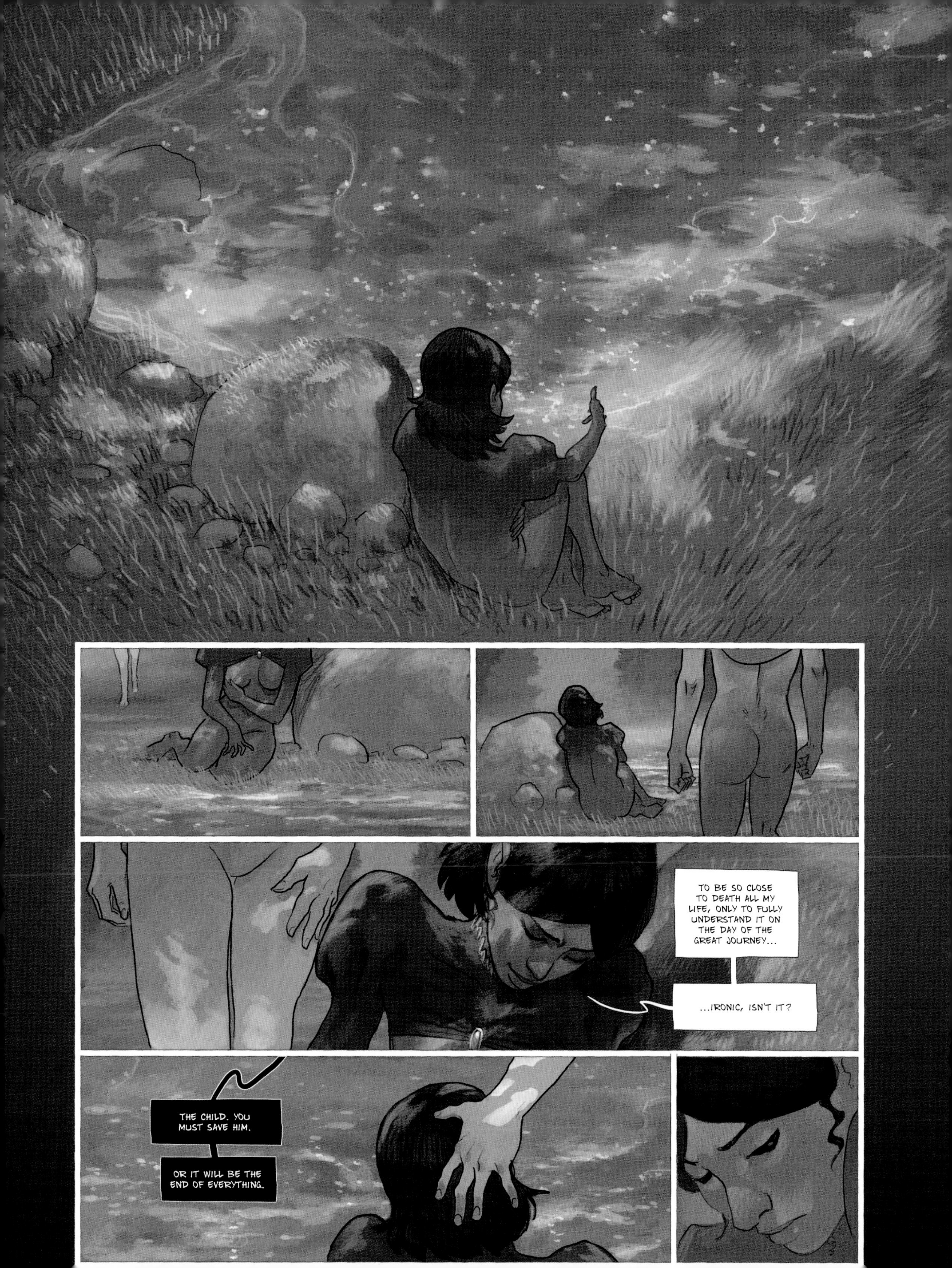
TO BE SO CLOSE TO DEATH ALL MY LIFE, ONLY TO FULLY UNDERSTAND IT ON THE DAY OF THE GREAT JOURNEY...
...IRONIC, ISN'T IT?
THE CHILD. YOU MUST SAVE HIM.
OR IT WILL BE THE END OF EVERYTHING.

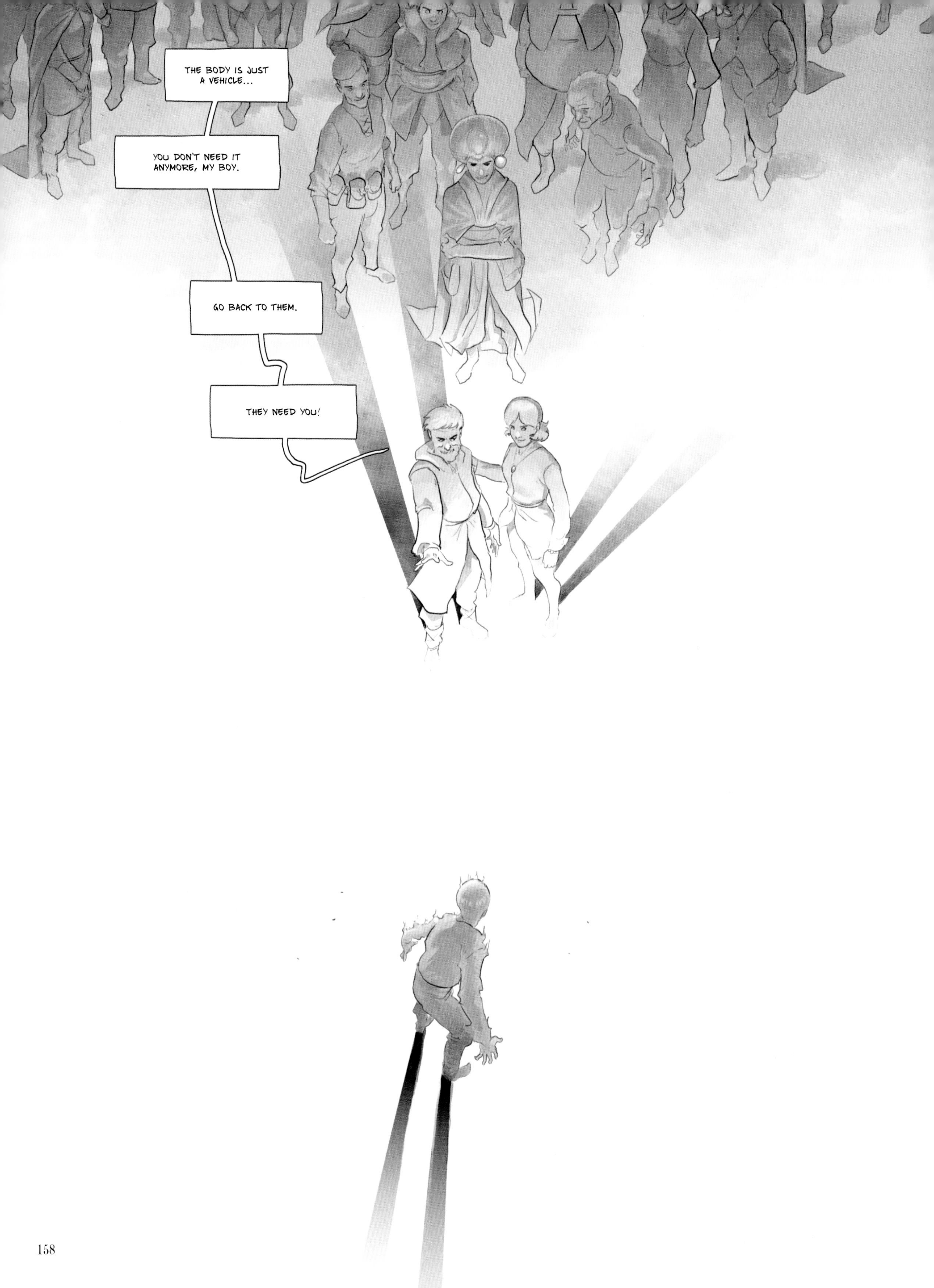
THE BODY IS JUST A VEHICLE...
YOU DON'T NEED IT ANYMORE, MY BOY.
GO BACK TO THEM.
THEY NEED YOU!

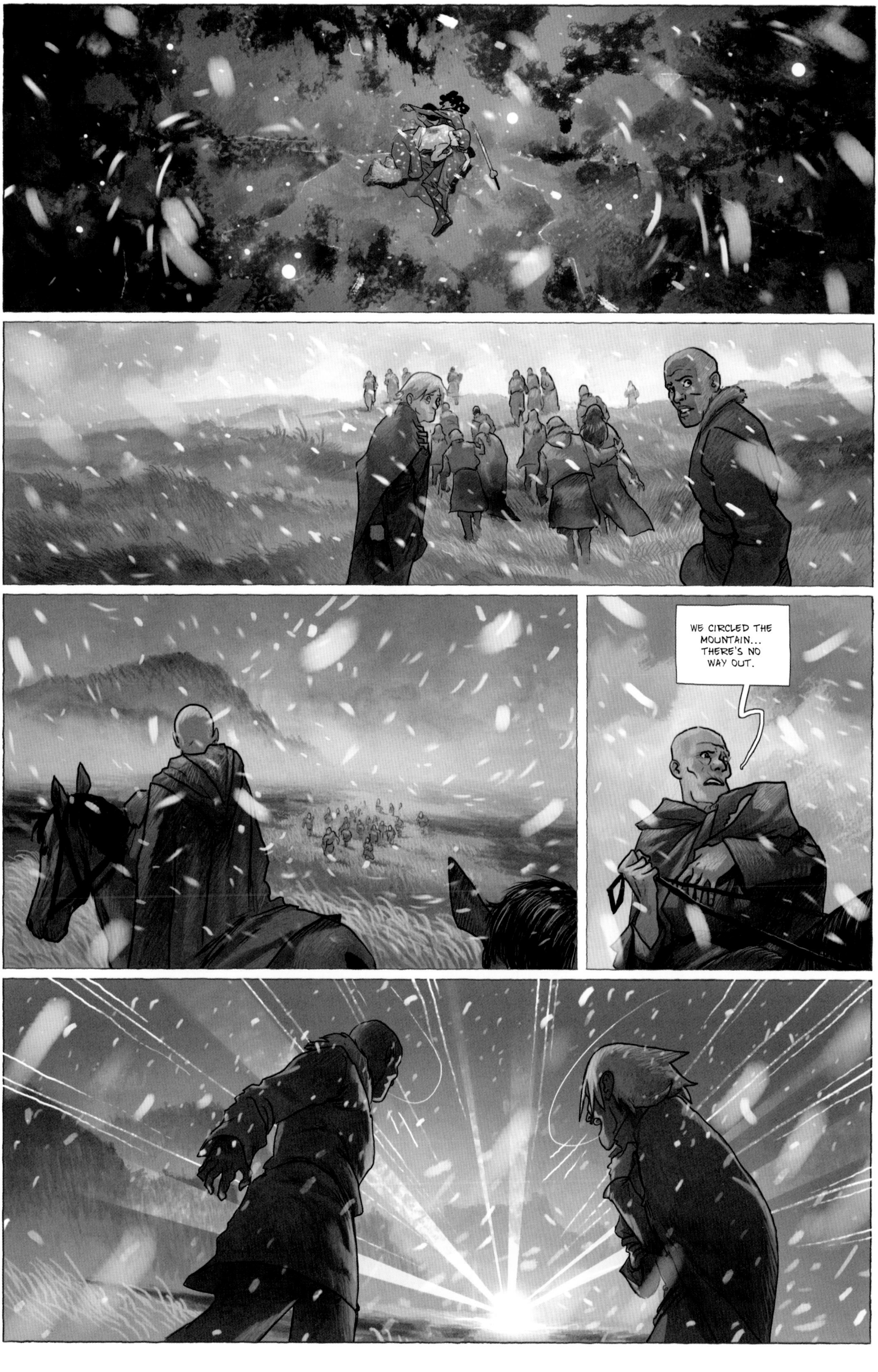
WE CIRCLED THE MOUNTAIN... THERE'S NO WAY OUT.

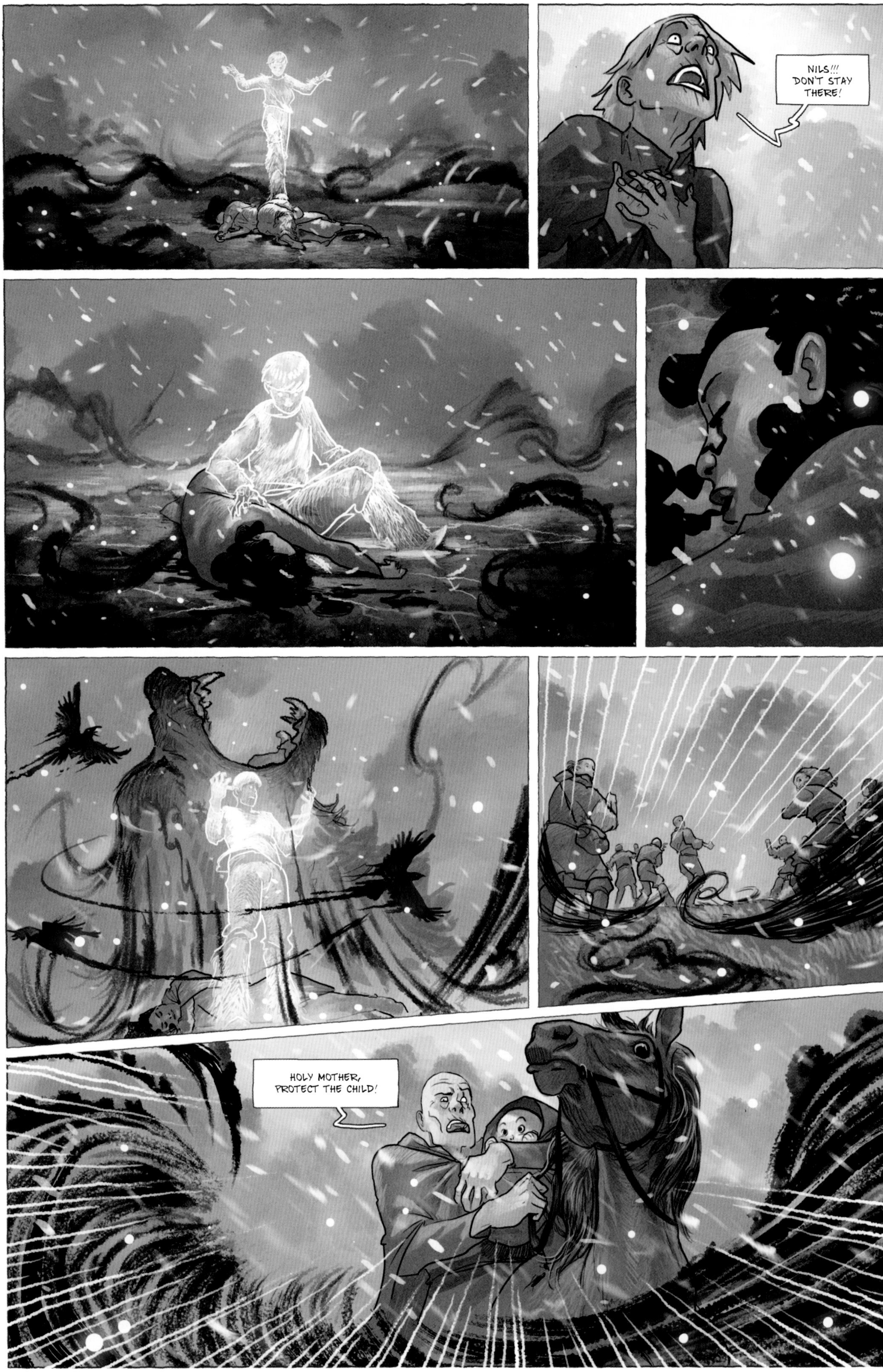
NILS!!! DON'T STAY THERE!
HOLY MOTHER, PROTECT THE CHILD!

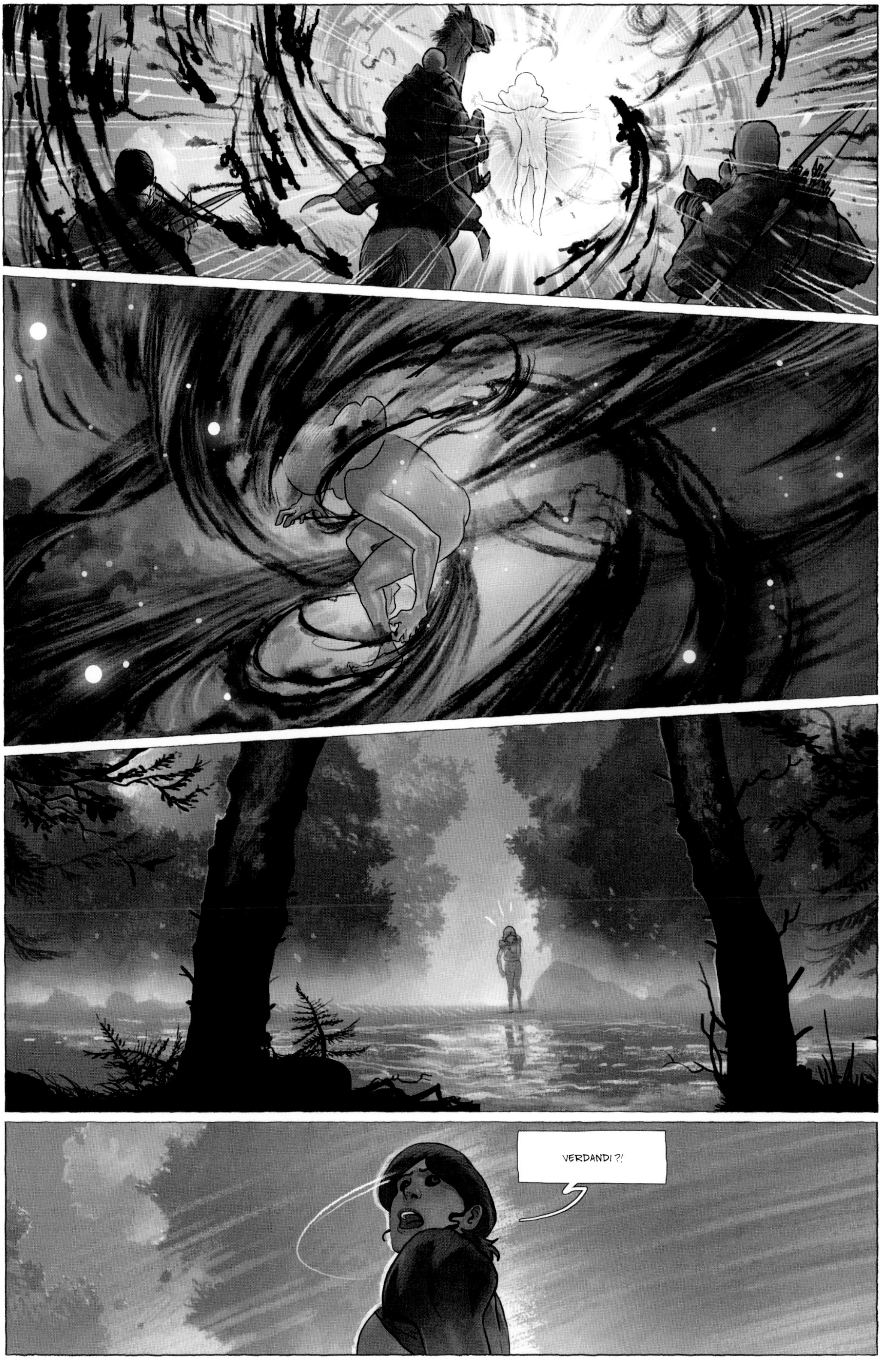
VERDANDI ?!

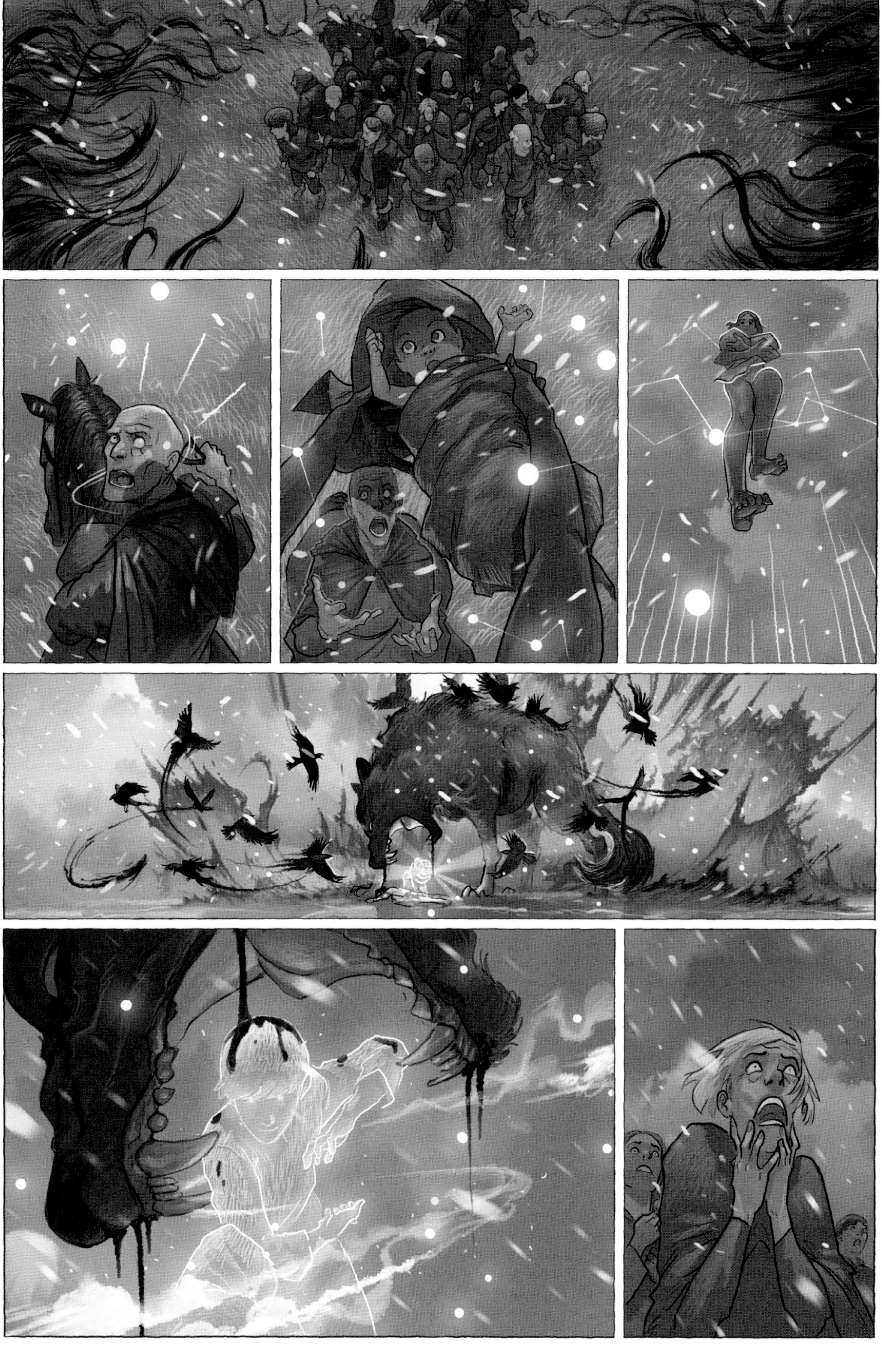

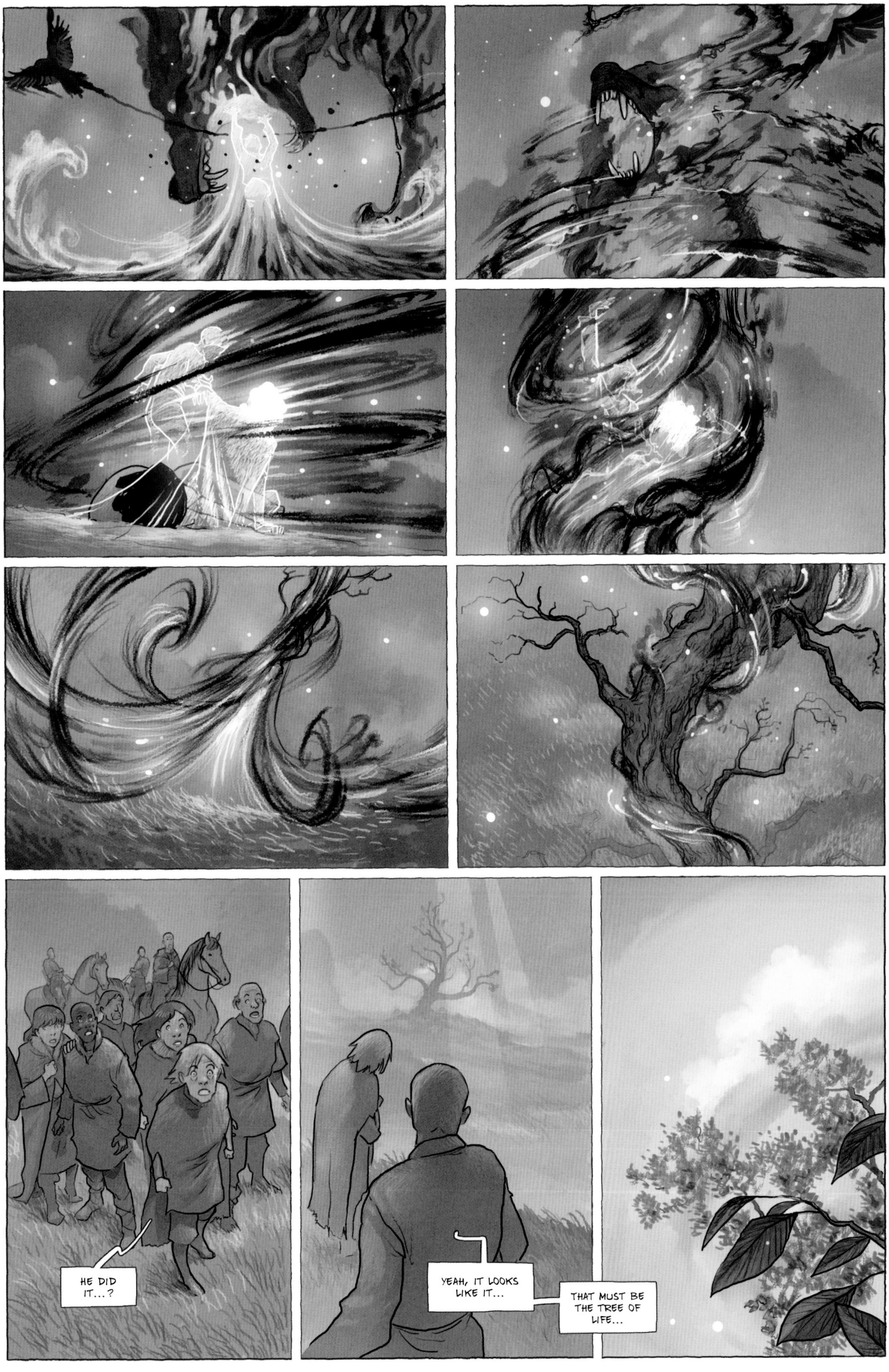
HE DID IT...?
YEAH, IT LOOKS LIKE IT...
THAT MUST BE THE TREE OF LIFE...

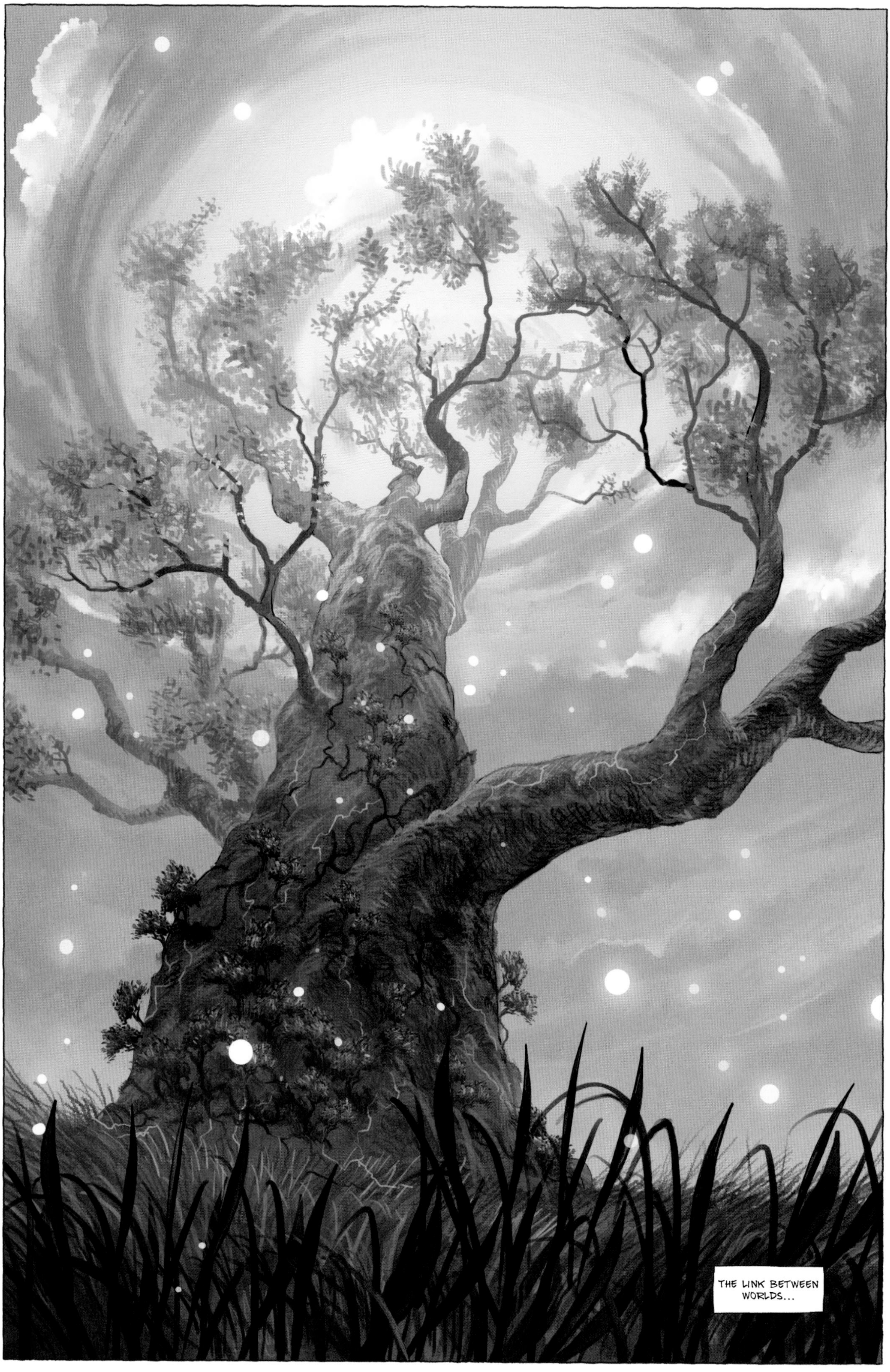
THE LINK BETWEEN WORLDS...

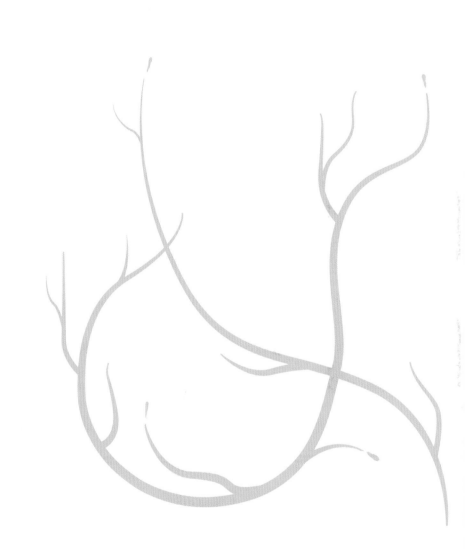

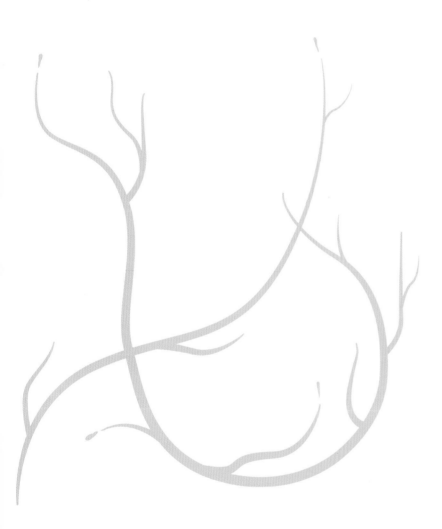

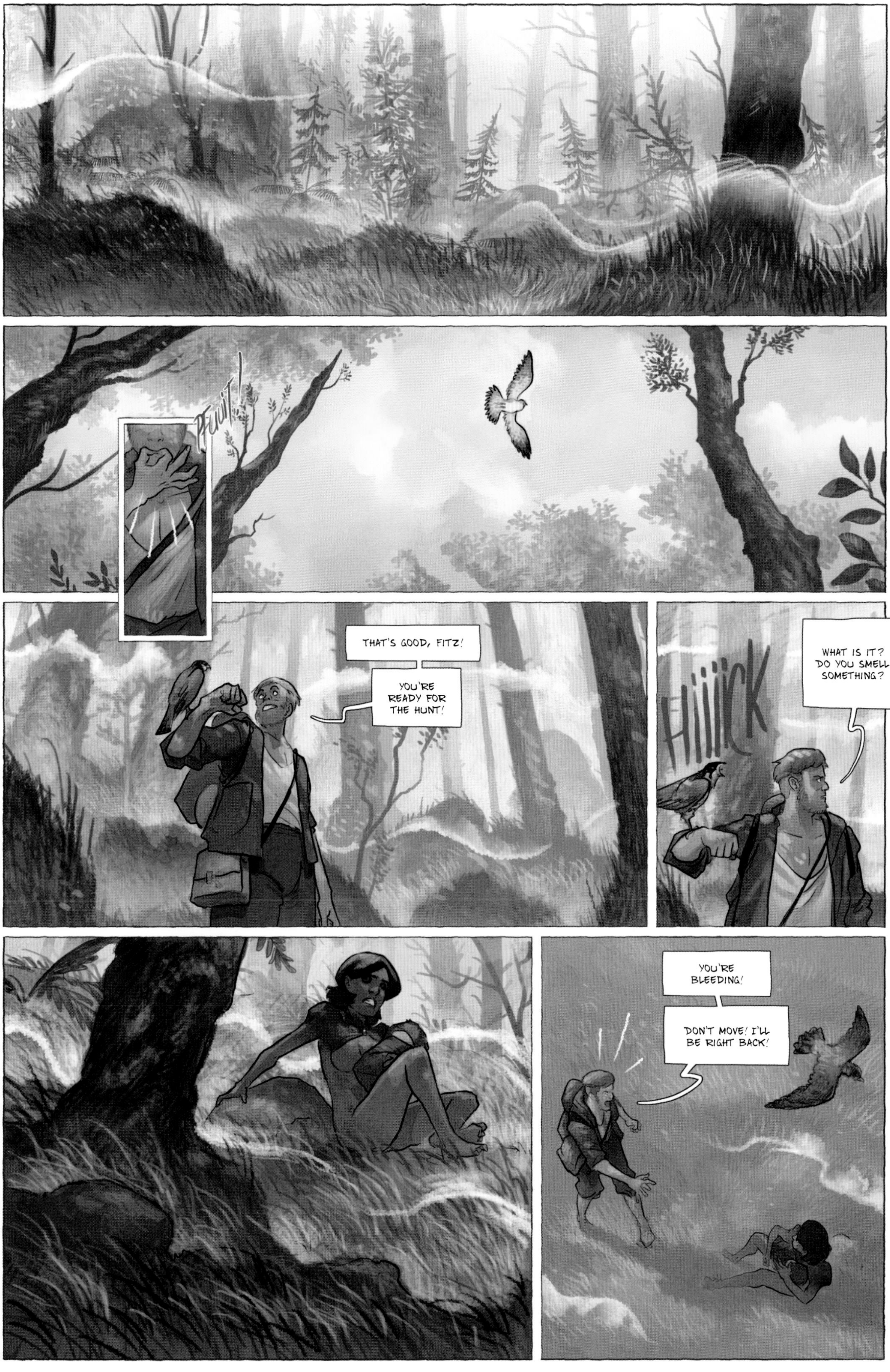
PFUUIT!
THAT'S GOOD, FITZ!
YOU'RE READY FOR THE HUNT!
HIIIICK
WHAT IS IT? DO YOU SMELL SOMETHING?
YOU'RE BLEEDING!
DON'T MOVE! I'LL BE RIGHT BACK!

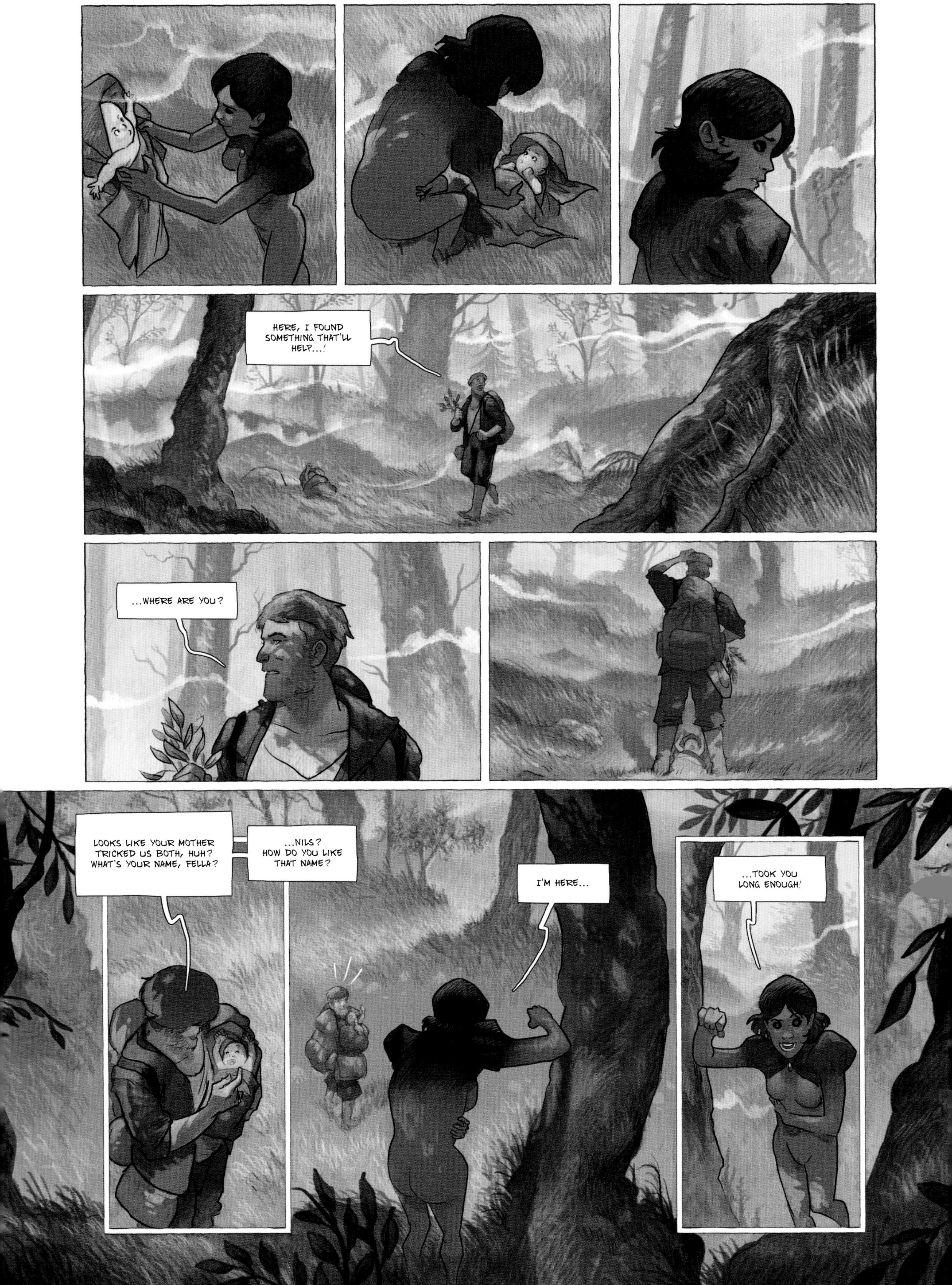
HERE, I FOUND SOMETHING THAT'LL HELP...!
...WHERE ARE YOU?
LOOKS LIKE YOUR MOTHER TRICKED US BOTH, HUH? WHAT'S YOUR NAME, FELLA?
...NILS? HOW DO YOU LIKE THAT NAME?
I'M HERE...
...TOOK YOU LONG ENOUGH!

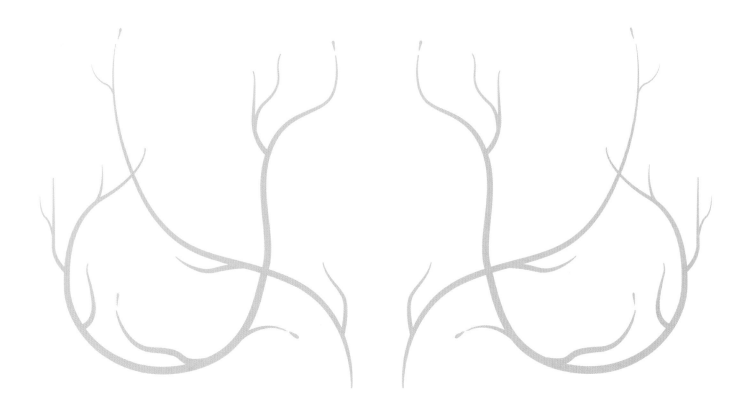

GALLERY

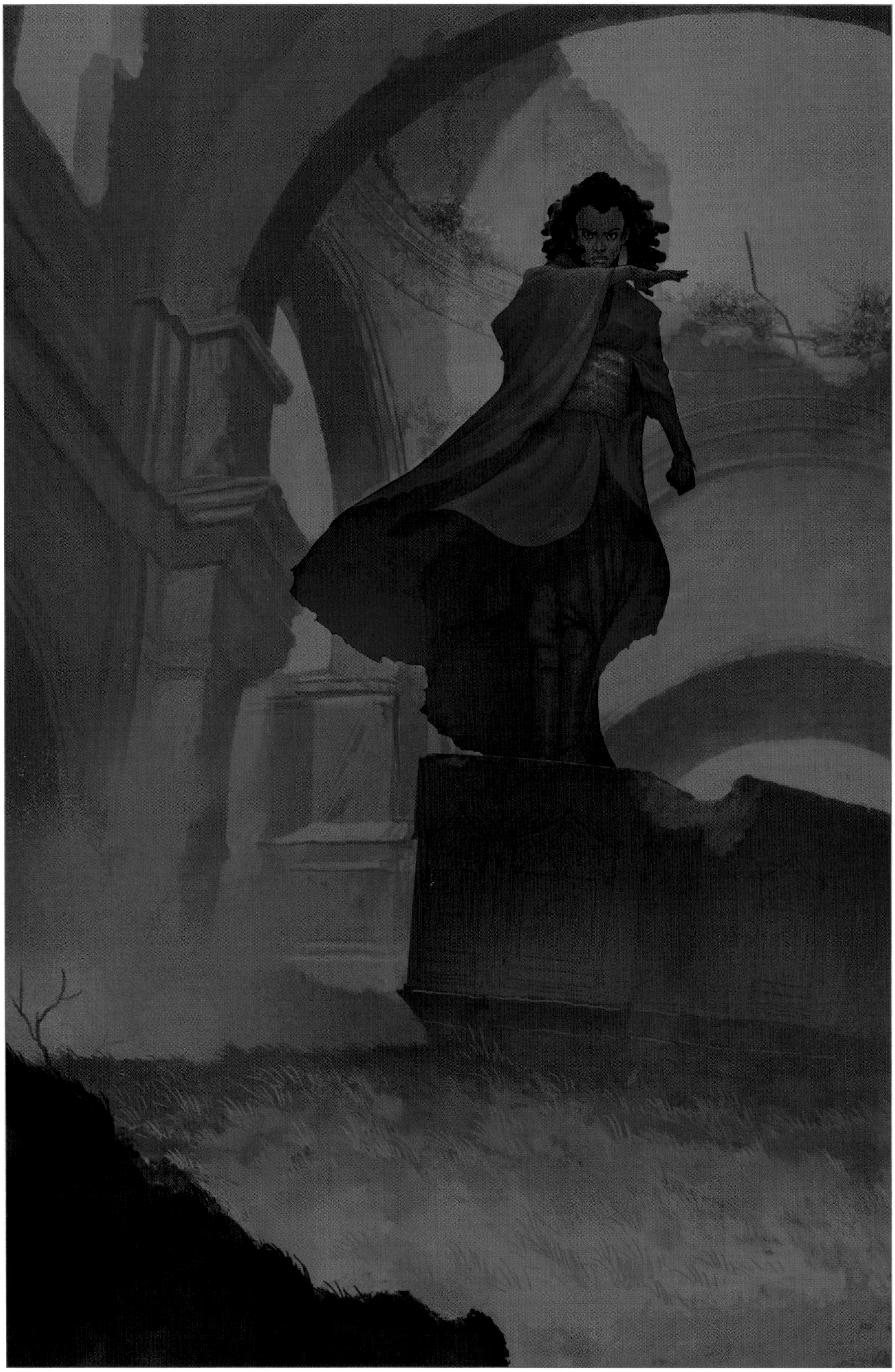

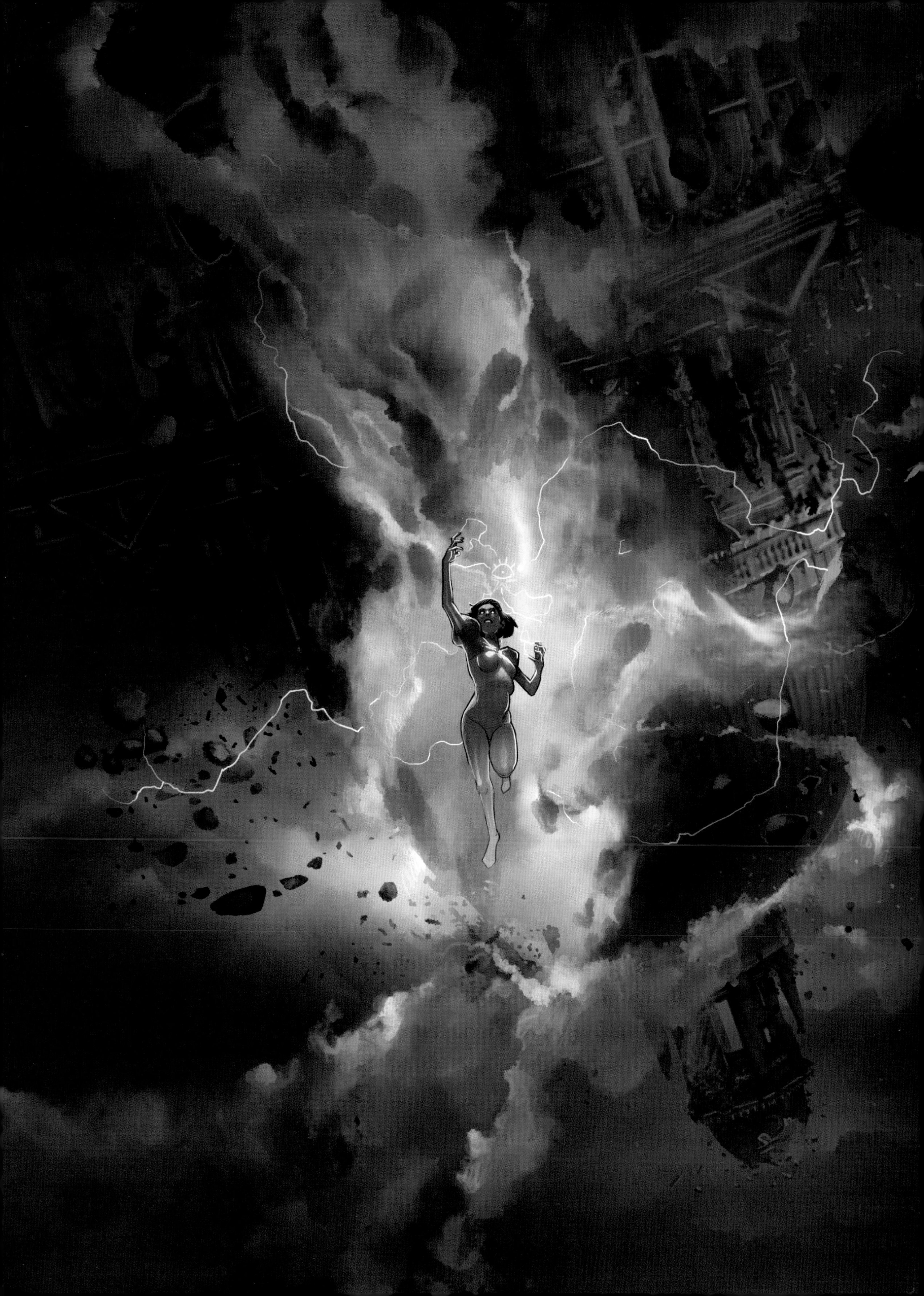

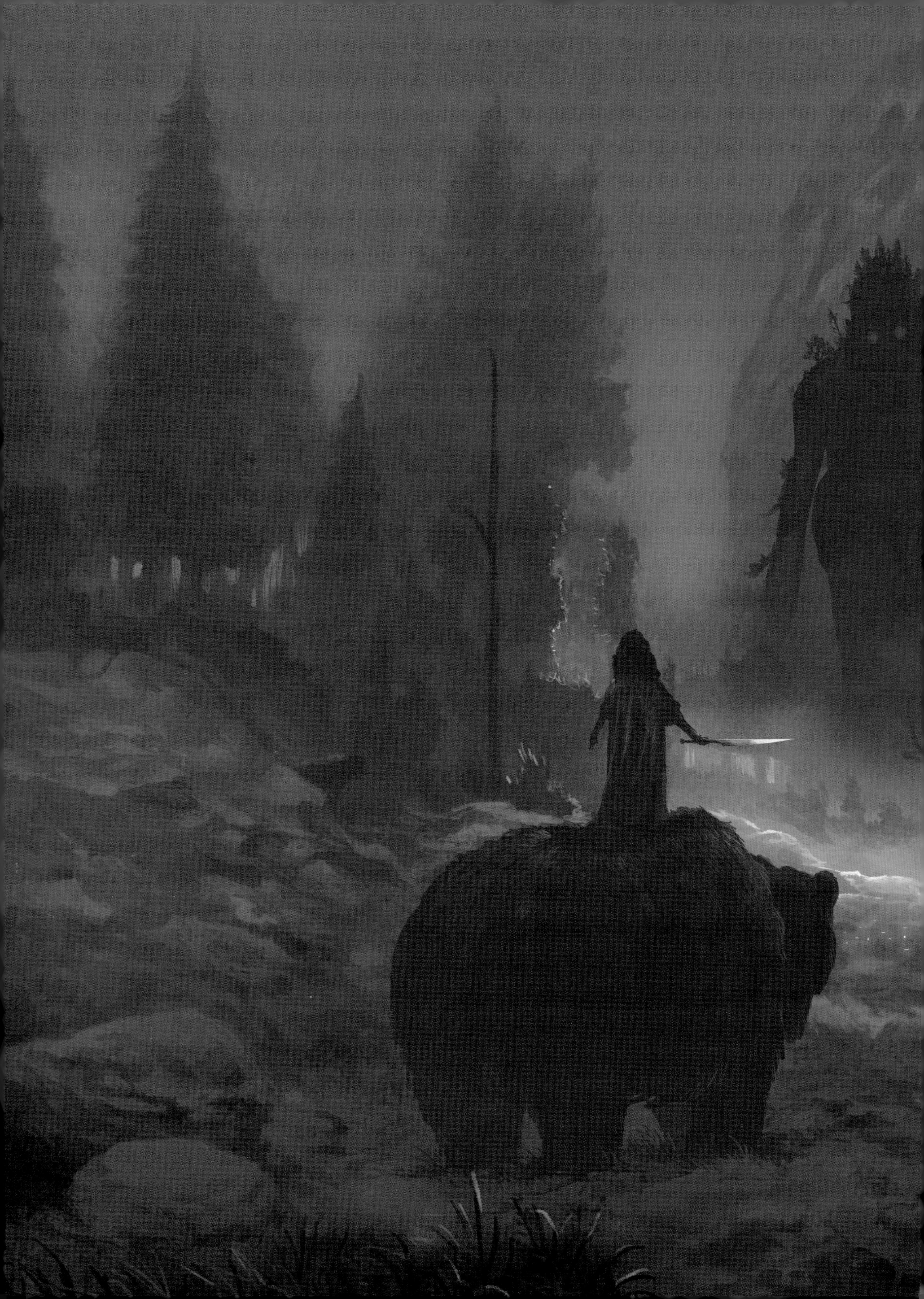

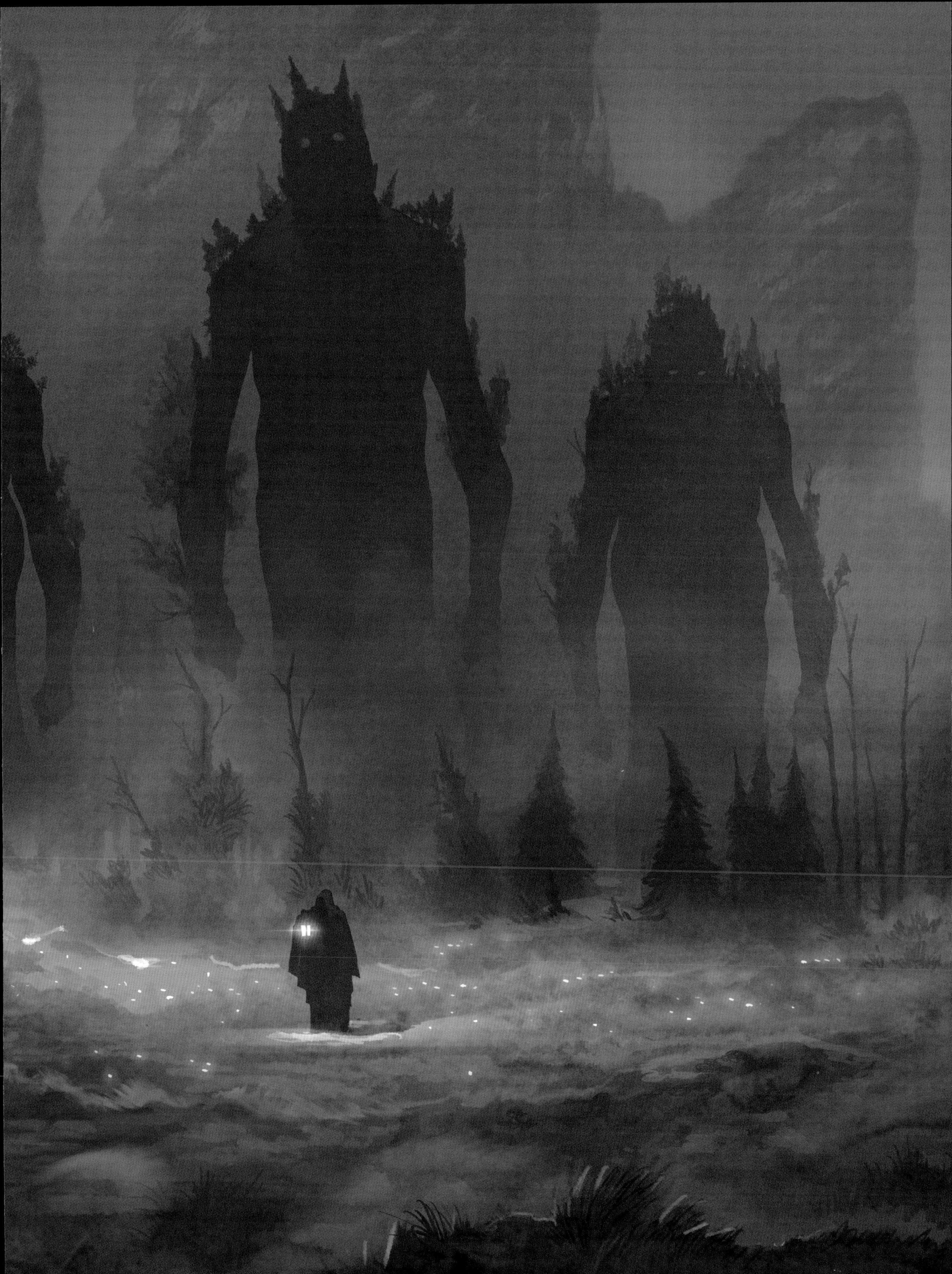

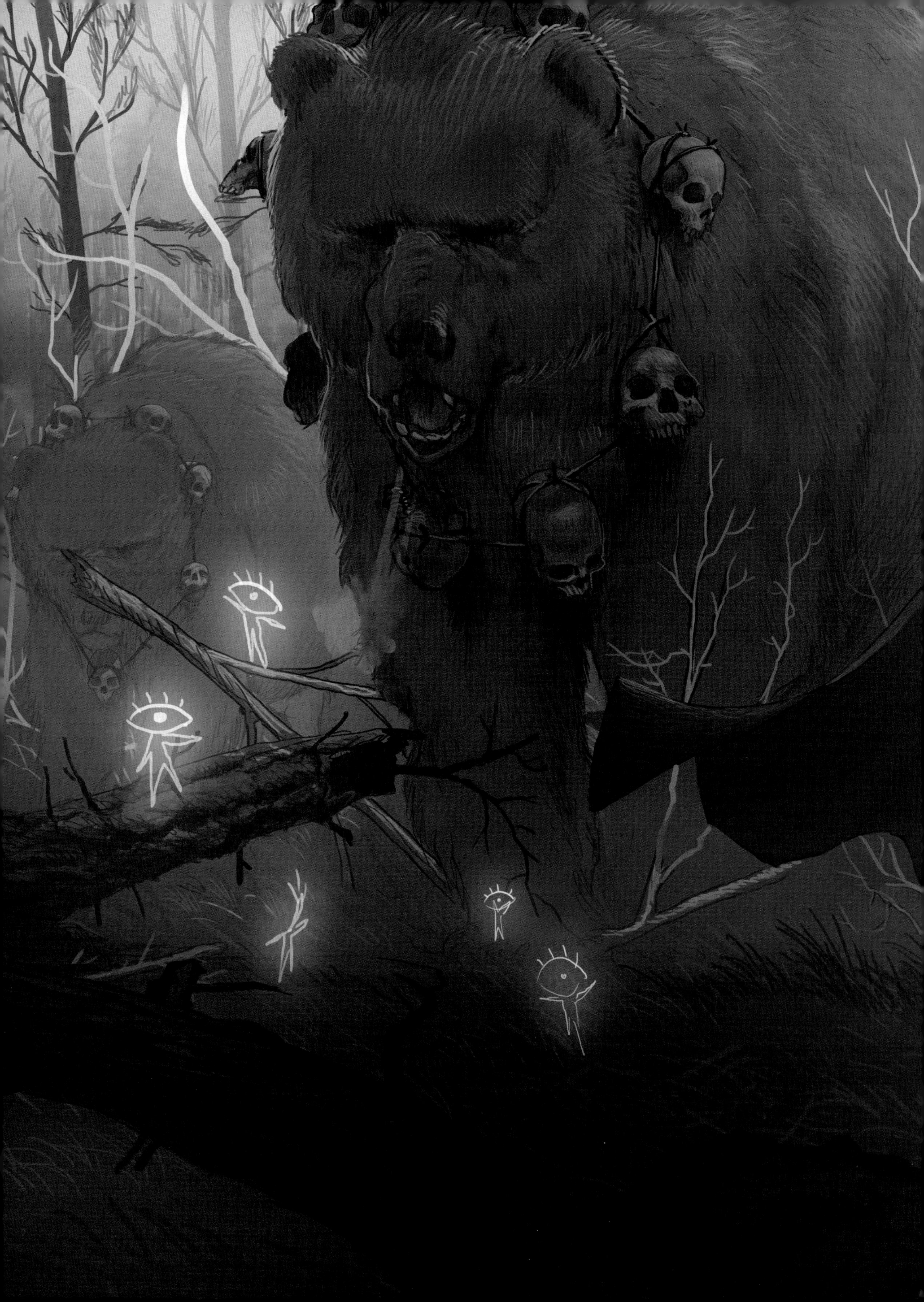

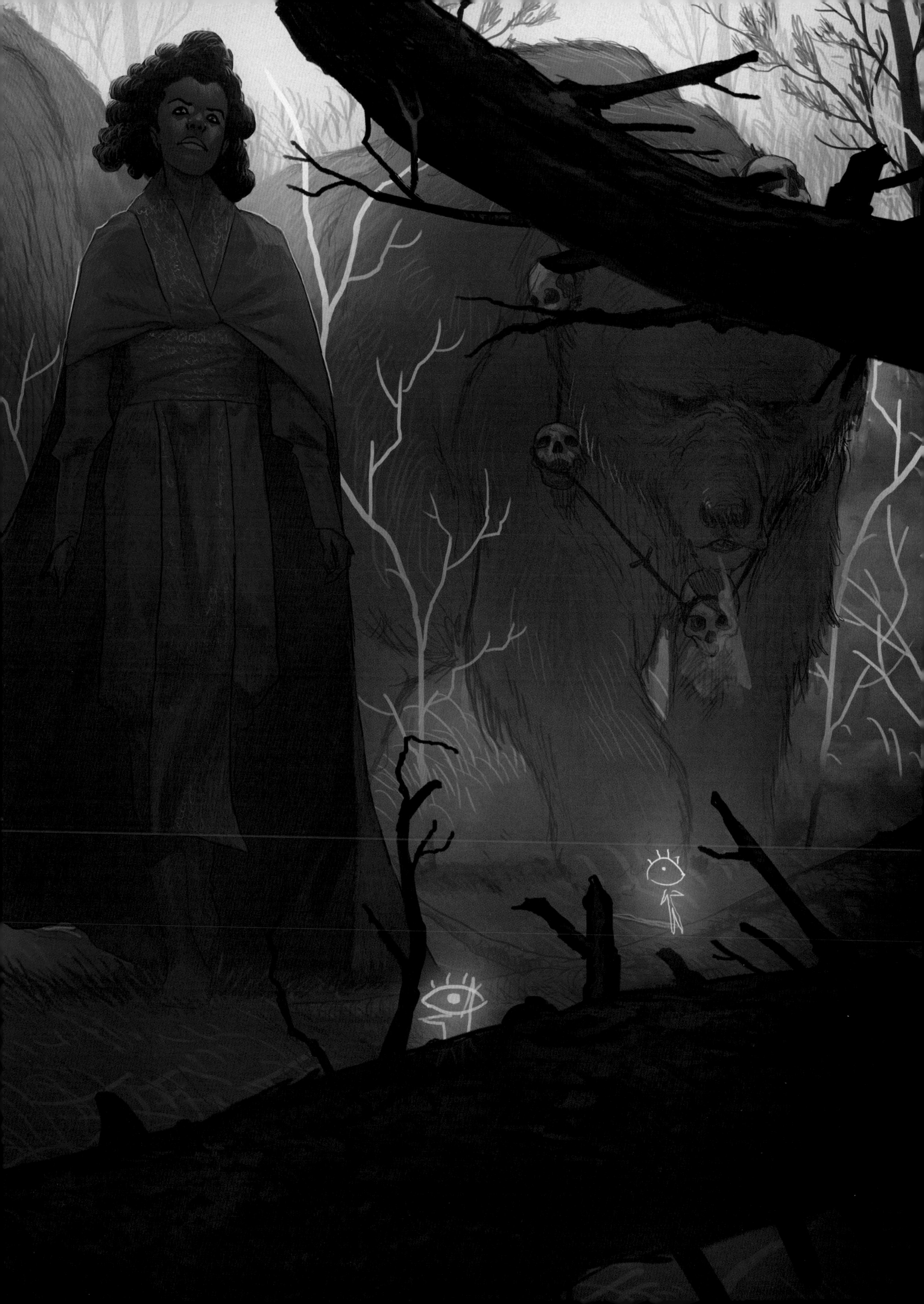

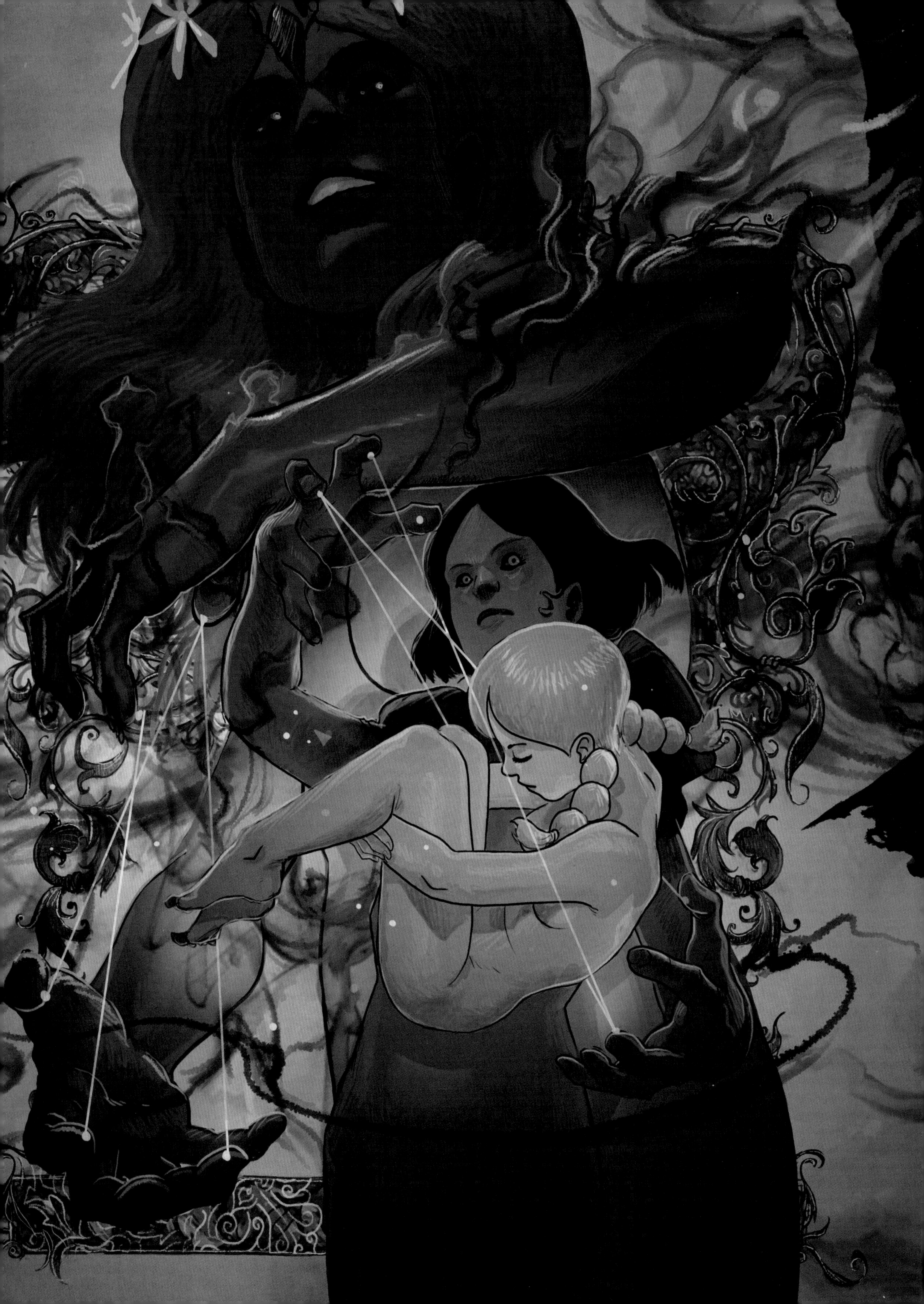

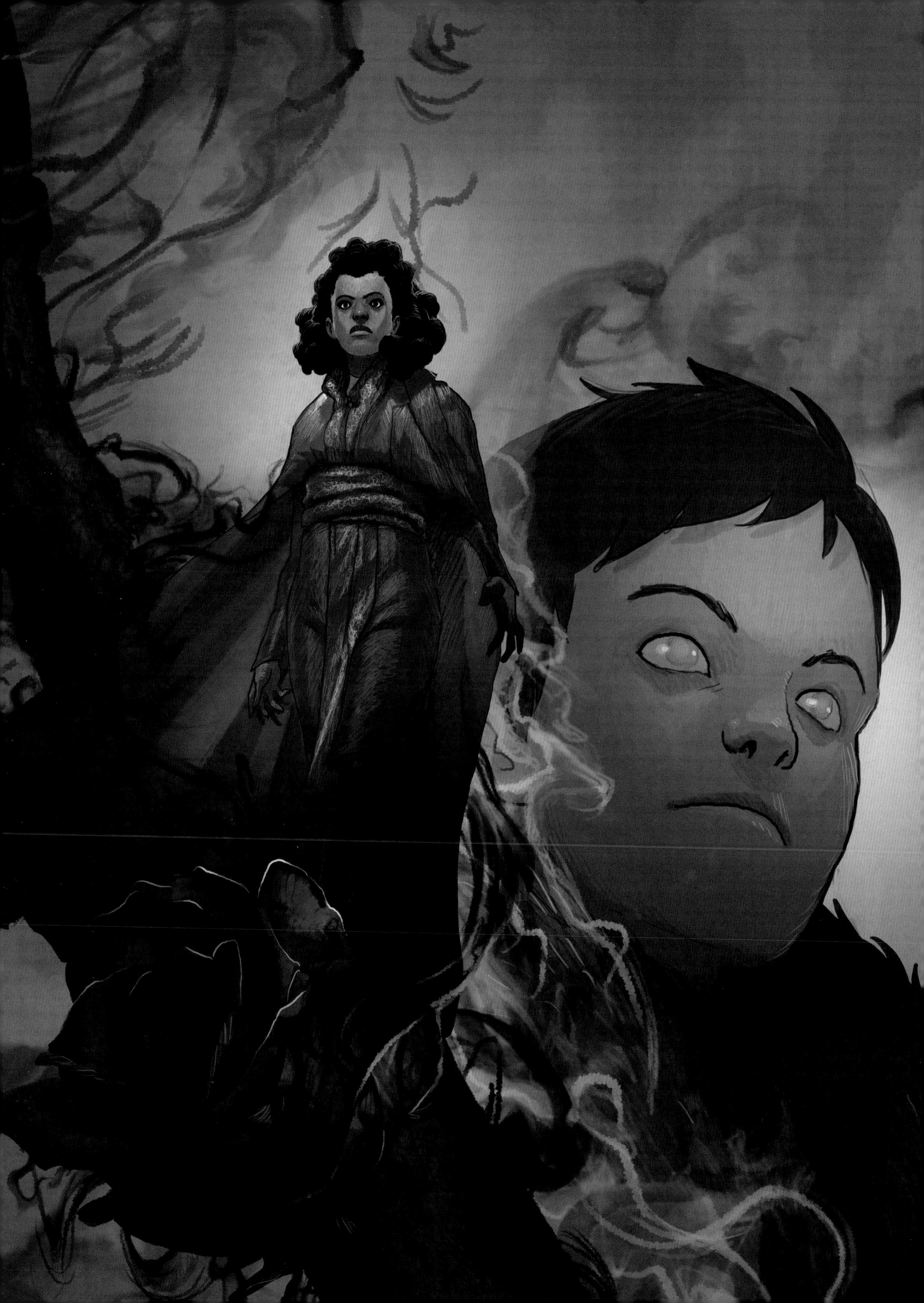

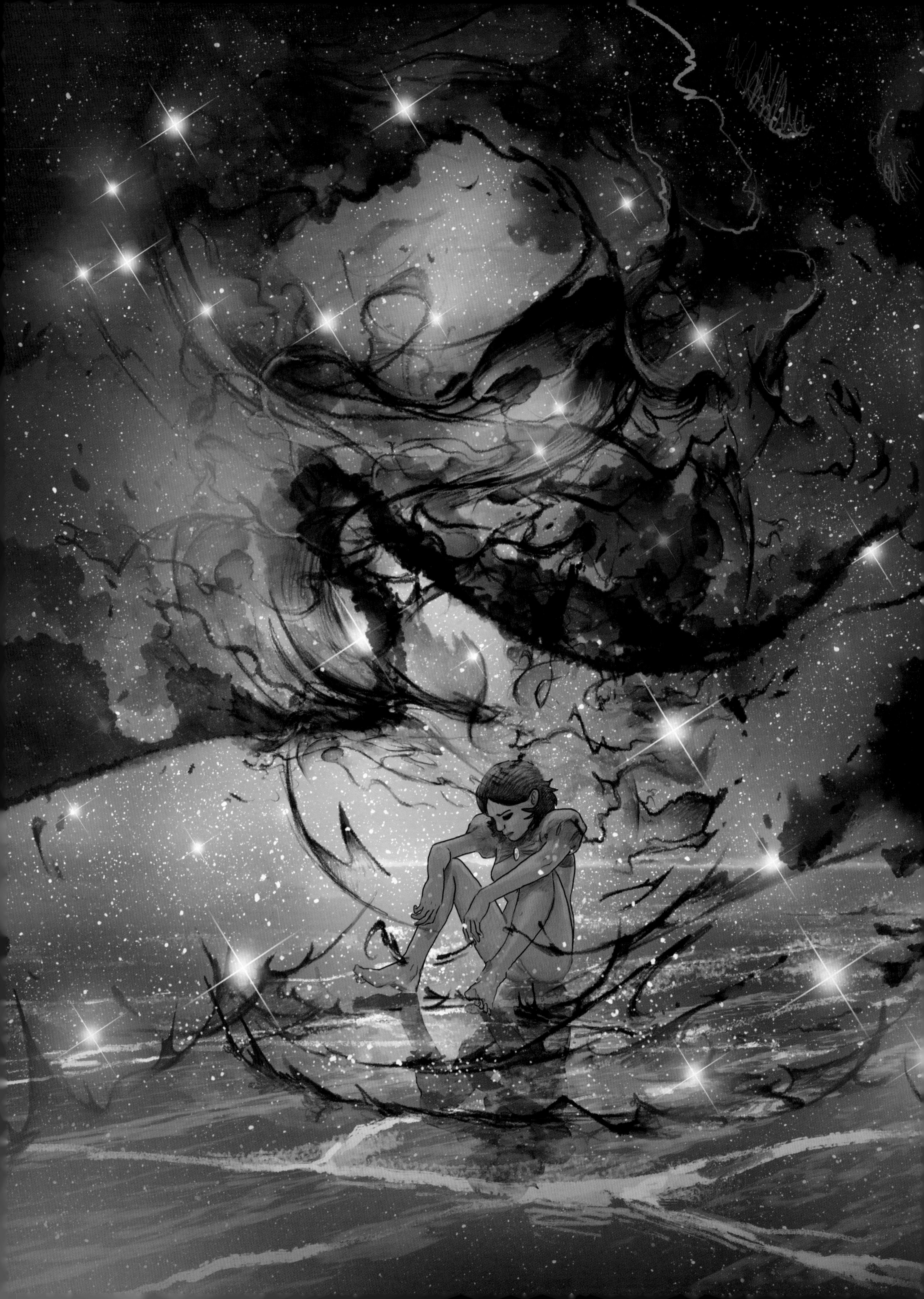

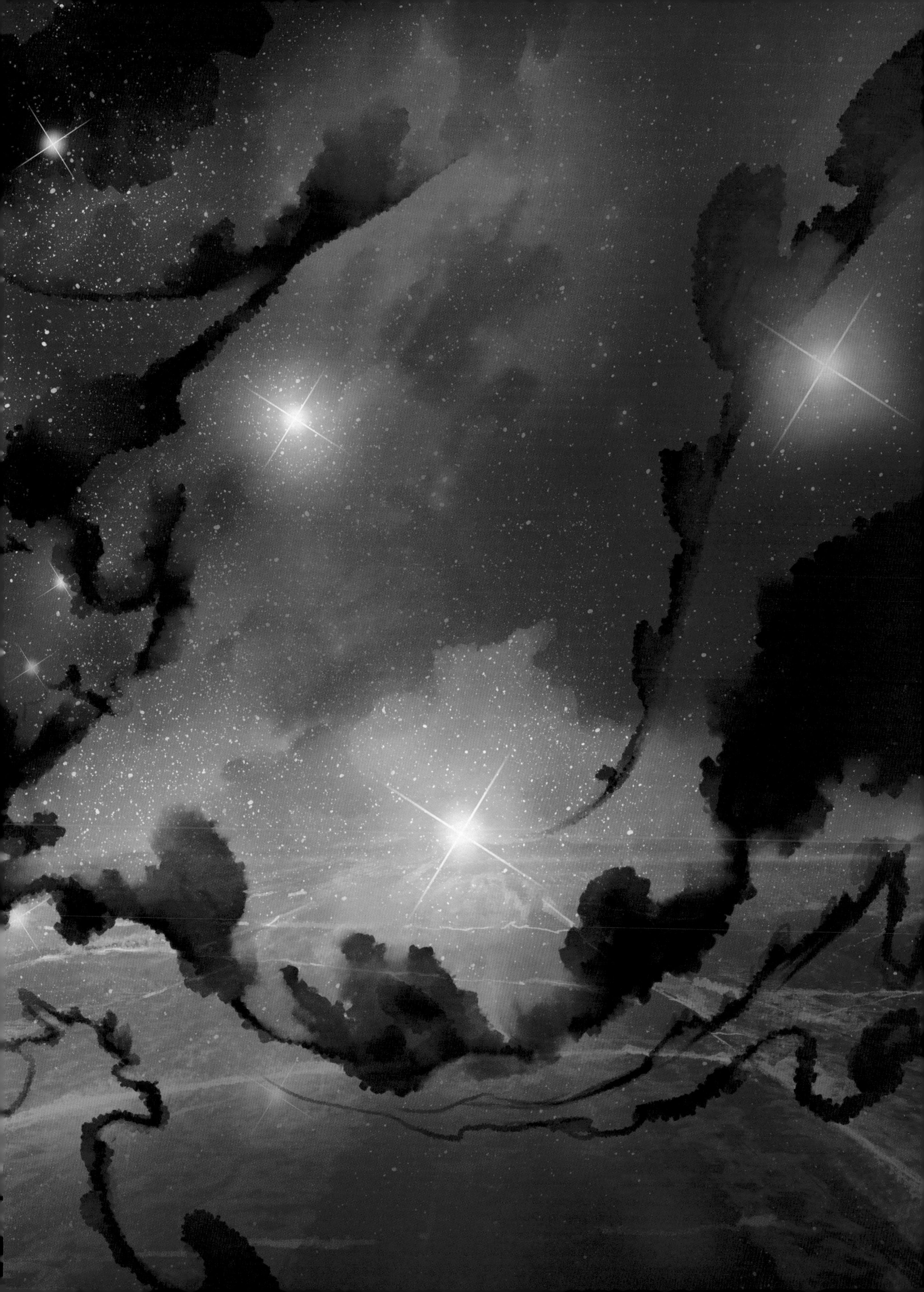

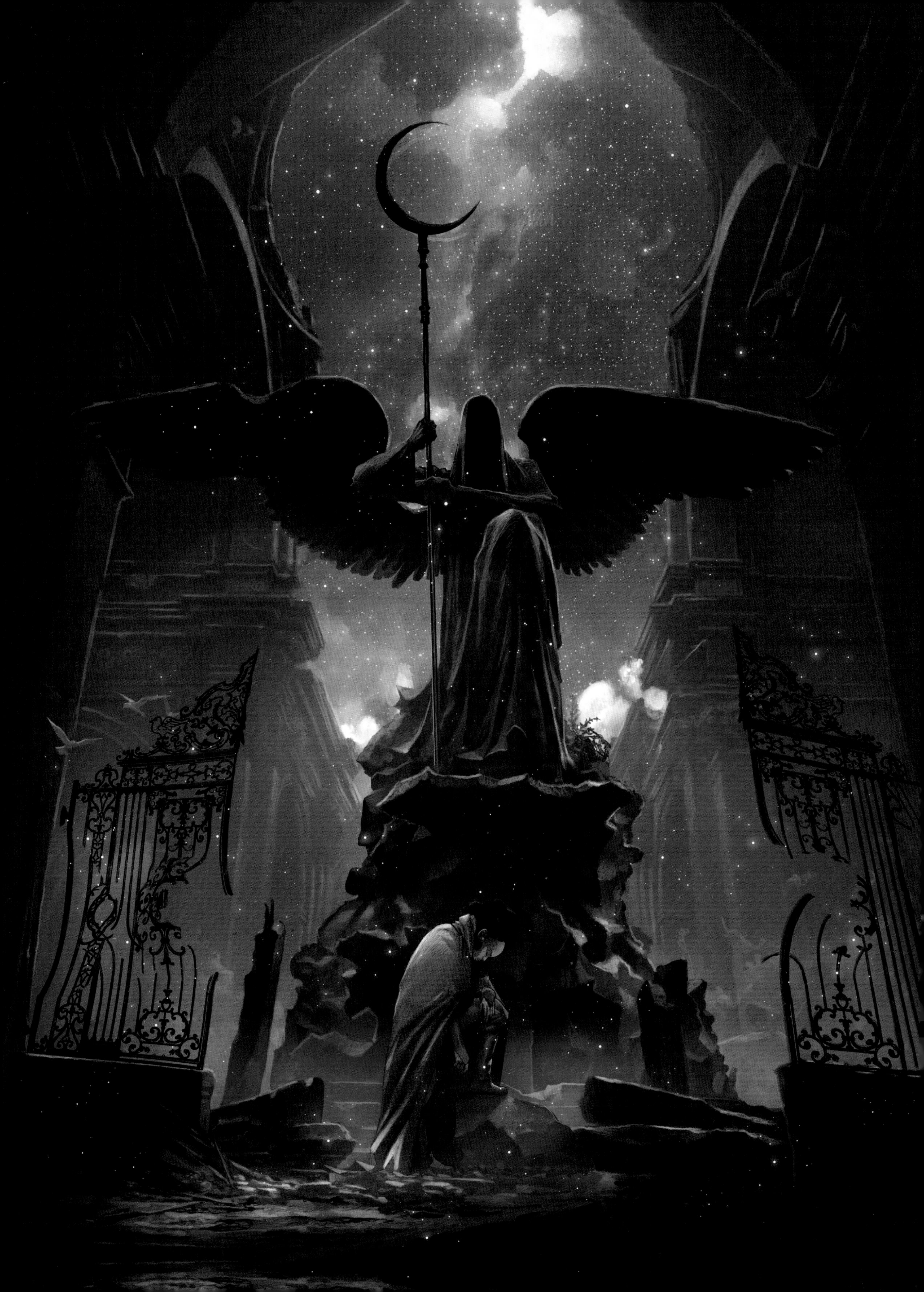

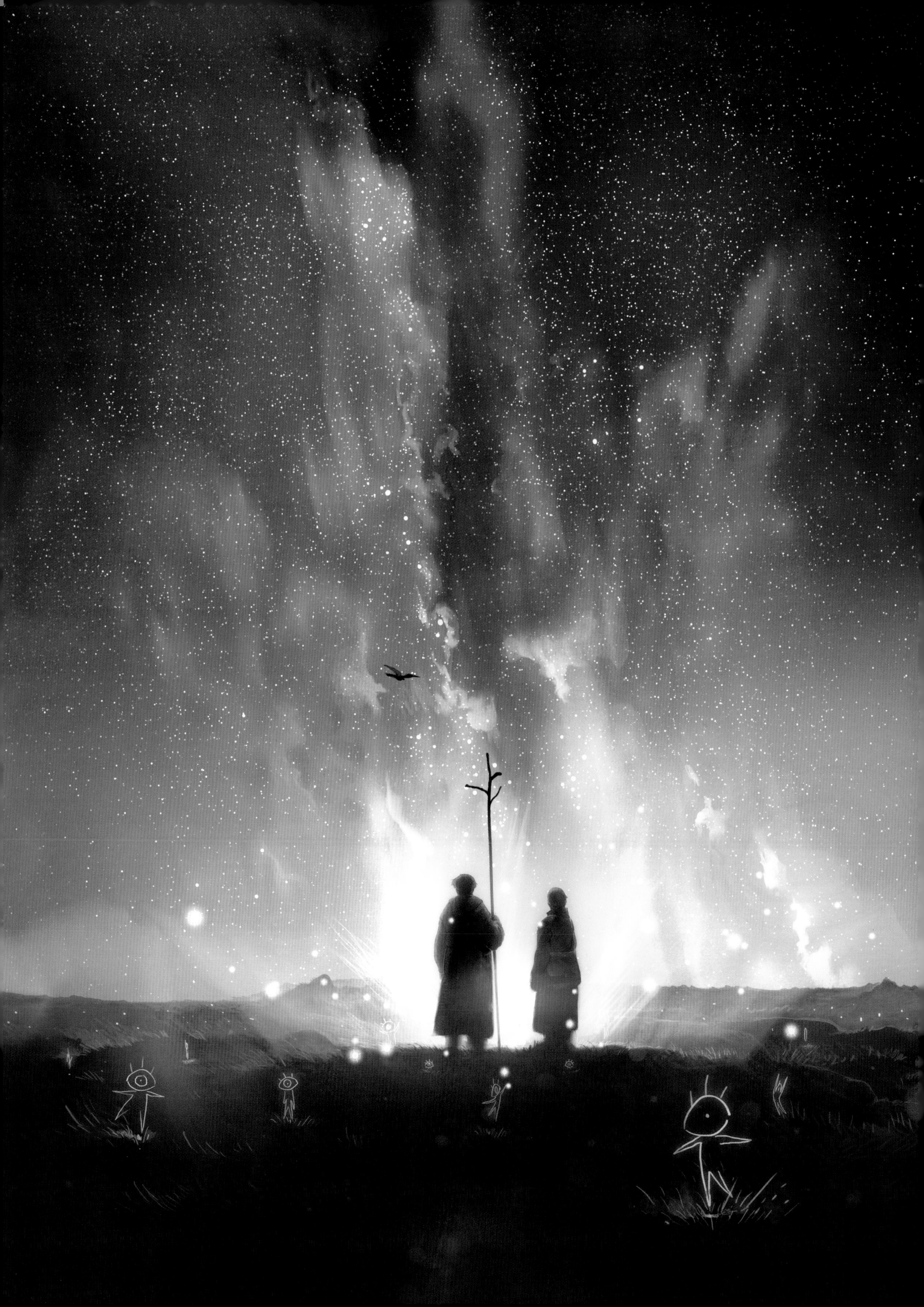

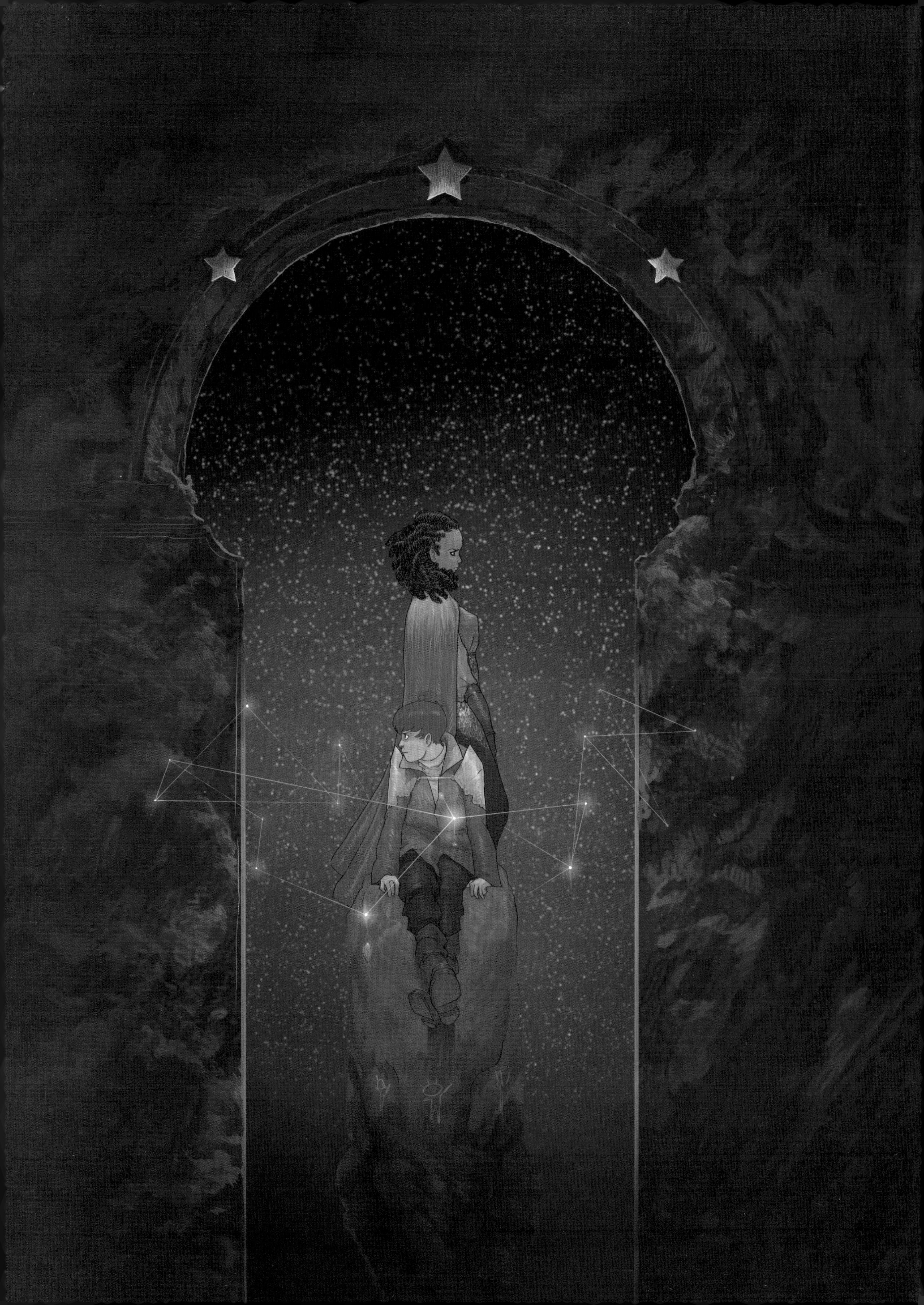

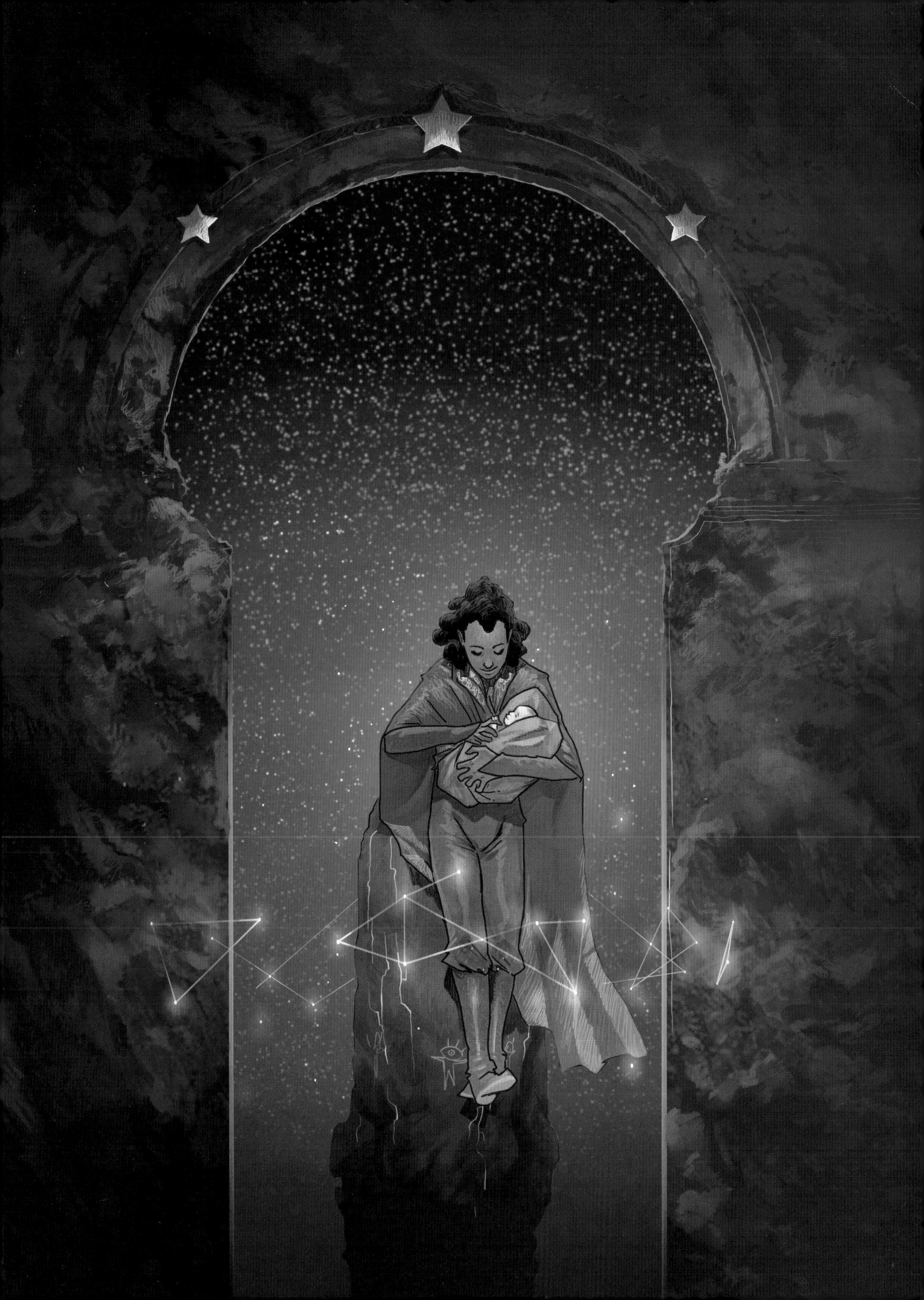

Translation by Jeremy Melloul
Localization, Editing, and Layout by Mike Kennedy

Chanted lyrics on page 66 from "I'm home", *a Plum Villlage Buddhist song written by Thich Nhat Hanh.*

ISBN: 978-1-5493-0815-4
Library of Congress Control Number: 2019914164

Nils: The Tree of Life, published 2020 by Magnetic Press, LLC.
Originally published in French under the following title: *Nils,* volumes 1 to 3, by Jérôme Hamon and Antoine Carrion © Editions Soleil,
2016/2018, in the Métamorphose collection directed by Barbara Canepa and Clotilde Vu.

Printed in China.

10 9 8 7 6 5 4 3 2 1